Heavy Metal

Heavy Metal

The Music and Its Culture
REVISED EDITION

Deena Weinstein

DA CAPO PRESS

Library of Congress Cataloging in Publication Data

Weinstein, Deena.
    Heavy Metal : the music and its culture / Deena Weinstein.— Rev. ed.
      p. cm.
    Includes bibliographical references (p.) and index.
    ISBN 0-306-80970-2 (pbk.)
      1. Heavy metal (Music)—History and criticism. 2. Music—Social aspects.
I. Title.

ML3534.W45 2000
306.4'84—dc21

                                                        99–045230

First Da Capo Press Edition 2000

Published by Da Capo Press
A Member of the Perseus Books Group
http://www.dacapopress.com

EBC 02 03 04 10 9 8 7 6 5 4

To Michael and Joey
Two Men Who STILL Play On Ten

Contents

Appreciation

I am greatly indebted to a multitude of generous people who helped to make this book possible in both its original version and in this new revised edition. They have come from all corners of the metal and academic worlds—musicians, fans, and mediators. Much gratitude goes to the legions of metalheads of all ages, genders, and races, from a variety of educational and religious backgrounds, who have shared their insight and pleasure with me. A shout out to those who have gone beyond the call of duty: Denis Chayakovsky, Jim DeRogatis, Joey DiMaio, Natalie DiPietro, Bill Eikost, Paula Hogan, Randy Kertz, Michael Mazur, Paul Natkin, Patrik Nicolic, Rodney Pawlak, Jeff Pizek, Kira Schlecter, and Tony Tavano.

Acknowledgments

Grateful acknowledgment is made to the following publishers for permission to quote from their work:

Straight Arrow Publishers, Inc.: Excerpts from "Money for Nothing and the Chicks for Free," by David Handelman, *Rolling Stone*, August 13, 1989. By Straight Arrow Publishers, Inc. Copyright 1989. All rights reserved. Reprinted by permission. Also excerpt from "The Band that Wouldn't Die," by David Wild, *Rolling Stone*, April 5, 1990. By Straight Arrow Publishers, Inc. Copyright 1990. All rights reserved. Reprinted by permission.

Los Angeles Times: Excerpt from "Heavy-metal hit wins new respect for Iron Maiden," by Dennis Hunt, *Los Angeles Times*, September 9, 1983. By Los Angeles Times. Copyright 1983. Reprinted by permission.

The Sun: Excerpts from "7 Tribes of Britain," by Les Daly, *The Sun* (London), October 2, 1991. Reprinted by permission.

Doubleday: Excerpt from *Soviet Women: Walking the Tightrope*, by Francine Du Plessix Gray, Doubleday, 1990. Originally appeared: "Reflections: Soviet Women," by Francine Du Plessix Gray, *New Yorker*, February 19, 1990. Reprinted by permission.

Permission granted to publish excerpts from personal correspondence with authors by Mars Bonfire, Gary Dray, and Michael Wedeven.

The Richmond Organization: Lyrics from "Suicide Solution," by John Osbourne, Robert Daisley, and Randy Rhoads. Copyright 1981. Essex Music Publishing International Inc. and Kord Music Publishing. All rights reserved. Reprinted by permission.

Photographs on pages facing chapters 1, 3, and 7 by Paul Natkin.

Photographs on pages facing chapters 2, 5, and 6 by Kathy Pilat, DePaul University, 1991

Photograph on page facing chapter 4 by Eric Adams.

Photograph on page facing chapter 8 by Frank White.

1

Studying Metal: The Bricolage of Culture

> *Sonorous metal blowing martial sounds;*
> *At which the universal host upsent*
> *A shout that tore Hell's concave, and beyond*
> *Frighted the reign of Chaos and old Night.*
>
> —*Milton,* Paradise Lost[1]

"Heavy metal: pimply, prole, putrid, unchic, unsophisticated, anti-intellectual (but impossibly pretentious), dismal, abysmal, terrible, horrible, and stupid music, barely music at all; death music, dead music, the beaten boogie, the dance of defeat and decay; the *huh?* sound, the *duh* sound, . . . music made *by* slack-jawed, alpaca-haired, bulbous-inseamed imbeciles in jackboots and leather and chrome *for* slack-jawed, alpaca-haired, downy-mustachioed imbeciles in cheap, too-large T-shirts with pictures of comic-book Armageddon ironed on the front."[2] So heavy metal music is described by Robert Duncan, a rock critic.

Baptist minister Jeff R. Steele is known for his lectures on the adverse effects of rock and roll. Certainly, few of his values are the same as those of Duncan or other rock journalists. But he shares a disgust for heavy metal, judging that it "is sick and repulsive and horrible and dangerous."[3]

Dr. Joe Stuessy, a professor of music at the University of Texas at San Antonio, testified about heavy metal before a United States Senate Committee. "Today's heavy metal music is categorically different from previous forms of popular music. It contains the element of hatred, a meanness of spirit. Its principal themes are . . .

extreme violence, extreme rebellion, substance abuse, sexual promiscuity, and perversion and Satanism. I know personally of no
form of popular music before which has had as one of its central
elements the element of hatred."[4] Professor Stuessy served as a
consultant to the religiously oriented Parents Music Resource Center (PMRC). His testimony to the Senate Committee also included
this observation: "Martin Luther said, 'Music is one of the greatest
gifts that God has given us; it is divine and therefore Satan is its
enemy. For with its aid, many dire temptations are overcome; the
devil does not stay where music is.' We can probably assume that
Martin Luther was not familiar with Heavy Metal!"[5]

In the early 1970s a rock critic characterized the quintessential
heavy metal band Black Sabbath as having the "sophistication of
four Cro-Magnon hunters who've stumbled upon a rock band's
equipment."[6]

A journalist in the *Musician* noted that most people see heavy
metal as "a musical moron joke, fodder for frustrated teens and
dominion of dim-witted devil-worshippers."[7]

A *Rolling Stone* review of a recent heavy metal album claims
that the singer's "voice rarely drops below a banshee soprano, and
the content of the lyrics is a hoot."[8] Eighteen years earlier a *Los
Angeles Times* reviewer described another heavy metal group as
having "a complete lack of subtlety, intelligence and originality."[9]

Lester Bangs, the only noted rock critic who had anything favorable to say about heavy metal at its inception, writes some years
later: "As its detractors have always claimed, heavy-metal rock is
nothing more than a bunch of noise; it is not music, it's distortion—and that is precisely why its adherents find it appealing. Of
all contemporary rock, it is the genre most closely identified with
violence and aggression, rapine and carnage. Heavy metal orches-
trates technological nihilism."[10]

An academic scholar who specializes in the history of the devil
concluded that "Overt Satanism faded rapidly after the 1970s, but
elements of cultural Satanism continued into the 1980s in 'heavy
metal' rock music with its occasional invocation of the Devil's name
and considerable respect for the Satanic values of cruelty, drugs,
ugliness, depression, self-indulgence, violence, noise and confusion,
and joylessness."[11]

In his social history of rock music, Loyd Grossman referred to the genre of heavy metal as "Downer Rock," commenting that its "chief exponents were Black Sabbath, a thuggy, atavistic, and philosophically lugubrious British quartet who became quite successful performing songs about paranoia, World War III, and other whistle-a-happy-tune subjects."[12]

Politicians have also passed judgment on the genre. Senator Albert Gore, during Senate hearings on record labeling, asked a witness "Do you agree that there does seem to be a growing trend, at least in the heavy metal area, that emphasizes explicit violence and sex and sado-masochism and the rest?"[13]

The mass media has joined the chorus of contempt. *Newsweek,* in 1990, ran the following advertisement for its upcoming issue on youth: "Is being a teenager still something to look forward to? Little kids think teenagers are really cool. But how cool is it to come of age in the age of AIDS, crack and heavy metal?"[14]

Heavy metal music is a controversial subject that stimulates visceral rather than intellectual reactions in both its partisans and its detractors. Many people hold that heavy metal music, along with drugs and promiscuous sex, proves that some parts of youth culture have gone beyond acceptable limits. To many of its detractors heavy metal embodies a shameless attack on the central values of Western civilization. But to its fans it is the greatest music ever made.

The severity of the denunciations directed at heavy metal and the disagreement exhibited by its two major opponents, the liberal-left rock critics and the religious right, concerning what to denounce are enough to pique a sociologist's interest. Why should a style of music have occasioned such extravagant rhetoric, not only from members of the lunatic fringe, but also from responsible elements on both sides of the political spectrum? Can a form of music that has attracted millions of fans for more than twenty years be all that dangerous? Does a form of music warrant being placed along with a dread disease (AIDS) and drug abuse? Are the critics of heavy metal really talking about music? If not, what is it that they are talking about?

The broadest purpose of this book is to show how sociology can inform public discussion of heavy metal. This book is not meant to be another voice in the controversy, but an effort to step back and reveal the elusive subject that is at the center of the controversy. In light of public debates over the advisability of censoring heavy metal music, this study is meant to show how heavy metal music is made, used, and transmitted by social groups. Only an objective inquiry can permit rational judgment about the merits of the proposals to limit the freedom of heavy metal's artists, audiences, and media.

The focus here is on the social dimension of heavy metal, not on the individual bands and personalities that are the usual concerns of almost everyone who writes about the genre. You do not have to be a fan or a detractor of heavy metal to read this book and gain an understanding of how this genre of popular culture is put together. If you have little or no acquaintance with the music, you can listen to some of the "suggested hearings" I list in Appendix A. If you are familiar with heavy metal, you will find that the specific examples that appear in the discussion reinforce and deepen the general analysis. You will also be able to think of other examples that substantiate or perhaps challenge the claims made in the text.

A Cultural Sociology of Heavy Metal

The field that explores the social dimension of forms of cultural expression is called cultural sociology. Generally, cultural sociology investigates the creation, appreciation, and mediation of cultural forms. In the case of heavy metal, that investigation involves artists, audiences, and mediators (those who bring the musicians and audiences together through such "media" as radio, records, and magazines).

Cultural sociology helps to clarify existing conditions that policies are intended to preserve or change. It does not, for example, join the debate over whether heavy metal is good or evil, a legitimate form of entertainment or a threat to youth. It examines how the music exists in a set of social relations. The basic message of cultural sociology can be put in a few words: know something about what you are discussing before you make policy about it.

Cultural sociology does not lend itself to a complete understanding of public debate and policy. It does not provide detailed clarifications of the value choices and ethical principles involved in alternative policies, in the manner of public ethics. It does not describe the dynamics of the policy-making process, in the manner of political science. It is not concerned with the impact of social policy, nor with the formation of new policies. It addresses a more immediate question: What are we making a public issue about?

Sociology of culture contributes to public discourse by exploring the factual assumptions of the parties involved in debate over policy. Most of this study will offer a sociological description of heavy metal. This description has value in itself as a contribution to cultural sociology. But this description also represents the kind of attempt at objectivity that public discourse, at least on this issue, needs the most.

In order to enlighten public discussion, the approach taken here must be comprehensive. No source of data or interpretation that is acknowledged to be part of cultural sociology can be ignored. This study of heavy metal is based on data drawn from a wide variety of sources based on diverse kinds of methods. Among them are participant observation (backstage, in recording studios, at basement rehearsals, on concert lines, in concert audiences, at record stores, on tour buses, etc.); the use of key informants among the musicians, the audience, and those in the media; unstructured interviews and questionnaire research; and nonparticipant field research (observing and counting). Also, the contributions of the scholarly literature and the media concerned with heavy metal have been consulted and integrated into the discussion where appropriate. No practice of cultural sociology is entirely alien to the following study.

The result of applying all these various methods is a description of the structures of heavy metal. Those structures are composed of relations between contrasting meanings and diverse social roles and functions. Heavy metal does not have a single meaning or even a single description. It is a compound of different elements. But it is not simply a hodgepodge. Heavy metal and many of the components that contribute to its making are "bricolages."

A "bricolage" is a collection of cultural elements.[15] It is not like a machine in which each part is specially adapted to contribute to the proper functioning of the whole. A bricolage is much looser than that. Its parts exist for themselves as much as they do for the whole. They are held together not by physical or logical necessity but by interdependence, affinity, analogy, and aesthetic similarity.

The comprehensive descriptions presented here are sociological bricolages.[16] They are constructed from the varied stock of data gathered by the many methods mentioned above. These descriptions are not works of artistic expression but attempts to honor the diversity of heavy metal. They can and should be judged for factual accuracy, logical consistency, and comprehensiveness, when those criteria are appropriate. But they should also be judged for their ability to reveal patterns that are generous enough to be faithful to heavy metal's actual complexity. Heavy metal is itself a bricolage, a loose organization of diverse elements. Only a sociological bricolage can reveal its complexities.

No single description does justice to the richness of the social dimension of heavy metal. Musicians, audiences, and mediators each grasp the whole in different, often contrasting, ways. They give three distinctive perspectives on the music, which cannot be put together into a single view. In the place of a unique view we must depend on a loosely seamed bricolage of viewpoints. As one reads about each participant in heavy metal's social dimension, one gets a distinctive vision of that whole dimension. These visions supplement each other but maintain their independence from the alternatives.

Genre

Heavy metal is a musical genre. Although some of its critics hear it only as noise, it has a code, or set of rules, that allows one to objectively determine whether a song, an album, a band, or a performance should be classified as belonging to the category "heavy metal." That code is not systematic, but it is sufficiently coherent to demarcate a core of music that is undeniably heavy metal. It also marks off a periphery at which heavy metal blends with other genres of rock music or develops offshoots of itself that violate parts of its code or develop new codes. Those seeking to investigate heavy metal need to be aware of the codes through which competent listeners appreciate the music and must be able to listen to it through those codes.

A genre of music includes at its minimum a code of sonic requirements that music must meet to be included in it. That is, a genre requires a certain sound, which is produced according to conventions of composition, instrumentation, and performance. For some types of music the sonic requirements in themselves define the genre. But most music also incorporates a visual dimension. Finally, some music has words that provide an added dimension of meaning. In the case of heavy metal, the sonic, the visual, and the verbal dimensions all make crucial contributions to the definition of the genre.[17]

Heavy metal, like other styles of music, was identified as a genre only after it had come into being. As Ronald Byrnside notes, musical styles "generally follow a pattern of formation, crystallization, and decay."[18] During the period of formation, the distinction between the new style and the styles out of which it erupts are still unclear. Later, in the period of crystallization, the style is self-consciously acknowledged. Its audience recognizes it as a distinctive style. But the boundaries of that style are not rigid. They expand, contract, and shift as artists, audiences, and mediators make new initiatives and change their various musical, social, and financial interests.[19]

To call heavy metal a genre means to acknowledge it as something more than a marketing category. It has a distinctive sound. It also has a stock of visual and verbal meanings that have been attached to it by the artists, audience members, and mediators who construct it.[20] Heavy metal has gone through what Byrnside calls the formative and crystallization phases. It has so far resisted decay, in which "the style becomes so familiar and certain things about it become so predictable that both composer and audience begin to lose interest."[21] Resistance to decay, however, does not mean the persistence of exactly the same pattern of meanings.

For a number of reasons, the most important of which is the growth of a subculture identified with the music, heavy metal has persisted far longer than most genres of rock music. It has also broadened. At heavy metal's peripheries, offshoots have appeared that are not yet independent enough to be called separate genres, and are therefore best called subgenres. The two main subgenres, thrash metal and lite metal, are treated in the following study in terms of their similarities to and differences from the core of heavy metal. Each of these offshoots changes or even breaks the heavy metal code in some ways, but still retains enough of this code to be placed in the same "family" with it.[22]

The family that includes heavy, lite, and thrash metal is called here simply "metal." When the term "metal" is used in the following discussion it normally refers to the loose bricolage composed of the genre of heavy metal and its subgenres. "Heavy metal" is sometimes called "classic" metal when references are made to the period after the eruption of its subgenres. Mapping the complexities of metal is part of this study, but that mapping is always done from a center, the core of the heavy metal genre.

The core of heavy metal—its sonic, visual, and verbal code—is defined in terms of the genre's period of crystallization in the mid- to late 1970s. From that period one can look back to the formative phase, identifying precursors and initiators, and also look forward to the phase of fragmentation (not yet decay), in which subgenres erupted. In the crystallization period heavy metal gained a core audience and became identified with a distinctive youth culture. The core of the heavy metal genre and its subcultural audience is the center of gravity of this study.

Transaction

The social dimension of heavy metal is a transaction between the artists, audiences, and mediators that enable the genre to exist. A transaction is a set of exchanges between participants. Each participant does something distinctive to contribute to the transaction and receives something in return from the other participants. Each one has its own independent interests and perspectives on the transaction: artists create and perform the music, audiences appreciate the music and make it the basis of a youth subculture, and mediators bring artists and audience together, usually for a price.

There is no overarching perspective on the transaction as a whole, only the viewpoints of the actors who put it together.[23] Once one has read chapter 2 of this work, in which the genre of heavy metal music is described, you could, in principle, read the following three chapters on the different participants in the transaction in any order you choose. All participants—musicians, audience, and mediators—are equally essential to heavy metal. No one of these three perspectives is more fundamental than the other two. Each one tells its own story of heavy metal. The order in which to tell these stories is somewhat arbitrary, but here the artist's perspective is presented in chapter 3, the audience's perspective in chapter 4, and the mediator's perspective in chapter 5.

The sequence of perspectives is meant to make sense in terms of how culture is socially constructed. One can imagine someone creating a piece of music that is never performed before an audience, but one cannot imagine an audience without any music to which to listen. Similarly, one can imagine artists and audiences getting together to perform and listen without benefit of mediators, such as record companies and concert promoters, but one cannot imagine such mediators without preexisting artists and audiences for them to serve.

The sequence artist-audience-mediator gives priority to culture over structure: an artist creates music for an audience and is connected with that audience through the offices of mediators. The accent is on the artists who create within the cultural form. But the transaction that constitutes heavy metal can be conceived in an alternative way, from a structural viewpoint. Here the sequence runs from mediator to audience to artist: the mediators deliver the artists to the audience in return for payment. In this view the artists mediate between the mediators and the audience.[24] The structural version of the transaction is used to describe a heavy metal concert in chapter 6. The concert is a special event in which all of the participants in the transaction are brought together in a common context of space and time, producing the closest approximation there is to a community of heavy metal.

Once the three perspectives on heavy metal have been presented and then have been adapted to the concert, the description of the social construction of heavy metal is complete. Then it is time to compare the sociological description of heavy metal with the descriptions of it in public debate. In Chapter 7 that task will be undertaken. The study ends with some reflections on why heavy metal has provoked such hostility from both the left and the right ends of the political spectrum.

Now we can begin at the beginning, before there was a heavy metal genre for the musicians, audience, and mediators to construct. Heavy metal erupted with new features that gradually distinguished it from the music present at its time of origin. But it had influences, precursors, and prototypes. Heavy metal crystallized, as Byrnside says, out of a formative phase.

2

Heavy Metal: The Beast that Refuses to Die

"Turn Up the Music"
—Sammy Hagar

The heavy metal genre erupted in the early 1970s from the wider cultural complex of rock music, which, in turn, had grown out of the rock and roll of the 1950s.[1] Rock and roll and rock are far too broad to be considered genres themselves; they must be categorized as formations within the field of musical culture that include varieties of genres and less crystallized subforms.[2] Neither rock and roll nor rock has a standard definition. Each is a bricolage that can only be defined or totalized from one of its aspects. Each aspect will have its own history or genealogy of its origins, which makes sense of what it is.

Rock History

Heavy metal has produced texts that offer their own history of rock and roll. Perhaps the paradigmatic text in regard to rock and roll's genealogy is AC/DC's song "Let There Be Rock."[3] For AC/DC, rock and roll was a genuine eruption, not a product of an insensible and continuous evolution of musical forms. Rock and roll was something uniquely new when it arose in 1955.

The progenitors of rock and roll were the musical sensibilities of two races, the whites and the blacks. The former provided the schmaltz and the latter provided the blues. "Schmaltz," which literally means rendered chicken fat, is used figuratively to refer to the sentimental and overemotional styles of pop crooners, and more generally to the way in which those styles are promoted and projected. "The blues" is that complex musical genre that expressed the joys and sorrows of African-Americans in a secular key. Pop is a dream machine, whereas the blues seek to portray life without illusion. According to blues singer Muddy Waters, "The blues had a baby and they called it rock and roll." What Waters does not mention—and AC/DC does—is that the father of this bastard child was schmaltz. In AC/DC's vision the unassuming and straightforward blues are given a shot of emotional hype, resulting in a hybrid music with emergent qualities that are all its own.

According to AC/DC, no one knew what the progenitors of rock and roll had in store, but Tchaikovsky heard the news. Here AC/DC acknowledges one of the founders of rock and roll, Chuck Berry, who in his 1955 song "Roll Over Beethoven" exhorts Beethoven to roll over in his grave and tell Tchaikovsky the good news that rock and roll has been born.[4] In the AC/DC song, rock is born as a concert, which gives it a power of immediacy. The song presents a series of ordinations that there be sound, light, drums, and guitar. This order of birth presents rock and roll from the viewpoint of heavy metal. Sound comes first: volume, a key emergent characteristic of rock and roll, was not a defining feature of pop or the blues. Next comes the stage lights that illuminate the band, the gods of the music. Finally come their instruments, the drum and the guitar. For heavy metal, rock and roll means the appearance of a sensual and vitalizing power that only heavy metal brings to its highest pitch, its perfection.

Rock and roll was superseded in the 1960s by rock, which was also a hybrid formation. Rock remixed rock and roll's constituents, adding a new, and this time around, less diluted shot of blues. New elements, especially folk music, were mixed into the blend. The rock of the late 1960s encompassed an incredibly diverse set of musical styles. Consider Woodstock. All the music performed at the Woodstock Music and Art Fair, held 15–17 August 1969, was considered "rock" by performers, audience, and promoters. Jimi Hendrix, Sha-Na-Na, the Who, the Jefferson Airplane, Janis Joplin, and Joe Cocker all belonged in the same fold. The audience appreciated it all as an undifferentiated musical style that was distinguished from other broad styles such as pop and folk music. A few years after Woodstock, however, young people would no longer use the term "rock" to name the type of music they favored. Asked for their preference, now they would refer to some genre or specific artist. The "rock" audience had lost its cohesion and fragmented into distinct followings for such forms as the art rock of Genesis and Yes, the southern rock of the Allman Brothers and Lynyrd Skynyrd, the singer-songwriter style of James Taylor, and heavy metal. The record industry encouraged the divisions as a marketing strategy, intensively exploiting the new, specialized audiences.[5]

The splintering of rock reflected the splintering of the youth culture. International in scope, the youth community of the 1960s had shared tastes in clothing, drugs, music, and social and political ideals. The culture had never been hegemonic, but for the media, for political and social authorities, and for many young people, even those who did not adopt its forms, the youth culture had symbolized the solidarity of youth. Although it grew out of the affluence that followed World War II, and although it was celebrated in the rock and roll of the 1950s, the youth culture's full emergence as a coherent and powerful unit of society can be traced to the civil rights movement of the early 1960s, the free speech movement that began on college campuses around 1964, and especially the antiwar movement that began in earnest around 1966. The youth culture achieved its most unified form in the period 1966–68. The decline and fall of the youth culture took place during the years from 1968 to 1972. Among the events that occurred in this later period were the police actions against mainly youthful demonstrators in Chicago, Paris, and Mexico City—among other places; the failure of Senator Eugene McCarthy's campaign for president; the assassinations of Martin Luther King, Jr., and Robert Kennedy; and the killings of students at Kent State and Jackson State universities. The Woodstock triumph of August 1969 was negated by the horror of Altamont in December of that same year. The breakup of the Beatles in 1970 marked the end of a group that had in many ways symbolized the youth culture. The final nail in the youth culture's coffin was the end of the draft. This backhanded payoff to the antiwar movement satisfied its more selfish demands, but in the process undercut its sense of idealism. Heavy metal was born amidst the ashes of the failed youth revolution.

A Genealogy of Heavy Metal

The eruption of the heavy metal genre, its formative phase, occurred during the years between 1969 and 1972. No one can name a specific date at which the genre became clearly distinguishable; its beginnings must be traced retrospectively from its phase of crystallization in the mid-1970s. At first what will later become the code of the genre appears in isolated songs. Then the work of a band or a cluster of bands begins to exemplify this code. Finally, the rules for generating the music played by such a cluster are self-consciously acknowledged and become a code for others to emulate. At that point the genre has achieved full being.

Heavy metal has many histories. There is no consensus on its precursors, basic influences, first full-fledged songs and bands, or developmental stages. There is even some debate about its name. Halfin and Makowski, in their book *Heavy Metal: The Power Age,* bemoan this lack of unity: "One of the many problems with Heavy Metal is that it comes in so many guises—one cringes and blushes in embarrassment at the thought of the pointless/countless tags attached to it."[6] Some commentators would have the genre begin as early as the mid-1960s, whereas others trace its origins to the early 1970s. There is even dispute about the time at which a band becomes historically relevant. For some it is the moment the band was formed, but for others it is the date of its first album release. This confusion is to be expected when treating a bricolage genre and an undisciplined discipline.

Histories of heavy metal also tend to vary according to where and when they were written. For instance, the title for which was the first real heavy metal band is a contest between Led Zeppelin and Black Sabbath. Americans tend to pull for Led Zeppelin, a band that has been popular in the United States for more than twenty years, but the British favor Black Sabbath. The American critic Pete Fornatale argues that "Without question, the members of Led Zeppelin . . . were the founding fathers of heavy metal. They set the standards by which all other groups who followed in their wake must be measured."[7] A British scholar counters, "arguably the first of these heavy rock bands [is] Black Sabbath."[8] Many others accord both groups an equal place as the initiators of the genre. A few commentators, generally American, put forward rival groups such as Iron Butterfly, Steppenwolf, or Blue Cheer, as in this dogmatic statement, "Blue Cheer . . . 1967 [was] the first of all heavy metal bands."[9] The present discussion will follow the majority of commentators and will grant precedence to both Black Sabbath and Led Zeppelin as the founders of heavy metal. The first albums of these two groups include much that later formed the sonic, visual, and verbal code of heavy metal.

Constant concern with drawing fine distinctions between who is within and who is without the pale of heavy metal is a staple of discourse among heavy metal critics and fans. For example, the genre's boundary line was the focus of a review of an album by a band called Fist, written in 1982: "This is a hard rock band as opposed to heavy metal. Metal evokes visions of Sabbath, Priest, and Motörhead, while hard rock is the Who, the Stones (sometimes), and Steppenwolf. Now, Steppenwolf was pretty heavy, but rhythmically they were doing things that could not be called heavy metal rhythms in a hard rock setting."[10] So much for those who think rock music is merely undifferentiated noise.

I asked a panel of heavy metal experts (some in the industry, others who have written academic works on the subject, and others who are serious fans of the genre) to nominate the groups that best exemplified the genre. They returned their written responses, but many of them also wrote supplementary letters or called me to express their concerns. They tended to recognize, at some level, that not everyone would agree with the way in which they as individuals drew genre boundary lines. Several strongly argued for their own demarcations. The brief history and description of heavy metal presented in this chapter is based neither on my personal sense of the boundary of the genre nor on the specific demarcation of some expert. Rather, the boundary line is replaced with a broad smudge. This visual metaphor allows for the recognition of a core of heavy metal groups for which there is broad expert consensus and a periphery of many musical types and specific groups that could be described as "more or less" heavy metal.

The debates over the boundaries of the genre underscore its complex heritage. Genres tend, as Byrnside notes, to go through a formative process in which they detach themselves from predecessors.[11] Heavy metal's predecessors form an amalgam of different musical styles and specific rock bands. Like the English language, which mixes Germanic Anglo-Saxon and Latin-derived French, heavy metal is primarily a blend of two sources, blues rock and psychedelic music. Anglo-Saxon provided English with its grammatical structure and most of its basic vocabulary, the words used by a rural population living in the everyday world. French contributed a considerable enrichment to its vocabulary. With the advent of the modern age, other languages have provided additional enhancements to English. Similarly, heavy metal's basic grammatical structure is provided by blues rock. This structure was ultimately derived from the American, urban, and electrified blues of artists such as Muddy Waters and Howlin' Wolf. Heavy metal borrowed its "grammar" secondhand from blues rock, with many modifications and already fully rocked up. The main mediators between blues rock and heavy metal were the British guitar-based groups, particularly the Yardbirds. That group's succession of lead guitarists— Eric Clapton, Jeff Beck, and Jimmy Page—revered the black bluesmen but did not slavishly imitate them. Another interpreter of the electric blues tradition, Jimi Hendrix, also exerted a powerful influence on the musical and performance features of heavy metal. Hendrix and Cream (Clapton's post-Yardbirds band) introduced some jazz elements, foremost among them extended instrumental solos, into their mix of blues rock. Heavy metal derived its basic song structure, its fundamental chord progressions, and its guitar riffs from the blues-rock tradition. Virtuoso lead-guitar techniques were a major legacy of blues rock to heavy metal.

Heavy metal added psychedelic/acid-rock music to the basic structure of blues rock.[12] Hendrix was already on to much of the psychedelic style, including its focus on visuals. He died before heavy metal became a well-defined genre, but he exerted an enormous influence on the eventual emergence of heavy metal through his personal charisma and talent, and through his embodiment of the two major traditions that formed the foundation for the genre. Psychedelic music was noted for its mysterious, drug-trip lyrics, and for the colorful clothes and lighting that marked its performances. Musically, it is jazzlike, but with a distinctive repetition of simple phrases. Using few and simple chords, it creates a very complex whole. Like nineteenth-century romantic tone poems, such as Smetana's "The Moldau," which aim at re-creating an object musically, acid rock tries to re-create an LSD experience. Acid rock was aimed not at one's legs or crotch, but at one's head. It wasn't dance music. Getting lost in the music was "getting" the music. This ecstatic use of music was taken up by heavy metal in a Dionysian key, for heavy metal revels in the powers of life.

The psychedelic source of heavy metal is discernible in the early work of artists who later adopted the conventions of the heavy metal genre. Judas Priest, a band that is unanimously judged to epitomize heavy metal, began as a psychedelic band. The group was formed in 1969 and added lead singer Rob (then called Bob) Halford two years later. The group's first release, *Rocka Rolla*,[13] belongs squarely under the head of what is termed hard psychedelic music. All of their subsequent albums, starting with *Sad Wings of Destiny*, released two years later in 1976, are quintessential heavy metal.

Further evidence of the influence of psychedelic music on heavy metal is provided by artists who shifted from that style of music to heavy metal. Lemmy Kilmister, originally with a British psychedelic band called Hawkwind, began Motörhead in 1976. Motörhead is a fast and very heavy metal outfit that is still going strong. The band's name was taken from a Hawkwind song, which it covered. Comparison of the original and the cover show that heavy metal is not continuous with psychedelic music, but a genuine eruption, even if it borrows elements from this predecessor. In the United States Ted Nugent also made the switch from psychedelic to heavy metal music. His band, Amboy Dukes, was a psychedelic group, with a 1969 hit song "Journey to the Center of Your Mind." Nugent's change was more gradual than Kilmister's, but by 1976, with the release of *Free for All*, he was squarely in the heavy metal camp. The relationship between heavy metal and hard psychedelia can also be traced with reference to Uriah Heep. Their first album in 1970 and most of their subsequent material (they, too, are still around) fall within psychedelia. But several of their songs fit clearly within the heavy metal genre. A few commentators even classify Uriah Heep as a heavy metal band. Mike Saunders, reviewing a Uriah Heep album for *Rolling Stone* in 1972, argued for the band's transitional position; their vocals are "psychedelic," he said, but "the guitar and rhythm section is English heavy metal rock."[14]

A final example of the linkage between acid and metal is the group Pink Floyd. Formed inthe mid-1960s, Floyd was a major originator of acid-rock music and was as well known for its light shows as for its acid-inspired, trip-evoking lyrics. They transformed themselves into an art-rock band with the megahit *Dark Side of the Moon*, released in 1973. Their concept albums of the latter part of the decade, *Animals* and *The Wall*, are musically closer to heavy metal.

Other influences and precursors of heavy metal can be noted. High volume as a feature of the musical aesthetic was originated by Blue Cheer and MC5, among other bands.[15] A thick, distorted guitar sound, pioneered by the Kinks on "You Really Got Me," is a metal staple. With characteristic immodesty, the Who's Pete Townshend contends that his group's sound, especially as heard on their *Live at Leeds* album, was responsible for the "gross, disgusting object that was Led Zeppelin."[16]

More generally, as an eruption from the music of the youth culture of the 1960s, heavy metal carried forward the attitudes, values, and practices that characterized the Woodstock generation. It appropriated blue jeans, marijuana, and long hair. It put rock stars on pedestals, adopted a distrust of social authority, and held that music was a serious expression and that authenticity was an essential moral virtue of rock performers. But in some respects heavy metal created a rupture with the ideals of the youth counterculture. The master word of the 1960s, LOVE, was negated by its binary opposite, EVIL. Colors shifted from earth tones and rainbow hues to black. Fabrics went from soft-woven natural fibers to leather. Heterosexual groupings became male-only clubs. The community of youth had fractured. The 1970s was called the "Me Decade." Those who attempted to preserve a sense of community became Deadheads or joined religious cults and became "Jesus Freaks." The heavy metal subculture was another alternative for an exclusionary youth community.

The Eruption of Heavy Metal

In its early formative phase heavy metal was not identified as a genre.[17] The origin of the term "heavy metal" is not easily traceable. Geezer Butler, longtime bassist for and founding member of Black Sabbath, said that Sabbath was the first band to have its music described as heavy metal: "It was around 1972. . . . it was an American critic. It was a derogatory term . . . 'this wasn't rock music. It was the sound of heavy metal crashing.' It was one of those wonderful reviews of our concerts. Someone in England just picked up on that and termed the whole thing heavy metal.'"[18]

The American critic Lester Bangs, who wrote for *Creem* and *Rolling Stone* magazines in the 1970s, has been credited with popularizing the term "heavy metal."[19] However, his landmark two-part article on Black Sabbath in *Creem* in 1972, which some writers claim is the source of the term, does not contain that term.[20] Muddying the issue further are statements that the term originates in William Burroughs's *Naked Lunch*.[21] Burroughs was one of Bangs's gurus and he is quoted by Bangs in the Sabbath article. But Bangs quotes Burroughs's *Nova Express*, where "heavy metal" appears, not *Naked Lunch*, where it does not appear. *Nova Express*, a piece of pornographic science fiction, includes a character called "The Heavy Metal Kid," a denizen of Uranus who has a metal face and antennae.[22] Given the themes of heavy metal lyrics, which include both sex and the grotesque, this derivation is not inappropriate. But it cannot be established with certainty.

The phrase "heavy metal" also was used in a 1968 song by Steppenwolf, "Born to Be Wild." This song was featured in the popular 1969 movie *Easy Rider* and became a biker's anthem. Motorcycle iconography has been a constant feature of the heavy metal genre from the biker fashion of black leather jackets to the use of motorcycles as stage props. The author of "Born to Be Wild," Mars Bonfire, writes, "I used the phrase 'heavy metal thunder' in 'Born to Be Wild' to help capture the experience of driving a car or motorcycle on the desert highway of California. At the time of writing the song I was intensely recalling and imaginatively enhancing such experiences and the phrase came to me as the right expression of the heaviness and noise of powerful cars and motorcycles. Afterwards I realized that I had been aware of the term 'heavy metals' from high school science. It is a part of Mendeleyev's Periodic Table that contains the elements with high atomic weights."[23] Elsewhere he writes, "As to the use of the phrase 'heavy metal' to describe a type of music my understanding is that it came about in this way: The recording of 'Born To Be Wild' helped establish a style of rock in which the vocal is sung intensely and with distortion and the guitar pattern is played intensely and with distortion and is of equal importance to the vocal. More records like this started being heard and a reviewer from one of the rock magazines (I believe *Rolling Stone*) noticing the stylistic similarities used the phrase from 'Born To Be Wild' to describe such music."[24]

There is no doubt that as early as 1971 the term "heavy metal" was being used to name the music characteristic of the genre's formative phase. In a review in *Creem* of Sir Lord Baltimore's album, *Kingdom Come*, Mike Saunders writes that the band "seems to have down pat all the best heavy metal tricks in the book."[25] He compared the group to Grand Funk, Free, MC5, and Blue Cheer, all of which are associated with hard psychedelia and are generally acknowledged to be precursors of heavy metal. But Saunders especially relates them to Led Zeppelin, one of the founding heavy metal bands. He uses the term "heavy metal" along with such synonyms as "heavy music" and "Heavy," which indicates that the term itself crystallized out of a formative discourse.

The term "heavy metal" has been widely accepted in Britain but has met with some resistance in the United States. American critics, especially those who find groups such as Black Sabbath and Judas Priest to be repugnant—that is, who detest heavy metal—try not to use the term. Instead they employ a broader category, "hard rock," in which heavy metal groups are included as a minor component with many others. In part, this usage is due to the wide popularity of the hard-rock radio format in the 1970s, when American critics were carefully attending to radio. Moreover, there were several very popular American bands that were similar to heavy metal groups but did not fully conform to heavy metal's code. Groups such as Aerosmith (first release in 1973) and Kiss (first release in 1974) were too melodic to be considered heavy metal in the 1970s. The term "hard rock" accommodated them, along with purer heavy metal bands. When the genre of heavy metal fragmented in the mid-1980s, one segment, lite metal, embraced Aerosmith's melodic vocal style while retaining specifically metal identifications, allowing Kiss and Aerosmith, which were still going strong in 1990, to be included in the now broadened metal genre. Still another reason for the American reluctance to employ "heavy metal" as a rubric is that the concert bills in the United States in the 1970s were not genre-specific. Heavy metal bands that toured the United States prior to 1979 did not use other, younger or less prominent heavy metal groups to open for them. There just were not many heavy metal bands in the United States at that time. Thus, a bill might headline Black Sabbath, with bands such as Alice Cooper or the Ramones in the opening slot.[26] During Black Sabbath's 1972 tour the art-rock group Yes opened for them. Thus, at that time, a concert featuring Black Sabbath was not strictly a heavy metal concert.

The teaming of disparate types of bands on concert bills was responsible for the further development of the heavy metal genre. Bands had firsthand experience with musical styles that were close enough to their own to invite borrowing. Thus, new influences helped to shape heavy metal as the decade of the 1970s proceeded. Alice Cooper, for example, can be credited with donating a horror-film visual aesthetic to heavy metal's bag of tricks. The dialogic process that creates a genre does not stop once that genre has crystallized. As George Lipsitz argues, "Popular music is nothing if not dialogic, the product of an ongoing historical conversation."[27]

From a historical perspective, the heavy metal genre can be roughly stratified into five eras.[28] Heavy metal erupts from 1969 to 1972 and begins to crystallize from 1973 to 1975. The golden age of traditional heavy metal, its full crystallization, occurs from 1976 to 1979.[29] Then from 1979 to 1983 metal undergoes a surge of growth in numbers of bands and numbers and kinds of fans, leading to an inward complexity and an expansion of its boundaries. This period of growth, finally, results in a rich diversity that crystallizes into fragments and subgenres after 1983. In the following discussion of the heavy metal genre as a code for generating musical culture, the emphasis is on the conventions that crystallized in the golden age and the growth periods. Those conventions are sometimes present fully and often present in varying degrees in the music created before the golden age and after the growth period, but they are frequently mixed with other elements in those periods. The emphasis here in defining heavy metal's code is to identify its core, which can be read back and ahead from the eras of full crystallization. The historical narrative will resume in the concluding section of this chapter, which discusses heavy metal's fragmentation.

The Code of Heavy Metal

Any attempt to define a genre runs into the problem that works of art, even the works created in the commercially based popular arts, are unique. Heavy metal, which has more than just a commercial dimension, is even more diverse than other genres. It is, in the broad sense of the term, a bricolage, which spans a multitude of differences. Each band must distinguish itself from other groups, at least for commercial purposes, which means that there is a multitude of "signature sounds." In addition, even though bands tend to keep within their signature sounds, their works—songs and albums—are expected to differ from one another. Finally, the genre of heavy metal has, over the years, become more diverse. Yet, for all the observable variety, there is a code that during the period of crystallization came to define the genre in such a way that it could be applied to generate new works exemplifying the genre and to identify works that fell within it. That code did not define the rules for generating every work that might fall under the rubric "heavy metal," as that term could be most generally used. But it demarcated a core of music that could be called, indisputably, heavy metal.

When heavy metal is called a musical genre in this study the term "music" is used broadly to include not only arrangements of sound, but other aesthetic and signifying elements that support the sound, such as visual art and verbal expression. The genre, in this sense, is a total sensibility based on sonic patterns but not exhausted by them. The codes provide the form of the sensibility and will be discussed here under the headings of aural, visual, and verbal dimensions of heavy metal. Other aspects of heavy metal's code, which relate more closely to the social transaction that constitutes the genre, will be discussed in the chapters on the artist, the audience, the mediators, and the concert.

The Sonic Dimension

The code for heavy metal involves several sets of rules that can be applied to generate a sound identifiable as heavy metal music. Just as rock and roll adopted many of the rules of rhythm and blues, exaggerating or simplifying some of them in the process, heavy metal's code has deep roots in the rock from which it emerged, specifically the blues-rock and acid-rock traditions.

Defining the code of heavy metal's sound does not describe that sound as it is experienced. As the often repeated phrase has it, writing about music is like dancing about architecture. Critics of all stripes constantly resort to similes and metaphors, often based in the other senses—especially taste and sight—when they discuss a piece of music. Much of the discussion of music in sociology is based on analyses of lyrics, because the verbal element is familiar turf for sociologists. However, understanding the heavy metal genre requires comprehending its sound. After reading the following discussion, the reader should listen to paradigmatic examples of the genre.

The essential sonic element in heavy metal is power, expressed as sheer volume. Loudness is meant to overwhelm, to sweep the listener into the sound, and then to lend the listener the sense of power that the sound provides. Injunctions such as "crank it up," "turn it up," and "blow your speakers" fill the lyrics of heavy metal songs. Black Sabbath's tour in the early 1970s was touted by the record company as "Louder Than Led Zeppelin."[30] At concerts the stage is loaded with stacks of amplifiers so that the decibel level of the instruments can be raised to the limit. The sonic standards of the concert are replicated in recordings. The kind of power that loudness gives is a shot of youthful vitality, a power to withstand the onslaught of sound and to expand one's energy to respond to it with a physical and emotional thrust of one's own. Heavy metal's loudness is not deafening, irritating, or painful (at least to the fan), but empowering. It is not just a "wall of sound," as detractors complain: it is an often complicated sonic pattern played out in high volume.

The essential element of complexity in the sound is the guitar work, which is embedded in an increasingly elaborate electronic technology that distorts and amplifies. The guitar is played as a lead instrument, a musical choice that stresses its melodic as opposed to its rhythmic possibilities. Absent is the jangly guitar sound that characterizes country-inspired rock music. The heavy metal guitar technique requires great manual dexterity, familiarity with a wide range of electronic gadgetry, such as wah-wah pedals and fuzz boxes, and the ability to treat sounds not merely as notes of discrete duration and pitch, but as tones that can be bent into each other.

The style of play owes much to blues-based guitarists who transformed the urban blues–guitar sound into rock. Following the blues-rock tradition, heavy metal guitarists are required to demonstrate technical proficiency. This emphasis on skill contrasts with the punk code, which emphasizes the simplicity of playing, the idea that "hey, anybody can do this, I just learned it two weeks ago." Punk stresses a leveling between fans and performers; heavy metal, with its guitar heroes, emphasizes distance.

Guitar solos are an essential element of the heavy metal code. A solo is a part of the song in which the guitarist does not compete with the vocalist, but may still be backed up by drums and bass. It is a rhetorical element of the code that underscores the significance of the guitar. The solo was a feature of blues-based rock. According to Eric Clapton, solos originated with Cream. The newly formed band had gigs to play. With only about thirty minutes of original material, they stretched it out by doing improvisational solos. The audiences loved this innovation and the solo became a convention.[31]

The guitar is moved along by a beat bashed out on a set of drums. The heavy metal drum kit is far more elaborate than the drum kits employed for many other forms of rock music. Like the guitarist, the drummer has a wide range of sonic effects to deploy, allowing the rhythmic pattern to take on a complexity within its elemental drive and insistency. The kit is miked to enhance volume and requires drummers to use both arms and legs. Prominence is given to the bass drum and the beat is emphatic, in the usual 4/4 time signature of rock. Both its tempo (often rather slow) and its emphatic stresses make heavy metal unsuitable as a dance music because it is too deliberate. Nonetheless, it involves the listener emotionally and physically. At its inception heavy metal was a slow, even ponderous, music, but by the end of the 1970s a wide range of tempos was permitted.

The distinctive bottom sound provided by the bass drum is greatly enhanced by the electronic bass guitar, which performs a more important role in heavy metal than in any other genre of rock music. Mainly used as a rhythm instrument, the bass produces a heavily amplified sound. Its contribution to the instrumental mix is what makes heavy metal "heavy." The genre was technically impossible before the 1960s because only then did the amplified bass sound become technologically available. The physical properties of sound are such that very low frequencies require far more amplification than higher frequencies to be heard at the same level of volume.[32] Due to the prominence of the heavy bottom sound, heavy metal has a tactile dimension. The music can be felt, not only metaphorically, but literally, particularly in the listener's chest.

No other instruments are part of the standard code, although keyboards are permitted. For example, the historical line that stretches from Deep Purple, through Rainbow, to Dio, which spans the full history of the genre, has made the keyboard integral to the sound. Keyboards provide a fullness that other bands achieve via electronic modifications of the guitar's sound. While keyboards do not violate the heavy metal code, other instruments, such as horns, orchestral stringed instruments, or an accordion would break it.

Heavy metal is not instrumental music in the sense of the nineteenth-century symphonic style. The heavy metal code always includes a singer. Yet the singer's vocal style has no connection to the tradition of the pop crooner. In heavy metal there is an intimate connection between the vocals and the instruments, with the voice participating as an equal, not as a privileged instrument. The voice is an instrument that challenges the prominence of the guitar. On record and in live performance, heavy metal's sound is the product of multiple inputs. Sound technicians adjust the relative strength of each component. Vocalist and guitarist are each accorded importance, but neither is allowed to eclipse the other. The two are dual foci, like the twin foci of an ellipse, around which the music is described. The relationship between the guitar and vocals is one of tension; they dynamically contend with one another for dominance but never allow this continuous competition to result in the defeat of either guitarist or vocalist. Like political parties in a two-party democratic system, guitar and voice must compete and cooperate, getting neither too close to nor too far away from each other.

More concerned with the total impact of the sound than with their individual success, the guitarist and vocalist are in an affectionate rivalry with each other. Examples of heavy metal groups with strong dual foci abound. Among the most famous are Led Zeppelin's vocalist Robert Plant and guitarist Jimmy Page, UFO's Phil Mogg and guitarist Michael Schenker, Rainbow's assorted singers in tension with guitarist Ritchie Blackmore, and Judas Priest's Rob Halford working with dual lead guitarists K. K. Downing and Glenn Tipton. Strong vocalists are always seeking strong guitarists and vice versa. The heavy metal vocal is a solitary function, as it is in the blues. But unlike the blues or even blues rock, heavy metal demands the subordination of the voice to the sound as a whole. The heavy metal vocalist is an individual and is not submerged in a vocal group. But the singer is also embedded in the band; the vocalist does not dominate the band and certainly is never its primary excuse for being.

The heavy metal code for the singer is distinctive. One major requirement is the explicit display of emotionality, which contrasts with the punk vocal principle of the flat, unemotional voice. But not all methods of emotional display are permitted. The plaintive, nasal whine of country music and the falsetto of doo-wop are rejected. The singing is openmouthed, neither gritted nor crooned. The range of emotions is wide, including pain, defiance, anger, and excitement. As in other features of the genre, softness, irony, and subtlety are excluded.

Simon Frith's understanding of rock vocals is especially relevant to heavy metal vocals because of their strong emotional component: "The tone of voice is more important . . . than the actual articulation of particular lyrics. We can thus identify with a song whether we understand the words or not, whether we already know the singer or not, because it is the voice—not the lyrics—to which we immediately respond."[33] Many fans and critics would agree that in heavy metal the lyrics are less relevant as words than as sound.[34]

The heavy metal singer's voice must also sound very powerful. It is amplified not merely by electronic devices, but by a robust set of lungs and vocal chords. Special sounds, especially screams, serve to emphasize the power and the emotionality of the voice. Led Zeppelin's Robert Plant and Judas Priest's Rob Halford are well known for their wails and yowls. The sounds are evocative and are probably derived from the blues "shouters" of the southern-based, post–World War II Chicago and Detroit blues traditions. Other singers use an operatic voice, although it cannot be pure toned. There must be a blues-tinged toughness in the voice. Ronnie James Dio's voice, well known in heavy metal circles for fifteen years, is an example of this gritty-operatic option. The heavy metal vocal lacks a mandated accent, such as the punk's cockney or country's southern drawl. In addition to its power, the emotionality of the heavy metal vocals is also a sign of authenticity. The importance of authenticity is a residue of the counterculture of the 1960s and is underscored by the dress code and the lyrical themes of the genre.

High volume, a wailing guitar, a booming bass drum, a heavy bass guitar line, and screaming vocals combine to release a vital power that lends its spirit to any lyrical theme. Popular music, taken as a whole, does not direct attention to any particular feature of a song. As John Street puts it, there is "uncertainty as to what matters in any given song: the sound, the tune, the words or the rhythm."[35] Styles such as disco, house, and salsa privilege rhythm. So does rock and roll, as the often parodied assessment makes clear: "It's got a good beat and you can dance to it. I'd give it a 9.5." In contrast, it is the lyrical element as a poetic expression or a call to arms that is most significant for the folk and folk-rock genres. For pop as a musical style and for advertising jingles, the melody is what counts. For heavy metal the sound as such—its timbre, its volume, and its feel—is what matters, what defines it as power, giving it inherent meaning.

The Visual Dimension

The sonic power of heavy metal is supported and enhanced by a wide range of visual artifacts and effects that display its inherent meaning. The visual aspect of heavy metal comprises a wide range of items including band logos, album covers, photographs, patches, and T-shirts; live performance visual elements such as concert costumes, lighting effects, stage sets, and choreography; and magazine artwork and music video images.

Heavy metal bands, more than other types of rock groups, use logos. These function in the same way as do the logos of multinational corporations, to provide fast identification and to convey a significant image. Logos serve to identify the band both visually and verbally, since most of them present the band's name in stylized letterings. Although each band tends to use a distinctive typeface, there is a similarity among those used in the genre. The code can be specified with reference to both positive and negative rules. Gently rounded typefaces are avoided, since they communicate an image of softness. The ubiquitous Helvetica typeface, which has come to dominate all manner of official signs from interstate highway information to logos of government bureaucracies, is also rejected. Helvetica, lacking embellishments of any kind, suggests neutrality, efficiency, and order, all of which are antithetical to heavy metal. The minimum requirements for a heavy metal typeface are angularity and thickness. The typefaces are more elaborate than mere block lettering, incorporating a multitude of oblique angles and rather squared off ends. Some resemble runic, Teutonic lettering.[36] Others have a menacing, armor-breaking mace or sawtooth appearance.

Typefaces are often embellished with a thunderbolt motif. Bands such as AC/DC and UFO, among others, incorporate the symbol of lightning, standing for released energy, into their logos. AC/DC has exploited the imagery to the fullest extent, placing a lightning bolt in the middle of its name, which itself refers to electrical currents. Tradition has it that AC/DC got the idea from the back of band member Angus Young's sister's sewing machine. The group has done albums entitled *High Voltage* and *Powerage*. The cover of the latter shows a very jolted Angus, electrical wires emerging from his jacket sleeves, illuminated by an aura of shocking light, which is also seen in his eyes and mouth. The typeface also looks as if it had been shattered by lightning.

Logos are used on album covers and the alternative media that accompany recorded music. They are also significant features of T-shirts, pins, hats, and patches—the merchandise bought and proudly worn by fans. Like the logos, the album covers serve the dual purpose of identifying the band and projecting its desired image, attitude, and emotion to the potential purchaser. On one level, album covers are marketing devices, not unlike the package designs for boxes of cornflakes or cans of soup. They serve to catch the eye of the potential consumer and to identify the product by both genre and specific artist. Heavy metal crystallized in the era when the album was the major medium for recorded music and when the album cover not only performed a marketing function but also served as part of the total aesthetic experience of being part of rock culture. Had the genre crystallized in the mid-1980s when audio cassettes, with their much smaller surface area, supplanted albums, an important part of the genre would never have emerged.

When one flips through rock albums in a store, it is easy to pick out the records released by heavy metal groups. Since the late 1970s the code for covers has been known by designers and fans, although not necessarily self-consciously.[37] The logos discussed above, with their distinctive typefaces, are one clue to the genre. The album's title is permitted to be in a different, rather ordinary, and smaller typeface, indicating that the band, not the particular song or album, is the significant unit of discourse in the genre.

The colors and imagery on the album covers enhance the power conveyed by the logos. The dominant color is black, used especially as the background for the other artwork. Red is the second most important color. The color scheme is not gentle, relaxing, or merely neutral. Rather, it is intense, exciting, or ominous. Whereas the code for pop and country albums mandates photographs of the faces of the performers, the fronts of heavy metal albums are not graced with close-ups of band members. The heavy metal code specifies that what is depicted must be somewhat ominous, threatening, and unsettling, suggesting chaos and bordering on the grotesque. This metatheme was expressed in many ways until the late 1970s, when the code narrowed to include the iconography of horror movies, gothic horror tales, and heroic fantasies; technological science fiction imagery; and impressions of studded, black leather–clad biker types. The bands often pose as bikers. Among the famous albums using the biker motif are Accept's *Balls to the Wall*, Scorpions' *Love at First Sting*, Judas Priest's *Hell Bent for Leather/Killing Machine*, Mötley Crüe's *Too Fast for Love*, W.A.S.P.'s *The Last Command*, and Motörhead's *Ace of Spades*.

The album covers, often reproduced on T-shirts, are designed to convey a mood or a sentiment. The visual imagery contextualizes the music or at least provides a clue to its meaning, a reference in terms of which to appreciate it. The impact is similar to that of the stained-glass images and filtered light that contribute to the total experience of listening to church music, or the psychedelic album covers and black-light posters that contributed so much to the acid-rock ambience.

Visuals are also an integral part of the heavy metal concert experience. Here, too, the genre did not create a code de novo but initially borrowed existing standards from the musical cultures within which it was embedded. Early performers adopted the "authentic" look of their time, wearing the "street clothes"—jeans (bell-bottoms were in fashion in the early 1970s) and T-shirts—

and long hair that served as the everyday uniform of the male members of the youth counterculture in the West. Gaudy Motown finery or British-invasion suits were ruled out as dress-code options. The look carried on the street-tough sensibility favored by the blues-rock crowd.

As heavy metal crystallized, the dress code was gradually modified. A second option, which became dominant among bands playing larger venues, was the biker look. Introduced into heavy metal by Judas Priest in the mid-1970s,[38] the metal-studded leather fashion was reminiscent of an earlier British youth culture, the rockers.[39] The look was originally introduced in the 1950s. Marlon Brando, in the movie *The Wild One*, made the leather jacket a symbol of both masculinity and rebellion. Rebellion against what? Brando's character, Johnny, replies: "Whaddaya got?" The motorcycle iconography is even more directly traceable to Steppenwolf's "Born to Be Wild," noted above as a source for the name of the genre. Similar to the biker style and derived from it is the style associated with the S&M subculture. S&M regalia definitely influenced the heavy metal look. As metal costume designer Laurie Greenan declares, "S&M was heavy metal long before heavy metal was."[40]

The third option for costuming, introduced around 1980, is spandex. Pants made of this material allow greater freedom of movement on stage and better display the athletic bodies of the performers, thereby promoting an image of vital power. The initial style of jeans and T-shirts evinced identification with the fans, symbolizing the performers' origins and loyalties. The next style, the biker look, meshed with a well-known symbol system of rebellion, masculinity, and outsider status that fit in with the other elements of the heavy metal culture. The members of the audience adopted the look for themselves, imitating their heroes. Spandex emphasizes the vitality that characterizes the genre. Male fans have not copied their band heroes by dressing in spandex. Spandex remains stage wear, a costume that serves to distance artists from their audience.

Clothing is not the only visual feature of concerts. Heavy metal retained, in a modified form, the elaborate light shows that were first initiated by psychedelic groups in England and in the San Francisco area around 1967. The technology of the live venue industry was fully exploited by the genre, adding intense, colorful, and increasingly varied overhead lighting, along with flash pots, fog, strobes, and laser beams to the concert experience. The album colors, featuring a dark or murky border surrounding red-hued images of chaos, resemble the concert aesthetic. The effect augments the sonic values, heightening excitement and the release of vital energy.

During the 1980s, music videos provided another medium for the visual expression of heavy metal's sensibility. The code for heavy metal videos was established early in the medium's development. The first rule is that concert footage or a realistic facsimile must be a strong element in the video. However, the medium of television cannot capture the aural power and general excitement of a heavy metal concert. TV is too domesticated in its ubiquitous position as a member of the household to simulate the all-inclusive concert experience. Its smaller-than-life screen and low-quality speakers cannot begin to approximate the sensory inputs of the live venue. To compensate for these deficiencies other visual images, sometimes forming a coherent narrative but generally not, are intercut with shots of the band playing and lip-synching, since the audio portion is not from a live performance, but is recorded in a studio. Visions of sexually provocative women, acts of revolt against figures of authority such as parents or teachers, and scenes of general disorder are usually intercut with the actual or simulated concert scenes. The common element in these images is the flouting of middle-class conventions. Rebellion against the dominant culture is the visual kick to compensate for the lack of the sonic power of the stereo system or of the live heavy metal performance. The ominous power of the album cover and the vital power of the stage costume is supplemented by the video's rebellious images.

The Verbal Dimension

The verbal dimension of heavy metal is at least as complex as its aural or visual aspects. As individual words or short phrases, verbal expression works on the levels of signification. The meaning of a word may be understood in its relationship to other words and/or singly as an evocative symbol. The three interdependent sets of expressions forming the verbal dimension are band names, album and song titles, and lyrics.

In part because heavy metal's unit of discourse is not a song or an album, but a band, the name of the band is a significant part of the genre. Fans display their genre loyalty with T-shirts and jackets emblazoned with the names of favorite groups. The band name serves both as a marketing device and as an artistic statement. To some degree, especially within heavy metal's subgenres, the band's name provides a context of meaning within which the titles and lyrics are interpreted.

A content analysis of the names of heavy metal bands must begin with the fact that the early groups took or created their names before the genre crystallized. Their names reflected general rock codes. The convention for rock bands in the 1960s was to adopt collective names, such as Kinks, Beatles, and Rolling Stones, rather than to create a name based on the personal names of members. Some early heavy metal groups, notably Deep Purple, began their recording careers by playing music that could not be termed heavy metal. UFO, which by the late 1970s was a typical heavy metal band, started out in the early 1970s playing rather spacey, psychedelic music. That accounts for their name, which was also the name of a British club that was "the" place for psychedelic music in the late 1960s. Judas Priest, formed in 1969, took a clever name that resonated with the norm of authenticity, of holding to one's principles rather than being seduced by financial rewards. The biblical figure Judas was a priest/disciple of Christ who sold out for forty pieces of silver. Albums that were ironically titled, such as *The Who Sell Out* by the Who (1967) and *We're Only in It for the Money* by the Mothers of Invention (1967), provided a context for Judas Priest's name choice.

Led Zeppelin's name also was not related to the genre of heavy metal. The group, formed by Jimmy Page after his departure from the Yardbirds, was originally called the New Yardbirds. According to legend, the Who's irrepressible drummer, Keith Moon, heard them and was not impressed. Their music would go down "like a lead zeppelin," he prophesied. Black Sabbath's name, adopted by the group in 1969, is paradigmatic for heavy metal. The band's original name was Earth, reflecting a hippie aesthetic. However, Earth was also the name of a cabaret band and booking agents tended to mistake the bands for one another. After a booking mistake that sent them to a business party at which the audience expected waltzes, the frustrated band members renamed themselves with the title of a song they had just written. *Black Sabbath* was the name of a British horror movie, starring Boris Karloff.[41] They expressly chose the new name to be a corrective to the "peace and love" credo that permeated the youth culture at the time.[42]

Heavy metal bands generally follow the rock convention of avoiding the use of members' names to name the group. In that sense, they remain true to the communal symbolism of the 1960s counterculture. When a personal name is adopted it is often because a key member has established a reputation in other bands and does not wish to relinquish that fame. But even then the personal name tends to be transformed into a collective noun. For example, the bands featuring vocalists Ozzy Osbourne and Ronnie James Dio are named Ozzy and Dio, respectively.

A glance at the names of hundreds of heavy metal groups shows some uniformities of signification and sensibility. A significant portion of the names evoke ominous images. Themes of mayhem and cosmic evil are prevalent. The following are some examples taken from different periods and subgenres: Abattoir, Annihilator, Anthrax, Black 'n Blue, Blue Murder, Dark Angel, Death, Death Angel, Forbidden, Grim Reaper, Iron Maiden, Lizzy Borden, Malice, Manowar, Mayhem, Megadeth, Nuclear Assault, Poison, Rogue Male, Savatage, Scorpions, Sepultura, Slayer, Trouble, Twisted Sister, Vengeance, Venom, Vio-lence, and W.A.S.P. There is no evidence here of 1960s-era flower power.[43] Religious allusions abound, with terms such as "angel," "hell," "sacred," and "saint" forming elements of band names. These names evoke their own sort of power: the power of the forces of chaos and the power to conjure and play with those forces.

Heavy metal album titles and the titles of the songs included on the albums reflect the same themes that the names of the bands do. Indeed, bands often title a song after their own name to celebrate or to make a statement about themselves. Debut albums tend to be eponymous, as is the case in many genres of popular music. The titles of albums are similar to the song titles. Indeed, album titles normally adopt the name of a song within the album.

The themes of heavy metal songs include the themes suggested by the names of the bands, along with many others. However, the album titles and particularly the bands' names provide a context in which songs are heard. They set up an emotional expectation and function the same way that familiarity with a person colors our understanding of that person's words or actions. The lyrics of any song are meant to be heard rather than read, and this judgment holds especially true for metal. Important words or phrases are more clearly articulated by the singer than the rest of the lyrics. They are embedded in the section called the chorus, which is repeated several times during the song, and are easily associated with the sensibility created by the band's name.

Heavy metal maintains a specific relationship between the voice and the words. As was noted above, heavy metal privileges the total sound of the music over any of its components, including the voice. The voice, indeed, is treated primarily as one of the musical instruments. Since vocal power is ordinarily valued more highly than clear enunciation, a song's inherent meaning of vital power is more important than any delineated meaning presented in the lyrics. The singer attempts to project an emotion that is appropriate to the lyrics, avoiding an ironical relation to them. Whatever the lyrics say, they are interpreted within a wider context of musical, visual, and verbal signifiers. The key phrases enunciated by the singer do more to convey a song's meaning than do the entire lyrics.

Analysis of heavy metal lyrics must be informed by figurative and contextual interpretation rather than by a literal reading. Lyrics are not intended to be tightly integrated systems of signifiers, although there are exceptions to this rule. Most lyrics are best understood as a loose array of fragmentary and suggestive signifiers.

Lyrical conventions are sufficiently shared by heavy metal artists and audiences to ensure a great deal of consensus on maximally competent readings. The clusters of themes discussed below are based on my listening to about 4,000 songs within the genre. Confidence in my reading comes from confirmation provided by discussing lyrics with a wide assortment of heavy metal fans, artists, and media personnel, and from reading about 150 heavy metal magazines and all of the academic literature on the genre. In addition, finding basic thematic similarities among the songs by a given group and among songs by groups sharing both musical styles and fans offers some internal validation of interpretations.

No single lyrical theme dominates the genre. According to Kotarba and Wells, the themes of heavy metal song lyrics span a wide range, "from Christian salvation to oral sex."[44] Indeed, Annihilator's latest album contains the song "Kraf Dinner," a paean to macaroni and cheese. A closer look, however, reveals significant core thematic complexes for heavy metal lyrics. Some themes are excluded. Broadway-musical optimism, the hopeful sentiment that "everything's coming up roses," and the confidence in a brighter tomorrow have no place in heavy metal. Also absent is the hope of the 1960s counterculture that "we can change the world, rearrange the world." There is nothing lighthearted in heavy metal's words. The verbal sensibility of the genre parallels its aural and visual dimensions.

What heavy metal takes seriously is power.[45] The sonic power of the music—its inherent meaning—contributes to every delineated meaning that appears in its lyrics. Any lyrical theme, even despair or suicide, is empowered by the heavy metal sound. The major themes of heavy metal fall into two clusters defined by a binary opposition: Dionysian and Chaotic. Dionysian experience celebrates the vital forces of life through various forms of ecstasy. It is embodied in the unholy trinity of sex, drugs, and rock and roll. The Dionysian is juxtaposed to a strong emotional involvement in all that challenges the order and hegemony of everyday life: monsters, the underworld and hell, the grotesque and horrifying, disasters, mayhem, carnage, injustice, death, and rebellion. Both Dionysus (the Greek god of wine) and Chaos (the most ancient god, who precedes form itself) are empowered by the sonic values of the music to fight a never-ending battle for the soul of the genre and to join together in combat against the smug security and safety of respectable society.

DIONYSIAN THEMES. Overcoming the cares of the everyday world and losing oneself in a pleasurable now with no thought of past or future, at least for a few moments, has been a goal sought and often achieved in all cultures. Sexual delight and the gratifications derived from intoxicating substances and music are human universals. They are not the invention of heavy metal nor of its musical forebear, rock and roll.

The romantic love so dear to pop music and the more general sentiment of caring and sharing associated with the counterculture are absent in heavy metal lyrics. The few songs about relationships describe those that have gone sour long ago. But love in its earthy sense of lust and sex is a staple of the genre. Some groups, such as AC/DC and the Scorpions, have many songs celebrating lust. Other bands, such as Black Sabbath, ignore the topic altogether.

Sex, in heavy metal's discourse, is sweaty, fun, and without commitments. It is generally not sadistic and is always exuberant. W.A.S.P.'s infamous "Animal (F**k Like a Beast)," a prime target of antimetal groups, and the Scorpions's "Animal Magnetism" stress the carnality and underscore the absence of a spiritual element in sexual activity. The sheer physical activity of sex is emphasized in a line of songs from Led Zeppelin's "You Shook Me" (a blues cover), through AC/DC's "Girls Got Rhythm," to Cinderella's "Shake Me." The influence of blues lyrics on this cluster of themes is obvious. It is the same blues thematic that entered rock and roll with songs such as "Shake, Rattle, and Roll." Indeed, the term "rock and roll" itself was a blues code word for sex. Since heavy metal is not a dance music, it does not make use of the word "dance," which was the main code word for sex in rock and roll and rock music.

Sex in heavy metal is anything but respectable, a truth made evident in such song titles as Krokus's "Mister Sixty-Nine" and the Scorpions's "He's a Woman, She's a Man." Women are rarely given personal names. They are essentially and exclusively sexual beings, often groupies such as the Scorpions's "Backstage Queen" or prostitutes such as those inhabiting Iron Maiden's "22, Acacia Avenue." Physical beauty is not important; some of the women celebrated in heavy metal song, like AC/DC's Rosie ("Whole Lotta Rosie"), who weighs more than nineteen stone (180 lbs.), and Krokus's "Smelly Nelly" would normally be considered unattractive or even sexually repulsive.

The special twist given to the theme of sex in heavy metal lyrics is to identify it with the core of its vital power, potency. When AC/DC sings "Shoot to Thrill" or Krokus intones "Long Stick Goes Boom," they are bringing sex under the sway of a more general Dionysian impulse. Sex is an emblem of youthful male power, a mark of prowess as well as pleasure.

The second member of the trinity of sex, drugs, and rock and roll does not fare so well in the lyrics of heavy metal. Despite the use of drugs by many members of heavy metal's audience and the celebration of drugs in psychedelic music, heavy metal has avoided the theme, perhaps because it does not resonate with the power of the music the way physical sex does. The most famous drug song in heavy metal is Black Sabbath's "Sweet Leaf," which was written at a time when marijuana use among youth in the West was at a peak. Appearing on Sabbath's 1971 album *Master of Reality,* the song celebrates marijuana for allowing one to know one's own mind. This lyric is not consistent with heavy metal's sensibility, but instead expresses the aesthetic of psychedelic music.[46] The few rousing drinking songs in heavy metal are, however, thoroughly Dionysian. Saxon's "Party Til You Puke" and W.A.S.P.'s "Blind in Texas" are wild musical and lyrical paeans to getting crazy drunk.

Far more important than drugs and even sex to the Dionysian side of heavy metal's lyrical output is praise of rock music. Writing and playing songs extolling the ecstasy that the music provides is almost a genre requirement. Most frequently the music is referred to by the terms "rock" or "rock and roll." These terms are not meant to refer to earlier music styles but to heavy metal's own sound, which is identified as the quintessence of rock. Will Straw, in his study of the genre, states that the terms refer specifically to the "performance and the energies to be unleashed."[47] The list of songs extolling and cheering the music is long and includes Rainbow's "Long Live Rock 'n' Roll" and "If You Don't Like Rock 'n' Roll"; AC/DC's "Rocker," "For Those About to Rock (We Salute You)," and "Let There Be Rock"; Judas Priest's "Rock Hard Ride Free" and "Rock Forever"; Saxon's "We Came Here to Rock" and "Rock the Nation"; Black Sabbath's "Rock 'N' Roll Doctor"; Keel's "The Right to Rock"; Krokus's "Easy Rocker"; Warlock's "Fight for Rock"; Sammy Hagar's "Rock 'n' Roll Weekend"; and Twisted Sister's "I Believe in Rock 'n' Roll." Some of these songs are specifically about live performances and others pay homage to fans. A few, particularly Motörhead's "Rock 'n' Roll" and Ozzy's "You Can't Kill Rock and Roll," celebrate the music for its power to make life meaningful and possible. Most of the songs, however, simply praise, pledge allegiance to, and defend the music. This is not a convention unique to heavy metal, but is a resurfacing of a widespread tradition in rock and roll. Rock, or rock and roll, is praised as music that is wildly pleasurable, Dionysian in the strict sense of the term.[48]

The most exciting aspect of heavy metal music, its high volume, comes in for special words of celebration, for example, in the songs "Long Live the Loud" (Exciter), "All Men Play on Ten" and "Blow Your Speakers" (Manowar), "Play It Loud" (Diamond Head), and "Turn Up the Music" (Sammy Hagar). In such songs the sonic power that most strictly defines heavy metal's inherent meaning achieves self-conscious delineation.

THEMES OF CHAOS. The second major thematic complex of heavy metal is chaos. Whereas Dionysian themes are not unique to heavy metal, references to chaos are a distinctive attribute of the genre. Chaos is used here to refer to the absence or destruction of relationships, which can run from confusion, through various forms of anomaly, conflict, and violence, to death. Respectable society tries to repress chaos. Heavy metal brings its images to the forefront, empowering them with its vitalizing sound. It stands against the pleasing illusions of normality, conjuring with the powers of the underworld and making them submit to the order of the music and nothing else. Robert Pielke, in an analysis of rock music in American culture, asserts, "Most evident in heavy metal has been the attitude of negation, with its emphasis on the images of death, satanism, sexual aberration, dismemberment, and the grotesque."[49] Pielke is correct about the images but not about the "attitude of negation." Heavy metal's insistence on bringing chaos to awareness is a complex affirmation of power, of the power of the forces of disorder, of the power to confront those forces in the imagination, and of the power to transcend those forces in art.

Heavy metal songs that have chaos as their lyrical theme are, at least in a sense, descendants of the blues. Happy talk is eschewed in both cases. S. I. Hayakawa's remarks about the older tradition apply to the metal songs that treat chaos: "There is, then, considerable tough-mindedness in the blues—a willingness, often absent in popular songs, to acknowledge the facts of life. Consequently, one finds in the blues comments on many problems other than those of love."[50] The blues were looked upon by church-going, gospel-singing blacks as "devil songs." Paul Oliver, a student of blues music, concludes, "Yet the blues is much concerned with death and is little concerned with birth."[51] The same can be said of heavy metal.

The discourse on chaos in heavy metal lyrics includes interest in disorder, conflict, opposition, and contradiction. It incorporates images of monsters, the grotesque, mayhem, and disaster. It speaks of injustice and of resistance, rebellion, and death. This constellation of themes can be understood as the inversion of the constellation revolving around Eros in countercultural music, which emphasized images of unity. That tradition accented the declaration or hope of community, of being at one with others, with the ultimate, and with oneself. For heavy metal, the reality of failed relationships overwhelms the utopia of harmonious and uncoerced order.

From another perspective, the themes of chaos can be understood in terms of the distinction between the sacred and the profane made famous by Emile Durkheim. Cultures differentiate ordinary, everyday life from a transcendent, sacred dimension. Working within Durkheim's scheme, others have proposed a division of the sacred into the sacred of respect and the sacred of transgression.[52] Chaos belongs to the latter category. Making it a lyrical theme is an act of metaphysical rebellion against the pieties and platitudes of normal society.

Quite obviously, then, heavy metal did not invent the discourse of chaos. Indeed, it has borrowed liberally from those cultural forms that already incorporated it. Heavy metal's major source for its imagery and rhetoric of chaos is religion, particularly the Judeo-Christian tradition. Although other religions speak to chaos, Judeo-Christian culture nourished the creators of heavy metal and their core audience. The Book of Revelations, that unique apocalyptic vision in the New Testament, is a particularly rich source of imagery for heavy metal lyrics. Not only are songs such as Iron Maiden's "Number of the Beast" inspired by its verses, but it provides a resonance, a cultural frame of reference, for the imagery of chaos itself. The other religious tradition from which heavy metal draws is paganism, the aggregate of the pre-Christian religions of Northern Europe. Since the use of so-called pagan images is judged by Christians to be a representation of chaos, such use by heavy metal bands serves as acts of rebellion.

Religious terminology is replete in heavy metal, from band names such as Grim Reaper, Armored Saint, Black Sabbath, and Judas Priest, to albums with such titles as *Sacred Heart* (Dio), *Sin After*

Sin (Judas Priest), *Heaven and Hell* (Black Sabbath), and *The Number of the Beast* (Iron Maiden). The lyrics make ample use of this religious-based terminology. The battle on earth between the forces of good and evil is a paradigm for the lyrical treatment of chaos in heavy metal. The songwriter is sometimes on one side, sometimes on the other, and sometimes just describing the excitement, profundity, or tragedy of the struggle.

Heavy metal's second major source of the rhetoric and imagery of chaos is secular entertainment. Literature, especially the gothic horror stories of Edgar Allen Poe and the fantasy of H. P. Lovecraft and J. R. R. Tolkien, has inspired songs. Iron Maiden's "Murders in the Rue Morgue," for example, is a liberal and literal borrowing from Poe's story of that name. Sword and sorcery and horror movies, from *Conan the Barbarian* to *Friday the 13th*, have also inspired heavy metal lyrics. Heavy metal's debt to these movie genres, which themselves increasingly use heavy metal songs on their sound tracks, is particularly noticeable on album covers, posters, and stage sets.

Some songs merely describe chaos in one or another of its forms. Mayhem, destruction, and carnage are evoked in songs about plane crashes and the human architects of chaos. Iron Maiden's "Killers" and "Genghis Khan" and Judas Priest's "Genocide" and "Ripper" take the descriptive approach. Another symbol of chaos is the monster. More common to movies than to heavy metal, monsters are anomalies, alien beings that do not fit into the existing order and thus lack relationships to others. They disturb normal society and often seek revenge against it. "Iron Man" and "The Green Manalishi (With the Two-Pronged Crown)" are favorite metal monsters.

Chaos can also be found in the society at large if one looks beyond its mystifications. In "Twentieth Century Man" the Scorpions depict contemporary life as "a jungle," where people are mesmerized by the media rather than connected to one another by love. Allusions to injustice and evil abound in the lyrics of heavy metal songs, indicating breaches of a moral order that the songwriter affirms. According to Iron Maiden, "Only the Good Die Young" in this unjust world. The privileged abuse their power. Rush comments about the power of the rich ("The Big Money"), who control with a "mean streak" and without "soul." In "Shot in the Dark" from *The Ultimate Sin* album, Ozzy Osbourne contends that those in power lack reason. Judas Priest in "Savage" repeatedly demands to know what they have done to "deserve such injustice."

The devil is frequently mentioned in heavy metal lyrics because he serves as shorthand for the forces of disorder. Hell, as both the home of the devil and the place of punishment for those who transgress, is used in heavy metal lyrics as a synonym for chaos itself. Many songs focus on the underworld: for example, Van Halen's "Running with the Devil," Judas Priest's "Saints in Hell," and Diamond Head's "Am I Evil?" (also covered by Metallica). AC/DC's canon runs from "Highway to Hell" to "Sin City."[53]

The attitudes expressed in the imagery of chaos and the rhetoric of transgressing order vary widely among songwriters and specific songs. While many of the songs about chaos are simply descriptive, others contain responses to it. Sometimes those responses are earnest pleas directed against the forces of destruction and sometimes they are expressions of playful delight in the imagery.[54] Although some lyrics issue strong challenges to the sources of disorder and urge listeners to fight the good fight (i.e., Manowar's "Dark Avenger"), most are more equivocal. Calls to rebellion, such as Rainbow's "Kill the King" and Krokus's "Eat the Rich," betoken symbolic resistance to injustice. Judas Priest defends "Breaking the Law" as a response to wrongs and injuries suffered at the hands of the powerful.

Weaker responses to chaos are plentiful. In a song detailing the tribulations of a persecuted pariah group, the American Indians, Iron Maiden cautions them to "Run to the Hills." Lyrics recount the hurt, the sadness, and the weakness that result from the various sources of chaos, ending with a feeling of alienation. This sense of not feeling connected to others, of being a "Stranger in a Strange Land" (Iron Maiden), is itself a manifestation of chaos. Chaos is not only "out there," but also located inside ourselves. When it becomes too powerful, it drives us crazy. Heavy metal lyrics are full of images of mental illness, of disorder within. Boundary words, terms that are applied both to external chaos and to mental illness, such as "confusion" and "derangement," indicate the interpenetration of the external world and our inner being. Images of mental illness abound in songs such as "Am I Going Insane (Radio)" (Black

Sabbath), "Sea of Madness" (Iron Maiden), and "Crazy Train" (Ozzy).

The extreme reaction of the weak and vulnerable to chaos, external or internal, is suicide and death itself. Death is the extinguishing of relations. Since order means relationship among things, death is ultimate chaos. Judas Priest's "Beyond the Realms of Death" describes the despair of someone cut off from the world. Venomously, the person defends his decision to cut himself off from the living. It is his escape from a world so full of "sin" that it is "not worth living in." Black Sabbath's "Children of the Grave" is about the death that will be brought by atomic warfare if the battle for peace is not won. This focus on vulnerability to the horrors of chaos is a very significant feature of traditional heavy metal. It became the centerpiece of thrash metal in the late 1980s.

The possible range of responses to chaos, which run from defiance, through rebellion and flight, to madness and suicide, all privilege the power of disorder. The lyrics indicate that despite human efforts to create order, their endeavors will be frustrated sooner or later. That judgment is presented with all of the power of the music behind it, fostering a sense that one is at least momentarily saved from despair by identifying with the truth of things. There is a deeper truth than the one presented by the respectable world. To accept it is to be empowered.

Chaos is deprived of much of its seriousness when its imagery and rhetoric become occasions for play. The attitude of playing with disorder is not a religious commitment to "Running with the Devil," but a delight in a sense of vitality that refuses to be repressed and suppressed. In AC/DC's "Hell Ain't a Bad Place to Be," "Bad Boy Boogie," and a host of other songs, hell becomes the site of a wild, enjoyable party. It symbolizes a refusal to conform to rules of respectability that repress vitality or to submit to those who wish to exert their domination over others. This reaction to chaos is Dionysian, sublimating it into pleasure through textual play and vindicating the power of art.

One of the most frequent terms in the lyrics of heavy metal songs, whatever their themes, is night. It is a symbol that is rich in meaning and has been employed by creators of culture working the high or the low road from the beginnings of literature. Night is a time of danger, obscurity, and mystery because in the dark of night the forces of chaos are strongest. But it is also the time for lovers and for bacchanalian revelry. Songs such as "Burning Up the Night" (Krokus), "We Belong to the Night" (UFO), "Living After Midnight" and "We Rule the Night" (Judas Priest), and "Turn Up the Night" (Black Sabbath) only hint at the frequency with which the term is used in heavy metal lyrics. Mötley Crüe's album *Too Fast for Love,* released in 1982, indicates that its creators understood the verbal code. Of the album's nine songs, eight specifically mention the word "night" in the lyrics. Since the lyrics of heavy metal songs center on evocative phrases, the importance of the word "night," with its rich evocative heritage, makes it a mediator between the two thematic figures of Dionysus and Chaos.

Under the cover of night everything that is repressed by the respectable world can come forth. What is that respectable world? For heavy metal's youthful audience that world is the adult world. It is no accident that those who testified against heavy metal at United States Senate hearings in 1985 were representatives of parental interest groups (PMRC and PTA), fundamentalist ministers, and physician-owners of psychiatric hospitals specializing in the treatment of adolescents. Heavy metal's inherent power, tied to rhetoric and imagery that puts forward themes that adult society tries to repress, is an act of symbolic rebellion, another chapter in generational conflict. The Dionysian themes and Chaos themes form a bricolage that is given coherence by the fact that both complexes conjure with powers that the adult world wishes to keep at bay and exclude from symbolic representation. It is as if heavy metal's opponents cannot stand to see and hear what they themselves have repressed paraded around them with joyous noise. In its final expression of power, heavy metal inverts and plays with the rhetoric of pastoral power, depriving it of unquestioned authority. It uses the rhetoric of the transgression of the sacred with abandon, redefining what is sacred and what is profane.

The Fragmentation of Heavy Metal

According to Byrnside, a popular music genre goes through phases of formation, crystallization, and exhaustion.[55] In the last phase artists repeat the success formulas of the glory days in a mechanical fashion, boring audiences and critics, and inspiring a new generation of creators to break new musical ground. The established genre then becomes a predecessor of a new one, just as it had drawn from predecessors in its own formative stage. Heavy metal has not followed Byrnside's trajectory. After going through phases of formation and crystallization, it did not become mannered. But neither did it simply perpetuate its golden age. Instead, after a spurt of growth, it began to fragment. Its main line, described in the section above, continued, but new lines were added that departed from some of the codes of heavy metal, but still acknowledged a close enough kinship to their predecessor to prevent them from becoming altogether new genres. Rather than being supplanted by new genres, heavy metal spawned subgenres. During this process, it became part of a wider genre complex, similar, though on a smaller scale, to the vast genre complex of rock, in which it erupted.

The period 1979–81 was marked by an explosion of new heavy metal bands on the British scene. The period became known as the New Wave of British Heavy Metal (NWOBHM).[56] No single musical or lyrical style was associated with the New Wave: each band tended to be rather unique. What all the new bands did share was a general heavy metal sensibility, along with youthfulness and a strong emphasis on visual elements. While many of the new bands continued the established heavy metal tradition, some tended to create specialized niches within the genre. The specialists tended to take elements of the heavy metal code and emphasize one or more of these features to the exclusion or at least the diminution of other elements. Two of these groups, Iron Maiden and Def Leppard, went on to achieve great success. Others, such as Venom, persisted with a more narrow following. The majority faded to black, although even some of these, for example, Diamond Head, left their mark on bands that followed them.

During the early 1980s many new bands were formed all over the world, and some of those that had been around for years were given a better hearing. The rock press duly took note of this phenomena, calling it a heavy metal "revival," "renaissance," and the like. For example, a writer in *Creem* stated in October 1980 that the genre "had pulled a Jesus Christ and was back in the saddle again."[57] The audience for heavy metal became much larger. Even the classic metal bands such as Judas Priest found themselves playing to much larger audiences. The media organizations, always alert to audience tastes, became more open to metal bands. The most public signal of the growth in popularity of the genre was US '83, a festival sponsored by Steve Wosniak in California. One of the three days of concerts was devoted to heavy metal. The featured bands included Ozzy, Judas Priest, Mötley Crüe, Scorpions, Quiet Riot, Van Halen, and Triumph. That day drew a far larger audience than did either of the other two days of the festival.[58]

The increase in numbers and variety of heavy metal bands in the early 1980s eventually gave rise to a fragmentation of the genre.[59] Subgeneric codes began to emerge. That is, the variety of bands began to close ranks around several sets of rules.

By 1983–84 two major subgenres were in place. Each emphasized a different feature of traditional heavy metal. One of them privileged the melody and the other stressed the rhythm. Heavy metal bands in the 1970s may have emphasized one of these musical elements more than the other, but they were heard and judged within the overall code of the genre. For example, the melodic and rhythmic elements were taken to extremes by the Scorpions and Motörhead, respectively. These bands were understood to be working out the possibilities within the genre's code, rather than challenging or attempting to alter it. In the 1970s no segregation of styles in terms of concert bookings, fans, and fanzines was apparent. All this changed during the 1980s. It was as if traditional heavy metal was a solution of various elements that finally became supersaturated and began to crystallize. The fragmentation of the 1980s included a lyrical as well as a musical component split: the melodic specialization took up the Dionysian legacy whereas the more rhythmically oriented level closed ranks around the legacy of Chaos.

Lite Metal

There is no legitimate, established authority, like the French Academy, that decides on the correct name for a musical style or genre, and there is no consensus on what to call the subgenres that crystallized within heavy metal. For the purposes of this analysis I will refer to the subgenre that emphasizes the melodic element as "lite metal." This term indicates the removal of the thick bottom sound of traditional heavy metal. Lite metal has also been referred to as "melodic metal" and "pop metal." Critic Philip Bashe called it "metal pop" in 1983, and identified its major exponents as Def Leppard and Van Halen.[60] Other prominent exemplars of this subgenre are Poison, Bon Jovi, and Ratt.

A host of pejorative terms for the new melodic style have been coined by heavy metal's traditional audience and by fans of the major alternative subgenre. These epithets include "poseurs," "false metal," "nerf metal," "poodle bands," "glam," and "commercial metal."[61] Chuck Eddy, in "Boogie Blunderland," asserts that nerf-metal heroes such as Def Leppard are "teen-pop, phony and wholesome as the New Kids but with louder guitars."[62] Evaluative bias aside, the words used to characterize lite metal by its despisers are useful descriptive terms, since they call attention to features of the genre. Reference to performers of lite metal as "poseurs" indicates that they are judged to lack authenticity. The code of authenticity, which is central to the heavy metal subculture, is demonstrated in many ways. Of all criteria—highly emotional voice, street (not crackerjack) clothes, and "serious" themes—lite metal fails the test of authenticity. The phrase "poodle bands" directs attention to the performers' hairstyles. Members of lite metal bands tend to have "big hair," which is ornately cut, moussed, and blow-dried. The development of lite metal was greatly aided by MTV, which, at least during its first few years, seemed to find extravagant hairstyles a good reason to include a band's video in its rotation, regardless of its musical style. Likewise, the term "glam" is a reference to visuals, pointing to lite metal's colorful costuming and its rejection or alteration of the black, working-class garb or outlaw fashions that were prescribed by the heavy metal code. Chuck Eddy notes that the glittery fashion of such artists as Prince and Boy George was central to rock in general when lite metal erupted: "The glamming of heavy metal has coincided with a decided glitter influence all over the rock spectrum."[63]

Lite metal's vocal style is sweet, with no growls or screams. It is characterized by much use of harmony, which shows the influence of Aerosmith and Kiss. The lyrics are also distinctive, centering on sleazy, raunchy blues themes. Cinderella's popular "Push, Push" exemplifies these features. Aurally, lite metal is a sweetened heavy metal. The subgenre is especially known for its power ballads, which are songs with just enough metal sound (the bass) to be heard as metal, but not so much metal sound that they will be detested by those who are turned off by traditional heavy metal music. Power ballads have been played on radio stations with formats that typically exclude heavy metal. They are crossovers, standing inside and outside the genre simultaneously. They sell albums to a nonmetal audience and enlist part of that audience into the true metal audience. Power ballads are similar in effect to the cover versions of black songs that Pat Boone and other white performers sang, in the process eventually bringing a wider, whiter, audience to rock and roll. The hard-rock format, a radio staple that passes in and out of wide popularity, found lite metal to be an acceptable addition to the sweeter Led Zeppelin tunes that had always been one of its features. Many lite metal bands have refused the metal designation altogether, opting for the "hard rock" alternative. Others have encouraged the use of both designations, one being aimed at the media industry and the other at fans.

Lite metal's verbal elements are more concerned with love and lust than with heaven and hell. Songs mention girls' names and are often addressed to a girl, which is a convention of pop music that serves to acknowledge and encourage the female audience. The influence of blues lyrics in lite metal is marked. It reflects the Dionysian strain in heavy metal and is reinforced by the blues-influenced hard-rock bands, such as Aerosmith, that merged into this subgenre. The sexual themes that heavy metal borrowed from the blues are even more prominent in lite metal. This subgenre also stresses the theme of Dionysian release, with the most intoxicating drug being the music itself. It minimizes the themes of chaos and the apocalyptical battles between good and evil. The real heavy stuff is removed.

The development of lite metal echoes the development of other trends in popular music, such as rock and roll in the late 1950s: "Some post-rhythm and blues music moved closer to mainstream white popular balladry while retaining many of the essential ingredients of rock 'n' roll, thereby creating a softer brand [with] the slightly less colloquial name of rock AND roll."[64] Another parallel is the development of the Nashville sound from country music: "The key to understanding the Nashville Sound is the recognition of what it is NOT. It is not corny or nasal. It does not include a steel guitar, fiddle or banjo. It is smooth, not rough; sophisticated, not corny; 'soft,' not 'hard' country music."[65] These changes all involved the excision of easily caricatured elements, especially those relating to socially problematic images: black, backwoodsy, or evil. The music's appeal was broadened by removing features that for one reason or another only spoke to a minority of listeners. A more "commercial" sound resulted and the success of the operation was confirmed in the market. Fans and critics may argue about the cultural merits of such musical transformations, but their financial triumphs are indisputable.

Speed/Thrash Metal

If lite metal results from the latitudinarian movement in metal, speed/thrash is its fundamentalist strain. Its dominant departure from heavy metal is an increase in tempo. As was the case for lite metal, there are many names for this subgenre. One is "power metal," which is used more in Britain than in the United States. This term underscores continuities with the heavy metal code rather than alterations in it. Power is the basic inherent meaning of heavy metal's sound and the major delineated meaning of its look and lyrics. Speed/thrash is also often referred to as "underground metal." Here the contrast is with commercial metal and its success in capturing a broad youth audience. The term "underground" refers to a social, not a musical, dimension—the pride of an exclusive subculture that rejects mass appeal. Speed/thrash can be understood as an attempt to reclaim metal for youth and especially for males by creating a style that is completely unacceptable to the hegemonic culture. Speed metal represents a fundamentalist return to the standards of the heavy metal subculture. But like all forms of fundamentalism, speed metal is at least as much a new beginning as it is a continuation of what it seeks to revive.

The speed/thrash subgenre erupted in California in 1981–83 with the formation of groups such as Metallica in the Los Angeles area and Exodus in San Francisco. By 1982 a "scene" had emerged, with fans enthusiastically sharing tapes of the bands' demos and bootlegs of their concerts. For many years the subgenre was signed only to independent ("indie") labels rather than to the larger ("major") companies. It was heard only on college radio metal shows rather than on commercial stations. On business grounds alone it deserved to be called "underground."

Speed/thrash was most directly influenced by NWOBHM groups, such as Venom, Diamond Head, and Iron Maiden, all of which made rhythmic innovations. But it also followed in a line already present in heavy metal's golden age. Moreover, speed/thrash bears the trace of the punk explosion. Punk began in England in 1975–76 and reached California four years later. It spawned hardcore, which was particularly strong on both coasts of the United States and bore many resemblances to the erupting speed/thrash style. Groups such as the Misfits, which was alternately called a horror-metal band and a horror-punk band, showed the possibilities for a blending of punk and metal. A more direct influence of hardcore entered the subgenre beginning in 1985–86, when groups such as DRI (Dirty Rotten Imbeciles) and Suicidal Tendencies created a style within a style, termed "thrashcore" or "crossover."[66] Its traces reinforced the punk-related elements that were already present in the subgenre.

Just as the related Jamaican musical styles of ska, rock-steady, and reggae are distinguished by an order of faster to slower tempos, so are thrash, speed, and traditional heavy metal. The intermediary, speed, is played by bands that belong either to speed/thrash or to classic metal, which continued to create and perform traditional heavy metal after that genre fragmented in the 1980s. That is, tempo is not enough to distinguish speed/thrash as a subgenre. Musically it shares the inherent meaning of power with heavy metal. Much of its rupture with its forebear is in the sphere of delineated meaning.

The speed/thrash subgenre can be understood to represent as much a transformation of attitude as a change in music. It pares away the arty, the fantastic, the overblown, and the heroic elements in heavy metal. There is an obvious similarity between speed/thrash's challenge to heavy metal and the contestation, initiated by Martin Luther and John Calvin, against the Catholic Church. Both movements charged that the established form had become corrupt through extravagance and both supported a return to the essential message, stripped bare of all adornment. In their clothes, their relationship to their followers, and their discourse, speed/thrash bands and the early Protestant leaders parallel one another. In the case of speed/thrash, fancy stage wear and elaborate props that set performers apart from their audience are replaced by street clothes (the original heavy metal uniform) and a simple stage. Similarly, the Protestant ministers exchanged the ornate clothing of church notables for a simple uniform and huge, ornate cathedrals for small-scale, simple churches. The distance between the artists and their fans was physically, emotionally, and attitudinally erased, just as the Protestants narrowed the distance between the minister and the communicants. Speed/thrash is a movement to go back to the basics, just as Protestantism stressed a return to biblical essentials.

Although speed/thrash provides some of the most Dionysian sounds ever invented by human beings, it overturns or ignores the Dionysian lyrical themes. It specializes in chaos. Sex is rarely mentioned, alcohol and drugs are judged to be bad rather than pleasurable, and, with a few exceptions, such as Exodus's mosh-pit anthem, "Toxic Waltz," there are no songs in praise of the music. Themes of lust and romance are ceded to lite metal.

Speed/thrash bends the discourse on chaos into specific images and cultivates an explicit rather than allusive lyrical style. It eschews the mystery, the nonspecific ominousness, that characterizes many heavy metal songs. Instead, lyrics focus on the bleak but concrete horrors of the real or possibly real world: the isolation and alienation of individuals, the corruption of those in power, and the horrors done by people to one another and to the environment. As the code of the speed/thrash subculture crystallized, groups took names that embodied it. Anthrax, Nuclear Assault, Slayer, Megadeth, Flotsam and Jetsam, Vio-lence, Sacred Reich, Suicidal Tendencies, Annihilator, and Sepultura are a few of the better known and typical band names in this subgenre. These appellations are suitable within the traditional code of heavy metal; speed/thrash is merely more restrictive than its progenitor.

Some of the bands in this subgenre introduce humor, political radicalism, and irony into their lyrics. Nuclear Assault's lyricist John Connelly claims that he now leaves no room for misinterpretation. Some of his early lyrics that were intended to be humorous had been taken the wrong way.[67] Much of the speed/thrash subgenre adopts the rhetorical stance of the protest song, with its tendency to acknowledge no view other than the singer's and to lecture listeners and leave them "no 'space.' "[68] The treatment of chaos also strongly resembles the content of protest songs. The injustice of the political order, illustrated by Metallica's album . . . *And Justice for All,* is a prime concern of speed/thrash lyrics. Environmental destruction has almost become as standard a theme for this subgenre as sex is for lite metal. Environmental concerns are expressed in songs such as "Inherited Hell" (Nuclear Assault), "Blackened" (Metallica), and "Greenhouse Effect" (Testament). The distance from Dionysian themes is probably best exemplified by songs about drugs and alcohol. No party-hearty attitude here: the songs condemn drinking and driving, as, for example, in the song "Emergency" by Nuclear Assault.[69] The subgenre has produced a multitude of diatribes against drug abuse: "Living Monstrosity" (Death), "The Needle Lies" (Queensrÿche), and "Seconds 'Til Death" (Stygian) are but a few. There are even songs championing animal rights.[70]

The response to chaos described in speed/thrash lyrics is along the line of retreat. Speed/thrash songs are replete with tales of alienation, such as Metallica's "Harvester of Sorrows." The more extreme reaction, suicide, is addressed head-on as an extension of the insanity thematic in traditional heavy metal. Indeed, the concern with suicide and death has become so strong that the speed/thrash subgenre has spawned a subgenre of its own, death metal. This style extracts an even narrower subset of traditional heavy metal themes than speed/thrash does, taking only the negative ultimates of death, gore, and evil as such. Death metal's horror movie depictions are the stuff that "whiten mother's hair." Vocalists in this style have a distinctive sound, growling and snarling rather than singing the words. Making ample use of the voice distortion box, they sound as if they had gargled with hydrochloric acid. The vocals contrast sharply with the usual high tenor of lite metal singers. Instrumentally, they use low-tuned guitars. Verbal cues alert one to this specialty. Bands with the names Death (United States), Coroner (Switzerland), and Sepultura (Brazil) issued albums titled, respectively, *Leprosy, No More Color,* and *Beneath the Remains.* By 1990 there were hundreds of bands, located all over the world, contributing to this fragment of a subgenre. Drawing upon the lyrical themes of chaos in traditional heavy metal, the focal concern of death metal is human misery, especially the triad of death, disease, and decay.

In the thrash/speed subgenre musicians interact with their audiences directly, hanging around with them before and after concerts.

Performers and fans dive into the crowd from the stage during the concert. Band members wear blue or black jeans and T-shirts, or skateboarding outfits (big shorts, high-top sneakers, and baseball-style caps worn backwards) on and off stage. Their hair is defiantly unstyled, unbleached, and long. Fans and performers, given the youthfulness of the band members and their fashion, are indistinguishable from one another. On stage, performers emulate the headbanging and moshing steps of their audience. The subgenre's underground image is best suited for small, grungy clubs. Those bands, such as Metallica and Anthrax, which have achieved enough success to allow them to play large arenas, have tried hard to overcome the commercial features inherent to performing in large venues.

Initially created as a fundamentalist revision of heavy metal's code, the speed/thrash subgenre has evolved into a cross between its heavy metal and punk/hardcore forebears. Since many of the rules within each one of these genres specifically contradict the rules of the other one, the stabilization of the speed/thrash code was not a blending of compatible styles. Speed/thrash is a bricolage of the second order, in which inherent musical meaning (mega-power) is combined with delineated meaning of failure and calamity. Such incompatibilities cannot be bridged logically, but coexist in compromise formations. For example, punk celebrates amateurism, whereas heavy metal requires technical expertise. Since a performer cannot be or look to be both amateur and expert, band members must appear to be one and then the other successively, or split the roles among themselves. The analysis of the amalgamation of opposed elements in speed/thrash would be an excellent case study of cultural transformation.

The Dispersion of Metal

Lite metal and speed/thrash have formed somewhat separate subcultures in addition to generating different musical patterns. The fans of one subgenre generally eschew the other one. Indeed, the styles of the two subgenres contradict one another in many ways. Musicians from one subgenre do not join bands in the other. Nonetheless, for several reasons, lite metal and speed/thrash have not become autonomous genres. Culturally, classic metal continues as a mediation between the two subgenres, carrying on the tradition to which they both pledge loyalty. Commercially, although booking agents for smaller venues keep the styles segregated, in large arena shows and in multigroup festivals bands from various subgenres play on the same stage.

Lite metal and speed/thrash have "family resemblances" to traditional heavy metal. Not only did they erupt from heavy metal, but the traces/influences of that genre—its sounds, visuals, thematics, and attitude, albeit modified or taken in part—are present in both of them. Heavy metal, in its traditional form, has not disappeared. It is still widely performed and very popular. More importantly, the classic metal style, which mediates between lite metal and speed/thrash, shares different practices with each of them. Lite metal and classic metal both create power ballads, and groups such as Whitesnake attempt to straddle the two subgenres. Thrash bands and classic metal bands both play songs that are termed speed metal.[71] Speed, as its name implies, increases the tempo of the song. By the late 1970s songs that would now be called speed metal were done by traditional heavy metal bands. Judas Priest's "Exciter" (from its 1978 release *Stained Class*) would have been a typical example of speed metal had the term then existed. The fragmentation of metal and the terminology that describes it are analogous to the way that biologists understand species differentiation. They reclassify breeds as separate species when intermediary types, which are capable of mating and producing fertile offspring with both extremes, become extinct. Classic metal, the intermediary, is still alive. Thus, in a retrospective of British metal, *Metal Hammer* magazine uses the tripartite division pure heavy metal, glam metal, and thrash.[72]

Another factor impeding the formation of autonomous genres from heavy metal is the presence of thematic diversity that crosscuts musical styles. In the 1980s white metal and black metal emerged. Their lyrical themes are at polar opposites to each other, one of them bringing the "good news" and the other the "bad news." Both include bands whose sounds span the full spectrum of metal.

White metal is more commonly called Christian metal. In part a response to the popularity of the heavy metal genre, it transforms the code of heavy metal to serve the purposes of Evangelical Christian sects and denominations. In part, also, Christian metal is a well-crafted missionary effort to recruit members and save souls.[73] The most well-known Christian metal group is called Stryper. The band has indicated that its name is derived from Isaiah 53:5: "with HIS stripes we are healed." Stryper debuted in 1985 with their album *Soldiers Under Command.* Its music style is classic/lite metal and its song and album titles fall within classic conventions. *To Hell with the Devil* was the title of their 1987 album and one of their popular songs. Another of their songs is called "The Rock That Makes Me Roll." However, one need only see the minibibles they throw to their audiences at concerts or listen to the words of their songs, replete with references to Jesus, to grasp their evangelical message.

At the other end of the musical spectrum from Stryper are groups such as Vengeance.[74] They play an extreme form of thrash metal, with demonic-sounding vocals. Many of their song titles ("Human Sacrifice," "Fill This Place with Blood," and "Beheaded"), their album's title, *Human Sacrifice,*[75] and their name fall squarely within the code of the thrash subgenre. But a closer examination reveals their religious mission. The human sacrifice refers to Jesus's death on the cross. The blood is that of the lamb, which was used ritually in the exodus from Egypt. The beheading is from The Book of Revelations, the source book shared with non-Christian metal groups such as Iron Maiden. Vengeance cites the chapter-and-verse sources of their songs on their lyric sheets.

By 1987 there were more than a hundred Christian metal groups, including Barren Cross, Bloodgood, Saint, Leviticus, Bride, and Messiah Prophet. One journalist, noting that their records are sold at both Christian bookstores and secular retail outlets, terms this subgenre a "musical-missionary movement."[76]

Black metal stands in thematic opposition to Christianity, not looking upward to heaven but setting its sights on the underworld. Satanic symbols and imagery have been a staple of heavy metal since its beginnings with Black Sabbath and Led Zeppelin. In the West there is no better symbol of rebellion. But groups such as Mercyful Fate claimed that they were not playing. Their claims to be true believers, followers of the lord of the underworld, were seen by many to be a commercial ploy. There are very few bands that could be called exclusively black metal, but the category is an acknowledged and logical one for the genre as a whole, inspiring songs, if not albums or the entire output of bands.

Heavy metal began as an eruption in the cultural complex or bricolage of 1960s rock music and a generation later became the core of its own complex of musical culture. The fragmentation or dispersion of heavy metal is a strictly intelligible process. Certain inherent and delineated meanings of the parent music are selected from it to the exclusion of others, and then the selected elements are intensified and/or blended with contributions from other genres or complexes of genres. The sound of heavy metal—its inherent meaning—includes a strong melodic strain and an emphasis on a heavy, rhythmic bottom sound. As has been shown above, lite metal intensifies the melodic component and blends it with elements of hard rock, diminishing the heavy bottom sound, while speed/thrash metal stresses the rhythmic component and blends it with elements of hardcore, subordinating and sometimes even effacing melody. On the level of delineated meaning, lite metal appropriates the Dionysian themes of its parent and speed/thrash the themes of Chaos, blending them with pop romance and social protest, respectively.

The eruption of subgenres in heavy metal is not, then, mainly a result of exogenous or contingent factors in its historical circumstance, but an instance of a normal process of endogenous cultural change. The diverse elements are there to be specialized and blended. All that is necessary is for an artist to sense a possibility and choose to work toward its realization. Of course, there is no reason why artists have to come along and loosen the bricolage of a genre, take some things out of it, add some things to their selected stock from elsewhere, and construct a new bricolage within the old one. But they do. Fragmentation of genres is the result of the encounter between artists and the inner complexity of genres. Genres are not so tightly coupled that they cannot be deconstructed, and artists are not such slavish mannerists that they do nothing but imitate their masters.

By spawning subgenres heavy metal became part of a wider cultural complex, just as it had earlier erupted from a wider complex. The new formation, called "metal" here, includes both heavy metal and subgenres within itself, each of its members being defined by distinctive codes that contain some or all of the elements of heavy metal's code. Heavy metal persists, after the subgenres have crystallized, as classic metal, carrying on the core of the musical culture. It is also ever present in the recordings of its classics, which are replayed and reissued, a library at hand to provide inspiration to new artists and a sense of tradition to fans. Finally, heavy metal is present in the traces that it leaves on the music produced within the subgenres that erupted within it. Those traces are deepened every time a new artist recurs to the classics, whether to cover a song, to continue the classic tradition, or to make a new departure from it; but they are present even when no such recurrence is made consciously and the artist draws only from a subgenre. The subgenre already is marked by a deep enough trace of heavy metal to keep the music produced in it kindred to its parent, if not to its siblings. The periphery can be referred to a core which is continually represented.

That periphery, however, tends to become very vague, ragged around the edges, and permeable to influence from the outside. It is possible for music to become so peripheral, through blending with other musical styles or by rejecting too much of the core code, that it can no longer be logically related back to the core. In that case it would have escaped the cultural complex, probably to enter a new one. The loss of definition on the periphery is particularly likely to take place as the normal process of cultural change occurs and new artists exploit special possibilities within subgenres to the exclusion of other elements of their codes, and most importantly when they begin to blend the subgenres with inherent and delineated meanings from codes outside metal. At that point forms of music will appear that will depart too much from the code of heavy metal to be recognizable as derived from it. If, as this further fragmentation happens, classic metal and the two major subgenres begin to decay, the cultural complex of metal will virtually disappear, except as a closed musical discourse. At present, the classic tradition and the two major subgenres are vital enough to ensure the continuation of metal in the near future. But the process of fragmenting and blending the fragments is already underway in the early 1990s.

A new surge of complexity has begun within metal that is making it lose its definition at the periphery. Lite metal deepens its flirtation/romance with pop, as some bands (e.g., Damn Yankees) incorporate string sections, alien to heavy metal's code, into their music. Other groups, influenced by blends of punk and funk are incorporating funk into metal (e.g., Living Color and Faith No More), often producing a sound the inherent meaning of which cuts metal's power with irony and takes away much of its force. Others (e.g., Jane's Addiction) introduce art rock into the mix, creating a reflective music that militates against metal's directness. Still others (e.g., Scatterbrain) play with the genre self-consciously, undercutting its stance and sensibility of authenticity. All of these developments are too germinal to include in the present discussion, but they indicate that metal is undergoing the normal process of cultural change, even as it retains its core.

The transformation of heavy metal from a genre into the core of a field composed of a genre, several subgenres, and an array of subgeneric fragments and proto-subgenres has been the work of artists, who explore the possibilities of cultural complexes and exploit some of them. The artist is the agent of cultural change and in being so is the initiator in the transaction of artists, audiences, and mediators that constitutes metal. Metal must reproduce itself to persist as a cultural complex and it does so through musical creativity and contrivance. In the most direct sense, without the artists there could be no musical culture. But the artists do not come from a world of their own. Indeed, they are enmeshed within the wider transaction, mediating between the two worlds of audience and mediators. They arise from the audience and then return to it through the offices of the mediators. The sociological study of the transaction constituting heavy metal begins with the artists and how they come to perform their initiating function through taking up an occupation.

Making the Music: Metal Gods

"It's a Long Way to the Top (If You Wanna Rock 'n' Roll)"
—*AC/DC*

Dressed in a black leather jumpsuit, standing stage right, with the spotlight on him, and his white flying-V guitar gleaming, Michael Schenker is playing the big solo in "Rockbottom." His group, UFO, is headlining at the Chicago Amphitheater in 1979. "Rockbottom" is one of those transcendent heavy metal songs. The vocalist, Phil Mogg, sings for less than one-third of its almost eleven minutes. The guitarist is in command throughout.

The ends of the guitar strings are untrimmed and they shine with metallic reflection in the lights; these flashing strings and Schenker's flying fingers are the only movements on the stage. Schenker's facial expression and bearing reveal his deep concentration. The guitar hero is totally focused on his playing, oblivious to the audience. Every member of that mainly male audience is standing in honor and awe. Many of them are playing air guitar, imitating Schenker's moves. It is almost as if they are participating in creating the glorious sound that fills the arena. Indeed, some of them would like to do just that, to become guitar heroes like Schenker, or to belt out the rhythms or sing the vocals up on stage.

The experience of the concert is charismatic. The artists on stage are rock-and-roll heroes to their fans, who adore and identify with them. The power of the band's music and the allure of its members life-style are an inseparable unity for the fan who aspires to become like them. He wants to make that music and live that life—to become one of those with the gift. The first step to becoming a heavy metal artist is to have a burning desire to be one. A person develops that desire by being a fan, a member of the audience. Interview members of a band and they will immediately reveal what bands most impressed them when they were sixteen. Indeed, it is part of the heavy metal culture to express enthusiasm for one's early allegiances.

As a form of musical culture, heavy metal can only be reproduced through the recruitment of artists to create and perform the music. Throughout the history of the genre recruitment has not been a great problem. The attraction of the image of the rock-and-roll hero, the metal god, has been sufficient to fire ambitions in heavy metal's fans. There are more than enough members of the audience who want a share of the heavy metal charisma for themselves to provide a steady supply of new artists. In other words, heavy metal artists arise from within its own precincts, just as its founders arose from within the precincts of rock. Heavy metal performers are not neutral specialists who perform a service, but, at least originally, passionate lovers of the kind of music they play. They are people who want to make their love for this specific rock genre their career.

From the point of view of the artist, heavy metal is a career that in its fullest realization becomes a vocation. This vocation includes total devotion to the music and deep loyalty to the youth subculture that grew up around it and from which the artist himself came. A heavy metal career may take the artist out of the subculture and into the routine and rationalized world of the media, and then back again to the subculture, where he once again joins the audience. Seen as an occupation, heavy metal is a serious and demanding struggle of committed and ambitious people who are also identified with and often devoted to a hedonistic life-style that reaches its peak in Dionysian ecstasy. The popular mind focuses on the hedonistic and rebellious displays of heavy metal's performers. In truth, such displays become secondary, and sometimes even antithetical, to the artists' primary desire to create and perform the music, which is a taxing job. Although attracted initially by a desire to share the charisma of heavy metal performers, artists must learn to love or at least to affirm a discipline of artistic practice and labor through which the products of the heavy metal genre are constituted. That discipline is culturally coded and socially organized. It is the structure, the site, of a hard struggle to make it to the top—

to the big stage, the peak at which one is charismatic—where one can become the inspiration for the next generation of metal gods.

The Code of Admission

The aspiring rock musician cannot enroll in a program of formal study or enter an apprenticeship program to prepare him for his career. The general education that provides the necessary skills for most white-collar employment does not develop the skills needed for rock artistry. Learning these skills takes ingenuity and perseverance. The time devoted to such learning is not subsidized by scholarships, but must be snatched from school and leisure time, and is paid for by sympathetic parents or the aspirant's own menial day jobs. The recruits for heavy metal performing are strictly self-selected and in large part self-motivated. Respectable society does not bless their choice of a career in heavy metal, nor does it provide the aspiring rock musician with the complex of public and private training and support systems it offers aspiring athletes, ballet dancers, and many other varieties of performing artists. The choice to pursue the path that leads to heavy metal performance can often be a frustrating one.

Talents and Skills

Becoming a heavy metal musician requires various abilities. Most important are the talents needed to create and perform music appropriate to the genre. In a sense the preceding chapter on the music was also a chapter about the artist. Those who try to make heavy metal their career must master its code, and must be able to create original music that conforms to the code or that expands the code from within without destroying it. The possession of musical talent and the willingness to develop it in conformity with the code are the distinguishing marks that separate aspiring artists from the air guitarists who live out a rock-and-roll fantasy. The desire to achieve charisma must take a distant second place to hard work and hard knocks as soon as the aspiring artist starts practicing. Such work may be gratifying because of the opportunities for creativity, sense of mastery, and experiences of social bonding it bestows, but it is still *work*, not Dionysian ecstasy. Heavy metal is a discipline, not a mere outburst of unformed expression. Heavy metal artists must first and foremost be willing and able to submit to that discipline.

Heavy metal artists need to possess many kinds of musical skills. Artists must be able to work both within the recording studio and on stage. In the studio one is allowed to make mistakes and to go back and redo inferior work. Song fragments or one song, rather than a set of songs, are the focus of concentration. Patience is at a premium, since doing multiple takes of a piece of music is the rule, not the exception. While making a record the members of a band do not have to integrate themselves into a tight unit. Indeed, they often play their parts independent of one another, recording in sequence rather than simultaneously. But each band member has to strive to keep perfecting his part. In contrast, live performance requires the ability to play through, without noticeable errors, many songs, in conjunction with other musicians. The performer has only one try to get it right. Instantaneous precision takes the place of patience. Technology cannot substitute for the cooperation and the sheer virtuosity required by the genre. Even in an era in which live shows are dependent on such sophisticated electronic equipment that the stage is really a mobile studio with lights, impressive performance skills are still needed for the live heavy metal show.

In addition to possessing performance skills, at least one member in a heavy metal band must know how to write and arrange songs. The code of the auteur in rock, initiated by the Beatles, has become obligatory for "real" rock musicians. True artists are supposed to create and play their own work, expressing their authentic selves. As a commentator wrote in 1971, "Today's contemporary artists are largely self-contained. They compose and perform their own material. They produce their own sessions in studios of their own choice. Production control is no longer 'in house.' It is in the hands of artists, writers, and production companies."[1] Heavy metal musicians maintain this ideology of the autonomous and authentic artist. A question directed at a metal musician, in which she was asked whether collaborating with a pop-oriented songwriter caused her trouble, implied that she had violated the heavy metal code of remaining autonomous.[2]

Musical talents are not the only capabilities required of heavy metal artists. They must also develop dramatic skills. Performance, live and on video, demands acting, the ability to express attitudes convincingly in standard forms. The moves, poses, displays of emotion, and expressions required by the performance code must be practiced and learned. In great measure heavy metal is a performance art, the projection of emotion through a set of sonic and visual conventions.

Heavy metal stage performance requires a dramatic and energetic rendering. Metal musicians are at the opposite pole from the members of a string quartet, whose formal and restrained bodies reflect a formal and restrained musical sensibility; or from the folksinger astride a stool, whose words overshadow sound and gesture. The heavy metal performer must translate the powerful, loud, and highly energetic music into his body movements and facial expressions. He must be acrobatically graceful enough to jump, leap, and generally bound about the stage.

Beyond having athletic prowess, the heavy metal musician must be skilled at projecting the emotions required by the performance code. He must look as if he were as highly touched by a song sung for the three-hundredth time as he was on the first singing, be able to simulate being engrossed in and challenged by a fretboard maneuver that has now become habitual, and smile and embrace with fraternal love band mates whom he may loathe and despise off stage.

The foregoing discussion of the talents and skills needed by the heavy metal artist takes us far away from the charisma experienced by the air guitarist identifying with his guitar hero. There is much artifice in the role as well as art and artistry, and there is much struggle, hard work, deferred gratification, frustration, and compromise to suffer as well as hedonic release to enjoy. Very few in the audience who would like to become metal gods have the drive or the multitude of talents needed to become one.

Ascribed Characteristics

Musical and dramatic talents, and the willingness to develop them, are the basic requisites of an aspiring metal artist, but they are not sufficient to give one even a reasonable chance of success. Heavy metal is not an equal-opportunity employer. Who you are, in the sense of ascribed characteristics over which you have little if any control—for example, gender and race—help determine whether you will make it to the big stage.

The code of the heavy metal star's physical appearance—the requisite body image—serves as a selecting mechanism, rejecting individuals who lack the requisite attributes. The advice to those aspiring to be heavy metal artists, if they are physically infirm or misshapen, not youthful, people of color, or women is "Abandon all hope!"

Rock is primarily a sound, but visual display has always been integral to its constitution as a cultural form. Elvis Presley's sneer, sideburns, and pompadour, the Beatles's Edwardian suits and "mop tops," Jim Morrison's black leather pants, Mick Jagger's pouty lips—these are only a few of the visual images that have contributed to the definition of rock culture. Commenting on an exhibit of photographs in *Rolling Stone,* Anthony DeCurtis remarked, "Your look is a way of presenting, revealing, concealing and interpreting yourself."[3] Of all of the personae of popular music, from the cowboy-clad country singer to the punk performer in shredded Salvation Army rejects, the heavy metal persona is most tied to appearance. At a heavy metal panel held in 1988 a public relations expert observed that magazines in Britain are more interested in the pictures of a group than in its sound. Meanwhile, magazines in the United States only take a band seriously if it has "got a British press."[4]

Heavy metal is inhospitable, if not hostile, to performers whose looks do not conform to its code of appearance. While that code places physical limits on who can be a successful artist, it also leaves some room for achievement and discipline. Having a powerful, young, and athletic-looking body is most significant for the lead singer, but such features are also important for other members of the group. The growing importance of videos through the 1980s produced a new requirement that the lead singer also have a handsome face: videos, with their close-ups, mercilessly revealed bad teeth, bad skin, and other unattractive facial features. Those who lack good looks and a good physique are severely hampered in pursuing a career as a metal artist, but even the well-endowed have to work on improving their natural physical assets. Many band members, especially those over twenty-five years old, engage in physical-fitness regimes worthy of Olympic athletes. Jogging is a popular method of maintaining the cardiovascular fitness needed to run around on stage for an hour or so each evening, and of keeping a trim look, with no beer belly or other visible flab. Jogging is widespread among band members because it requires no special equipment, except for a pair of running shoes, and can be done wherever the tour bus stops.

Backstage chatter is as likely to be about stomach-flattening techniques as about guitar electronics. The muscular upper torso required by the genre, highlighted by a stage costume that usually features exposed arms and bare chests, takes more than jogging to create. A set of weights is often tucked aboard the tour bus or in the equipment van. Some artists take up a sport; Bruce Dickinson of Iron Maiden, for example, is a top-rated fencer.

The bald or even those who simply lack luxurious manes of hair are at a disadvantage in heavy metal. Long hair, an emblem of the hippies of the late 1960s, is the norm. Shoulder-length or longer hair, cascading loosely, mats with sweat as concerts progress, showing the audience that the artists are exerting themselves. It is a part of the costume that cannot be removed, and it therefore reinforces the ideology of authenticity, inherited by heavy metal from the 1960s. Heavy metal performers are supposed to perform in a manner that reflects their "true being." The artist is not supposed to play a part like an actor, who can remove all traces of a role in the dressing room and merge into the crowd as an ordinary human being. The heavy metal performer's personality is supposed to be identified with his art; he announces his independence from the compromises of respectable society by such outward signs of inward grace as long hair and tattoos.

Metal fans can name exceptions to some of the requirements of the appearance code, but they are known and teased as exceptions, serving to prove that the code is generally operative. For example, Ronnie James Dio, former lead singer with Rainbow and Black Sabbath, and now the front man for his eponymous band, is particularly short. The heavy metal press almost always alludes to his diminutive size in its references to him. Much comment was made when Judas Priest's main man, Rob Halford, traded his blond locks for a closely cropped style. Derisive comments are also made about the enlarging paunches of aging notables such as Ozzy Osbourne. These comments serve to enforce the code, but also reflect the fact that the physical ideal is generally approximated by artists.

Heavy metal is a preserve not only of the youthful and the physically well endowed but also of white males. The genre is widely acknowledged by fans and artists to have been heavily influenced by a black artist, Jimi Hendrix. But until the late 1980s there were almost no black heavy metal musicians. (Exceptions such as the late Phil Lynott of Thin Lizzy can be counted on the fingers of one hand.) The image of the heavy metal star as a hypermacho, athletic, strong, lustful, and musically competent individual certainly corresponds with white stereotypes of the black male in the West. Indeed, Hendrix (dis)played these characteristics to the hilt. But historical circumstance made heavy metal the "white-boy blues."

Heavy metal originated with white, working-class bands in the industrial cities of England. The American blacks who might have joined its ranks were excluded from its inception by geography. Once the music reached the United States in earnest, in the mid-1970s, it encountered a situation of cultural self-segregation by American blacks, which blocked them from appropriating it. For blacks, the period following 1968 was one of disenchantment. Martin Luther King, Jr., had been murdered and civil rights and antipoverty legislation had not visibly improved the lives of African-Americans. The black community turned inward, in great part as a response to the so-called benign neglect policy of the Nixon administration. Cultural expressions of isolationism could be seen in the rise of black-oriented radio stations, movies, and especially music. Segments of the black community actively denounced artists who played "white" music, especially rock music. Hendrix himself came in for criticism from fellow blacks before his death in 1970 left the rock community without any black superstars.[5] Meanwhile, the audience for heavy metal in the 1970s was made up mainly of blue-collar, white, adolescent males, a group not known for their sympathy for blacks. Thus, the post-1960s social retrenchment made heavy metal an unattractive option for aspiring black musical artists.

By the end of the 1980s, however, as metal continued to fragment and absorb other musical elements, black and Hispanic heavy metal musicians were no longer novel. Hispanics tended to specialize in the speed/thrash subgenre. Blacks also could be found in those groups, but they concentrated especially in the funk-oriented metal made by groups such as Living Colour and 24-7 Spyz. That is, they brought the contribution of their separate musical culture to metal, grafting themselves on to it.

The barriers confronting women in heavy metal are more fundamental than those encountered by blacks. The predominance of whites in the genre is mostly a historical accident, whereas the bias against women is rooted in the delineated meanings of heavy metal music. No racist themes match the macho ideology of the genre. The antifemale posturing of heavy metal stars relates less to misogyny than to a rejection of the cultural values associated with femininity. In Western culture, as feminist scholars have noted, masculinity and femininity are dichotomous and mutually opposed cultural forms into which men and women are forced to fit. Men are supposed to be powerful, tough, and strong, whereas women are supposed to be delicate and weak. Simone de Beauvoir, in her widely respected reading of the gender code *The Second Sex*, asserts that the masculinity/femininity binary opposition reflects the subject/object opposition. Masculinity means being active and femininity means being passive. Men act, women are acted upon— through sight, touch, or merely imaginative transformations. Power, the essential inherent and delineated meaning of heavy metal, is culturally coded as a masculine trait.

Reinforcing the cultural barrier is the presence of women on the heavy metal scene who define themselves as providers of sexual services to band members. Groupies are commemorated in lyrics and on videos, and are the standard role models for women in the heavy metal culture, fitting the image of the woman in heavy metal's ideology. Not only passive, they are also one-dimensional. They epitomize, as the metal subculture often does, tendencies that characterize rock culture more generally. Rock, indeed, has been permeated with sexism. For example, in an analysis of the full range of MTV programming, researchers concluded that "The depiction of . . . gender roles in rock videos appears to be fairly traditional. Females are portrayed as submissive, passive, yet sensual and physically attractive."[6] Women have never been important factors in rock music. Alan Wells found that "female artists have accounted for approximately 10 of Billboard's top 50 annual singles" for the period from 1955 to 1985.[7]

The obstacles in the way of female metal artists have been surmounted by very few individuals, and then only in the 1980s. Girlschool, whose debut album was released in 1980, was the first and for years the only all-female metal group. The eruption of lite metal, with its accent on fashion, made the code of visual appearance more favorable to women. The styled, colored, permed, moussed, and fluffed hair of glam-group members is reminiscent of the androgynous/transsexual fashion of such 1970s acts as the New York Dolls.[8] The members of the female group Vixen look almost indistinguishable from the members of the leading male glam group, Poison. Indeed, metal wags, who are not fond of this style, say that the stunning girls in Vixen are not half as pretty as the boys in Poison. Lite metal's stress on the vocalist has also been helpful to women, who have traditionally gained success in popular music as singers.

According to Matt Snow, "The highway to hell is a merciless thoroughfare for the all-girl heavy metal band. Male counterparts regard you with deep suspicion, record companies run a mile and hordes of pimply youths attempt to infiltrate your bedroom. According to Vixen, a fast-rising quartet from Los Angeles, the only way up is to out-macho the men."[9] Snow describes their act: "Janet wields the mike stand with aplomb. Jan unleashes several solos in the time-honoured guitar-hero manner; we enjoy Share's thumb-busting showcase; Roxy enjoys her drum solo."[10] However, despite their conformity to the code, Vixen had difficulty getting a record contract and "had to play innumerable live showcases to prove they weren't faking."[11]

The presence of women in metal bands, either as the lead singers fronting male instrumentalists, such as Doro Pesch and Lita Ford, or in all-female groups, does not mean that the macho image of the metal artist has been subverted. Indeed, one might argue that quite the opposite is the case. The female metal artists do not transcend their primary role as sexual objects. Tight leather pants on a man does not signify the same thing as tight leather pants or, more frequently, tight leather micro-miniskirts on a woman. Lita Ford's outfit was once described as "the Folies-Bergès-through-a-meat-grinder costume."[12]

Choreography is also cued to gender stereotypes. Betsy, lead singer of a group called Bitch, recounts how the band's stage moves included the guitarist and the bass player putting their instruments between her legs, after which the guitarist kicked and banged her with his guitar—"your basic family show!"[13] The bottom line was tallied by a panelist at a 1988 seminar on women in metal: "I'm saying sex sells."[14]

Seemingly the best that women can do is to make fun of the sexism while embodying it. Metal is not heavy on humor, but one female group calls itself the Cycle Sluts from Hell. A female artist, the Great Kat, is audaciously trying to beat the boys at their own game. Trained as a classical violinist at Julliard, Kat, who played Kreisler's "Liebesfreud" at Carnegie Hall, is a speed-metal guitarist. Her style evokes the image of Paganini as a headbanger. She is trying to have it both ways, performing feats of technical virtuosity in her décolleté leather and studs outfit.

The Band as a Social Unit

Supposing that our air guitarist has the talents and ascribed characteristics, and is willing to work hard to develop the skills required of a heavy metal artist, he still needs something more. The heavy metal artist cannot go it alone: he must be a member of a group. Metal, following the rock tradition, is group-oriented. The band is both a symbol of community and a practical necessity to produce the heavy metal sound. Pop singers and some rock and rollers, such as Chuck Berry, can perform with a band put together for the occasion, since the focus is on the vocalist. Folksingers, such as Joan Baez or the early Bob Dylan, can accompany themselves instrumentally because the folk code stresses the delivery of lyrics, not the overall musical sound. But metal's dual emphasis on strong singing and highly proficient guitar work, backed by a powerful bass and drum sound, cannot be achieved by one person. The total sound is all-important, and it can only be created through disciplined cooperation. Even when a heavy metal band has an individual's name, there is, at least for touring, a real group. Bands such as Ted Nugent, Ozzy, Dio, and the Michael Schenker Group are genuine collective efforts despite having an individual's name.

The size of the heavy metal band varies from three to six members. The minimum requirements are a lead guitarist, a drummer, a bass-guitar player, and a vocalist. If there are only three members the singer also plays an instrument, usually the bass. The vast majority of groups have either four or five members. When a fourth instrument is present, it is a rhythm guitar or, less frequently, keyboards.

Heavy metal bands and rock groups in general are complex social forms. Sociologists divide groups into primary and secondary types, but rock groups do not fit well into either category because they share features of each. Primary groups, such as the ideal modern nuclear family or a pair of friends, exhibit "intimate face-to-face association and cooperation . . . the sort of sympathy and mutual identification for which 'we' is the natural expression. One lives in the feeling of the whole and finds the chief aims of his will in that feeling."[15] In contrast, the small secondary group, for example, the employees of a business office or restaurant, is based not on common feelings but on accomplishing a joint task. The German sociologist Ferdinand Tönnies distinguished between *gemeinschaft* (community) and *gesellschaft* (association). In the former, relations are based on the mutual identification of the members, while in the latter, relations are based on the special services that they perform for one another.

Many rock groups, including those within the heavy metal genre, are formed by groups of teenage pals. Since their original basis is friendship, such rock groups begin as pure primary or *gemeinschaft* groups. As the members develop their talents and perfect their individual and collective skills, they may begin to try to "go for it" and become successful rock professionals. They do not initially lose their bond to one another. Over time, however, some of the original members may be asked to leave or are forced out so that they can be replaced by others whose musical skills, ideas, look, or contacts better serve the collective ambition. Sometimes, too, a more successful group woos away a promising band member. In rock groups that have achieved some measure of renown, new members are more likely to be recruited not on the basis of friendship but for their talent and skill. Whatever the original basis for the group, problems of group cohesion and order are always present. In addition to possessing creative and performance skills, therefore, the musicians must be skilled in the art of interpersonal relations.

Whether they have a hands-on manager, group members have to learn on their own to negotiate their relations with each other and the division of their tasks. Knowing how to organize and sustain a band is neither taught nor learned through example, since the internal workings of a group are, press interviews notwithstanding, private matters that are often unacknowledged in public forums by the participants. Moreover, what one learns as a member of one group does not transfer well to another one, for "Each group's manner of operation—even much of the language used in coordinating activities—is constructed from the unique interactional history of its membership."[16] A band is like a modern marriage, in which there are few if any behaviors expected of the partners, who must cooperatively and creatively construct a life together. When members leave and are replaced, the construction of a common life must begin anew, almost from scratch.

The difficulty of forging the interpersonal relations that constitute a band as a social unit makes each member more valuable than his musical and performance abilities might at first glance indicate. In a mass production system workers who are inconvenient for any reason can be easily replaced by others. In bands, on the contrary, each member is costly to replace. Thus, if a member is having troubles, due to drugs, alcohol, or women—the three most common problems—the other members need to wait patiently until such difficulties are resolved, or to intervene to lend their assistance.[17]

The strains of interdependence among members of a group are probably responsible for the rancorous accusations that are often made when someone leaves a band. Interdependence also partly explains the legendary solidarity of some groups. For example, Def Leppard's drummer lost his hand in an automobile accident, but he was not replaced. The band waited for him to heal and then returned to record and tour rather triumphantly with a one-handed drummer. In a less dramatic case, the Scorpions's distinctive vocalist, Klaus Meine, suffered severe throat problems. He required surgery and could not work for a long time, and it was not clear that he would recover sufficiently to take up his role with the band again. The rest of the band waited patiently and Meine recovered fully. Led Zeppelin broke up when drummer John Bonham died rather than try to replace him, but that is an exceptional case for a successful band. When Bon Scott, the talented and alcoholic singer for AC/DC, died, he was mourned but nonetheless successfully replaced by Brian Johnson. Metallica went on to greater fame with a replacement for bassist Cliff Burton, who died when the band's touring van overturned. Ozzy sincerely mourned the gruesome death of guitar-ace Randy Rhoads, but went on to find a replacement.

The difficulty of constituting a band as a cooperative social unit is shown by the vast array of tensions within groups. The rock community refers to these tensions as "ego problems" or "attitude." For several reasons, heavy metal is probably more prone than other musical styles to personality clashes. First, humility is not a virtue in metal stars. The performance code requires one to be loud and proud, even extravagantly boastful. Metal acts demand strong and assertive stances. Some band members may begin to become their personae; others are typecast from the beginning. Second, the virtuosity required in heavy metal performances, especially from the frontman singer and the lead guitarist, encourages the musicians to behave as prima donnas. The best heavy metal music skillfully holds the guitarist and vocalist in their respective orbits, but sometimes one of the two begins to dominate the other. While privileging the total sound over any of its components, heavy metal also accents individual virtuosos. Band members need to contribute to the common sound even as they work to distinguish themselves. Such a structure is a perfect breeding ground for "ego problems."

Thus, it is no wonder that heavy metal groups seem to undergo frequent personnel shifts. The magazines report and the fans prove their stuff by quoting the outcomes of such musical-chairs activity. Metal's adherence to the rock ideology increases the possibilities for group tension. Rock groups were supposed to work in a communal fashion with each member having an equal say. Consensus democracy in a small, task-oriented group is particularly difficult to achieve when skill levels, creativity, and will are not equally distributed. Some groups give credit for the songwriting to the whole band when only one or two members actually write the material. Assigning royalties is a tricky problem in the context of the democratic ideology.

There are bands that do not attempt to be democratic and in which it is understood that one member is in charge. Generally the person in the leadership position was responsible for forming the band initially and is more experienced and often more famous than its other members. The median between democratic organization and one-man authority is organization according to reciprocal superordination and subordination: those with expertise in one area lead when that area needs work and follow others in areas outside their realm of expertise.[18] This median type of organization is probably the most common form.

Cooperation among the members of the band, no matter how difficult to achieve, is crucial to many aspects of making heavy metal music. Band members have to learn to be tolerant of one another's limitations. "The secret of group operation is, very simply, the shared knowledge that one has to be bad before being good. The cooperative understanding at practice sessions must operate with no negative sanctions for mistakes, and in fact must be conducive to the correction and amendment of another's playing."[19] For the highly produced sound of much metal, especially the styles other than thrash, such cooperation is not as central as it once was. To a great degree, the technological apparatus can replace willed solidarity. There is some disagreement about whether good stage performances can be realized without strong interpersonal bonds within the band. Bennett's assessment is that, at a minimum, interpersonal difficulties must be held in abeyance: "*getting up for the gig* is a very delicate part of the group's ceremonial invocation of unity. The hours and minutes before going on are carefully negotiated between members to exclude from attention any issues of conflict and tension that might actually exist between them, and, in particular, the moments before a performance are spent in close physical proximity to one another with alcohol, dope, or simply in-group conversation as the ceremonial sacrament."[20]

Even if the group learns how to work harmoniously, it normally faces financial barriers to success. More than other styles of music, heavy metal demands a significant financial commitment. The genre requirements of technical virtuosity, very strong amplification, and visual hi-tech polish make heavy metal the most expensive musical style to create. Not only is the initial investment substantial, but there are recurring costs for upkeep. Established bands maintain technicians on their payrolls to keep their complicated and expensive equipment in good repair. The unique combinations of electronic gear and instruments used by each band require skilled workers to assemble and tune them. On tour, specialized workers travel with the band, setting up the equipment on stage each night. Transporting the amplifiers and drum kit—the bulkiest equipment—is costly. Heavy metal also demands a visually appealing stage show. Costs for lighting effects, fog machines, stage sets, and backdrops, and costs for their transportation and setup are also substantial. Stage wear—the studded black leather or the fancy spandex—is still another expense. The great capital expenditure required to do everything according to the code is too high for most new bands to undertake. Usually a new band starts small; as it earns money, either from gigs or from the day jobs of its members, it slowly adds to what it has.

Unlike bands in most rock genres, heavy metal groups cannot easily finance their initial phase by playing at local venues. There were few if any metal clubs in the United States until the late 1980s; even today there are still not many in proportion to the number of fans of the genre. Club patrons generally want dance music and one cannot dance to heavy metal. In addition, rock groups generally start off by playing cover tunes; only gradually, as their local fame grows, do they add original material to their sets. But this is not an option for heavy metal groups, since the genre's code demands original compositions. And even if covering other bands was not ideologically problematic, it would not have been effective in the period before the late 1980s, when the genre received little radio play or television exposure. As the genre became more popular, these obstacles began to shrink. For example, Slayer, an extreme thrash metal group, began by playing covers at clubs.[21]

Another way to start out is to be a "tribute" band, covering, indeed imitating, one band exclusively. Groups such as Black Sabbath, Rush, Led Zeppelin, and Pink Floyd have tribute bands. But as a career option the tribute band is a dead end. Record companies want bands that can both play and create. Cover bands do not display songwriting talents and therefore do not get signed.

During the explosion of heavy metal in the early 1980s many of the new groups were described as "street metal." Their musical style tended to reflect the faster rhythms that evolved into speed/thrash. But the distinguishing feature of street metal was a stripped-down visual presentation. These bands did not try to compete with the elaborate shows put on by Judas Priest, the Scorpions, Black Sabbath, UFO, and the rest of the bands that had been in business for many years. Street clothes were worn for performance and, with the exception of some colored lighting, stage enhancements were minimal. The new style cut down the start-up costs of a group.

During the same period other groups began to seek outside financial backing. As the genre of heavy metal came out of the closet into more general visibility in the mid-1980s, financing a fledgling but promising metal band was seen in some quarters as a possibly lucrative, albeit risky, investment.

The majority of the members of heavy metal bands that started before 1980 came from working-class backgrounds. They were little different from their fans. Indeed, the heavy metal press tends to stress humble origins. Black Sabbath, they constantly remind readers, were Birmingham "toughs," AC/DC came from a working-class environment, and Led Zeppelin's Jimmy Page was brought up in a London slum. In contrast, many of the groups in the 1980s came from rather comfortable middle-class circumstances. The initial financing for a band is now likely to come from the parents of one or more of the members of the band. In 1988 the leader of a still struggling and unsigned band mentioned that the band was financed by the $30,000 that his parents had saved for his college education. Additional financing for the necessary gear is sought from record companies. Major-label contracts, especially for new groups, include monies for equipment.

Financial issues are a constant source of stress for all but the few bands that have "made it." But even they are burdened with large expenses, which grow as their stage shows become more elaborate. Sometimes unscrupulous managers foist unfavorable contracts on naïve bands, which never receive the rewards for their later success. Financial anxieties can lead to tensions among group members, which are piled on top of the "ego problems" that already exist. Starting up and gaining momentum is the most difficult phase of the heavy metal artist's career.

The Production of Heavy Metal

Most bands never make it beyond the start-up and early momentum phases of the drive to success. The obstacles prove to be too great to surmount. Disharmonies within the group, lack of financial resources, personal problems, fatigue, waning enthusiasm in the face of frustration, inability to make hard decisions to sacrifice weaker members, and lack of the requisite talents and skills all contribute to failure. Most bands never sign a record contract. They are the losers in a Darwinian struggle for access to the facilities of the mediators: the record companies and the concert promoters. The successful band must be accepted into the media because the media control the means to attracting a large enough audience to sustain a career as a metal musician and to become a metal god, bringing charismatic experience to hordes of devoted fans.

The losers have often gone through a great deal of sacrifice and frustration before they call it quits or their bands dissolve around them. A writer for a metal magazine observed that while there are very few success stories "there are literally thousands of tales of rock 'n' roll heartbreak and disillusion."[22]

The conditions of the struggle are often quite unpleasant. As heavy metal has increased in popularity since the mid-1980s more and more air guitarists have been inspired to give a career in the genre a try. Thousands have packed their gear and headed west to Los Angeles, the major metal Mecca in the United States.[23] Once there, they are subject to the pay-for-play policy of the local venue owners. If they want to have an audience, create a buzz, and be seen by record company executives, they have to pay for the privilege. The A&R staffs of the major and many "indie" record companies are located in the area. Often the band is reduced to shilling on the street to get people to come in and see them. They really have no other option.

The buyer's market in metal creates pressure on aspiring bands to conform to commercial codes of aural and visual acceptability, and to adopt an instrumental approach to achieving success. In reaction to this pressure, the sense of community that characterized the band at its inception is apt to give way to the realism of a task-oriented work group, whose members are chosen for their talents and skills. The halo of authenticity that surrounded the group's "own music" is likely to tarnish as changes are made in the band's sound to make it more promotable. At worst the band members will become abject slaves to the commercial codes of composition, appearance, and performance. The choice to go for success carries great penalties for the losers. They need to be able to sustain themselves by their love of the music even after all is said and done, and by a sense that it was worth the try to go after a dream. Even for the "winners," those who get signed, it is still a long way to the top.

There are thousands of unsigned metal bands.[24] But, for rock as a whole, even if a band gets signed to a major label, it has only a 15 percent chance of breaking even.[25] Many metal bands sign their first contract with an "indie," which provides them with less financing, studio time, promotion, and marketing potential than a major would give them. But it is a genuine milestone for a band to be signed by any company. Signing proves that a group is at least minimally fit to participate in the great institutionalized competition for the status of metal gods and all of the rewards that go with that status. They will have access to a studio to record an album and tours will be booked for them to promote that album. They have shown that they can keep their act together, manage their finances adequately, and master musical, dramatic, and athletic skills sufficiently to convince someone else in the business that they have promise. If our air guitarist has reached this point, he is no longer merely an aspirant but has become a participant in a production complex. He is no longer, socially, merely a member of the subculture from which he came, but has now been drawn into a specialized work environment.

The record company is the artist's major connection to the system for producing and disseminating culture to impersonal audiences. By signing a contract with an organization in the entertainment industry the artist takes on a new dual role as a producer/product for a commercial enterprise. Indeed, through the contract the band itself necessarily becomes a commercial enterprise with claims and obligations. The heavy metal band is, economically, a typical form of late capitalist enterprise in the entertainment industry. The band is not strictly proletarian because it owns some of its own means of production, but it is not fully petit bourgeois either, since it does not own all of them, including some of the most crucial elements. Unless it is already at the top, it pays a premium in its contract terms to secure access to key facilities, such as the studio and the arena.

The buyer's market in metal is reinforced by the oligopoly of the record industry's major labels, which pits the large number of competing bands against a tiny group of buyers. Bands are quasi-independent enterprises that are at a disadvantage in their encounter with concentrated economic power. Even when one of a band's members is a skilled entrepreneur the group lacks clout until it reaches the top. It has to make terms with the mediators who own the only road that leads to success, and invariably such terms always favor the mediators. But also invariably the band is delighted to make such terms.

The group's role in the production complex is to create and perform music in accordance with sonic, lyrical, appearance, and performance codes that are based on shifting mixtures of the codes of the heavy metal subculture and the predominantly commercial media, and their own conceptions of what the music should be. When the contract is generous enough, band members devote themselves to their enterprise on a full-time basis. They become self-conscious artists and musicians, and develop an occupational subculture that translates the requirements for success into their own unique discipline. They struggle more than ever, but they have made it through the door.

Creating the Product

The successful band must play a unique version of the genre. They have to have a "signature sound," an aural fingerprint. That sound is their's alone, even though it may be similar to that of other bands. The signature sound is like the unique style of a painter (distinctive brush strokes and a special palette of colors, for example), by which art dealers and museum curators assign authorship to a given canvas. A band ordinarily begins by faithfully re-creating or at least imitating what other groups in the genre are playing. But it needs to find a distinctive sonic niche if it wants to achieve true success.

The development of a unique sound is an emergent characteristic, reflecting the musical interests, influences, and personalities of the band or its dominant member. It also is an essential marketing device—a commercial identification and an aural logo. Record companies need to market products that are both differentiated enough from competing products to attract attention and thus consumers, yet close enough to known products to appeal to a reliable established market. On one level, the signature sound is like the blue beads or the green flakes put into detergents to set off one brand from its all-but-equivalent competitors. Artistically, the signature sound represents a compromise formation between full self-expression and total fit with the code of the genre. A *Hit Parader* piece claimed that the group Krokus had been hampered in its quest for success because it had not fully established "an instantly recognizable sound. [They were handicapped by their] chameleon-like quality to mimic other bands, like Priest and AC/DC."[26]

All commercially viable popular music genres require a distinguishing sound from their artists. In the blues, each performer puts his or her own stamp on a canon of standard songs. In its formative and crystallization periods heavy metal did not encourage such cover versions. There were a few, such as Judas Priest's "Green Manalishi (With the Two-Pronged Crown)." Priest kept the same slow tempo and eerie menace of the song's original version, but crunched up—metalized—the overall sound. Indeed, there were so few covers in the early periods that serious fans of the genre were able to name them all. In the current phase of fragmentation, however, cover versions have become more acceptable. Lite metal groups, in particular, desire to make "crossover" records that appeal to radio programmers who serve a general audience. The familiar song rendered in a distinctive way aids in gaining general acceptance. In addition, younger bands often exhibit an impulse to pay homage to their older heroes. Such impulses did not exist in the early days when each band was a pioneer, creating a new musical sensibility.[27]

Despite the growing acceptability of covers, heavy metal artists are still expected to write their own songs. The requirement of authenticity, which heavy metal inherited from the rock culture of the 1960s, demands expression of the artist's unique imagination. The rock star's code is the binary opposite of the pop star's. In the musical world of pop, songs are written and chosen for the artist by others and are performed for a heterogeneous audience, not an audience with a core subculture. But "in rock, there is the ethos of self-expression which draws an intimate tie between the personal and the performance. . . . Rock and pop stars play to different rules."[28] The pop star is not motivated by a desire for self-expression, which simultaneously expresses the sensibilities of the audience.

An ideal for the heavy metal musician, authenticity is impossible to fully achieve. First, it will probably be to some extent incompatible with the requirement of a "signature sound," which must be distinctive but not too different from what is already popular. This may not be too much of a problem for a performer because the love that young artists have for the genre motivates them to conform to its code voluntarily and enthusiastically. But even if a band is comfortable working within the code, not all of its members will be equally capable of expressing themselves. In many cases, one or perhaps two members will be creatively dominant, leaving the others to follow their cue. In other cases, the band will develop its music collectively, giving no one a chance to express himself fully, but allowing each to have a share in the emergent sound.

Who is really responsible for creation is often hard to determine in heavy metal music. For about a century, songs in the United States have been defined legally as written entities; copyrights are always based on sheet music. The majority of heavy metal songs, however, do not exist in written form, and when they do they were often transcribed by an outsider. Since heavy metal arose in the era of tape recorders, musical literacy has not been necessary for musical creativity or performance. Indeed, even if the initial creation was written down on paper the song as performed would never fully represent the notation. The musical notation system that was developed during the Renaissance and perfected in the nineteenth century is clearly inadequate for heavy metal. For example, it cannot indicate when the guitarist bends a string or how he uses the variety of distortion pedals. The screams and growls of the vocalist, embellished with electronic devices, are also not part of the standard notation system.

The many specialized contributions of each band member to the total sound blur individual authorship. Authenticity tends to come out partially, as it does in jazz, where there is "the attitude that each player [is] a creative musician, shaping his part into something that reflected his own skills and personality."[29] John Street expresses a similar understanding of rock music: "In rock, composing songs is not a matter of writing so much as playing. The writer may have a melody and some lyrics, but what we hear as the finished product often owes much to the way the group has chosen to present the song."[30] The guitarist who devises his guitar riffs for the instrumental break may not receive formal creative credits, but he has composed music.

The lyrical component of the music is usually written and is often created by only one member of the group. Considerations of authenticity aside, heavy metal required fresh lyrical material from its inception because it broke new thematic ground in popular music. The themes of chaos discussed in the preceding chapter needed original lyrical expression.

Composing the music that one performs runs against the division of labor that characterizes social activity in the modern world, from factories to football fields. With the band as the basic creative unit, each group has its own methods of carrying through the process of composition. Since credit for songs is influenced by ideology, financial concerns, and relations within the group, the public attribution of credit is not necessarily an adequate indicator of who was involved in creation. Generally, in heavy metal, the lyrics are written by the vocalist and the music by the lead guitarist. But this is just a tendency and not the norm, either in a statistical or a regulative sense. Many ways of organizing the creative process are used. For example, the drummer of Rush, Neil Peart, writes the group's lyrics, and the singer, Geddy Lee, and the guitarist, Alex Lifeson, compose the music. In Manowar, in contrast, both lyrics and music are created by bassist Joey DeMaio.

There are some bands in which several members each compose lyrics and music for songs. Each member of the Scorpions, for example, writes songs, and the band as a whole selects those which "they most believe in."[31] In Metallica each of the members brings in his ideas for songs. These ideas are not written down but are recorded on tapes. Lars Ulrich, the drummer, hums his ideas to vocalist/guitarist James Hetfield, who plays and records them on guitar. Together the band listens to all the tapes and the best parts are collected on a master "riff tape." This tape serves as the source for the album's songs.[32]

Performing the Product

Once songs have been composed, the band must perform them both in the studio and live in concert. For heavy metal, both the studio and the concert venue are essential sites for performance. This situation stands in sharp contrast to that prevalent in other musical genres, which privilege one or the other site. For pop music the studio dominates and live performances are attempts to recreate the sounds achieved there; despite the technical sophistication typical of modern concerts, often studio-produced sounds cannot be duplicated on the concert stage. The current controversy over lip-synching at concerts by Milli Vanilli, Madonna, and New Kids on the Block is a rock critic's tempest on a turntable. Pop audiences, especially those whose major source of music is MTV, demand replication of the recorded song in concert. Because music videos use studio recordings as sound tracks, and because audiences expect pop concerts to duplicate music video sound, lip-synching is inevitable for some songs. In contrast to pop, punk and blues privilege the live performance. Recordings are valued to the degree that they capture the feeling of the live performance.

Rock, at least in terms of the standards of criticism that emerged after the Beatles moved into the studio in earnest, holds up the well-produced recorded version as the test of a band's ability. Music critic Jon Pareles affirms that "most rock is ruled by recording."[33] He estimates that 70 percent of the time rock bands attempt to re-create their records on stage. Heavy metal, however, breaks from rock in this regard by valuing the live concert performance at least as highly as the studio performance. Thus, the heavy metal band must cultivate two separate sets of virtues: the studio requires patience, whereas the stage demands endurance.

THE STUDIO. Heavy metal came into existence at the height of the musician's power in the recording studio. James Coffman notes that the musician had little control in the studio in the preceding era: "Within the structure of the recording industry, at least until the late 1960s, the musician was usually subjected to the direction of other corporate employees during the rehearsal, recording and 'mixing' of the product."[34] During the 1970s, however, until the recession hit the record business, rock musicians had the upper hand, hiring producers, selecting recording studios, and making decisions on aspects of production ranging from what songs to record to the album's cover art. In the 1980s the independent producer stepped into the driver's seat. Metal musicians prefer to work with producers who specialize in the genre. One or more members of the band will often also be involved in the production, preserving some of the artistic control required by the code of the heavy metal artist.

Modern studio technology, which permits the recording and subsequent electronic manipulation of discrete sounds, allows heavy metal to insist upon virtuosity. Notes that are missed, by guitarist or vocalist, can be redone again and again. Recording engineers and producers have as much, if not more, to do with the final product as the band. It is quite possible for a group of musicians to record without ever seeing one another. Indeed, the final product can be—but usually is not—left to the producer and the recording engineers. Thus, the linear progression and the simultaneity of parts that constitute a live performance are abandoned in the studio.

The amount of time taken to make an album varies considerably. The general tendency is that more "commercial" work takes longer than "underground" material: the more melodic lite metal subgenre involves more studio work than does the thrash subgenre. Overall there is immense variation in production time. Studio time is expensive, which means that successful bands can afford to prolong their stay and generally do. Record companies are willing to provide more funds to bands with a proven track record. For example, Poison's first album cost $30,000 and was recorded in twelve days. Not only did the band have more time to record its subsequent release, *Open Up and Say . . . Ahh!*, but "the budget had increased tenfold."[35]

Black Sabbath's debut album was done in twelve hours.[36] However, heavy metal albums that have taken several months to record are legion. For example, Anthrax's *Spreading the Disease* required more than five months of studio time.[37] Heavy metal recording is usually more time consuming than recording the average rock album, since the genre puts a premium on technical perfection, the appearance of virtuosity, and the total sound, which must balance the distinct contributions of each musician.

Whether the music is recorded with all band members in the studio at the same time or with members there separately, the process requires serious work by all concerned. Songs need to be written, arranged, and rehearsed prior to entering the studio. Once there, parts are played over and over again to achieve a polished performance. Once the music is recorded, those involved in mixing and editing have days or weeks of careful and concentrated work ahead of them. Studio work is not a public activity. Photographers and journalists do not give the fans reports on the making of records. It is the other performance site, the concert, that they show to the world. The contrast between these two locations is marked.

On stage at the concert charisma reigns. In the studio the technical rationality of the late capitalist production complex dominates. The whole is analyzed into parts and then put together deliberately by a team of specialists. In the studio authenticity is reduced to a concern that the final sound should be affirmed by the band.

THE CONCERT. Heavy metal bands cannot rest on the laurels of their recorded efforts. They must do well on stage. Groups begin by playing live; initially, the studio is an alien environment. For extroverted personalities, like our air guitarist, being on stage is the reason they wanted to become metal stars. For others, who were attracted by the private experience they had with the music, live performance is a difficult discipline. One of the reasons why performers use drugs is to overcome stage fright. One performer extolled the virtues of a bit of heroin by saying "it just relaxes you, but it doesn't take your muscle coordination away."[38] The ubiquity of alcohol, backstage and on stage, at metal concerts not only mirrors the fans and upholds the Dionysian image, but provides relief from stress. The show must go on, whether one is in the mood for it. John Lord of Deep Purple lamented that if one does not feel like playing, "that's tough tittly, isn't it?"[39] In this sense heavy metal performers are no different from musicians in many genres.[40]

On stage the performers can get full and immediate feedback about their music, something they can never have in the studio. Musicians are aware of the audience's reaction to what they are doing. Heavy metal is a populist art form, despite its commitment to artistry and virtuosity. The musicians cannot feel satisfied with their work unless an audience of fans, rather than critics or other musicians, praises it. Further, since the performers have shared a pariah image with their fans, they have not set mass success as their goal. Mere numbers of record sales do not serve as a yardstick of a band's excellence. Success can only be confirmed by a more total and direct appreciation.

Live concerts are one-night affairs for the fans, but not for the bands. Partly because of the capital expenditure required to put together a live show, bands play a series of concerts. Like medieval troubadours, they travel to their audience. The tour resembles a "ten-countries-in-ten-days" vacation package. The schedule is grueling. The band plays one city each night, using most of the time between shows to get to the next city. Groups that are just starting may travel in a van, with their equipment taking up any possible sleeping space. At small venues one can hear band members say before the final song, "Remember, we need a place to stay tonight." After all, medieval princes put the troubadours up for the night at their castles.

Successful groups usually travel on well-appointed tour buses that have sleeping berths, usually stacked three high. Sound systems, microwave ovens, and refrigerators are standard equipment. Nonetheless, the bus is tightly packed with people and equipment, and provides no privacy. Band members need to get along harmoniously with each other not merely to play tightly on stage, but to tolerate living together on the road. The tour entourage, whether packed in a van or strung out over several buses, tends to resemble a commune.

Life on tour stands in marked contrast to the traditional middle-class life-style. Most people's nine-to-five work time is when the band sleeps. The members cannot take care of the normal responsibilities of everyday life such as getting clean clothes. Such tasks have to be done by others.

The press coverage of a tour stresses the wild excitement, the image of "Bad Boys Running Wild." Photographers are backstage taking candids (or shots posed to resemble them) of the "Backstage Queens" with the band. Band members pose with drinks in hand and perform high jinks with one another. Stage shots show sweaty, ecstatic musicians. To emphasize the hedonistic aspect of Poison's tour, their press agent released a statement indicating that the band had installed a condom machine on the tour bus.[41]

Press coverage typically reveals the public aspect of the tour, obscuring, ignoring, or hiding the dull routine. Mostly the band has to "hurry up and wait." The members wait to do their sound check, wait for appointments with the media for interviews or for in-store appearances, wait for the stage to be ready for them to go on, and wait for the bus to be repacked with equipment and personnel before things can get moving to the next city. The nuts-and-bolts of touring tends to wear a band down. The tough routine contrasts sharply with the charismatic image of the metal god.

The concert is crucial to a band's success. It sells the latest album and the band to its audience and provides direct feedback from the audience that allows the band to assess how to alter its work. Touring permits record-label people to see or hear about unsigned bands. The metal media play an essential role in the tour. They advertise the concert and thus bring in the live audience. They review and photograph the concert, promoting the band beyond the audience who came to see and hear it. The band has to be accessible and rather pleasant to the numerous deejays, photographers, and writers for metal magazines that they hope to encounter along the way. Much of the work of a tour goes on backstage.

Touring takes up a major portion of the year for the typical heavy metal band. It is not unusual for bands to be on the road far more than they are at home. The normal work of a creator-musician is done on the road too. New songs have to be written and proficiency on one's instrument enhanced. Bands are notorious for including "life-on-the-road" songs in their second album, since they have had to tour constantly in support of their debut release. Thus, one of the only things that they can write about authentically is life on tour. Guitarists are noted for noodling around with their instruments on the bus. Randy Rhoads, a great heavy metal guitarist who died while touring with Ozzy Osbourne, used to practice constantly. Moreover, he would prearrange to get guitar lessons from local instructors when he was on tour.[42]

Creating new musical material and getting it ready for performance, studio work, and touring are the artist's work cycle. The band that is signed, has successful first and second albums, and gains a following in the metal subculture(s) goes through this cycle recurrently and can be said to have achieved at least a modicum of success. Its members will have made heavy metal their full-time career and will have developed an occupational culture standing somewhere between the youth subculture from which they came and the rationalized and instrumental culture of the entertainment industry that controls the essential means of their musical production and distribution. The cycle can be intrinsically rewarding for those who have a vocation. They will enjoy the ability to create and perform, and will take the trials and tribulations, the interpersonal problems, and the dull routine as incidentals that accompany doing what has captured their devotion. Others will look more to extrinsic rewards to sustain them, but none will share any more a full identification with the air guitarist in the audience. It is a long way to the top and that way is filled with hard work, calculation, compromises, and at least some disillusionment. Yet almost no one who ever makes it to the top regrets it or wants to leave that position, even to retire to luxury.

Success

What is it about success that is so alluring? Financial rewards are ample for the top groups, but wealth does not seem to be the prime motivator for the heavy metal band, the reason why it struggled and sacrificed. Often success in terms of records sold and arenas filled does not translate into a financial windfall for the group. Unscrupulous managers can profit handsomely at the band's expense and record companies are well known for their "killer contracts," in which increasingly expensive costs of production and promotion are deducted from any royalties earned by the band. Then, too, receiving large sums of money is not quite the same thing as getting rich. Prudent investment is not the typical response of young, working-class, modern-day sybaritic troubadours. Band members are likely to spend extravagantly. In "Finding Fame without Fortune" Leigh Silverman concludes that "living to excess is part and parcel of the rock and roll philosophy."[43]

There are, of course, heavy metal bands whose members are exclusively motivated by money. I once heard a band that I thought was awful and asked someone who knew the members personally how they could play such rot. It was a rhetorical question, since I fully expected to be told that they liked how they sounded. But instead I was informed that they disliked their music almost as much as I did, but thought that their sound would bring them success. My friend used the term "prostitutes" to describe them. Shortly after this conversation the band signed a record contract and has since achieved some financial success. It is not, however, typical of heavy metal bands. At least publicly, metal artists do not aspire to become "Tattooed Millionaires."

Some heavy metal artists define success artistically. They wish to create and play great music that expresses their being authentically and that will be recognized as excellent by those who can appreciate their art. But although a purely artistic motivation is present in heavy metal, it is not a dominant concern. The air guitarist dreams of being a star and the successful heavy metal artist glories in being one.

A metal god is not a mere celebrity, someone who is famous just for being famous. He has won renown for his artistry and is a compelling force because of it. He is charismatic. Fans are the devoted and enthusiastic followers of him and his band because they acknowledge their special gifts. The band gains and maintains its charismatic authority by constantly proving itself in concert and in its recorded output. Max Weber's discussion of the power of war lords and religious founders, whose authority is gained outside the traditional or legal-rational framework of everyday life, applies to the metal gods.[44] Of the types of charismatic leaders, heavy metal stars come closest to the shaman. They are seen to have extraordinary gifts, which they cultivate, and to be able to achieve states of ecstasy. When they do so they are judged and felt to be "plugged into" the divine, mediating between the mundane and sacred worlds.

The experience of Dionysian ecstasy is the shamanistic state associated with the heavy metal concert performance. To achieve this state before a vast audience and then to communicate it to that audience is the pinnacle of success. This is what the air guitarist who set off on a metal career yearned for, to create that power, to feel that power, to communicate it, and to be adored for his efforts. Let Bruce Dickinson of Iron Maiden describe it: "Performing is a release, a kind of high. The music really gets me worked up. It's the kind of music that makes people react. I don't want to see them clapping lightly. I want to see them go crazy, just like me."[45]

The charismatic moment, repeated over and over again, is the intrinsic draw of the metal career. It redeems all the hardships and compromises. But charisma also has its price. Charismatics must constantly demonstrate their gifts and manifest their charisma through their life-style. They eschew the rational, careful, staid behavior that characterizes the daily routines of most people. Their separation from the everyday world involves a rejection of the dominant norms for a respectable adult life. Living in impoverished squalor in L.A., hoping for a break, or throwing money away on extravagances such as expensive cars, demonstrates a lack of concern for financial security. Wildly promiscuous sex backstage flouts social norms of prudence and responsibility. One never hears people claiming that their pursuit of heavy metal stardom was done solely to get "chicks for free," and when asked about the ubiquitous groupies, the usual riposte is, "It's a dirty job but someone's got to do it."[46] Nonetheless promiscuity is part of the star's mystique.

Squandering wealth and engaging in unrestrained sex are ways in which the metal gods exhibit the themes of Dionysian ecstasy, rebellion, and chaos in their actual lives. Their lives are emblems of their music to the fans, who are never told about the grind of being part of a production complex. Most deeply, the metal star incarnates the inherent and delineated meanings of the music through his rejection of safety and caution, and his defiance of death. Prudence has no place in the life-style of "Living After Midnight." Vitality is to be expended, not hoarded. The best proof of one's charisma is dying from some excess of "sex, drugs, and rock and roll." Fatally overdosing on drugs or alcohol, or dying while on route from one concert to another are great career moves. The charisma of the dead musician is enhanced and his aura rubs off on his band mates who survive him. Heavy metal expects a Dionysian existence, extreme affirmations of vital energy, from its artists to underscore their charisma. They live and die in swings between creativity in a technical complex and ecstatic consummation. They both produce their music and incarnate its meanings.

The choice of the metal god is to "burn out or fade away." This is an endgame career decision that comes in the prime of one's life. Heavy metal, more than pop and most other forms of rock, is a young man's game.[47] Success can only last when it is translated into the fame that comes from "burning out," dying at the height of one's powers. For those who refuse to "die with your boots on," there is usually a slow fade to black.

Unlike many pop stars, metal gods are not pushed off their pedestals by newcomers. The audience, which shares a subculture at its core, is loyal and basically conservative. But success still unravels in myriad ways. As the star ages, the charismatic life-style begins to lose its allure. Young bodies can endure the alcohol, drugs, and lack of sleep that tend to ravage the organism on the other side of thirty. The detoxification of bands such as Mötley Crüe and Aerosmith owes as much to the band members' advancing ages as to the antidrug crusade in the United States. But "clean" bands are placed in an uncomfortable position. As a reporter commenting on the Crüe put it, they do not emphasize their sobriety because they do not want "to give up their well-crafted hedonistic image."[48] Of course, the drugs and alcohol were not only used to build an image, but were integral to the life-style of the band members. The act of cleaning up the act is not only difficult to perform but may change the act itself.

The youthful-looking body and high energy level also become increasingly difficult to maintain as stars get older. Loyal audiences will put up with lame performances, but only for so long. A receding hairline and middle-age spread are incompatible with being a metal god. Rock in general has permitted its artists to age, and grey-haired rockers such as Billy Joel and Don Henley prosper. Heavy metal also has some indulgence for aging, and people like Ozzy Osbourne and Ronnie James Dio still draw devoted audiences. But as these singers and other performers grow older they tend to hire very young guitar players into their bands to maintain a presence of vitality. Indeed, Dio remarked in 1990 that his new band, including an eighteen-year-old lead guitarist, had made it possible for him to revisit cities, in which he had performed many times, with a renewed excitement, a feeling that he was just starting out.[49]

The most damaging erosion of charisma is the inner disaffection that the metal god may begin to feel for the life-style. That is, he may begin to find Dionysian rebellion less attractive and be drawn to a more staid adult life. Even if music remains front and center, a family or some hobby may conflict with touring. Few artists are able to continue being enamored of Dionysian vitality and pleasure indefinitely. But since their sound and lyrics must conform to the heavy metal code, they become inauthentic. Singing words that once expressed oneself but no longer does puts the heavy metal star in a compromised state. By the age of thirty-five he may still be working within the same signature sound and lyrical theme that he had begun with eighteen years earlier. The form that once promised expanded creativity may by now have been thoroughly exhausted and so be felt to be a straightjacket. But that signature brought him and the band to the top, and if it is abandoned or much modified the band is likely to lose the loyalty of its fans. Some musicians, such as Bruce Dickinson, have tried to have it both ways, staying with their band and also launching a solo career in which they experiment with new creative directions.

Ultimately, no one who lives long enough can both survive and conform to the codes of heavy metal. But despite all of the tendencies encouraging a fade-out, metal gods try to hang on for as long as they can. They do not lose their desire for the limelight and, more importantly, they do not lose their taste for creating and performing music, and for the charismatic experience. They are artists and rock-and-roll heroes, and they want to perpetuate their success. They are also moved by the loyalty of their fans. Few forms of music create as deep a bond between artist and fan as heavy metal does. Some of what made the air guitarist seems always to remain in the metal god. Despite all of the experiences that take him away from his roots, he seems never to become fully cynical. Perhaps the text of Chaos saves him from that. He is not a disillusioned utopian. He has experienced what for him is the best that can be hoped for.

The heavy metal god does not ordinarily mix with the audience. He is a charismatic figure, not a comrade. But sometimes he goes back to the audience out of which he came, hanging out in the parking lot or on the sidewalk outside the concert venue with his fans. He will rap with them, sign autographs, let them take pictures, and simply share his charisma in a democratic way. He has come full circle and rejoined his subculture. Tomorrow night he will take to the stage, inspiring another generation of air guitarists to set out on the long way to the top and to refresh the genre with a new supply of gods.

4

Digging the Music: Proud Pariahs

"Denim and Leather"
—*Saxon*

A journalist describes some California metal fans, guys standing around in a parking lot, in the following way: "They were white kids, stoners, fifteen and sixteen years old, and they wore the obligatory heavy-metal T-shirts. But, more than anything else, their hair set them apart, flowing from their heads in such lush cascades that I was reminded of a Breck-shampoo advertisement. Every ounce of protein in their bodies appeared to be concentrated in their scalps."[1]

Travis is big, in a lean and beefy sort of way, with a kind and intelligent look. He is well-groomed, ready to go for a job interview without needing a hair cut. An honor-roll math major at a Chicago university, Travis is a great Metallica fan, even by the standards of Metallica fans, who tend to be a knowledgeable and devoted bunch.

Researchers studying the headbangers at a Houston club noted that "[The] most common attire consisted of black jeans and black T-shirts with heavy metal band logos printed on the front and back. Long hair, not arranged in any particular style, is de rigueur."[2]

For a sociology of culture, the audience is essential to the constitution of an art form. Art can be created without reference to an audience, but it cannot become involved in a social system without one. The power of the audience can, in certain cases, reach the point of determining the content and form of the art. In that case the art becomes the servant of the audience's more general cultural values and mythologies. In contrast, sometimes the audience is simply a mass, created by the manipulations of the entertainment industry. Then the audience serves the industry through the art. In most cases there is a mix of both relations. In order to determine what kind of audience heavy metal has, it is necessary first to consider how audiences can be conceived. Only then will it be possible to define the metal audience in a sociologically pertinent way.

Defining Metal's Audience

Within the domain(s) designated by terms such as "popular culture," "mass culture," "the popular arts," and "mass media," assessment of the nature and function of the audience is often biased by aesthetic preferences. Critics and researchers reveal an unfortunate tendency to interpret the audience in terms of the supposed merits of the cultural form that it appreciates. Aesthetic evaluation, based on unexamined assumptions about the cultural form, is used to pigeonhole the audience. This approach was carried to near panic proportions in the period following World War II, by cultural critics such as Theodore Adorno, Edward Shils, and Dwight Macdonald. Although one can safely say that none of these defenders of the traditional "high culture" had listened to heavy metal, they surely would have judged it and its audience negatively. Alan Bloom, who belongs to the contemporary group of cultural elitists, reserves a special circle in hell for rock music. His 1985 diatribe against rock damns its audience in no uncertain terms.[3] Priests of the high culture dismiss rock as "brutal culture," "masscult," or, more generally, mass culture.

There will be no attempt here to engage the elitists in a war of value judgments. Their approach is normative and the present discussion is sociological. It is necessary to note, however, that elitist criticism, by denigrating the audience, is unable to take it seriously and to see it on its own terms. Sociology cannot be dismissive in this way if it seeks to understand its subject matter.

From a sociological perspective it is useful to consider whether the audience for heavy metal is a "mass," in an analytical sense of that term.[4] For Herbert Blumer, a mass consists of people from a wide variety of social positions, the members of which are not only physically separated from one another but have little, if any, interaction of any sort; they are basically anonymous individuals.[5] In Blumer's sense the heavy metal audience is not a mass since its members come from a narrow range of demographic positions and are often known to one another through their abundant interactions, especially at frequent live concerts and in peer groups that foster devotion to the music. Will Straw remarks of the heavy metal audience that its members have "coherent and consistent taste patterns." They are distinguished in that respect from "casual audiences," whose members have "eclectic" tastes.[6]

Mass audiences for music are generally understood to be "passive recipients of already interpreted songs, nothing more than a collection of isolated 'cultural dopes.' "[7] But work done by Stuart Hall and his associates in England, and Denzin[8] and Grossberg in the United States, among others, challenges the view that rock audiences are passive. Contesting the mass model, writers such as Hebdige, Willis, and Grossberg describe how the audience defines and interprets the music, "bringing it into its own already constituted realities, or 'uses' it to satisfy already present needs."[9] The practices and fashions of the heavy metal audience, and its standards for and readings of the music, reveal a very active stance.

If the metal audience is not typically mass, what is it? According to the conventional wisdom, "folk" culture is the opposite of mass culture. The former exists outside the systems of the corporate economy, while the latter is a product of that economy. Most, though not all, of heavy metal exists within a commercial frame. But there is also a profusion of amateur groups, without professional intentions and/or possibilities, which mediate between the world of commerce and the "folk arts." In folk culture, the distinction between artist and fan is blurred. The performer is not a member of a specialized occupational group, but merely a more talented audience member. The air-guitar stance, assumed by members of the heavy metal audience, both at home alone with their records and at concerts, is a symbolic representation of the connectedness of the artist and the audience. The ideology of metal as a folk art permeates the heavy metal culture, yet the heavy metal world is not a true folk culture.

Neither the locus of a folk culture nor the passive recipient of mass culture, the metal audience stands somewhere in between. Like all spatially dispersed modern audiences, it is not homogeneous, though, as will be shown later, it has a distinctive, persisting, and well-delineated core. Indeed, community is highly valued in the ideology of the metal audience and is visibly represented by its dress code. But close up one sees a myriad of differences. There are subsets of heavy metal music, each with its own partly divergent audiences, distinctive modes of interpreting the music, and variations in the ways in which the music is incorporated into the lives of its devotees. There is metal for born-again Christians and for practicing Satanists, each of whom read the music using codes external to it. Within the music's code some fans are sophisticated readers, while others are extremely literal. Writing about rock audiences in general, Willis concludes, "It is clear that different groups can be involved with the same cultural items and yet take different homological meanings and effects from them. It is also clear that what a particular group makes of a particular item can change over time, so that what was once accepted is rejected."[10]

Geographic, temporal, and subgenre variations may be associated with more or less distinctive metal audiences. One cannot assume that the audience for heavy metal in England matches such audiences in the United States, Japan, or Poland. The metal audience in the late 1980s may not be the same as it was in the mid-1970s. Similarly, the audience that follows classical metal artists such as Judas Priest, Iron Maiden, and Ozzy may not be the same as the audience for thrash metal artists such as Anthrax and Nuclear Assault; and neither of these audiences may overlap with those who appreciate the lite metal "hair bands" such as Poison and White Lion.

Intelligent analysis demands an awareness of these and other distinctions within the audience, as well as a realization that these differences may be more or less significant. In the description of the audience that follows, common characteristics will be stressed, but attention will also be given to significant variations.

Methodological barriers to getting a fully accurate understanding of the metal audience may exist. The research on which this chapter is based relies mainly on intensive participant observation and unstructured interviews. These methods are restricted by space and time restraints, so they have been supplemented with readings in professional literature and the rock and metal press, and with interviews of people who have witnessed metal audiences in other contexts than those to which I have been privy. Yet despite these precautions I have a sense of tentativeness. For example, Kotarba and Wells in 1987 reported that metalheads at metal concerts in a club played air-guitar to get girls.[11] This interpretation did not square with the meaning of any air-guitar playing that I had ever seen. I asked people in the metal audience about Kotarba and Wells's conclusion, and they laughed it out of court. Either Kotarba and Wells misinterpreted their evidence, or the metal fans they observed are different from those with whom I had contact. Similarly, whereas Will Straw contends that metal fans do not read magazines or collect albums, I found a significant proportion of them doing both. Indeed, some of the most avid buyers of used records in the Midwest, at the time that Straw was writing, were metal fans. Was this pattern different among those whom he observed? In light of the fact that the record companies say that their metal back catalogues have always sold well, I find confirmation of, but do not have total confidence in, my observations.

As a distinctive social formation, sharing elements of mass and folk culture, the metal audience is usefully understood in terms of the sociological concepts of "taste public" and, particularly, "subculture." The idea of taste public was elaborated and employed by American investigators; the idea of subculture is British in origin and, thus far, application. The differences between the two phrases reflect different intellectual perspectives.

As defined by Herbert Gans, "taste cultures . . . consist of values, the cultural forms which express these values . . . and the media in which these are expressed."[12] "Users who make similar choices of values and taste culture content [are] . . . *Taste Publics*, even though they are unorganized aggregates rather than organized publics."[13] The audience for heavy metal is more than an "unorganized aggregate," but it is not fully organized. A taste public is "defined primarily in terms of shared aesthetic values, rather than because [its members] choose the same cultural content, for they may choose it on the basis of different values."[14] Gans's work directs inquiry to the common set of aesthetic values shared by the audience for heavy metal.

The concept of subculture is broader and more useful for the present discussion than that of taste public.[15] The theory developed in Britain stresses the activities of the audience, not merely the values of its members. Subcultures are not only contexts of appreciation, but also of the creation of a way of life, including a certain style. One author, discussing members of the Rasta subculture, found that they were typical of those belonging to other youth subcultures since they "were mostly quite young, drew inspiration from music, identified positively with each other, dressed similarly and, most important, emphasized their difference."[16] The work on British music-based youth groups emphasizes the relationship between music and style: "Subcultures create styles which become living art homologous with musical form and which creates its own intoxication."[17] The metal audience is articulated into a subculture with a distinctive style and activities. It is constituted by its members, but is not fully their own.

Of course, the members of a music-based youth subculture are only a subset of the wider audience for the relevant genre of music. Brake notes that "Membership is a difficult problem because there are always righteous, full-time members and part-time adherents, and outrageous styles reduce marginal membership."[18] Grossberg also notes that "being a particular sort of rock fan can take on an enormous importance and thus come to constitute a dominant part of the fan's identity."[19] For any music-based subculture it is an empirical question as to what proportion of the audience for the genre is made up of members of the subculture.

It would be foolish to estimate the ratio between membership in heavy metal's audience and membership in the heavy metal subculture. That ratio varies over time and place, and according to the range of music that is included within the genre. However, some generalizations about the relations between these two sets can be made. The ratio was far higher in 1979, when there was little mass-media exposure of heavy metal, than it was a decade later. The ratio is reduced when groups such as Led Zeppelin or Kiss are included in the genre, since these groups attract fans otherwise unconnected with the genre. Where the audience is crystallized into the demographics most associated with an appreciation of heavy metal (where white, blue-collar, male youth form the audience), the ratio will be higher. As heavy metal embraces musical styles from the heaviest to the lightest, from the growled and snarled to the sweetly melodious, from themes of evil and mayhem to those of love (romantic, lustful, and even religious), the ratio declines.

The Core Audience and Its Subculture

The metal audience can be described in terms of its demographics, the set of structural positions valued so highly by market research.

The stereotypical metal fan is male, white, and in his midteens.[20] As one journalist writes, "heavy metal fans are usually white working-class males between the ages of 12 and 22."[21] Most are also blue collar, either in fact or by sentimental attachment. This is an accurate external description of the vast majority of enthusiasts for the genre, from its beginning through the mid-1980s. Further, these characteristics form a consistent pattern across geographical settings, although the Japanese and some Latin American fans could not be designated as "white."

Tastes in popular culture have traditionally been associated with structural position. The point here is not merely to describe the metal audience in terms of its members' positions in the larger social structure (the market-research approach), but to understand how the demographics translate into the constitution of a distinctive subculture that coconstitutes the metal genre. Heavy metal is not unique in having a demographically specific audience. Pop groups such as New Kids on the Block and the Osmond Brothers have equally narrow audiences, though of a rather different composition. The significant difference between the metal audience and any other narrow audience is that its core is a rather elaborate and long-lived subculture.

To say that the core of the metal audience belongs to a persisting subculture is to go beyond demographics to the level of social groups. The term "subculture" implies an integrity that includes and organizes a variety of elements. The subculture as a whole is more valued by its members than are any of its parts. Each part finds its relative place within the whole.

One might ask whether this description really fits the metal audience. After all, we are talking about a subculture that is named after a musical genre. Perhaps the audience is a sheer creation of the genre and its commercial mediators. Although that is what some disparaging critics like to think, it is not true. Music is the master emblem of the heavy metal subculture, but it is not its meaning. Indeed, from the aspect of the audience, the music is a function of the life-styles and mythologies of a youth group, and must be consistent with those life-styles and mythologies in order to be appropriated by the group. The youth subculture that forms the core of heavy metal provides parameters for the music. Within those bounds artists are free to create and the music industry to promote.

But they must honor the culture by, at the very least, appearing to serve it.

Most of the discussion of the audience here will be presented as a general description of the core subculture and its members, leaving out the factor of historical change. This procedure is justified because, on the whole, the subculture remained remarkably stable through the mid-1980s, and continued to be an important, perhaps dominant, factor in the metal audience afterward. But in order to understand the independence of the metal subculture, it is necessary to note briefly how it arose.

Roots of the Metal Subculture

The heavy metal subculture is a direct outgrowth from the youth culture of the 1960s. By the late 1960s the youth culture had spilled beyond its origins in the fusion between political protest and romantic hedonism to become a style and a mood, a fashion and an ethos, which could be appropriated by youth outside the colleges and the middle class, the sites at which that culture originated. One subgroup of youth was especially attracted to the ethos of the youth culture, particularly its attitudes of disrespect for authority and its hedonism. Blue-collar, white, male youth found in the styles and hedonistic pursuits of the 1960s youth culture a means of justifying and enhancing their normal rebelliousness against conforming to the disciplines of a social order that did not provide them with privileges or an attractive future. They adopted the long hairstyle, the casual dress, the drugs, and the psychedelic music of the prevailing youth culture, but they preserved their traditional machismo and romance with physical power, which were epitomized by the images of the outlaw biker gang. This hybrid youth subculture, a melding of hippie and biker, began to appear in the late 1960s, but it was unorganized and had no unique forms of self-expression. It was a nondistinctive part of the scene.

At the same time that a blue-collar variant of the youth culture was forming, psychedelic music was getting harder. Indeed, the manager of Blue Cheer, one of the hardest psychedelic groups, was a former Hell's Angel; straddling two worlds, this manager's career demonstrates that a hybrid subculture was crystallizing on the level of its music in the late 1960s.[22] As the broad 1960s youth culture collapsed and fragmented at the turn of the new decade, both the blue-collar long-hairs and the psychedelic bands were left stranded. Eventually they found each other with the help of the music industry and the result was a heavy metal subculture, in which both audience and music became essential to one another's definition. The music became the prime representation or emblem of the youth group's identity because it cohered with the life-styles and mythologies of that group. The important thing to note here is that the subculture was not a fabrication of the popular-culture industry, but existed, in germ, before heavy metal music as a distinctive genre erupted.

The heavy metal subculture, then, is a legitimate offspring of the 1960s youth culture, inheriting and preserving some of its central symbols, attitudes, practices, and fashions, and carrying them forward into the next historical period. Indeed, it might usefully be considered as ruled by an ideal that fuses two of the most powerful signifying events of the 1960s, Woodstock and Altamont. Woodstock, the utopia of peaceful hedonism and community, and Altamont, the dystopia of macho violence, exemplify the polarity of the 1960s youth culture. The heavy metal subculture borrows from both of them, never effecting a genuine reconciliation of the utopian and dystopian oppositions, but creating, instead, a shifting bricolage of fashion, ritual, and behavior, which includes elements of each partner in the binary opposition.

Thus, the heavy metal subculture basically represents a preservationist and conservative tendency, the first 1960s nostalgia movement, arising amidst the decay of the 1960s youth culture. Why a segment of white, blue-collar, and male youth should find an ideological home in a nostalgic utopia is partly explained as a response to declining economic opportunities for that group, whose members faced increasing disadvantages in their lives. They were ripe for a rock-and-roll fantasy rooted in the high times of the recent past. Also, as the general youth culture, which was dominated by white males, fell apart, white, male, and heterosexual youth became socioculturally de-centered by emerging movements of women, gays, and nonwhites. Nostalgia for centricity, then, also had its part in the metal subculture's conservation of the 1960s.

Considered from the viewpoint of historical sociology, heavy metal music is the master emblem of the subculture of a well-defined segment of youth. Not all those who form the audience for metal are white, male, blue-collar youth. Not all white, male, blue-collar youth are members of the metal subculture. But the core of the metal audience is a subculture whose members have those demographic characteristics, not by chance, but because heavy metal music came to express the utopian desires, the life-style, and the discontents of a structurally defined segment of youth. There could have been no heavy metal music if there had been no incipient subculture ready to guide and embrace it.

As an expression of a distinctive segment of youth, the metal subculture valorizes the demographics of its membership. Masculinity, blue-collar sentiments, youthfulness, and, to a lesser extent, "whiteness" are values shared and upheld by the metal audience. Moreover, many of the other features of the heavy metal subculture are strongly related to or implicated in these demographically derived values.

It is difficult to determine which of the four demographic factors is the most important in determining the subculture. Together they describe a social position that should be understood as a whole, not analyzed into its components. There are also interrelationships among the factors. Since they constitute a complex, the act of discussing them separately should be recognized as an act of abstraction. Yet there is a general order of importance, moving from maleness, through youthfulness, to whiteness, to blue-collar sentiments.

Male

Heavy metal is a form of rock music, sharing with that larger category an array of features. Various authors have commented on the male orientation of rock culture in general.[23] Although it is most evident in metal, "Rock's following tends to be male; pop fans tend to be younger and female."[24] Frith and Horne argue that in Britain rock was a predominantly male interest because, in part, the leading British rock musicians of the 1960s had an art-school background. The romantic ideology that was rampant in these schools stressed a bohemian ideal, which was both masculine and somewhat misogynistic.[25] Heavy metal artists did not come from the art schools but were, like their fans, steeped in the rock ideology. In some sense metal is the Ur-rock practice, taking to an extreme many of the ideals of 1960s rock.

Not merely rock, but youth culture as such, tends to be male-oriented. In his comparative study of adolescent culture in the United States, Canada, and Britain, Michael Brake concluded that it is "male dominated and predominantly heterosexual, thus celebrating masculinity and excluding girls to the periphery."[26] Some commentators note two different adolescent cultures, distinguished by gender, "each with its *own* distinctive characteristics, style, and world view, in which boys are encouraged to settle career and personal identity issues first and foremost, whereas girls are taught that their primary developmental task is to attract a husband and prepare for caring for a family."[27]

One can go even further, arguing that males, in contrast to females, tend to form bonding groups with members of their own sex. Writing in 1963, Jules Henry observed that in the United States "Boys flock. . . . Boys are dependent on masculine solidarity within a relatively large group. In boys' groups the emphasis is on masculine unity; in girls' cliques the purpose is to shut out other girls."[28] Male culture, for Henry, was centered around sports: "The faithfulness of boys to sports is a striking characteristic of American life. As the season for each sport arrives, the boys are out in the field or in the street playing it with dogged loyalty, and the patter of information about the game is a counterpoint to the determined, excited play. There is a total, almost a religious, community of sport among boys, in which maleness, masculine solidarity, and the rules of the game are validated, year in and year out."[29] His observations—if one substitutes "watching" for "playing"—also apply to male adults. Substitute "music" for "sport" and one gets an idea of the intensity of the heavy metal subculture.

"That the audience for heavy-metal music is heavily male-dominated is generally acknowledged, and statistically confirmed."[30] Even a marginal metal group such as Aerosmith had an all-male following during the 1970s. Steve Tyler, the group's singer, bluntly acknowledges this truth: "It used to be the only girls at Aerosmith shows were the ones who came to blow us on the bus." His band mate, Tom Hamilton, agrees: "We used to call our fans the blue army, . . . We'd look out and all we'd see were these stadiums full of guys in bluejeans, a sea of blue."[31]

But the heavy metal audience is more than just male; it is masculinist. That is, the heavy metal subculture, as a community with shared values, norms, and behaviors, highly esteems masculinity. Whereas other youth cultures and audiences, such as the early-1970s glam rock following that coalesced around David Bowie, and the mid-1980s pop audience for Culture Club and Michael Jackson, countenanced play with gender, heavy metal fans are deadly earnest about the value of male identity. Masculinity is understood in the metal subculture to be the binary opposite of femininity. Much like the religious fundamentalism that denounces heavy metal, the metal subculture holds that gender differences are rooted in the order of things: it is perilous even to question, let alone play with or breach, the boundaries.

Influenced in part by the British biker subculture and the related, though more diffuse, American "greasers,"[32] the masculinist model predated metal. Willis's analysis of the motor-bike boys defines the model: "Their appearance was aggressively masculine. The motorcycle gear both looked tough, with its leather, studs and denim, and by association with the motor-bike, took over some of the intimidating quality of the machine. Hair was worn long. . . . Tattoos on the hands, arms and chest were extremely common."[33]

Interpretations of such boys-only groups abound. A feminist assessment understands these groups in terms of male bonding, through which "men learn from each other that they are entitled under patriarchy to power in the culture."[34] Whether this indicates the strength of patriarchy or is a defensive response to the weakening of male hegemony is debatable. In light of the fact that music-based masculine subcultures came into their own at approximately the same time as the late-twentieth-century women's movement was reaching its peak, one should not dismiss the idea that these subcultures have a defensive nature.

Insofar as male youths have a different set of problems than their female counterparts, expressive activities such as music mean different things to each gender group. Women are part of the problem for males, not only because they are objects of lust but because they symbolize repressive authority in the persons of the mother and the teacher. Even a generous reading of the Freudian Oedipus model, where the mother disappoints as a failed love object, allows for an understanding of the misogyny and male chauvinism that are so prevalent among adolescent males. Young males are, at a minimum, ambivalent regarding women, seeking to escape from maternal and other forms of female authority and fearful of being viewed as "mama's boys," and yet attracted to women sexually. Childhood socialization patterns, in which boys are allowed freer rein than girls, make the transition from youth to adulthood more difficult for males than for females. The expected adult role in Western industrialized society is closer to the female pattern of low aggression, stricter conformity to the "rules," and supervision by adults, such as spouses. Heavy metal music celebrates the very qualities that boys must sacrifice in order to become adult members of society.[35]

The male chauvinism and misogyny that characterize the metal subculture are tempered by its sense of community. Females who do not flaunt their femininity, that is, who dress in jeans and black T-shirts, and who even more importantly display a love of the music, are often welcomed and treated as equals at such events as concerts. Open hostility of various sorts is displayed toward females who do not conform to the dress and behavior codes. Women who dress in "provocative" attire, such as miniskirts and high heels, are either denounced as sluts waiting to have sex with the band or are ogled as obnoxiously as they might be by the most chauvinistic construction workers. The distinction made by the metal subculture between women who dress and behave according to the masculine code and those who fit feminine stereotypes indicates that it is the culture of masculinity, not biological differences, that is of greatest significance.

The masculinist element in metal subculture is not merely relevant to the attitudes toward and treatment of women. There is also an attitude of extreme intolerance toward male homosexuality. Heavy metal fans "are often vehemently opposed to other forms of music and to acts that display the slightest hint of ambisexuality. Headbangers are notoriously homophobic . . . and generally regard any act that does not go in for metal's much-macho posturing as beneath contempt."[36] The term "homophobic" is embedded in a psychoanalytic theory that interprets hatred as an emotional response rooted in fear. Whether it is appropriate for characterizing the metal subculture is a debatable point that cannot be resolved here.

During the 1970s the British Skinheads carried the animus against homosexuality into the activity of "Queer Bashing."[37] The metal subculture did not incorporate this violent practice, but expressed its abhorrence for gays by means of more acceptable cultural practices, such as an impassioned loathing for disco music.[38] The relevance of and hostility toward homosexuality in the heavy metal subculture is in some sense a reaction of resistance by masculinist interests against the change in dominant values. The gay culture, the source of the mass popularity of disco and disco fashion, came to be admired in the 1970s by the hip culture mavens. At that time, too, the gay rights movement came into its own. Gays "coming out" of the closet were seen by many traditional males as flaunting their "gay culture."

The masculine mystique that characterizes the metal subculture has many roots, the most important of which is simply the general sexist bias of modern and more generally human culture, which is intensified by the special insecurities of youth. This general tendency is fortified in a historically specific way by the social, cultural, and economic marginalization of white, blue-collar males in the post-1960s era. The heavy metal subculture is usefully interpreted as a defensive reaction of members of this group as their standing and security declined. In this sense the masculinism of heavy metal is the same sort of dialectical negation of the forces unleashed by the 1960s as is the fundamentalist agenda (which also includes masculinism) of metal's most vigorous foes. But this dialectical negation is not complete. A masculinism that coexists with and is expressed by long hair and the S&M paraphernalia of segments of the gay subculture bespeaks a compromise formation, a bricolage, an unconscious drive to synthesize binaries, to carry on the 1960s, when, for a moment, male supremacy, hedonism, and the rejection of established authorities and codes all seemed to be mutually compatible.

Youth

The metal subculture is also characterized by the midadolescent age grouping of its membership. That metal's audience is overwhelmingly young is not surprising. Audiences for rock music traditionally have been teenagers. For example, a study published in

1984 of 1500 twelve to eighteen year olds who were representative of the national population "found that almost 81% of the students cited music as an important part of their lives. Music was the sample's fourth highest ranked hobby."[39]

Rock music in general responds to the ambivalence of youth. "Caught between the moment of suspended freedom and the transition from dependency to responsibility, the typical dualistic consciousness of youth is modified by the counter-tendencies to sink back into childhood and to advance towards adulthood."[40] "Teenage culture is, in part, an authentic response to this situation, an area of common symbols and meanings, shared in part or in whole by a generation, in which they can work out or work through not only the natural tensions of adolescence, but the special tensions of being an adolescent in our kind of society."[41] People seem to become members of youth subcultures at a structurally meaningful time: "[Membership] occurs in the period between, or near to, the end of the school career, usually at a point when education is perceived as meaningless in terms of a young person's work prospects, and lasts until marriage."[42]

Heavy metal's subculture emerged from the wreckage of the youth counter(sub)culture of the 1960s. The great consensus following World War II was shattered in the United States by the civil rights movement and then the antiwar movement. The youth subculture, an amalgam of the so-called hippie movement and the free speech movement on college campuses, and a wide assortment of commercial and community-based groupings, emerged in the second half of the 1960s. It spread around the world, including Britain, where it merged with class-based youth subcultures. Symbolized by the audience at the Woodstock Festival in 1969 and by terms such as "the generation gap," the youth culture was never as all-encompassing as the media, always eager to woo baby boomers nostalgic for their lost youth, would have one believe. But it was a genuine cultural phenomenon that, as it broke apart, released a host of related social and cultural movements, including heavy metal.

A series of events beginning in 1968, some of which were meant to repress the counterculture, shattered its fragile unity. The litany for the United States includes the police riot at the Democratic National Convention in Chicago in 1968, the deaths and disorder at the Altamont Concert in 1969, the National Guard's shooting of students at Kent State University in 1970, and the end of the draft. Cultural icons died too. "The hippie counter-culture confronted its own demise most dramatically in the deaths of Hendrix and Joplin. With the break-up of the Beatles, the murder of a participant in the 1969 Altamont Rock festival . . . the degeneration into drug-ravaged slums of . . . Haight-Ashbury and New York's East Village, it became clear even to its adherents that 'the dream' was over."[43]

The ensuing fragmentation, which led to what Tom Wolfe mischaracterized as the "me decade," was the environment in which the metal subculture surfaced. Grossman, in his social history of rock music, characterizes heavy metal, which he calls "downer rock," as a response to the antiyouth crusade. "It appeared that society had formally declared war against the young and Heavy Rock brought forth Downer Rock, a particularly appropriate genre for the times."[44]

At least as serious as the undoing of the youth counterculture, and concurrent with it, was the radical change in the meaning of the term "youth" in social discourse. Beyond and indeed in place of its use in referring to a biological or a social group, "youth" became a cultural signifier, referring to a style and a spirit. Through the 1960s the notion of "youth" was anchored to its biological and social definitions; that is, the youth culture belonged to that group in the population that was undergoing adolescent maturation and was moving socially from childhood to adulthood. But then the youth culture got co-opted into the general leisure culture and lost its moorings in a particular age group. It became what semioticians call a "floating signifier," a designation or identification that could be taken up by anyone as the emblem of a life-style. It became chic for adults to take up aspects of the youth culture in the mid-1960s, but afterwards a youthful image, as defined by the leisure culture, became a normalized component of anything else that might be "chic" or "trendy" or "hip" or "in."

The fundamental marginalization of young people is reflected in the change of "youth" from a signifier that once designated their particular state of being to a signifier for a cultural category. Having been set loose from its biological and social moorings, "youth" drifts around them, drawing upon their significance but only so much as to remain acceptable for appropriation by anyone of any biological age or social position. "Youth" as a cultural category has been eviscerated and sublimated into a commercialized spirit of "youthfulness." In the process of becoming a floating signifier, available for appropriation and manipulation, "youth" became detached from young people. Youth in the sense of young people in a special biological and social predicament became marginal to "youth" as a cultural code of beliefs, values, sentiments, and practices.

Young people responded to the extortion of "youth" in a variety of ways. Mainly they merged into the youthful leisure culture as its distinctive representatives. Others, reacting in the manner of tribal peoples who have become deracinated, dropped out of society into depression, becoming heavy users of alcohol and other drugs, and sometimes committing suicide. Some entered cults and authoritarian sects, which set themselves sharply off from the general culture. Still others formed subcultures that raised the symbolic stakes too high for the general leisure culture easily to co-opt them.

The heavy metal and punk subcultures are the two dominant examples of youth attempting to create and hold onto their own distinctive and unassimilable culture. The significance in both subcultures of hairstyles demonstrates the raising of symbolic stakes. Cashmore argues that punk's major feature was the valorization of youth: "Punks decried anyone or anything connected with the established social order as boring old farts (BOFs). They regurgitated the impulse behind the mod slogan of the 1960s, 'I hope I die before I get old.' "[45] Although dissimilar on the surface, the heavy metal and punk styles were united at their core by the desire to constitute themselves as unacceptable to the respectable world. They could not be modified, in the way that clothes can, to allow for weekend warriors. Metal and punk required permanent stigmata. The subculture was inscribed on the body. More recently, as metal has itself become somewhat of a floating signifier, thrash metal, a kind of hybrid of metal and punk, has arisen as an exclusivist youth subculture by emphasizing elements unacceptable to the vast majority of adults.

Both the metal and punk subcultures borrowed heavily from prior youth cultures. In a highly oversimplified summary, punk took a rave-up beat from early rock and roll, and cobbled it together with inverted features of art-rock conventions. Metal appropriated musical, visual, and performance elements from the hard-rock/biker and the psychedelic musical subcultures. Whereas punk's transformations were understood, internally and by the critics, as progressive, metal's appropriations were interpreted, from within and especially from without, as retrograde. Indeed, the heavy metal subculture initially was a movement to preserve the best of the youth counterculture even as it died. Beyond the musical components, heavy metal perpetuated the sense of community, the use of marijuana, and the visual element of performances, among other values and practices. The conservativism of the metal subculture, so abhorred by the critics, is rooted here: "there are few things as conservative and hidebound as a crazed Heavy Metal fan."[46] The metal subculture selected only a small portion of the 1960s youth culture to preserve, but what it chose was genuine. Perhaps the critics of metal simply do not like to be reminded that the 1960s contained both more and less than they wish it did.

What happens to heavy metal fans when they become adults? The metal subculture does not fully include those metal fans who are no longer in their teens. Commentators contend that "Heavy metal was consumed by one generation of teenagers after another; attending a concert, one would rarely find anyone over the age of eighteen or nineteen. Heavy metal, with its deafening volume and proud hostility to cultural and aesthetic niceties, is the primary music of teenage rebellion and, almost by definition, something a listener outgrows."[47]

Not everyone seems to outgrow it fully, but evidence of adult metal fans is hard to come by. Adults are not studied as an audience for rock music, except as potential players in the marketplace. It is the high school and college students, who are easily and cheaply available to researchers, whose preferences are measured by sociologists. However, observation of the audience at classic metal concerts in the late 1980s (Ozzy, the regrouped Deep Purple, and Motörhead, among others), revealed a few people who were well past their youth. The rest of the audience not only tolerated these generational oddities, but saw their presence as an affirmation of the metal culture itself.[48] The same is not true of audiences for lite metal groups, such as Poison and Ratt, nor for speed and thrash metal groups such as Anthrax, Slayer, and Nuclear Assault. Lite and thrash metal audiences tend to be uniformly adolescent.

The adults who continue to appreciate metal rarely use the metal media, except for playing their old albums. They do not attend many, if any, concerts; do not buy new metal releases or metal magazines; and do not call in requests on the radio. Many do not even play their albums all that much, but they have not thrown them out either. Once part of the metal subculture, they are now like wistful emigrants, living a continent away in another world than their own.

White

The members of the metal subculture are predominantly white, except in countries with overwhelmingly nonwhite populations, such as Japan and Brazil. The performers of metal music are also overwhelmingly white. As was the case for maleness, "whiteness" is not merely a demographic category but has a cultural significance. That significance is not overtly or even necessarily covertly racist. Indeed, it is less an affirmation of "whiteness" than it is an absence—an obtrusive absence—of blacks.

For Hebdige, "the succession of white subcultural forms can be read as a series of deep-structural adaptations which symbolically accommodate or expunge the black presence from the host community."[49] An affection for black music, found in mid-1950s American teenagers and in early 1960s British youth, was not merely a taste for the inherent features of the music. It also included the delineated aspect of the music's "black" association, with its connotations of rebellion. Youth was attracted to black music in part because of the myth of the "negro," who was seen to be unrepressed, especially sexually—a "natural man." Prior to rock and roll, trad jazz in the United Kingdom also worked to fuse blackness with rebellion: "For young whites . . . it served as a suitable vehicle for musical protest because its relative musical simplicity and its atavism offended their elders, as did its racial connections, and these shocking factors could be reinforced by the myth of the red light origins of New Orleans jazz and the less mythical association with gangster speakeasies of the prohibition era."[50]

Heavy metal emerged at a time when the position of blacks in Anglo-American society was undergoing massive changes. The black power movement in the United States, with its separatist, white-rejecting strains, was in full flower. At the same time, civil rights legislation started to have an impact in housing, in schools, and in the workplace. This, coupled with the severe downturn in the economy, led to a strong sense of resentment against blacks by marginal whites. The situation in Britain was different. Prior to World War II there were few people of color in the British population. In the 1960s Commonwealth subjects from the Indian subcontinent and the Caribbean islands began to move to Britain in large numbers. The out-in-the-street culture of the latter group, in conjunction with the severe recession in Britain in the 1970s, elicited racist sentiment from working-class whites. In the general climate of social tension, white youth had to look elsewhere than black culture to shock their elders.

In both Great Britain and North America, one could look over the vast sea of thousands of faces at a heavy metal concert and fail to find one black person. By the mid-1980s, when a few brave blacks started to enter the arena, they were in the company of their white buddies. I recall speaking with an articulate and intelligent black college student, an avid metal guitarist. His favorite band, Rush, was coming to town, and although he would have loved to have seen them, he was too intimidated to go (He did get to attend their concert the next year and reported no problems.)

The experience of this black fan points up the fact, already noted in the section on maleness, that the metal subculture tends to be tolerant of those outside its core demographic base who follow its codes of dress, appearance, and behavior, and who show devotion to the music. Neither sexist, ageist, nor racist on principle, the metal subculture is exclusivist, insistent upon upholding the codes of its core membership.

Hispanics rarely joined the heavy metal subculture until the late 1980s. The fragmentation of the youth subculture in the early 1970s, which had integrated some elements of Hispanic music (for example, Santana), led to the emergence of a new wave of separate Hispanic music. Salsa and its variants were the musical base of the Hispanic youth subculture. There was nothing in the metal subculture that symbolically excluded Hispanics. Indeed, a number of symbols found in some segments of metal were present in some Hispanic cultures, especially the symbolism of death. In communities in the United States where Mexican youth are in the majority, notably in south Texas, the audience for heavy metal is rapidly growing and the metal subculture is taking root.

Although the white demographic base was not given cultural expression primarily as a racial value, either in the prowhite or the antiblack sense, metal has been associated with a strong ethnocentrism bordering on xenophobia. But while the Skinheads acted out similar hostilities by "Paki-Bashing," making racial violence central to their subculture,[51] the metal subculture was not aggressive in the same way.

Many of the symbols, especially the visual ones, of heavy metal are derived from medieval northern Europe, ancient Anglo-Saxon, and Nordic mythologies. Thus the heavy metal subculture is less a racially based than a cultural grouping, drawing on the symbols of particular ethnic traditions. Emerging at the time of a "discovering and celebrating one's roots" mania among racial and ethnic groups, particularly in the United States, the valorization of "white" into heavy metal subculture can be interpreted as the creation of the semblance of an ethnic group for individuals who were perceived to be nonethnics in the Anglo-American context. Jon Epstein, studying a group of junior high school students in 1990 in North Carolina, found that their musical preferences were closely allied with race. Blacks preferred rap, whites metal.[52]

Blue Collar

It is generally accepted that the members of the metal subculture are predominantly male, young, and white. Some commentators add that they also tend to come from working-class/blue-collar backgrounds.[53] This observation is more accurate concerning England than the United States. Class consciousness and class segregation are far more pronounced in Britain than in the United States. Much of British leisure culture is class-based, whereas America has far more mass entertainments, which are enjoyed by people over a wide range of income levels, occupational statuses, and other class-related positions. Thus youth subcultures that are related, in part, to leisure culture, are more class-based in Britain than they are in the United States.[54] But in a cultural sense, heavy metal has a class signification wherever it appears. For the United States, it might be most accurate to say that metal partakes of a blue-collar ethos.

Blue-collar mythologies replace the romance of black culture in metal's syllabus of rebellion.

During the 1970s the working class(es) in the West were under siege. The fierce economic "stagflation," caused in part by the OPEC oil cartel, seriously hurt those working at manufacturing jobs. Working-class youths could no longer expect to follow their fathers and uncles into the nearby factories. Unions, particularly in Britain, were undermined by legislation restricting their rights.[55] The recession was felt to be especially severe because it stood in contrast to the recent boom times of the 1960s. The structural position of youth is most influenced by upturns and downturns in the economy. Punk in England was one response to the deteriorating conditions and heavy metal was another. "The days of affluence were over by about 1976,"[56] a year that saw the full flowering of both of these youth subcultures.

In addition to suffering straightened economic conditions, the working class was culturally threatened by the growing hegemony of a middle-class/mass-culture life-style in the mass media. In the United States many blue-collar families migrated from their "rust belt" surroundings, dislocating the sense of community that had existed there for several generations. Brake argues that "Subcultures try to retrieve the lost, socially cohesive elements in the parent culture; they attempt to relocate 'in an imaginary relation' the real relations which those in subcultures cannot transcend."[57] Thus, just as the heavy metal subculture was a response to the collapse of the 1960s youth culture, it was also a response to the cultural marginalization of the working class.

In terms of many of its values and mythologies, the heavy metal subculture is blue collar. The expectations for blue-collar young males is that they will sow their wild oats in a "period of intense emotion, colour, and excitement during the brief respite between school and the insecurities of the early days of working and settling down into marriage and adulthood."[58]

The heavy metal audience was never exclusively working class. The older metal fans, those in their late teens and early twenties, were more likely to be blue-collar workers, but a significant portion of high school–aged adherents came from middle-class families.[59] Nonetheless, blue-collar culture permeated the heavy metal subculture. The separation of the sexes, the boisterous, beer-swilling, male camaraderie, among other features, are rooted in blue-collar folkways. Hebdige interprets part of the heavy metal subculture as a "football terrace machismo,"[60] a distinctly male, working-class culture.

By the 1970s the blue-collar romance had the same appeal for middle-class youth that the black fantasia had for an earlier cohort in the 1950s. Blue-collar culture was disreputable. Parents who felt that their middle-class affluence was insecure were outraged when their kids became déclassé, just as earlier generations of parents had been appalled by their children adopting "negro" music and styles, or the hippie life-style. American youth cultures, succeeding one another over decades and embracing a variety of styles, all rebel against the bourgeois culture. The process has been aptly characterized as "prestige from below."[61] The middle-class kids who embraced metal were not from the upper reaches of their class. They were centered in the lower middle class, whose members are the most insecure in their standing. There could be few things more threatening for lower-middle-class parents than to witness their sons aping blue-collar manners and espousing blue-collar values.

The class composition of the core metal audience is working and middle class, but the metal subculture is steeped in the blue-collar ethos. Ethos, however, need not and does not translate in this case into a political stance. The members of the metal subculture normally do not have the sense of themselves as political actors in the way that the punks did.[62] This is a major reason why they are not admired by the graduates of the counterculture who became the dominant popular music critics. In the metal subculture, blue-collar style and sentiments are tied to political attitudes, but these are not progressive in any conventional sense, basically amounting to a cynical animosity toward those in positions of governmental authority. There is a strongly shared antibourgeois sentiment, but this is a remnant of the youth counterculture. For fans, perhaps the worst thing that can be said about a heavy metal band is that it has "gone commercial."[63]

The demographic unity of the metal subculture shifted in the mid-1980s. The differentiation of heavy metal into rather distinctive subgenres, especially in the United States, described in chapter 2, paralleled these demographic changes. Overall, the heavy metal audience became de-differentiated. The age group widened on both ends of the midteen norm and wider ranges of the middle class became involved. In addition, nonwhite, especially Latin American, groups entered the audience; and evangelical Christian youth got their own subgenre of metal. Chicago has even given birth to a Gay Metal Society, which might seem to deconstruct the subculture altogether. Most importantly, females became a significant segment of metal fans. This has led in the Chicago area to the formation of the Chicago Women's Rock Club, the motto of which is "Let 'em know that you're no bimbo." These changes in the demographics of the audience did not impact on each of the metal subgenres uniformly. The audiences for classic metal, which continued traditional heavy metal, lite or pop metal, and speed/thrash metal were as differentiated as the distinctive forms of music that they appreciated. See Appendix B for the relationship between type of metal and gender.

The classic metal audience maintained the demographics described above for the heavy metal subculture, but not as strictly. The audience for thrash/speed metal, particularly those examples of it that integrated many punk elements, became exclusively male and concentrated at the lower end of the age group. Lite metal audiences became almost undistinguishable demographically from pop-rock audiences: they were teenaged, middle class, and included significant percentages of females. Indeed, males were in the minority of the audiences for some groups, such as Ratt, Poison, and White Lion.[64] The group Bon Jovi was seen to be the major innovator of lite metal, creating a music which, while specifically aimed at a female audience, did not fully alienate the males.[65]

The appearance of thrash metal and lite metal at approximately the same time is not a coincidence. The integration of females into the metal subculture through the lite subgenre aided the rise of thrash. Although gender issues do not account for the existence of thrash, the subgenre did spawn a basically male subculture at a time when not only metal, but other traditional male bastions, such as football and stock car racing, were being de-gendered. That is, thrash is a dialectical negation of the de-gendering tendency, attempting to restore the maleness of the traditional metal subculture.

A survey of high school students in a northeastern American city in 1989 reached a conclusion that was unanticipated by the researchers: "Surprisingly, gender is not related to liking heavy metal."[66] Preferences do not amount to membership in the subculture. Nonetheless, this does indicate a shift in the gender distribution of the metal audience, which correlates with the fragmentation of the music into subgenres.

Despite the demographic changes of the 1980s, the original makeup of the heavy metal audience—male, midteen, white, and blue collar—left a deep trace on the metal subculture(s), which continued to valorize and culturalize these demographic categories. For example, female "headbangers" of the 1980s look the part of the male fantasy of the "whore-bitch," the cliché constantly presented in metal videos.

As a valorization and culturalization of demographic categories, the metal subculture is a child of its time. In a world in which all groups have been de-centered, marginalization tends to become a universal condition. The metal subculture follows the black and Chicano movements in making a strong sense of negative marginality a badge of honor by taking as its name an epithet hurled against it. It is a cultural defense for maleness, a ghetto for youth when "youth" no longer signifies the young, a white preserve by default, and a stylization of blue-collar leisure culture. It is the reproduction of a world that never was, but in constituting itself as this yearned-for world it has become a real force in the lives of individuals and even in the environing society. It cannot make the world at large over, but it provides that world with some of its significance and meaning.

The Human Geography of Metal

In the 1970s the heavy metal subculture was, for the most part, geographically restricted. It originated in Britain, in part because it was British bands that pioneered many features of the genre. In addition, during the last half of the twentieth century, British youth have been more involved in distinctive subcultures than the youth of other countries. Strong class consciousness in British society and lack of opportunities for geographical mobility for British youth contributed to the crystallization of youth subcultures, including heavy metal.

England is split not only along class lines but also along a north/

south axis. The heavy metal subculture thrived in the northern parts of the country, particularly in the industrial midlands. Cities such as Birmingham spawned artists and audiences. London, in the south, was never a metal mecca, except when touring bands got to play at its arenas. The heavy metal subculture was probably in existence by 1973 in England, although setting exact dates for its appearance is as difficult as establishing the precise moment when heavy metal music emerged.

Several years later the United States could be said to have a fully articulated heavy metal subculture. Here too the audience was not evenly dispersed, but was concentrated in the large cities of the American Midwest, as well as in medium-sized cities and blue-collar suburbs. These sites were areas where lower-middle-class and working-class whites were more likely to be found. Large coastal cities tend to embrace more "hip" styles. Metal, even when it was new, was definitely not hip, and, as the 1970s continued, the image of metal as antihip became a cliché. Canada's metal subculture, centering in the Toronto area, was fully in place by the late 1970s.

In Europe, Germany's metal subculture emerged in the mid-1970s. It was large enough by 1981 to have had an important impact on record sales in the country.[67] The spread of the genre initially ran along the northern tier of the continent. By the early 1980s there were well-established metal subcultures in all of the Scandinavian countries, and small ones in parts of Italy, France, and Spain.

Poland seems to have been the first country in the former Eastern bloc to develop a serious heavy metal subculture, partly because the Polish government, in contrast to other iron curtain regimes, permitted the music to be heard. Indeed, the state-run radio stations actually offered heavy metal programs. The appeal of the music to Polish youth is highly complex, mixing more political motives with the basic metal ethos found in the West. With the decline of Soviet imperialism, metal is being avidly taken up elsewhere in Eastern Europe: "When the wall gave way last November [1989], East German rock and roll fans hit West Berlin's record shops with flying deutsche marks and sticky fingers," picking up albums by such metal artists as Bon Jovi, AC/DC, Metallica, and Led Zeppelin.[68]

The spirit of glasnost has allowed Soviet youth access to heavy metal and subcultures are forming there. Their presence was confirmed in 1989, when Ozzy Osbourne and other metal artists performed in Moscow. One hundred noisy motorcyclists "buzzed the Ukraine hotel early one morning until Osbourne indulged them with an appearance."[69] The metal subculture in the Soviet Union is heavily male. In 1989 Francine Du Plessix Gray studied Soviet women and found that they lived in a different world from that of Soviet males. Reporting on a conversation with a teenaged girl, she wrote, "Apart from books, her favorite distraction was ballroom dancing—waltz, tango—but her male friends disdained such music and liked only heavy-metal rock, which she detested."[70]

The Japanese took to heavy metal the way they have taken to so many forms of Western leisure culture. Heavy metal subculture was strong enough to encourage major metal tours to include Japan in their itinerary (often combining it with a trip to Australia). As mass merchandising becomes worldwide, metal has gained followers elsewhere in Asia. For example, some computer software pirates in Hong Kong have developed a taste for the music; the owners of a software shop are reported to pass the time bargaining with customers, smoking, and listening to "heavy metal bands (Iron Maiden and Led Zeppelin are favorites)."[71]

Heavy metal subcultures have grown up, during the 1980s, in many places, such as Brazil and Mexico, that are far from their core sites. What is needed for the emergence of the metal subculture is enough affluence for adolescents to have a youth culture. Indeed, David Handelman argues that whereas the punk rebellion in England "was fueled by lower-class anger and social unrest," heavy metal seems "a particularly middle-American-youth phenomenon," because "in America the average middle-class Joe can afford some form of the good life. . . . So instead of roaming the streets, alienated youths cruise the malls, more bored than angry. . . . And heavy metal has caught on as a sort of Lite punk: it smells and tastes like rebellion but without that political aftertaste."[72] Although Handelman is referring to the lite metal of the late 1980s, the audience for which expanded beyond metal's core audience, his remarks point up the need for elements of a consumer society to exist in order to sustain the hedonistic component of the metal subculture.

But affluence alone is not sufficient for the spread of the metal subculture. There must also be a decline of the native culture's pull on its youth. If the strength of the dominant religion is strong or if a sufficiently severe political struggle absorbs the identity and commitment of adolescents, heavy metal subcultures will not arise, because there will be alternative channels to hedonism into which youthful aspirations and discontents can flow. For example, the pull of Islam seems to be strong enough, even outside the Middle East, to preclude metal from getting a foothold among Moslem youth. Also, much of the iconography of heavy metal is related to northern European pagan cultures, so where there is native resonance with those symbols metal is more likely to be adopted. There are, however, many points of contact among the world's mythologies and romances. For example, in Japan it was easy to read the Samurai tradition into metal heroics. Similarly, the focus on death in Mexican and Brazilian culture resonates with speed/thrash metal imagery in particular, especially with that variant known as death metal.

The spread of metal beyond the West, attended by the diffusion of its subculture, has caused a change in that subculture, making it less provincial. Metal's popularity in non-Western areas has become a cause for rejoicing in the metal community since it demonstrates the universal appeal of the music. For example, Iron Maiden's trip to Poland in 1984 was greeted in the metal press as proof of the existence of an international metal community. Bands denote their playing schedules as a "world tour," albums are recorded with titles such as *World Wide Live* and *Maiden Japan,* and performers crow about being the first to play in Poland, the USSR, and elsewhere. Here, as at the origins of metal, the demographics of the heavy metal audience are valorized and culturalized. But it is no longer the same audience, although it is still preponderantly young and mostly male.

Just as during the 1980s metal began to appeal to new groups within its core sites, it also became rooted in new sites. But as it has spread it has not lost its ethos. In a social irony, the music that preserved a utopia for a provincial and restricted group has now become transnational, addressing youth throughout the world who feel thwarted by technological society and frustrated by its demands. If metal is reactionary, it seems that reaction has a firm place in the contemporary cultural bricolage.

The Elements of the Heavy Metal Subculture

A subculture unites its members on the basis of very specific objects and practices, which make the members distinctive both to others and to themselves. The romantic and utopian themes of the heavy metal subculture, which often make it appear to be a quasi-religion, generate emblems, icons, rituals, and symbols that are particularized as are those of any religious faith. Straw's conclusion that the members of the heavy metal audience "exhibit coherent and consistent taste patterns which distinguish them from the casual audiences for eclectic, trans-generic examples of rock music"[73] is an understatement for those who belong to the core of the subculture. For them, the subculture is the basis of a visible and unique community that nurtures an inner spirit and set of experiences.

The Music

Music is the master emblem of the heavy metal subculture. It is its official raison d'être. But the apparent centrity of the music is deconstructed when what is meant by the term "the music" is examined. Is it the sounds, and, if so, which ones or combinations of them? Is it the lyrics and, if so, does that mean equating lyrics with poetry? Is it the visual elements that have always accompanied the sounds, such as album covers, stage settings, and music videos? Finally, does the music include the memories of the social relations that it seems to nurture? With reservations, all of these questions can be answered affirmatively. "The music" is a bricolage.

The cultural object itself, heavy metal music, is described in chapter 2. Here my specific concern is to explain how the members of the heavy metal subculture integrate the music into their wider life-style. What meanings do they give to it? How do they interpret it? What are their standards of criticism? Love for a certain kind of music is not something inborn, timeless, or spontaneous; such love is nurtured in social relations. In 1982 an Italian terrorist group kidnapped and proceeded to torture an American brigadier general by making him listen to AC/DC. Torturers and tortured, along with the general American public and mass media, held the same negative judgment of AC/DC.[74] But metal fans found the incident bizarrely amusing, since they willingly expose themselves to the same music and find it to be pleasurable. It evokes certain emotions in them and expresses and epitomizes their subculture; it has, in Lucy Green's terms, both "inherent meaning" as a directly valued experience and "delineated meaning" as a signifier of a lifestyle that runs beyond musical expression.[75]

For the heavy metal subculture the sonic elements of the music take precedence over its textual, visual, or social components. One basic standard is the decibel level of the music. Loudness is valued as an end in itself. References to this feature abound, from the oft-quoted "If it's too loud, you're too old," to song titles such as Manowar's "All Men Play on Ten," which refers to the loudest setting on amplifiers and stereo tuners. One metalhead is quoted as saying, "The whole point of heavy metal music is to get out of your mind. The music is always so loud I can never hear the words, but it is just a basic noise to blast your brains out."[76] Although not all fans would agree completely, no one at a metal show would think of complaining that the music was too loud. Those who wear ear plugs, beloved by critics and essential for some musicians, do so surreptitiously.

Pitch is also significant. The audience appreciates the bottom sound, the source of the term "heavy" in "heavy metal." As a result of the massive amplification of the music and the properties of sound that require lower sounds to be amplified with extra power to be heard equally with the rest of the range, one can physically feel the bottom sounds. They resonate in the chest cavity, creating a sensation cherished by metal fans. The music's sensibility embodies and epitomizes the culture. The heavy bottom sound connotes masculinity. As in other forms of youth music, notably punk, loudness, the source of the power so valued in metal, is a signifier of rambunctious adolescence.

The genre features of a strong vocalist and a technically proficient lead guitarist, whose work is allowed to stand out, are insisted upon by the audience. Fans comment on the guitarist most of all and bands are often evaluated according to the relative greatness of their guitarists. The guitar riffs are a counterpoint to sheer loudness and a heavy bottom sound. They are precise, often elaborate, and require much dexterity on the part of the performer. At concerts the audience falls silent and listens in rapt attention to a great guitar solo. Here the music is not merely a noise to blast one's brains out, but a pattern of sounds that evokes emotions, illustrating once again the complexity of metal as a cultural form.

Lyrics

The subculture's standards for lyrics are less precise, less articulate, and less shared. Bands such as Iron Maiden and Rush are highly esteemed for their eloquent and meaning-charged lyrics. Groups such as Judas Priest are appreciated for words that give vent to the intense feelings of their fans. Nevertheless, heavy metal is not a genre that privileges lyrics and its followers do not evaluate them as elements in a coherent, fully articulated, worldview.[77]

The research on lyrics indicates that adolescents neither attend to, know, nor understand the verbal texts of even their favorite songs.[78] A sample of adolescents was asked in the mid-1980s whether they attended to the lyrics or to the sound of a song. The results of the study indicated that 12 percent claimed to attend to lyrics carefully, 58 percent stated that they were most concerned with the "general sound" of a song, and 30 percent said that both the lyrics and the general sound were significant to them.[79] Females seem to be more attentive to lyrics than males.[80] No similar study has been made of members of the heavy metal subculture, but the impression that I get from interviews and conversations is that a large majority of metal fans would agree that, for them, both the lyrics and the sound are important. About a third would cite the music alone. Reviewing the literature on lyric comprehension, Roger Desmond concluded that the research shows that about one-third of adolescent listeners can grasp the meaning of the words in popular songs.[81]

One of the ways in which members of the heavy metal subculture show their commitment to the genre is to know the lyrics. In metal the lyrics are usually included with the albums, particularly by those groups whose lyrics have more substance than merely "Let's party!" and "I'm hot for her." Thus, heavy metal fans are more likely than other adolescents to be familiar with the lyrics of their favorite songs. Desmond indicates that only those who are most committed to a type of music or a particular band are able to recall lyrics.[82] But at metal concerts one can hear the audience singing along with the vocalist. In conversation, key phrases from songs are quoted. However, being able to recite lyrics does not imply that one understands or adequately interprets them.

One evening I got a chance to test how well lyrics were understood. I was in the midst of hundreds of rabid fans of the Canadian group, Rush. All were spending the night in the parking lot of a large arena, waiting in line for the ticket office to open at 10:00 the next morning. Most of the fans had arrived well before midnight and stood or sat in the mild night air. The hours were spent socializing with one another, and the major topic of conversation, of course, was Rush. During one conversation I asked two fifteen year olds if they knew Rush's album *2112*. At that time, in 1982, the album was over six years old. "Of course!" came the answer. Everyone in the parking lot knew that album. Did they know the side of the album that was a set of songs telling a story of 2112?[83] "What? Of course!" was their reply, in unison. Having discussed the song-set with other Rush fans over the years and having used it as a text in a social theory course I taught, I was intimately familiar with the lyrics. "What's it about?" I disingenuously asked. The inarticulate responses made it clear that narrative was not these fans' strong point. Others came over to join in. I let them all talk. Two of those in this initial grouping could fully quote all the lyrics, which is no mean feat. But to speak the words was not necessarily to interpret their meaning, and they knew it. In frustration they asked me what the album was about.

As I described and then explained the story, my efforts were greeted with much enthusiasm. One fan tried to challenge my interpretation, but I was able to show him why his was inadequate. The group dispersed, but shortly afterwards someone else came up and said, "I heard that you really know 2112." He was the first of a long line that kept me fully involved until the sun came up. I shortened the query, merely asking each the same question: "Which side is Rush on, the priests or the dreamer who found the instrument under the waterfall?" The story is about a theocracy that crushed people trying to express themselves by making their own music. Rush, proponents of romantic individualism, were undoubtedly against the priests. Each person I asked had a 50 percent chance of being right, merely by chance. Yet over 70 percent chose the priests.[84] All claimed that they knew the lyrics and many could quote them. The evidence that older listeners understand lyrics better than younger ones was not true for this group, whose ages ranged from fourteen to twenty.[85] Other interviews and conversations with metal fans, however, suggested that the general pattern (more understanding as age increases) seemed to hold true.

Most Americans can recite the words to the "Pledge of Allegiance" and the "Star-Spangled Banner," but they may not reflect very much on their meaning. Knowing the words is part of a ritual that affirms solidarity with the nation, even if the words are only known by rote. Similarly, knowing the lyrics to the songs of one's favorite group is a pledge of allegiance to the group and a sign that one is a devotee in good standing.

The metal magazines do not dwell on the lyrics. Some reprint them, but few offer interpretations. Attention to lyrics should not, however, be equated with either recall of lyrics or interpretation of them. The words of a song function for listeners, in metal and in rock in general, more as isolated words and phrases than as integral poetic texts. Meaning is obtained from evocative words: "evil," "black," "night," "death." These utterances are easily distinguishable in the overall sound, are mentioned more than once in a song, and are often more clearly articulated by the singer than other lyrical passages. Creative reading, attending to certain words or passages and ignoring others, is less individualized than it is a function of reading through the metal code.

Lyrics can, and in metal do, also serve a function that is unrelated to providing meaningful symbols, singly or as statements. They provide the opportunity to hear a singer, a human voice. The voice is another instrument in the mix, but in addition it is the primary means of communicating human emotion, again providing a counterpoint to the sheer loudness and resonating bottom sound. Musical instruments can evoke emotional responses in the audience (in metal the guitar often substitutes for the voice by "wailing" and "crying"), but the voice directly expresses emotion. Frith argues, "We can thus identify with a song whether we understand the words or not, whether we already know the singer or not, because it is the voice—not the lyrics—to which we immediately respond."[86]

In the heavy metal subculture vocalists with powerful and emotional voices are highly valued. Although they are a notch lower in the pantheon than lead guitarists, great singers such as Ronnie James

Dio, Ozzy Osbourne, Queensrÿche's Geoff Tate, and Manowar's Eric Adams constantly evoke praise for their pipes. The standard in metal is both a powerful voice that seems to be able to fill an arena even without microphones, and a voice that not merely betrays but is centered on the transmission of emotion. Rob Halford of Judas Priest is well known and lauded for his ability to make spine-chilling screams, sounds that come from another world. In subgenres, such as death metal, the words are not sung as much as they are growled. Although Frith argues that for all rock "tone of voice is more important . . . than the actual articulation of particular lyrics,"[87] this statement is especially true for heavy metal.

Appreciation of heavy metal music does not focus on the individual song, as is the case for pop music. Carrying on a practice of the 1960s counterculture,[88] the album is the basic unit of appreciation. Fans will discuss the merits of the various albums made by a group. There is a large measure of consensus among heavy metal fans concerning which album presents the best work by any given group.

The visuals of heavy metal music—the band logos, album covers, posters, performer's costumes, and stage sets; including the merchandising of these visuals on T-shirts, pins, and banners—also help to constitute the subculture. These images and icons, discussed in chapter 2, are noted here as expressions of the sensibility of the heavy metal subculture.

The Styles

As the master emblem of the heavy metal subculture, the music has a privileged place within it. But the subculture is not exhausted by the music. It also has nonmusical elements that form a distinctive style, giving the core audience a relative independence of and initiative in relation to the other actors in the transaction that constitutes metal. Through the components of its style the core audience becomes essential to determining what metal is.

The term "style" refers to the whole range of ways in which the body is displayed, animated, and chemically influenced. The elements of style are not created de novo, but are borrowed, with or without resignification, from other youth cultures and from the dominant culture. The elements of metal style are mainly derived from two late-1960s youth cultures: motorcycle culture (the bikers in Britain and the "outlaw" gangs such as the Hell's Angels in the United States)[89] and the hippies. As noted earlier in this chapter, it is no coincidence that heavy metal musical and performance styles were cobbled out of the music of these two subcultures.

Metal style is not comprised of arbitrary components, but neither is it unitary. It is a bricolage of its parent cultures, with special additions of its own to mediate the conflicts within its inheritance. The components of style serve social, social-psychological, and symbolic functions. Style differentiates insiders from outsiders, allowing individuals to create identities. By providing forms for expressing attitudes, values, and norms, style takes on the character of a readable text.

Those elements of style that are revealed as visual adornments of the body, are referred to as fashion. More so than in other youth subcultures, heavy metal fashion is male fashion. Although not all female members of the subculture share the same styles as the males, all metal styles are inscribed by the masculinist ideology. The following discussion of metal style, then, demands a special, explicitly secondary, discussion of female style.

Heavy metal fashion involves the metal uniform of blue jeans, black T-shirts, boots, and black leather or jeans jackets. Boots were joined by athletic shoes around 1980, along with baseball caps with band logos. Jeans have become the universal youth fashion, spreading from American teens in the 1950s around the world. With black boots, the outfit is also a blue-collar uniform.

T-shirts are generally emblazoned with the logos or other visual representations of favorite metal bands. The shirts are worn proudly and metal fans feel free to direct brief remarks or a thumbs-up gesture to others wearing shirts depicting a group admired by the viewer. T-shirts that are tour shirts, ordinarily sold at concerts, are more highly valued than those bought in stores, and shirts from long-ago tours are the most highly respected of all. The shirts are a visible sign of allegiance and commitment to a band and more generally to metal as a genre. The older the shirt, the longer one's commitment. Other ads on shirts are quite acceptable to the metal audience, particularly those for Harley-Davidson motorcycles. This brand is the top-of-the-line motorcycle, big, powerful, and expensive. Few heavy metal fans own Harleys. The Harley is a metal icon, a link with the bikers and thus a symbol of their culture.

Two types of jackets are worn by members of the metal subculture. Best known to the general public is the black leather motorcycle jacket. Basically it is made with heavy leather and has several oversized chrome zippers, including those on pockets and sleeves. Marlon Brando wore such a jacket in the 1950s movie *The Wild Ones*. Until recently, when the fashion industry discovered biker jackets and created a wide range of modified versions for upper-middle-class adults, the black leather jacket served as a masculine emblem. The jeans jacket, a legacy of the hippie, is more popular than the black leather jacket in terms of prevalence. These jackets are not only far less expensive than leather, they are also light enough for summer wear. Both kinds of jacket provide spaces for an array of patches, buttons, pins, and homemade artistic efforts.

The patches (embroidered band logos) are sewn on to the jackets. They range in size from about three inches to over a foot long. The buttons, from one inch to three inches in diameter, carry logos or reproduce the album covers of favorite groups; a person rarely wears just one. The fabric painting and sometimes embroidery (embroidered jackets are more popular in Britain, where sewing is not stigmatized as a nonmale activity, as it is in the United States) depict band logos or band-related icons, such as Motörhead's demonic mask.

Pins and rings, which are usually made of pewter or silver, are widely worn, depicting icons associated with heavy metal in general, rather than specific bands. Prominent designs include skulls, skeletons, snakes, dragons, and daggers, maces, and other instruments of pre-gun mayhem. These are symbols of chaos, danger, and outlaws, and are deeply rooted in Western mythology. Leather-studded gauntlets and wrist bands are also worn. Other items of jewelry adorning some metal fans include earrings and necklaces, generally with dangling crosses, although males with earrings are in a distinct minority. The crosses worn span a wide variety of designs from elaborate Celtic to thick iron and simple thin silver, but all are Christian symbols and are explicitly seen as such by their wearers. The Christian signifiers in which the metal subculture is steeped may not function the same way that they do in the discourses of mainline churches, but they are not arbitrary. A significant part of metal's mythology revolves around the more apocalyptic strain of Christianity, especially the Book of Revelations.

Closely related to the pins and rings, but more colorful, are the tattoos, which are key trademarks of the members of the metal subculture. Dragons are among the most popular icons, along with a wide array of other chaos/monster figures. The usual location of the tattoo is on the arm, since T-shirts permit it to be seen there. Women's tattoos tend to be smaller than men's, and are inscribed on a number of parts of the body, including the arms, the upper back, and the area right above the breast. The tattoo is a special mark of loyalty to the metal subculture; it is permanent. It pledges the very body of the adherent to the subculture. The larger and less concealable the tattoos, the more they demonstrate allegiance.[90]

The body of the member of the metal subculture is also bound over to the subculture by hairstyle, which can be considered as a voluntary stigma.[91] From the beginning the metal hairstyle for males has consisted of one simple feature: it is very long. Long hair is the most crucial distinguishing feature of metal fashion. Describing some of his audience to a reporter, a metal musician said that they are "kids with real long hair and leather jackets; you know, the metal heads."[92] A researcher depicting the audience at a venue playing heavy metal stated that "Long hair, not arranged in any particular style, is de rigueur."[93]

Long hair is significant because it cannot be concealed. It is the one feature that excludes "weekend warriors," those with a part-time commitment to heavy metal. Long hair—especially as the other traces of counterculture fashion faded away—became a real sign of heavy metal dedication, a willingly embraced cross to bear. It functions to define the boundary of the subculture.

The metal hairstyle is not past-the-ears long, in the manner of the Beatles, who provoked comment when they invaded the United States in 1964; nor is it the shoulder-length cut that was fashionable in the late 1960s among college students. Metal hair is down-the-back long, similar to and derived from the hippie, counterculture hairstyle.[94] The beards also favored by the counterculture did not, however, enter the heavy metal subculture. Beards became associated, after World War II, with the intelligentsia, and that signification clashes with the blue-collar ideology of metal. Long hair did not have such connotations and, thus, could be appropriated directly, serving as a symbolic connection to the counterculture.

Just as other elements of metal, such as the demographics of its audience, began to diversify in the 1980s, so did the metal hairstyle. The advent of music videos as a significant factor in popular music, more than any other cause, created a new metal hairstyle.[95] This second style is still very long, but it is cut in a shag or layered manner. Moreover, it is styled after each washing with mousse and blow dryers. The new style has not supplanted the old one, but has been adopted mainly by metal audiences and artists that favor lite metal and by those classic metal artists with wide appeal.

Long hair has reference not only to a prior subculture but to distinctive body movements, which are a functional alternative to dancing. Youth music, in particular, accords danceability high importance, as evidenced by 1950s rock and roll, the dance-craze songs of the 1960s, such as "The Locomotion," "Twist," and "Monkey," and disco and punk music in the 1970s.

Dancing is alien to heavy metal for two basic reasons. One is the continuation of the tradition of the youth counterculture. The audience for psychedelic music and for folk-inspired political protest songs listened while seated, to better concentrate on the lyrics. Second, dance is understood in the modern West as an erotic activity. As a masculinist and overwhelmingly masculine grouping with an extreme heterosexualist ideology, the heavy metal subculture stresses male bonding, not male-female pairing. Thus, it did not appropriate dance as it had been traditionally understood. It also could not redefine dancing, as the punks did, by making it an individual rather than a dyadic activity, because of its valorization of community. Yet heavy metal music is based on a strong, regular beat that calls forth movement from the body. One might sit still for folk or psychedelic music, but only the motor-impaired or those who are extremely repressed will not move to the sound of heavy metal songs.

The solution to the problem of body movement was to create a code of gestural response to the music that could be shared in common. One of the two primary gestures is the arm thrust, usually a sign of appreciation but also used to keep time with the rhythm. The other primary gesture, called headbanging, involves a downward thrust of the head with a gentler upthrust. The move is distinctive enough to metal to serve, by metonymy, as a designation of the metal audience: "headbangers." Done correctly and with long, loose hair, the downward thrust repositions the hair so that it falls down around the face as one faces the floor. The upthrust neatly repositions it down the back. As one headbanger remarks, the feeling achieved by headbanging is diminished if one does not have long hair: "Shaking your head about to the music wouldn't feel the same if your hair wasn't flying all over the place."[96]

The metal subculture also fosters the ideal of a specific body type, even if that type is not achieved by the majority of the subculture's members. Muscle building is a hobby of many metal fans; their concentration on their arms creates the look of the idealized blue-collar worker, similar to that iconized in the socialist realist paintings of the Stalinist era. This is not the yuppie-type, health-club body, trim, with a flat stomach. Indeed, among older males in the audience, beer bellies are a commonplace. Individualizing the purchased T-shirt is a frequent practice, particularly by ripping off the sleeves, which is often done in public after purchasing a new shirt. Among blue-collar workers and some baseball players, ripping off the sleeves was practiced by those whose upper arm muscles were so overly developed that sleeves would cut into their skin.

The body type of the typical metal fan is mesomorphic, in contrast to the ectomorphic type found in the punk and hardcore subcultures. A number of factors probably account for this observed difference. Some of them involve the types of movements encouraged by the two subcultures, which are related to the musical differences. With the melding of punk and metal into thrash, these differences are evident in the same venue. The people who stand near the stage, moshing and slam-dancing, are generally skinny, gangly, and more likely to have short hair. Those off to the sides, headbanging or merely standing there, have far more muscle mass, and tend toward the beefy.

A distinctive demeanor and expression are also nurtured in the metal subculture. The familiar insult that metal fans are "slack-jawed," evincing a look of dull stupidity, needs to be examined. In part it is an accurate characterization of the faces of those emerging from a heavy metal concert, but it also probably could be used to describe anyone who has just spent several hours enjoying ecstatic physical activity. The look also reflects the impact of the drugs (downers) and beer consumed by metal fans. But it is also related to the attitudes of the metal subculture.

Heavy metal is not cool. It is not hip. As a social construction, the facial expression of the member of the metal subculture toward outsiders is a rejection of hip-ocracy. Look at the countenance of those who are into a cool and a hip subculture, and you will notice an expression of studied indifference common to the former, and an expression of sneering alertness for the latter. The slack-jawed look is neither indifferent nor alert. It often accompanies the self-described state of being "wasted." If you are wasted, you are not available to the everyday world, nor are you setting an example for it. You are simply out of it. The other key expression of the member of the metal subculture, the eager look of the ardent enthusiast, is only for insiders. This face is put on not only at concerts, but while listening to favorite songs or even talking about admired artists or their work. Parents, teachers, and the world in general are not privy to this second expression.

The walk of metal fans is less distinctive than their gestures and expressions. It is not the walk of the fleet-of-foot athlete or the graceful gait of would-be dancers. The term "lumbering" might be an appropriate adjective for a walking style that resembles the movement of a weight lifter. It reflects the masculinity of the culture.

The metal style is a surprising blend of the assertive and the laid back, a blend that can be traced to its dual origins in the biker and hippie subcultures. The same person can by turns be ecstatic and wasted. These extremes are probably only possible for young, resilient bodies, which are also capable of absorbing intoxicants and bounding back to vitality. Alcohol and drugs play a role in the heavy metal subculture, defining another aspect of its independence from determination by the music and setting restrictions for the music.

Metalheads' substances of choice are beer and pot, the former taken over from the bikers and the latter borrowed from the hippies. Use of other "downers," especially Quaaludes, is not uncommon. Drugs and alcohol are commodities to be bought and consumed, but they are also symbolic objects, the meanings of which are integrated into the rest of the subculture. Further, they are mediating materials, physically or at least psychopharmacologically, standing between the user and the external world.[97]

Ingestion of massive quantities of beer has remained a constant feature of the metal subculture. In Britain, metal festivals are notorious for the urine-filled containers tossed at acts that are not appreciated. Fearful of flying bottles, or at least worried about insurance costs, American venues serve only paper or plastic containers. These are often outsized, with quart tubs being the containers of choice. Beer-induced urination has influenced at least one venue in the United States to spread large amounts of kitty litter in the area near the stage.[98] "Beer drinking and hell raising" is a motto of the metal style.

Beer and pot are not ritualized substances for concerts only. Hanging around, in their rooms or out in the street, metalheads drink beer and smoke pot. A high school junior who entered the metal subculture in 1978 in Chicago told me that it was mainly the pot that attracted him. The music, at least initially, was secondary. He listened to it because "it just went well with the dope." Since the "War on Drugs" began in the late 1980s, the use of marijuana has markedly decreased at concerts. Prior to that time the aroma of pot permeated the air.

The use of pot and downers in the heavy metal subculture works well with some aspects of the music. Although metal is not drug music, specifically intended to augment a drug experience in the manner of psychedelic music, it is conditioned in part by the sensibility fostered by "downers." Metal's guitar solos are a modification of psychedelic music and are best appreciated while in a laid-back mood. That marijuana is outlawed also adds to its appeal, corresponding with the "outlaw" image of metal itself. Further, the danger of arrest for possession of a controlled substance works, like the stigma of long hair, to enhance group solidarity.

Drugs are an important part of the metal subculture, but they have never gained the symbolic centrality that they had for the youth counterculture. In his excellent ethnological analysis of British hippies, Paul Willis concludes, "Drugs were just about the central topic of conversation on the scene, and great stress was laid on knowledge of various types of drugs."[99] "Though drugs were only keys, they were still accorded a kind of sacred place in the head culture. Their use was surrounded by ritual and reverence."[100]

In the metal subculture drugs are less fetishes than means to the experience of getting wasted, which involves a unique mixture of activity and relaxation, in which the heavy music is counterpointed by the downer drugs. The aim is not to take "a journey to the center of your mind," as it was for the hippies, but to reach a state of physical and emotional catharsis. That is, drugs are not valued as providers of self-knowledge or of exotic experiences, but as a source of release through ecstasy. Here the subculture is greater than its discrete components, each component contributing to a distinctive experience.

The metal style, from the clothes and hair, to the formed and moving body, is male. A summary reading of heavy metal fashion reveals menace, male menace. It is of, by, and for males. Yet there have always been some girls among the sea of boys at heavy metal concerts. Attendance at concerts is the central ritual of the metal subculture. The vast increase of females, especially at lite metal concerts, has already been noted. But it remains the case that most of the female fans are marginalized in the sense that they are less likely to attend concerts. Their activities take place, as is the case for most girls, in the home. There they can listen to the music, read the magazines, and be active in the fan clubs.[101]

Females in the metal subculture are at all times, as Bashe states, "divided between those who dress like the boys and those who try to emulate the bitch goddesses they see in their heroes' videos."[102] Thus, some girls wear the jeans and black metal T-shirts, along with black leather or jeans jackets. Others are attired in leather miniskirts, spiked-heel shoes, and an array of cleavage-revealing tops. Both outfits are generated by the masculinist code, either as male fashion or as male fantasy.[103] The point is that there is not a metal style that females can wear as subjects the way that their male counterparts can. The same item, be it a black leather jacket or very long hair, is read differently, does not have the same meaning, when the wearer is female.

Women are also fond of wearing spandex pants, favored by many metal performers, but not emulated by male metal fans. The pants graphically display not only the gender, but also the anatomical differences between the sexes. Heavy metal style is masculine, and women who want to become members of the metal subculture must do so on male terms. This situation is not unique to, but is extreme, in the heavy metal world.

The Solidarity of the Metal Subculture

Women are aliens in the heavy metal subculture because of their otherness. Males do not bond with them through identification. The desire for community (a mechanical solidarity in Durkheim's sense) is a value central to the heavy metal subculture. For youth groups in general, from ghetto gangs to cliques in middle-class high schools, the feeling of belonging to a community of people "like you" is basic.[104] In the case of the heavy metal subculture, nostalgia for the worldwide youth culture of the late 1960s adds to the premium placed on community. But the definition of the community is not exactly the same as it was in the counterculture. A blend of biker and hippie signifiers, it can be likened to an enormous male-bonding group.

The valorization of community does not, of course, mean that a community, in any strong sense of that term, exists among the far-flung members of the metal subculture. The facts indicate that the members of the subculture tend to lack any active political stance, that their ideals are hedonistic, and that they are widely dispersed geographically. All these realities prevent the subculture's members from cooperating in sustained, practical projects or from extending their interests beyond a shared love of the music. That love gives rise to mutual recognition when members of the subculture meet, but, for the most part, "community" among members of the subculture in general is attenuated and narrow. A stronger and more multifaceted community exists in small peer groups and an approximation to communion emerges at concerts. In both cases male bonding is a prominent element of the solidarity.

Even if he has a girlfriend, a heavy metal fan prefers being with his buddies when participating in the metal culture, whether the activity is seeing a concert, listening to records, or talking about the music or the performers. Many of my informants sneered at the types of music—often as different from heavy metal as possible—that were favored by their girlfriends. Why, when heavy metal was so crucially important in and to their lives, did they choose a girlfriend who did not share their musical taste? The responses were more or less articulate, along the lines of "she's a girl." They not only expect girls to dislike metal, but seem to prefer that it be that way.

A study done on Indiana University students by Zillmann and Bhatia helps to explain this response. The investigators showed students videos of people who were to be judged as potential dates. Several versions of the video were prepared, varying only the musical tastes expressed by the potential dates. Thus the same potential date was seen by some groups as preferring classical music, by others as favoring country, by others as liking soft rock, and by others as preferring heavy metal. Zillmann and Bhatia found that a penchant for heavy metal boosts a man's chances with women, but severely reduces a woman's desirability to men. Women preferring heavy metal were judged to be the least sexy, cultured, beautiful, and exciting. The researchers speculate that the features of heavy metal ("emotionally excessive rock music") are associated with those who prefer that style. Males are enhanced by this association, since masculinity and power are linked to the music's emotionality. In contrast, power is judged to be antithetical to femininity.[105]

The shared demographics and especially their valorization and culturalization serve to unite the subculture. They are the matrix in which the members of the subculture become an ongoing social formation with distinctive social practices that create a solidarity.

Some of the social activities that constitute the small groups and transient communions that embody the metal subculture are directly rooted in that subculture. Primary among them is the live concert experience. A plaintive letter sent to *Circus* magazine gives some indication of the significance of concerts. The writer, an eighteen year old, lived in Nebraska, far from any concert venue: "I live, eat and breathe metal, but I've never been to a concert."[106] Like the religious rituals analyzed by Durkheim and Eliade, concerts are, for the audience, celebrations of the subculture itself. The physical expression and social transmission of the culture, somewhat unmediated by the mass media, occurs here. The audience feels itself as one quite palpably.

The lack of a heavy metal radio format and, for the first decade of the subculture's existence, the lack of other mass media serving heavy metal necessitated interpersonal recruitment into the subculture. A consequence of the absence of institutional mediation, which allows for participation of isolated individuals in a subculture, was to strengthen the role of the peer group in the constitution of the metal subculture. Ask any heavy metal fans how prior to the mid-1980s they found out about their favorite band, and the response is the name of some friend or an older brother who "turned them on" to the group. Years later they still recall, with much gratitude, that person. The bonds between particular people are extended to loyalty to the subculture, giving that subculture an endurance and persistence that other subcultures that depend upon institutional mediation lack.

The heavy metal subculture is noted for being culturally conservative, a characteristic that can be traced in part to the importance of interpersonal relations in its constitution. Its standards and its music, its styles and performers, transcend several "generations" of adolescent audiences. Record labels and concert promoters did not have to worry about new trends: the old bands continue to sell their back catalogues of albums and to sell tickets to their current concerts without needing much promotion. Cashmore asserts that heavy metal is "a dinosaur of youth culture, surviving its contemporaries and lasting seemingly without change into the 1980s."[107] Changes are, indeed, resisted by the audience, a reality that demonstrates the residual power of the audience over the constitution of the music. For example, when Judas Priest attempted to modify its sound, using elements associated with pop disco, the fans denounced the *Turbo* album. Chastised, Priest's next effort, *Ram It Down,* was a return to their traditional sound.[108]

The development of new metal expressions in the mid-1980s (lite metal and thrash) was also met with much hostility. Lite metal bands were called, among a host of other derogatory terms, "poseurs" and "poodle bands." Cries of "death to false metal" emphasize the heretical nature of innovation. This conservatism, rooted in romantic preservationism, creates an ongoing subculture, sharply distinguished from the mass culture of pop music. Pop is a sound made by a bubble that bursts almost as soon as it emerges. Metal shares conservatism with several other music-based cultural groups, such as Deadheads and fans of country music.[109] Older members initiate younger ones into the rituals and the lore of heavy metal, fostering a stronger sense of community than short-lived subcultures.

One should not underestimate the impact of the constant barrage of ridicule heaped upon metal as a factor engendering solidarity among members of the subculture. "The more the music was ridiculed . . . the more firmly welded together the audience became, and the more desperately it attached itself to [the music]." Ronald Byrnside was referring to rock and roll in the 1950s, but his remark is even more applicable to heavy metal.[110] The unremitting disdain shown by rock critics, from the beginning, for the genre and its adherents enhanced the solidarity of the subculture. When the genre was losing much of its cohesion in the mid-1980s—because of genre changes and the impact of MTV—the PMRC's attack on metal worked wonders to reinvest the subculture with a strong solidarity. Tipper Gore's name was mentioned in scorn at so many concerts that it quickly became a cliché. Recrimination and ridicule of heavy metal has only underscored the proud pariah status of the subculture's members, resonating with the outlaw imagery found in the music's lyrics and the visual elements and fashions of the subculture.

The solidarity of the heavy metal subculture is due in no small measure to the fact that it is a seed around which peer groups can crystallize. Most junior and senior high schools in the United States are divided into cliques, which differentiate themselves from one another on a number of bases that may overlap, such as social class, major interests, and school achievement. Cliques must adopt conventions of style that set them apart, "much as various aboriginal tribes mark themselves with symbols of inclusion and exclusion, with tattoos and ritual inscriptions."[111] In schools there is pressure "to accept a tag stating your name, rank and musical preference."[112]

In 1990 a varied group of midwestern college students consisting of people who attended high school since the mid-1970s, was asked to describe the characteristics of those who attended their high schools and listened to heavy metal music. All respondents were able to do so. Most referred to cliques that were not identified by musical preference. With the exception of those who graduated before 1978, the term "stoner" and/or "burnout" was the designation used. Moreover, musical preference was perceived to be associated with a number of other features, such as use of marijuana, distinctive fashion, and school achievement.

A 1989 graduate from a public high school writes, "The heavy metal listeners were known as 'stoners,' 'headbangers,' 'druggies.' Characteristics—males—long hair, one earring (skulls and crossbones, daggers, etc.), ripped jeans, dirty old high tops. Females—

long hair—either very 'poofy' or flat feathered sides and long in back, a lot of makeup—especially around the eyes—dark black eyeliner 'raccoon eyes,' many earrings and also ear clips, tight faded jeans or tight short skirts and the skimpiest tops allowed or concert T-shirts. Both [males and females] heavy metal concert T-shirts (usually black) with skulls and other 'evil' symbols; many also had vulgar or offensive language. They were the trouble makers in school, often being sent to the dean, in school suspension, detention after school, etc. They were also typically in the more remedial type classes whether they needed to be there or not."[113] A 1984 graduate of an upper-middle-class high school in Indiana agrees with this description: "The kids who listened to heavy metal music were referred to as burnouts. The burnouts generally had long hair and wore black clothes. Around school they could always be found in the smoking block, a section designated for smoking. The burnouts did use marijuana a lot but I don't believe any more so than the other groups."[114]

Another student, a 1982, suburban, middle-class graduate reports, "In my high school, the kids who listened to heavy metal (Led Zeppelin, AC/DC, etc.) music all dressed in a similar fashion—old blue jeans, concert T-shirts, untucked flannel shirts, and longer hair than most. They were withdrawn from the 'activities-oriented' crowds and the only overlap was for boys in some sports. In retrospect, they were a pretty close-knit group and did most things together."[115]

These descriptions support the view presented here that the heavy metal subculture is distinctive and marginalized from the mainstream. A 1989 graduate from an upper-middle-class suburban high school makes this point clearly: "There were heavy metal, burnouts, students that definitely stood out in relation to the majority of the 'normal students.' They stood out because they wore long hair—possibly greasy—and tight jeans. They usually smoked in the bathroom and on occasion drank in the bathroom. Some of them, more than likely, used marijuana."[116]

School peer groups are cohesive units, reinforced by day-to-day interaction and shared social circumstances, and by common leisure pursuits and fashions. The statements above show that the heavy metal subculture is not merely a set of signifiers and practices referent to a musical form. It is much more a total life-style that includes music as a prime component, but uses the music to express and foster a sense of life. It is important to remember, however, that not all of those who follow the music are visible members of the subculture.[117]

The place of music in constituting peer groups and the youth subcultures that form their matrices has not been studied systematically. Most of the literature relates to crime and delinquency, and therefore gives a biased reading of the peer group. We do have studies that look at musical preferences and relate them to demographics and (self-reported) delinquent acts.[118] Such work, however, does not reveal whether the delinquency is caused by the music or the musical preference is caused by the delinquency, or whether both are caused by one or more other factor(s). Other research finds heavy metal to be the favorite format of students in vocational tracks and of those with emotional and behavioral disturbances.[119] A study of a group of adolescents called "The Stoners," who were involved in or professed a belief in the occult sciences and/or Satanism, indicated that they were also deeply involved in heavy metal rock music and street crime.[120] This fragmentary literature is at best suggestive.

The mass media's sensationalized descriptions of youthful murderers often include reference to musical preferences that fall outside the mainstream. The unsophisticated reader tends to interpret this information as indicating that those who listen to those forms of music are likely to be emotionally disturbed, Satanists, or murderers.

Roe, studying Scandinavian high school students, argues that the peer groups are fundamentally "achievement-related subcultures [that] may then form distinct orientations toward the media in general and preferences for certain kinds of music as well."[121] He finds that "low school achievement leads to a greater involvement with peers, leading to a greater preference for socially disapproved music."[122] American and British students who are members of cliques associated with the heavy metal subculture are not distinguished by their academic excellence. Roe contends that the music functions to express symbolically "alienation from school."[123] The sense of alienation in general and an active dislike of school in particular is one theme that does characterize heavy metal, speaking to the marginalization of its core audience.

Peer groups mediate the full array of cultural phenomena to their members. They are the collective bricoleurs selecting such specifics as a subset of bands, preferred readings of lyrics, and details of fashion from the whole of the heavy metal culture. Within the heavy metal peer group—a group of teens who are friends and all "into metal"—there is some degree of specialization. Each member tends to specialize in the band they hold to be the best, although they are careful to say they appreciate all of the groups favored by their friends. The metal subculture is polytheistic. Fans genuflect before all the metal gods, but also reserve special worship for one or a few personal favorites. When talking about a group, a person will often defer to the expertise of a friend whose god is that group. "You gotta speak with my buddy Paul. He's really into Nuclear Assault and knows all about them." The constant chatter on which is a group's best album or which lineup worked best reflects deference to specialized authority: "Well, my friend Jim, who is really into Maiden, says that *Number of the Beast* is their best album." When the peer group is very small, with only two or three close friends, they may all be into the same band. But even here specialization continues to be important. One member of the group is judged to be the most knowledgeable about the band, in terms of gossip or knowledge of which song is on which album.

Metal Style

The music is taken seriously by the metal subculture. It is the master emblem of the subculture, epitomizing what is precious and good in it. That is why the subculture is accurately designated by a musical term rather than by another special term, even one that preserves its binary character, such as a "hippie/biker" subculture. It would be true to call it a hippie/biker subculture but that term would not indicate that the music provides an experiential, aesthetic, and mythological, though never a logical, synthesis of the opposed elements. If the core personal type cultivated by the subculture is the proud pariah, then it is the music that supplies the pride. In the case of metal as a music-based youth subculture, the music legitimizes and transvalues pariah status, and then redeems it. Thus, metal is, in one sense, just an element in a wider hippie/biker culture, but, in another sense, it is what gives that subculture its integrity.

"Loud and proud" is a metal motto. Pride is instilled in the core metal audience, on the level of meaning, by the way in which the music represents the subculture to its members through signifiers. Metal bands make it a point to mythologize themselves, continually stressing their musical prowess and their exemplary exploits. Boasting is no sin in the metal world. Artists boast about themselves, fans boast about artists, and artists boast about their appreciative and loyal fans. The praise of the band for its audience fills its members with an esteem they often receive nowhere else. It is a validation of themselves.

But the band does more than praise the audience. It also creates the aura of the hippie/biker subculture through lyrical messages, appearances in public and on videos, and reports of its life-style in the metal magazines and the more general press. As John Clarke observes about youth subcultures in general, each of their symbolic objects "must have the 'objective possibility' of reflecting the particular values and concerns of the group in question as one among the range of potential meanings that it could hold. It also requires that the group self-consciousness is sufficiently developed for its members to be concerned to recognise themselves in the range of symbolic objects available."[124]

Flaunting the life-style valued by the metal subculture—sex, drugs, and raising hell—with pride before its fans, the band romanticizes and idealizes that life-style, and, even more importantly, legitimizes it. The signifiers of pariah status—everything that the respectable world condemns about metal's audience—are endowed with the highest value. The pariah is transvalued into, as Ozzy Osbourne calls his own persona, "a rock and roll rebel," someone who rebels against the established authorities through rock and roll, who finds a positive ground to contest established authorities in metal music itself and in the subculture that, under this aspect, the music serves. As legitimator of a youth subculture, the genre of metal music is shaped by the core audience, coconstituted by it, more than it is under any of its other aspects. Metal must present the subculture to its members in an appealing way. Otherwise it cannot make the pariahs proud and transvalue their status. That is, the members of the group must recognize themselves as valuable "in the range of symbolic objects available."

The legitimizing function, however, is not the only way that the music instills pride in its core audience. If there was nothing about the music that gave inherent meaning to the audience rather than merely hyped-up delineated meaning to romanticize its life-style, the pride fostered by metal would be empty because there would be nothing to be proud of. But the members of the metal subculture are convinced that metal music is great. It is great as music for what it does to them—how it draws them into it, excites them, and finally leaves them wasted, completely spent, having burned the potlatch of their youthful vitality and purged their emotions.

Those who claim that metal does not evoke a great experience are met with disbelief by an enthusiast. Their judgments on metal cannot be taken seriously and the rest of their judgments on life are therefore suspect. The deepest pride of the member of the metal subculture is to be an appreciator of great music. The music is viewed as a gift of the artist. The obligation, willingly undertaken, of the appreciator is to give the artist loyalty. And here an anomaly appears in the conventional account, in both popular and academic literature, of the metal audience. Some of the same adolescents who are called "downers" or "burnouts" are the ones who memorize lyrics, specialize in groups to follow, and make fine judgments about the merits of the music. In this realm, at least, they do not merely live for the moment, withdraw, take the easy way out, fall into depression, or make trouble. Here they are certain of their standing and are willing to exert effort to keep something worthwhile going. They transcend hedonism, even if ironically, in the name of hedonism, which is what all authentic lovers of a cultural form do. Under this aspect of pride, the music does not serve the subculture, but the subculture serves the music.

This reciprocity of service, music-to-subculture and subculture-to-music, is the inner form of the music-based subculture, of which the heavy metal subculture is a paradigmatic example. Metal is *the* music of the members of its subculture, it is *their* music. And it is theirs in many ways—as an idealized representation of the life-style of their subculture, as the music that provides them with cherished experiences, and, because of those services that it renders to them, as something that they can serve through their loyalty. Metal represents, legitimizes, and redeems the members of its subculture. That is the meaning of metal for its audience.

Transmitting the Music:
Metal Media

"The Spirit of the Radio"
—Rush

The third actor in the triadic transaction that constitutes metal is the communications media. The media form a bricolage of all of those means by which artists and audience are brought together. They are mediators, providing facilities to the other two parties to the transaction. They range in the performance of their function from servants of the other parties to their effective masters.

Importance of the Media

The media that coconstitute heavy metal can be arrayed on an axis from mass to specialized. The mass media appeal to an undifferentiated audience. They must be fit to enter the family rooms of the preponderance of the population and, therefore, must develop a code for screening and filtering cultural objects that originate with some degree of independence from their culture-fabricating and culture-promoting apparatus. That is, if a new cultural form is not compatible with the code of the mass media it will either be excluded from them or will be transformed by them to bring it into line with that code. In contrast, the specialized media, especially when they serve a subculture, do not create their own codes to filter and screen cultural objects; instead, they adopt the codes of differentiated and relatively self-conscious audiences.

In the case of metal, the distinction between mass and specialized media illuminates a cultural conflict in which the mass media struggle to dilute the distinctive and often confrontational style of the genre, and the specialized media tend to fortify the particularity of the subcultural core audience by defending the traditional standards of the genre.

Whether a medium is mass or specialized depends upon the audience at which it is directed, not upon its technological character, the means by which, in Marshall McLuhan's terms, it "extends the senses." Radio, for example, can be either mass or specialized, depending upon whether it seeks a general audience or a special one. The "top-40" format is a use of radio as a mass medium and a two-hour thrash-metal program broadcast on a college station is a use of radio as a specialized medium.

Most of the media—mass or specialized—in the United States are commercial. Some specialized noncommercial media, such as fanzines or college radio stations, do exist; they will be discussed later in this chapter. The basic purpose of the commercial media is to make money, and they may pursue that aim either by seeking to maximize the size of their audience or by seeking to attract the loyalty of a specialized audience. In the latter case conflict between the medium and the cultural form it mediates does not occur. In the former case conflict does occur whenever the prospective object-to-be-mediated does not fit the mass code.

Without going into great detail, the mass commercial media seek to mediate cultural objects that are safe, undemanding, nonconfrontational, and inoffensive. Their aim is to carry or publish nothing that will make someone turn off or turn away from the medium. When appropriating culture that has not been fabricated within its own apparatus, the mass media deploy various practices to transform it to meet the code, such as burlesquing it, sentimentalizing it, driving it to the absurd, making it bland or blander, reframing it, and sweetening it. Mass commercial media have no respect whatever for the content or form of a cultural object or for the critical standards of a specialized audience. For the mass commercial media, music is a product and a commodity, and the audience is merely an aggregate of listeners to be sold or delivered to sponsors. The mass media will produce and play what their managers believe will get them the largest or most profitable audience.

As actors in the transaction of metal, the commercial media bring together artist and audience, taking a profit for performing a service and, in the case of mass media, attempting to shape and control what they mediate. Although the ideology of rock, inherited by heavy metal, denounces business, seeing it as at best a necessary evil, metal arose within a cultural environment that was already coconstituted by the commercial media. In principle, one must grant the possibility that artists and audiences can find one another without recourse to the offices of secondary media. But the commercial media were present at the conception of rock and roll in the 1950s. The same condition of affluence that makes distinctive youth subcultures possible also creates a potential youth market for the media to serve/exploit. Viewed as an economic event, rock and roll was in large part a commercial redirection of certain styles of black and country music to a white, urban and suburban, youth audience, one whose commercial success from the very beginning depended on modifying those styles—even homogenizing them—to capture the target market. Simultaneously, a youth culture began to emerge around the new music. Which was the tail and which was the dog is impossible to determine. The triad artist-audience-media as coconstitutors of musical culture helps to define rock and roll, and every form of youth music that follows in its train.

By the time heavy metal emerged both rock artists and rock media were generating musical styles independent of the musical origins of rock and roll. At one extreme forms of rock could emerge that were self-consciously noncommercial, while at the other extreme forms could be totally fabricated by the commercial apparatus. But no form could be indifferent to commerce.

The heavy metal subculture took up the hippie rejection of "commerce," but heavy metal was, from its inception, mediated to its audience by the "commercial apparatus"[1]—it was a sales category.[2] Metal did not spring from a subculture, but was put into contact with one through the offices of the commercial media, indeed, initially, of the large record companies, which created first the possibility of an Anglo-American metal audience and eventually the reality of a worldwide metal audience.

A host of rhetorical conventions creates a sense of "you and me against the world" between metal's performers and fans. The stance is reminiscent of a scene in the movie *The Godfather*. The scene is set in rural southern Italy. A boy and girl romantically stroll together, lost in one another. The camera pans back, disclosing the chaperons, under whose watchful eyes the two were brought together and allowed to be with one another.

Changes in the Media

Over the past two decades the position of the media in heavy metal culture has undergone many changes. Some of those changes are related to shifts within heavy metal culture, such as stylistic transformations of the music and growth and diversification of the audience. Other changes are internal to the rock industry. Initially heavy metal was a pariah, deprecated by rock magazines, tolerated only for its cash flow by record companies, rarely played on radio, and never seen on TV. Two decades later the commercial status of the music had been radically transformed in a Cinderella/Rocky-like trajectory. *Newsweek* summed up this change in 1989: "Heavy metal, for years the scourge of America's pop scene, now dominates record sales, with the latest albums of just five metal bands together selling more than 30 million units in the United States alone. . . . Once banished from the traditional media, heavy metal has crashed radio play lists, invaded MTV and earned its own category in the Grammy Awards."[3] In terms of the relative power of the three elements constituting heavy metal culture, commerce was the weakest component during the first decade of metal's existence. It is now far more important in constituting the cultural form, but it is still far from being dominant.

A series of major trends characterized the transformation of the media's position in metal culture. Most generally, the quantity, forms, and functions of the media expanded. There has been an increase in the number of organizations concerned with heavy metal, ranging in size from small venues to multinational megaconglomerates, some of them exclusively mediating metal. The kinds of secondary media with heavy metal content have expanded from records alone to all of the forms available in the entertainment industry. The functions performed by the media have come to extend far beyond the primary service of bringing the music to the fans. A secondary mediation, parasitical to the primary one, is to let the audience know about the music, to promote it: hype engulfs and permeates all of the commercial media. In addition, commerce began to mediate relationships within each of the three constitutors of metal, first among the audience members, then between the business-sector organizations, and finally between artists and the media.

These changes were not gradual. Allowing for fuzzy boundaries, the shifts in the media's position within metal culture define three periods. The first, lasting until about 1979, is distinguished by metal's marginalization by record companies and its exclusion by the rest of the rock industry. The second period, beginning around 1980 and ending around 1983, is marked by the formation of autonomous heavy metal organizations and by a stronger acceptance of metal by mainstream record companies. In the third era, starting around 1984 and not yet over, metal entered the mainstream. These periods will be distinguished within the following discussion of the various aspects of the media.

Radio

Radio, at least until the late 1980s and the stunning success of MTV, has always been the most decisive secondary medium for determining the form and content of music that falls under the umbrella of rock.[4] Music that makes it on to commercial radio must be consistent with a code that is engendered internally by that medium. Music that is excluded from commercial radio is freer to develop its own conventions or to honor the codes of a subculture. The constraints on music are greatest in mass commercial radio, which seeks a relatively undifferentiated audience and is able to capture it only by making sure that what it carries is inoffensive to listeners. For much of metal's history commercial radio was, by and large, seeking a mass market. Metal was exiled from the medium because, although it had a devoted audience, many of its themes and sounds were offensive to large segments of the mass audience and to critical opinion within the secondary media. That exile had a positive result: it allowed metal to preserve many distinctive elements and to avoid dilution.

The power of radio over the bricolage called "rock music" is pronounced. Rock and roll in the mid-1950s and rock a decade later could not have come into being without radio. Obviously, the record industry is also crucial to the existence of rock, but radio distributes the recorded sound to an audience and promotes the purchase of records.

Radio has not merely been decisive in connecting an audience with an artistic creation. It has also had significant influence on the formation of the music itself. As a major gatekeeper, radio plays neither all music put out on records nor even a random sample of this music. It selects what it will carry according to its own code. For example, when the makers of recorded music know that the radio programmers will only play a song of a certain duration, they make their songs fit that time range. Similarly, they will adjust their product to comply with radio's restrictions on lyrical themes, instrumental sounds, and so on. "Since songs need radio exposure to become popular, record company decision makers will try to anticipate what radio station decision makers want to play when they are producing and releasing records. Since radio stations work within formats, this serves as a form of pressure for record companies to work within formats as well."[5] Scholars have argued that the form of music that became known as "sixties rock" was to a large extent conditioned by the underground/progressive/free-form FM radio format of the 1960s.[6]

Given the centrality of radio to rock music, the fact that during its first decade of existence heavy metal received virtually no airplay has many implications. The heavy metal subculture was not served by a radio format in the 1970s. In Britain state-controlled radio had no room for heavy metal. In the United States the chances of hearing any heavy metal on the radio ranged from slim to none. The only metal-affiliated band to get radio exposure, and quite a bit at that, was Led Zeppelin. This was not really an anomaly, since the songs by this group chosen for play, such as "Stairway to Heaven," were only on the fringes of the metal genre. Zeppelin was widely popular, attracting audiences with no interest in or affiliation with any aspects of the heavy metal subculture.

Heavy metal was exiled from the radio for several reasons. Metal's themes and sounds, as noted above, were offensive to segments of the mass audience. But more generally and perhaps more importantly, in the 1970s heavy metal's core audience was not the target audience desired by station managers; that is, advertisers did not find fifteen-to-eighteen-year-old males to be as desirable an audience as eighteen-to-twenty-five-year-old males and females. As the decade continued, the most desired audience became even older, in part due to the advancing age of the massive baby boom generation. As *The Wall Street Journal* noted in 1980, "The current teen market is smaller, has less money."[7]

The progressive/free-form format was dominant on FM until about 1973. The hip-progressive mentality that characterized this format excluded much of heavy metal for several reasons. Black Sabbath, the major force in metal at that time, was judged to be philosophically unacceptable, since the group rejected the key word of the progressive format, "love," in favor of "evil." Sabbath did not attract middle-class hippies: it had a blue-collar following with less income. The rock critics defended the progressive format's standards and, as will be shown in chapter 7, they rejected heavy metal in no uncertain terms.

As the progressive format declined in the mid-1970s it was replaced by the very successful AOR (album-oriented rock) format. A highly rationalized format based on market research, AOR established consultants as the major radio programmers. AOR was group-focused rather than song-focused. Still, it was a mass format, excluding anything that might offend the listener and cause him or her to change the station. A staple of AOR was what has since been called "corporate rock." As a style of music it shares some features with heavy metal, but it appeals to pop themes of romantic love rather than to the symbols and values of the metal subculture. Corporate rock has been described as a "uniform style of tenors singing over a slick, melodic, high-velocity sound sweetened with whooshing synthesizers."[8] It was very popular in the United States, especially in the Midwest.

AOR also included the ubiquitous staple of FM, Led Zeppelin. Indeed, "Stairway to Heaven" is the one song that critics of AOR consistently point to as typifying the content of that format. Some other popular heavy metal groups, such as AC/DC, received AOR play. By 1981, in the evening at least, one could find songs by Judas Priest and Ozzy Osbourne in the AOR rotation. Some AOR stations focused on the harder edge of rock music, playing corporate rock and popular heavy metal songs, shifting the format slightly to hard rock and appealing to a new youth audience who had little emotional investment in the 1960s. But this very partial reception of metal by radio was short-lived.

The AOR format began to suffer in the early 1980s when it faced competition from a variety of alternative alphabet formats such as AC (adult contemporary), UC (urban contemporary—a euphemism for black pop music), and especially CHR (contemporary hit radio—a modification of top-40 AM). Hard rock, including anything even vaguely heavy metal in sound, began to be eliminated as stations sought to appeal to an older and often a more female audience. One California station advertised its transformation with the slogan, "The Ecstasy without the Agony." In 1983 in Chicago the major FM AOR/hard-rock stations began pulling their AC/DC and Ozzy albums out of rotation and stopped sponsoring heavy metal concerts. By the mid-1980s the "classic rock" format was a dominating presence on the radio.[9] Heavy metal was excluded from any "classic" status.

The lack of a heavy metal radio format or of a format that included a large proportion of metal music has been a major factor in the constitution of heavy metal, an absent presence in that constitution. Exile from the airwaves led to an emphasis on the live concert as a way to disseminate the music and promote record sales: "Many heavy-metal bands took to the road in lieu of radio support, cultivating their audiences that way. Aerosmith, Blue Oyster Cult, and Ted Nugent stayed on the road more than forty weeks out of the year."[10] Bands had to rely "on massive amounts of touring."[11] This made them conscious of their reliance on loyal fans, binding them closer to the metal subculture.

Radio defined mainstream music. Metal's fans and artists were angered that their music "did not receive the kind of radio airplay its popularity entitled it to."[12] But rejection by radio permitted the cultivation of the proud-pariah image of the metal subculture. By virtue of its exclusion of metal from its formats, radio was seen as rejecting metal's audience.[13] The audience gained solidarity in dialectical response to the exclusion.

The record industry was also influenced by metal's exile from the airwaves. Although they were not averse to having one or two metal bands on their rosters, the companies did not actively seek to sign artists in the genre. As a general rule, "Record companies avoid signing artists or groups whose music does not appear to fit into one of the established radio station formats."[14] The companies would only touch those bands that could generate their own promotion through touring to appreciative audiences. Heavy metal bands were signed only after they had generated their own audiences through live appearances. In contrast to the procedure for other styles of music, the golden ears of company A&R staffs were not deployed to determine which heavy metal bands were signed. Thus, metal bypassed the two sets of gatekeepers guarding the heaven of mainstream rock. The ideology of populism persisted within heavy metal culture by virtue of the exclusion of the music from the mass media, an exclusion that bound artists and their core audiences together as proud pariahs.

The bonds forged between artist and audience, and within the audience, led to the often-observed imperviousness of metal to changes in musical fashion during the 1970s and early 1980s: "The form appears to be immune from trends and fickleness in the recording industry. No matter who or what is dominating radio airplay or the top of the charts, there are always heavy metal bands filling arenas, out-selling substantial numbers of albums."[15] That is, the major result of metal's exclusion from radio was to increase the power of the metal subculture itself for determining which artists would be successful and what kind of music they would play. Of course, the fact that there was a male, white, and blue-collar youth subculture that valorized its demographics through its music of choice contributed, in the first place, to metal's exile.

Due to metal's exclusion from the air waves, metal artists had no incentive to make their musical style conform to the codes of radio.[16] The AOR format that dominated radio during the 1970s was the antithesis of the underground/progressive/free-form of the 1960s. The latter was self-consciously the antithesis of AM radio's top-40 format, with which, therefore, AOR shared many features. Heavy metal, as an exiled music, could maintain a wide variety of "underground" characteristics rooted in the 1960s. Raised on "underground" music, the metal artists of the 1970s found no reason to alter many of its conventions. For example, artists did not have to restrict themselves to the two-and-one-half-minute song required by radio. The length of a rock song, because of the repetitive structure of the music, is an easily varied convention: "There are no extended phrases building to an eventual climax but, rather, the same strophic, melodic patterns over and over, with no real end. The music could go on for an indefinite length of time; the length of the song was obviously dictated by the requirements of the recording industry, not by anything about the music itself."[17] Classic metal songs of the 1970s were rarely less than four minutes long and were usually much longer. For example, the studio version of Black Sabbath's "War Pigs" runs eight minutes and that of "Iron Man" five minutes. Judas Priest's "Sinner," Rainbow's "Catch the Rainbow," and UFO's "Love to Love" all run close to seven minutes. By increasing the length of their songs on records, bands are able to simulate the concert experience in which songs have a longer duration than they do on mass-commercial radio.

Other AOR conventions could also be breached. Radio privileges vocals over instrumentals. The relative volume of the two is therefore adjusted in the mixing process during record production so that the voice can be heard above, not within, the instrumental portion. Metal, however, with its reliance on a heavy bottom sound, often privileges the instrumental over the vocal. Also, made-for-radio songs have short nonvocal sections, whereas heavy metal songs have strong, purely instrumental components. Lengthy guitar solos are the rule rather than the exception.

Not having to worry about creating hit songs targeted to radio's expectations and restrictions, the metal artist's focus could remain on the album as the unit of creation and appreciation. The value of the album over the individual cut even endures in the 1980s when metal finally found its way on to the airwaves. Klaus Meine, lead singer and writer for the Scorpions, said in 1987 that the group did not wish to write "hit singles" for a "radio oriented public," but wanted to create their "own music and write hit albums."[18] That same year Ozzy Osbourne remarked, "Record companies say 'We need a hit single, you've got to get commercial, you've got to get a pop song.' I say 'Screw that.' Do what you want to do. Do what your heart tells you to do. Get into your own groove."[19] Authenticity is equated in metal with disinterest in commercial appeal, especially as reflected in a radio hit. Rush's "Spirit of the Radio" declares that the "coldly charted" medium demands "endless compromises" that "shatter the illusion of integrity."

Trying to create hit singles often leads artists to subordinate their skills and standards to specialists—producers, songwriters, technicians, etc.—who have proven track records. However, if an artist has no desire to create a hit single or it is ruled out by the genre, specialists who know what is "hot" are not needed. The music remains substantially under the control of the artist, perpetuating the reality and the ideology of authenticity, in which the performer is also the creator. Metal is one of the few types of music in which an album can "go platinum without a boost from a hit."[20]

When members of the audience hear the music on their own turntables or tape players, rather than as singles on the radio, whole albums or album sides necessarily become their prime units of appreciation. They also tend to share more musical information with friends.[21] Metal fans display their knowledge of albums by recalling not only which song is on which album, but where on the album it appears. Despite the freedom to do so, artists rarely organize albums around concepts through which the songs are related to one another thematically. Queensrÿche's *Operation Mindcrime* and Rush's *2112* are two of the few exceptions.[22]

The importance of the concert and of the album in shaping the standards of heavy metal is shown by the proportion of "live" albums released by heavy metal bands in comparison to the proportion of such albums released by artists working in other genres.[23] One group, Motörhead, has released *three* live albums: *No Sleep Til Hammersmith, What's Wordsworth?*, and *No Sleep at All.*

Of course, the sound on such "live" albums is not really the same as the sound heard by someone present at the concert. Albums are remixed, that is, the relative volume of vocals and instrumentals is made to conform more to recorded-music values, and retouched, so that some instrumental parts are "sweetened." But with longer versions of the songs, audible audience reaction, and often remarks by the singer directed specifically to the crowd, the live album is a reproduction of the concert and an emblem of the consequences of metal's exile from radio in the 1970s. It simulates the bond between artist and audience that was forged in the years of exile.

By 1980 the role of the secondary media in constituting metal seemed to have stabilized. Metal's core audience was reliable and easy to service, so the large record companies made the genre one of their specialized offerings, reaping consistent profits from it. Radio continued to ignore the genre, leaving metal artists and the audience to form their own bonds with one another based on the inherent meaning of the music—its exuberant power—and the delineated meaning lent to it by the youth subculture that had crystallized around it.

But moments of equilibrium are always brief in contemporary life. As metal's artists and audience coalesced into a distinctive social form, expressed by a well-defined subculture, membership in that subculture began to grow. In addition, the first cohorts of metal fans grew older but did not surrender their devotion to the music. A "new wave" of metal bands appeared, especially in Britain, and audiences for metal expanded, though the demographics remained constant and the musical style was not significantly altered.

In this new period of incipient growth (the early 1980s) commercial radio continued to ignore metal. If anything, it was pushed even farther beyond the pale than previously, as consultants fine-tuned formats to reach an older youth market. But simultaneously an underground metal movement arose in the United States on noncommercial, college radio, independent record labels specializing in metal emerged, and grassroots metal publications began to appear. The fragmentation of taste publics and music-based subcultures began to impinge upon college programming, where the formerly full-time "progressive"/alternative format began to be dotted with speciality programs. For several hours each week heavy metal in all its glory could be heard on the radio, commercial-free. The major record companies were not eager to work with the college stations. Deejays, deeply committed to the music and members of the metal subculture, brought in their own records and tapes, and found that the new independent record companies, springing up to catch the new wave, were pleased to send them new releases. The independents, often founded by young people with a passion for metal, provided the stations with free passes for their artists' concerts, getting free advertising in return. Metal had finally gained a purchase, outside the large-scale commercial media, on the airwaves.

During the mid-1980s sheer quantitative growth in the audience and outlets for metal precipitated a qualitative change, ushering in the present period. College stations proliferated.[24] Metal programs could be found at Penn State, Lehigh, Kent State, Wesleyan, Auburn, Hawaii, Rutgers, and Cornell, among dozens of other universities. Junior colleges were as likely as public and private universities to offer a few hours per week of heavy metal on their stations. At least one college station, WSOU at Seton Hall University in New Jersey, which covers the New York City area, converted all of its programming to metal. In 1990 there were two thriving metal programs on college radio in Chicago. One, based at WZRD at Northeastern Illinois University, is on the air Wednesdays from noon to 4:00 P.M. The other, "The Steel Mill," on WNUR, Northwestern University's station, airs from 2:00 to 4:00 on Saturday afternoons. The college-based programs rely strongly on releases from independent record labels and have tended to support the thrash end of the metal style-spectrum in the late 1980s. Indeed, thrash, the offshoot of metal that consciously tries to make itself unassimilable by the commercial electronic media, is confined to late-night ghettos by them, if it is played at all. It needs the college stations for radio exposure. These stations still honor the codes of the free-form format, such as deejays playing what they like and discussing the meaning of the songs after playing them.

Organizations were created to mediate the college radio programs. The CMJ *(College Media Journal)*, a trade organization for college radio, created a separate metal report in which playlists from college metal programs are presented and summarized. The CMJ's annual conference, held in New York, added a separate set of events, the Metal Marathon, in which heavy metal artists, record-label executives, and journalists served on panels and interacted with the college metal deejays.

Commercial radio got in on the heavy metal action too. For example, in mid-1985 in the Chicago area, WVVX began broadcasting an evening heavy metal program called "Real Precious Metal." The program was underwritten by concert promoters who saw a metal show as a good way to advertise their frequent and lucrative heavy metal concerts. However, the format is now explicitly called, Hard-Rock/Heavy-Metal. In 1989 another heavy program began in the same area on WSSY, an AM station, under the rubric "G-Force." Independent commercial metal shows, however, continue to be few in number and are usually confined to evening time slots. But they indicate that commercial radio has now become a specialized medium for metal.

Another commercial radio enterprise that began in the mid-1980s has had a significant impact on the heavy metal industry. Called Z-Rock, it is a twenty-four-hour-a-day heavy metal radio format. The

broadcast studio is located in Dallas, Texas, but the deejays head-
quartered there are heard all over the United States. The signal is
sent via satellite to about twenty local stations in market areas
ranging from New York City to Fresno, California.[25] The record
companies like Z-Rock because, rather than dealing with dozens of
programmers, they only have to convince one programmer to include their releases in his playlist. Both artists and record companies
view inclusion on Z-Rock's Top 50 as a confirmation of success.
Program Director Pat Dawsey observes, "Z-Rock shows the via-
bility of both the format and the music." The station maintains a
toll-free request line, linking together the nationwide audience. The
line takes about 13,000 calls per month from a predominantly male
audience.[26] (See Appendix B.) Z-Rock has recently changed the
name of its format, originally "Hard Rock and Heavy Metal," to
"Hard Rock Radio." The subgenres of metal are not equally represented. Speed/thrash is segregated, being played primarily on a
separate late-night, one-hour show called "Headbanger's Heaven."
The format name change to eliminate the term "heavy metal" indicates that even specialized commercial radio has the mass aspirations associated with AOR, and will indulge in diluting the genre
whenever its programmers believe they can do so without surren-
dering their core audience.

A show called "Metal Shop," which radio stations may purchase
to air at any hour they choose, is also in syndication. Not only
does it feature a wide variety of heavy metal songs, but it provides
information on upcoming tours and releases, histories of groups,
and styles of metal. This specialized service allows stations without
any metal expertise to air a credible metal show. It is positioned
between the college and the commercial metal programs.

Commercial stations with a CHR or revised AOR format also
jumped on the metal bandwagon in the late 1980s by integrating
some metal songs into their general playlists. The new receptivity
of mass-commercial radio to metal is not only due to the exploding
sales of metal releases (see Appendix C), but, more importantly, to
the changes in the genre that stimulated those sales. Most of the
metal played on mass-commercial radio belongs to the subgenre of
lite metal, especially the "power ballads." The industry term for
such recordings is "crossovers."[27] Exposure on these stations, of
course, fosters still higher sales and permits the symbolism of the

metal subculture—in large part preserved by lite metal artists—to filter into the mass culture in a diluted form. The largest factor in the reception of metal by CHR is another secondary commercial medium, MTV. The metal groups included in medium-to-heavy rotation on MTV are the same groups played on CHR radio, both because the radio programmers look to MTV to read audience preference and because MTV exposure increases record sales, which also interest radio programmers. A rock journalist adds, "In some sense, the reception of radio to metal was not only that MTV proved the music's appeal, but that radio had been in the doldrums, with an increasingly conservative AOR format aimed at the older end of the 'youth' market."[28] That is, a definable and broad-based youth market reappeared, partly generated by MTV and partly a result of larger sociocultural processes than the present study can treat.

Just as the absence of heavy metal from the radio in the 1970s shaped the genre, its inclusion has altered it. Conforming to radio standards is the price of admission. Heavy metal bands have begun to employ professional songwriters. Producers with "proven hits" are in demand and often have dominant roles in the recording process. Bands attempting to retain control over their work are wary that their integrity will be "sacrificed on an alter of shine and polish."[29] The producers, paid a fee plus royalties, have a vested interest in adding "shine and polish" in order to create hits. Songs are tailored for the radio. For example, in 1988 a guitarist complained that a cut on his latest album had originally been five and a half minutes long. The record company, Chrysalis, found that the radio program directors refused to play it because of its length. "So something had to be taken out and . . . it was part of my guitar solo."[30]

Despite the immense increase of metal on commercial radio stations, the vast preponderance of the genre, in terms of bands and styles, is not given airplay. In this sense, even in the 1990s it continues to be true that metal is popular "despite little to no radio play."[31] The most obvious evidence for this assertion is Metallica's experience. The band's 1988 release, *And Justice for All,* sold more than a million copies despite the fact that it was not aired on the radio.[32] A journalist for *Spin* concluded that "No other rock band with an album in *Billboard*'s Top 30 could complain of so little airplay."[33] Exclusion from radio allows Metallica to continue in the tradition of the proud pariah: "Remaining true to a tough identity incompatible with MTV, AOR, or even college radio, Metallica are the first in years to build a big career in American rock disregarding the dictates of all three. They've called their own shots, kept their integrity, and rallied their support on the strength of their music and non-image."[34]

British radio was far more resistant to heavy metal than even American radio. The "Friday Night Rock Show" on BBC One was the only game in town for the harder types of rock.[35] Its coverage of metal in the 1980s was extensive and earned the respect of the metal subculture. A British fan noted that only two deejays, Tommy Vance and Alan Freeman, were "worth mentioning as champions of heavy metal."[36] As a nonprofit broadcast the "Friday Night Rock Show" can and does treat the albums from independent companies with as much, if not more, consideration, than those from the majors.

Since the deregulation of local radio in Britain in 1988, the commercial radio system has allowed for some further rock broadcasting.[37] In many areas hard rock gets only a once-a-week show. A syndication company, Radio Radio, delivered throughout Great Britain and Northern Ireland via satellite, has a late-night Saturday and Sunday show that includes a good deal of heavy metal in its hard-rock format. Greater London Radio, which can be heard through much of southeast England, also has a weekly heavy metal show.

Its period of exile from the radio over, heavy metal and its lite metal offshoot are members, though not of the first rank, of the chorus of pop genres filling the commercial airwaves. Its success in gaining airplay is fundamentally due to the internal development of lite metal as one of it subgenres. Lite metal brought in a female audience and a telegenic fashion that were made for MTV. In turn MTV was the relay for commercial radio's acceptance of metal. In lite metal traces of the subculture of metal's core audience remain, such as the irreverent bad-boy image and much of the fashion, but they are often relatively faint. That is, acceptance by radio has meant the sacrifice of much of the subculture that had coalesced during the years of exile.

Of course, the subculture has not disappeared. Not only does the classical tradition of metal continue, retaining its core audience, but the subgenre of speed/thrash, which emerged at about the same time as lite metal, carries the proud-pariah image to its extreme, replacing the hippie with a punk component and fashioning itself self-consciously as a cultural form that is unacceptable to the mass media.

Metal has lost the unity that it gained in its exile, mostly because of internally generated changes in the art and the audience, and in the artist-audience relation. Those changes have made the codes of the media far more important to the constitution of metal than they were previously, either through the need to submit to them or the will to reject them. Expanding beyond its core audience and the practices, symbols, and values of the subculture supporting that core, metal is more of a floating signifier than it was in the past— that is, it is more vulnerable to appropriation by the media, but it is also more open to artistic experimentation.

MTV

A decade ago one could never have imagined using the words heavy metal and television in the same sentence. It is not that TV has been inhospitable to rock music. Far from it.[38] From the appearances of Elvis, the Beatles, and the Rolling Stones on the "Ed Sullivan Show," to "American Bandstand," and guest spots on "Saturday Night Live," "television has always promoted rock 'n' roll"—the most successful performers "know how to communicate on the tube."[39] But mass commercial television has always demanded safe, domesticated performances of rock. Bad-boy images had to be compromised to get on the tube. For example, the Stones's "Let's Spend the Night Together" was sung on Sullivan as "Let's Spend Some Time Together."

The 1980s made the occasional mating of television and rock into a marriage without the possibility of divorce. The impact on heavy metal has been profound. It has had repercussions for each of the coconstitutors of the metal culture: the audience, the artists, and the other media.

MTV began in August 1981. There had been and, continue to be, other television shows that featured music video clips. Within two years, however, MTV had gained a near-monopoly on the new combination. By January 1983 it had hit the New York and Los

Angeles markets.[40] As the station grew with the cabling of America, many rock styles were presented in video form. Heavy metal bands, with hairstyles that rivaled those of "A Flock of Seagulls" and Cyndi Lauper, received much play during 1983 and 1984. At least since Judas Priest started wearing studded-leather clothes, heavy metal has had a strong visual element. As such, it was a natural for MTV.

Among the first groups to be shown were Quiet Riot, Mötley Crüe, Twisted Sister, Dokken, and the Scorpions. One scholar contends that most of MTV's videos borrow much of the visual iconography of heavy metal. The master figure of that iconography is the "bad boy," essential to rock from its beginnings and made into a self-conscious style by the metal subculture. That style became a paradigm for videos in general. Thus, the actual metal videos had no problem winning inclusion on MTV.[41] Indeed, the great discovery of MTV was that the styles, fashions, and symbolism of heavy metal attracted a far broader range of youth than those included in metal's core audience. The metal style of appearance and comportment, if not the metal ethos, affected youth culture as a whole. It was as though a broad audience had been waiting for a new fashion, for the simulacrum of a youth culture combining glamour and rebellion, glamorized rebellion and rebellious glamour.

By early 1985, however, MTV's management cut back on heavy metal videos because of intense pressure from religious fundamentalists[42]: "MTV claimed it wanted to program more music on the 'cutting edge'. . . . The real reason for metal cutbacks, as most of the industry saw it, was that MTV was bowing to the pressure of various conservative watchdog groups who had been complaining about heavy metal."[43] Nonetheless, at the end of 1988 heavy metal remained an integral part of MTV's programming. Not only were metal videos played in regular rotation, but a special late-night heavy metal program, "Headbanger's Ball," was added: "The channel got an immediate reaction. 'We were just trying to be more sensitive to what was breaking,' says MTV's Lee Masters. 'The thing about hard rock is, its audience reaction is much faster with the fans than in just about any other genre. We played Whitesnake, the phones rang, the product went out of the store, and it was instant.' "[44]

Many commentators have noted the impact of MTV on the sales

of metal records[45] and the acceptance of the music on mainstream radio.[46] In 1983 MTV was more influential than radio in the record-buying behavior of twelve to thirty-four year olds.[47] In 1984 Dee Snider of Twisted Sister said, "MTV was responsible for the resurgence of heavy metal."[48] In 1985 Bashe wrote, "Heavy-metal groups began ascending the charts. . . . MTV's acceptance eventually provided acceptance from rock radio."[49] Sales figures tell the story: "MTV 'discovered' metal in 1984. Metal's market share was eight percent in 1983, and then rose dramatically to twenty percent in 1984."[50] Since 1985 sales and radio acceptance have grown even further.

MTV's influence on sales can be illustrated by the story of *The Real Thing*. Released in June 1989, it was Faith No More's third album. It made a small dent in the marketplace but by the beginning of 1990 it had yet to appear on *Billboard*'s charts. Because one of the cuts on the album received a Grammy nomination, MTV began to air the video for that song in March 1990. By July 1990 the album was certified gold and was on *Billboard*'s list of the top twenty albums in sales.[51]

The marginalization of heavy metal by mainstream radio and rock magazines made MTV's promotional possibilities all the more attractive to the record companies, which began to sign telegenic groups. It is not unusual for metal bands to send photos and often videotapes along with or instead of their audio demo. What is true for rock in general is even more applicable to metal: the record companies resist signing bands that are not "video friendly."[52] Lack of songwriting ability can be taken care of by assigning that job to specialists. Choreographers can be called in to enhance lackluster visuals.[53] Poor musicianship can be masked, since the technological development of the studio and even of the concert-arena-as-studio can compensate for deficiencies of virtuosity. Metal bands acknowledge the sales impact of the video channel. They implore their fans at their concerts to call up MTV and request their video. Bands, especially those playing the harder forms of mainstream metal, are in a ticklish situation. They need to avoid the appearance of being concerned with commercial goals. In an interview, Gary Holt, guitarist for the thrash metal band, Exodus, described his recent video: "There won't be any silly things like walking down hallways singing at the camera."[54]

The record companies first saw videos as a cheaper alternative to the intensive touring that had previously been required to introduce and promote a new group. A British journalist notes that videos allowed bands to escape the need to tour in order to build a base of fans.[55] For the more pop-oriented bands the new marketing technique was cost-effective. They traded the loyalty of the core audience that is created by intensive touring for the more transient celebrity status of the pop star.

As MTV, with its general youth audience, became the tool of choice for promoting a band, access to it became a highly competitive struggle fought with dollars. A 1982 *Billboard* article mentioned that "Video clips . . . don't come cheaply: it costs between $20,000 and $40,000 to produce a typical example."[56] Of course, by 1989 the expense of making a video was significantly higher. That year the cost of a Poison video was $190,000. With elaborate pyrotechnics and a large rig, it was shot on 35 mm film. New bands, with as much as $70,000 to spend on a video, find it difficult "to compete with the Bon Jovis and Poisons of the world."[57] Videos encourage bands to emphasize the "production values" that have always been associated with metal, but which had in the past always been held subordinate to the music. As a rule, only established bands on large labels can successfully compete in the arena of production values, leaving smaller bands and independent record companies at a distinct disadvantage. In the first half of the 1980s MTV not only gave metal as a cultural form access to the other mass media, but also "broke" many new bands. Today, however, new bands without much financial clout are shut out.

As the videos increasingly stressed Hollywood and Madison Avenue production values, they became more than merely marketing techniques to promote bands, though they have retained their primary function as marketing tools. Frith argues that companies now see videos as "entertainment services," that is, as products to be sold to individuals and to be licensed to those who show them to the public.[58] Originally videos were provided free of charge to broadcasters. Now they are licensed to them for a fee.

Musicians must spend much time and effort on their visual images if they want the broad popularity among youth delivered by MTV. The two offshoots of heavy metal, lite metal and speed/thrash, are distinguished as much by visual image as by musical style. Thrash bands eschew the glammed-up gimmickry, styled hairdos, spandex, and glitz that characterize the metal bands that gain MTV play. Thrash also renounces the clichéd poses of heroism and romantic sensitivity. [59] In contrast, most of the lite metal or melodic metal groups have rather elaborate and distinctive visual presentations of themselves. The split in the music preceded MTV's impact, but the popularity of the lite metal subgenre owes much to television exposure.

The longer songs typical of the years when metal was exiled from the radio are excluded from MTV. The video clips run from three to five minutes. Part of Metallica's image of integrity is rhetorically reinforced by composing longer songs. As drummer Lars Ulrich said in 1986, "We're showing the industry that you can write eight-minute songs, you can be honest with yourself and your crowd, you don't have to put a huge, pretentious thing on just to come across and relate to the people out there."[60] But outside the subgenre of speed/thrash there are few, if any, bands like Metallica. The melodic and romantic strain of metal is drawn into conformity with the pop codes of the mass commercial media; only the hard strain of metal perpetuates the exclusive subculture that heavy metal had in its years of exile.

Music videos mediate between audience and artist in markedly different ways than do live concerts, radio, and records. Videos perform multiple functions: "They must gain and hold the viewer's attention amidst other videos; help establish, vitalize, or maintain the artist's image; sell that image and the products associated with it; and perhaps, carry one or several direct or indirect messages."[61] No other medium for rock music seeks so many different effects simultaneously. In order to have the possibility of fulfilling its multiple aims, the video must de-center the music itself and privilege a general impression or attitude.

One of the significant features of the MTV video is the aggressive discontinuity of the images. They are similar to TV advertisements and, increasingly, to TV newscasts. The videos' pace and cutting resemble ads. Indeed, videos are often created by advertising directors.[62] They have the same form as ads: "Interest and excitement is stimulated by rapid cutting, intercutting, dissolves, superimpositions, and other special effects."[63] During the first years of MTV, media commentators often saw the videos as a new art form and analyzed them according to the standards of film criticism.[64] Today, they are increasingly acknowledged as conventionalized promotional devices, essentially commercials. "Its an advertising campaign."[65] There is no reason to expect videos to conform to any but advertising conventions, since they were first developed as promotional tools and have never outgrown those origins, though new uses have been found for them as "entertainment services."

"Videos function like advertising in which the signifier that addresses desire is linked to a commodity."[66] That commodity, in the typical video, is the band itself. But it could be any other product, as is demonstrated by the ads that such rock stars as Lou Reed, Eric Clapton, and George Thorogood have made. With their music used as the sound track, the circle is closed; the ads seem like nothing other than music videos. The advertising industry, claims *New York Times* rock critic Jon Pareles, is "eager to blur boundaries, to point out that rock itself is a commercial product."[67] Metal performers have not, as yet, been the stars of advertising campaigns for beer, cigarettes, motorbikes, or any other mass-consumption products.[68] If they ever do make ads for anything other than themselves, they will severely undercut metal's code of authenticity, opposition to established authority, and separateness from the rest of society. So far, it has been "easy for them to resist temptation that wasn't being offered."[69]

The visual characteristic of the MTV video is discontinuity. Cuts, scenes, color and black-and-white frames, and concert footage and conceptual shots are rapidly juxtaposed. Catching the eye, music videos privilege sight over sound. Even though the narrative line, such as it is, is carried mainly by the song, the audience's attention is diverted and drawn in by the quick-paced visuals. MTV stands for music television, where the noun refers to a visual medium and the modifier refers to the art of shaping sound. The logo for the station follows the advertising principle of the big lie: the "M" looms large, engulfing the tiny "TV."

The prominence, indeed predominance, of the visual component of MTV means that the song is read through the visuals, not through the lyrics or the music.[70] If we only hear the song, our interpretations are not given to us: we must actively create them. Some argue that videos stop viewers from thinking for themselves by telling them what to think and "what to see in the words."[71] Others believe that rock videos preclude rather than provide understandings, supplying associations instead of allowing the audience to free-associate. They are "series of retinal quickies, too punchy to be subliminal, too scattered to have true impact."[72] MTV encourages a passive interpretation that is alien to both the audience and the song's creator. Metal bands rarely have any say in the creation of the video "concept," which is the province of the producer or director of the video. Directors often have concepts prior to ever hearing the song or knowing about the band for whom they are to create a video. MTV mediates between artist and audience by imposing a producer's or director's concept along with the music. The concept provides a further discontinuity on the level of signification, deconstructing the song by supplementation. Desmond notes a wide disparity between lyrical meaning and video interpretation of that meaning.[73] The music video is a typical postmodern cultural form, overdetermined by heterogeneous signifiers and underdetermined by their fragmentation. It ends up doing too little by trying to do too much. But, like an ad, a video can create a generalized attitude such as excitement or glamour.

Metal bands are able to resist to some extent the tyranny of concept over music because their videos must contain ample concert footage. Seeing the band play on stage does not predetermine the interpretation of a song, although, of course, some hints are given. And they are given by the performers themselves. Their stage performance may be directed, choreographed, and coached by others, but explicit meanings are not conveyed by playing music; that is, musical meaning is not illustrated. The significance of the concert in heavy metal culture is continued in the videos: "heavy metal videos always have to contain moments of live performance (whatever the surrounding story line) in order to capture and acknowledge the kind of empowerment that is involved in the concert itself."[74]

The ubiquity of concert footage, however, has the unintended consequence of changing the concert experience. The excitement of seeing a favorite band for the first time or of seeing their new stage set is considerably diminished for the audience when its members have already seen a facsimile on television. Excitement, at least the intensity of emotion that it encourages, is an important aspect of heavy metal concerts. The entire rock industry acknowledges that "the music videos are disappointing people when they go and see the live performers, because the performers live aren't as interesting."[75] Recognizing the impact of their videos, bands are forced to create more and more elaborately exciting stage sets to pique the interest of their now somewhat jaded audiences, adding to the cost of a concert tour and becoming more dependent on specialists hired from outside the metal community. At the same time, they have to re-create the video experience to satisfy the expectations of their fans. Thus, the live concerts become the imitation, more precisely the simulacrum, of the videos. Following Georg Simmel's discussion of the triadic relation, at the post-MTV concert artist and audience interact directly, but they also interact indirectly "from their common relation" to MTV.[76] Here the mediator may have become the most significant coconstitutor.

MTV influences not only the audience's appreciation of metal but also the composition of that audience. Demographically, the metal audience became younger, more socially heterogeneous, and more female.[77] The record companies realize that the female, MTV-influenced audience is not the traditional following for their metal groups: "The core audience is the males who buy the band. They don't tend to be as fickle as teenage females—they know before a record comes out that they're gonna buy it. The idea is to sustain that core audience and then take the upswing as well."[78] That is, the video must be a compromise formation between the need to serve the values of the metal subculture and the need to attract the new peripheral audience. Lite metal is a self-conscious attempt to make itself that compromise, through its musical style (melodic), its visual presentation (the shag haircut), and its image/attitude (the cute bad-boy).

There is some evidence that females watch more MTV than males do.[79] Their entry into the audience has not had impact on the masculinist code of metal. The depiction of women in metal videos in particular tends toward the extremes of traditional stereotypes. Females are portrayed as "submissive, passive, yet sensual and physically attractive."[80] The metal subculture may have been corrupted, fragmented, and redirected by MTV, but it has not been fundamentally altered.

MTV attracted younger and also more hip and middle-class segments of youth into the metal audience. The cable-connected television exposed people to a culture that one previously entered only by personal introduction. Now someone could affiliate with metal through the media, bypassing the metal subculture or participating in it vicariously in the very partial version of it presented on the videos. When the media take over as recruiters, the sense of solidarity among audience members is reduced and their standards of appropriate behavior, for example, at concerts, are altered. Most concert behaviors prescribed by the metal subculture do not make it into the videos. But the new audience learns what to wear to a concert and how to respond to it through the videos: "MTV is almost a subliminal fashion show."[81] The moussed and shag-cut hairstyles affected by the metal musicians are imitated by their fans, and although the males do not adopt the colorful spandex often seen in the videos, females are influenced to dress like the "bitch goddesses" so pervasive in metal clips.[82]

Metal on the family television also attracted viewers who reacted against the music and its visual presentation with vehement anger. Fundamentalists, such as those who formed and supported the PMRC, were not amused by what they saw on MTV. The PMRC's "filty fifteen" list mentioned nine heavy metal bands including AC/DC, Black Sabbath, Def Leppard, Judas Priest, Mercyful Fate, Twisted Sister, Venom, and W.A.S.P.[83] These moral critics of metal were effective in greatly reducing the amount of heavy metal on MTV, at least for a time. Had MTV never existed, metal's current enemies might never have known about it: "The atrocity tales have become numerous as the medium of the music video to some extent lifted the veil of secrecy surrounding the 'great noisy unknown.'"[84]

In response to the attack from the right, MTV began to require that a copy of the lyrics be submitted with each video. It has created a Program Standards Department, not unlike the old Hays Commission for movies, that seeks to weed out videos that seem to sanction or even feature illegal drugs, alcohol "abuse," "gratuitous" violence, or "explicit, graphic or excessive" sex.[85] The impact of the visual images, not the musical sounds or the lyrics, was what caught the attention of metal's opponents. Metal became a target in part because of the "increasing noticeability of music lyrics as they are acted out in video forms for millions of viewers."[86] This is particularly ironic, since, as has been noted, the visuals often have little or nothing to do with the lyrics.

MTV's troubles with the right wing stem from the fact that it is an inherently socially compromised medium; that is, it is neither a mass medium appealing to an undifferentiated audience and, therefore, capable of generating its own codes to exploit that audience, nor a specialized medium serving a distinctive subculture. Rather, it is in between, a medium primarily for young people in general, but readily accessible to those of all ages who have access to cable TV. It can neither be as bland as the AOR format on commercial radio nor as uncompromising as a metal show on college radio, making it the perfect mediator of a specialized music to the mass media and to a wider audience than the core audience of that music. MTV must be rambunctious enough to draw in the young, but not too threatening to anger their elders. That is, MTV must dilute the signifiers of music-based subcultures, but it cannot replace or even significantly transvalue those subcultures. Granting its importance as a coconstitutor of metal, it is dependent on the recording industry for its product, which must suit the sales strategies of that industry. Thus, it has had a large impact on musical culture, especially by tacking the visual sensibility of advertising on to music, but it has not created a new musical culture or new music-based subcultures.

What MTV has done is to select those elements within each genre of youth music that are compatible with its compromised structure while excluding the rest. Lite metal, for example, originated prior to MTV as an internal development of the melodic side of the genre. MTV selected it for play because it was the form of metal most congenial to a broad youth audience, defined in terms of age, sex, and class. By doing so, it made lite metal more distinctive than it might have otherwise been, exacerbating the fragmentation of the cultural form of metal without eliminating the sense of that form altogether. Similarly, by basically excluding the harder side of metal, MTV intensified the differentiation of thrash as a self-consciously confrontational music. Z-Rock copied its "Headbanger's Heaven" from MTV's "Headbanger's Ball," the first weekly ghetto for harder metal, aired late at night once a week. But even "Headbanger's Ball" offers little thrash. The most far-reaching effect of MTV, then, has been to intensify the differentiation of metal into subgenres by making one metal style commercially viable, indeed, lucrative, and another stridently noncommercial, hastening the implosion of the heavy metal genre.

Given the diversity of musical taste among youth, MTV does not find it advisable to exclude the music of any youth taste public, including heavy metal. The broad youth audience that it serves requires a rotation that includes many genres of music. No youth subculture is known for its catholic taste and metal audiences are well known for intolerance: "Fans of hard rock and heavy metal were not enthusiastic about the frequent appearance of new wave bands on MTV in the middle 1980s, and some of them refused to watch for that reason."[87] In other words, MTV was too much a mass medium to serve the members of the metal subculture.

Videos

The video need not be confined to MTV, but can be a specialized medium when it is sold or rented as a product to individual buyers. The pattern is the same as it was when radio had exiled metal: fans buy their own product.

The assortment of metal videos for sale is extensive. Some are collections of a group's videos, such as Judas Priest's *Fuel for Life*. Released in 1986, it includes ten "hit, classic and rare" videos spanning the years 1980 to 1986. *Ozzy Rules* offers eighteen minutes of videos based on songs from one of his albums. Concert videos sometimes are devoted to one band, sometimes to a variety of bands. Combat Records, for example, released the *Ultimate Revenge 2* video in 1989; it includes live concert footage from five of the label's "not ready for prime time" (MTV) groups: Forbidden, Death, Raven, Dark Angel, and Faith or Fear. These groups have little in common with the lite metal/hard rock favored by MTV; they represent the speed/thrash subgenre. Another "indie" label, Metal Blade, released a compilation tape of some of its groups, *Enigma Metal Reel/Fall '87*. Included are videos by Death Angel, TSOL, Trouble, Poison, Stryper, Lizzy Borden, and Anvil. These groups run the gamut of metal. The video in this case is less a retail product than a promotional device directed at the industry itself, a showcase for the record label.

Iron Maiden's *Live After Death* video shows, according to the copy on the package, "Maiden in concert at their ferocious best, performing with the most elaborate stage and lighting production yet."[88] Many of the statements on video packages stress the visual appeal of the contents, using phrases such as "makes for compulsive viewing." There are also documentary-style videos, such as Dokken's 1986 *Unchain the Night*. The viewer is taken offstage and backstage, as well as stage-front. It is one of many examples that follow the model of Led Zeppelin's *The Song Remains the Same*,"[89] whose video package proclaims: "And with the sounds are the sights." A newer format is the metal video that copies the magazine. A 1989 tape/"issue" of one series, called "Hard and Heavy," contains more than one hour of interviews, music videos, and cartoons.

Metallica deconstructs the various video formats in *Cliff 'em All*.[90] Not only is the video done in honor of their recently deceased band member, Cliff Burton, but it combines home footage and bootleg material with made-for-TV but never-used videos. Given their role as upholders of the integrity of metal in the face of a sellout of gargantuan proportions, they had to explain themselves on the package: "Well we finally went and did what we always talked about not doing. Releasing a vid!! . . . First of all this is not your typical shit home video done with high-tech 10 camera production and sound. . . . The quality in some places ain't that happening but the feeling is there and that's what matters!!"

Movies

Of the various visual media, movies have had the least engagement with heavy metal. Movies, because of their production and distribution expenses, require a mass audience. Since heavy metal appeals to a limited audience, it cannot be a Hollywood staple. Nonetheless, it has made some inroads: "Metal music's in . . . just about every Horror film and 'youf' movie made in America."[91] Even Judas Priest's cover of Chuck Berry's rock-and-roll-star anthem, "Johnny B. Goode," was used in a little-known movie of the same name.

Two movies were released during the 1980s that not only used, but were about, heavy metal. *This Is Spinal Tap*, released in 1984, with a soundtrack album on a major label, was a humorous history of a hapless heavy metal band.[92] It was written and directed by Rob Reiner, who played the radic-lib Meathead on the popular 1970s television program "All in the Family." Penelope Spheeris's *The Decline of Western Civilization, Part 2: The Metal Years* came out in 1988. It featured interviews and performances by a variety of heavy metal and hard-rock bands, most of which were highly visual, even for metal. Among them were Alice Cooper, Ozzy Osbourne, Aerosmith, Poison, Motörhead, Lizzy Borden, and Faster Pussycat. Both films were in the documentary form, but, of course, *This Is Spinal Tap* was a comic mock-documentary. In a typical postmodern twist, after the picture's release the "fictional" group portrayed in the movie was in such demand and the album sold so well that the actors got together and went on a concert tour as Spinal Tap.

Both movies had the same problem. They had to attract both a metal audience and an audience that had no affiliation with that musical form. Heavy metal, however, is not either loved or ignored, but loved or hated. How could antagonistic groups be satisfied within the confines of the same picture? The solution, well-known in the mass media since the breakdown of the great consensus of the 1950s, is overdetermination, the "something-for-everyone" story line. "All in the Family," for example, had to appeal to both the liberal and conservative elements that divided the TV audience in the 1970s. The liberals in the audience viewed Archie Bunker as a buffoon and his son-in-law, Meathead (played by Reiner), as enlightened. In contrast, the conservatives saw the Meathead as the buffoon and Archie as the ultimately triumphant common man.

Spheeris and Reiner provided pleasure to the metal audience by focusing on their music, their musicians, and their culture. But they provided at least as much pleasure to metal detractors. In both movies the artists were portrayed in a markedly unflattering light. Spinal Tap was depicted as a bunch of pretentious, bombastic boozers. Spheeris's groups were shown in the throes of their alcoholically dissipated and dissolute life-styles. Their shows were rampant with shtick. The subtext of each film was the case against heavy metal. Reiner's, reflecting the progressive, hip remnant of the counterculture, is a cultural criticism, emphasizing the unsophistication of the metal artist. Indeed, a damning review of a "real" metal group's efforts was titled "Look Out, Spinal Tap: Here Come the Scorpions, Heavy Metal's Latest Heroes."[93] Spheeris's movie, which was released in the wake of the PMRC's attacks on heavy metal, is basically a moral criticism, emphasizing the artist's depravity. Spheeris denies that the genre has any other message than " . . . being rich and famous and getting laid."[94] Metal's experience with the movies shows how resistant it is to assimilation into the codes of the mass media.

Magazines

The history of heavy metal's involvement with the print media generally parallels that of its relations with radio; a period of exile was followed by one of incipient connections, which was, in turn, succeeded by a period of firm and extensive linkages. In the 1970s the mainstream rock magazines mainly ignored the genre when they were not trashing it: "The response of American rock criticism to Heavy Metal in the early-mid 1970s was consistently a negative one."[95] Straw argues that one result of this treatment was the emergence of a "discourse of populism" among heavy metal musicians, who responded to the critics' contempt by accusing them of elitism,[96] thereby strengthening the proud-pariah image of metal and bonding the artists more closely to the metal subculture.

In Britain "the only major music paper to promote heavy metal was *Sounds*."[97] Geoff Barton, editor of *Kerrang!*, the preeminent heavy metal magazine of the 1980s, was an alumnus of *Sounds*. In the United States *Creem* did not uniformly repudiate the genre the way *Rolling Stone* did.[98]

By the early 1980s, coinciding with the new wave of British heavy metal and the growth spurt in the heavy metal audience worldwide, specialized heavy metal magazines began to appear. The oldest is *Kerrang!*, begun in 1981. *Metal Forces* and *Metal Hammer* started up in the middle of the decade, joined later by *RAW*. In the United States *Aardschok America* began in 1985 and *RIP* a year later. In addition, several long-established general rock magazines have changed format and now cover metal almost exclusively. All fourteen of the feature stories in a randomly selected *Hit Parader* from 1989 were about metal groups. Similarly, all of the articles in a 1986 issue of *Circus* were about metal bands.

Hard Rock from France, *Metallion* from Canada, and *Heavy Rock* from Spain are examples illustrating the presence of metal magazines throughout the world. Wherever metal subcultures exist, there are also metal magazines, including all of Western Europe, Japan, North America, Australia, and, more recently, Eastern Europe, and Latin America. In addition to the publications mentioned above, some of the metal magazines available in 1989 were *Livewire* (Germany), *Morbid* (Norway), *Revenge* (Brazil), *F.E.T.U.* (Japan), and *Grim Death* (New Zealand). Some of the major magazines, such as *Kerrang!*, are read in many countries. Thus, fans are linked to one another transnationally by these magazines. The value of the worldwide metal community is promoted and achieved by this medium. The rhetoric expressing transnationalism is captured in the names of some of the periodicals. The British *RAW* stands for "Rock Action Worldwide," and the subtitle of another British magazine, *Metal Hammer*, is "The International Hard Rock and Heavy Metal Magazine." The latter lists its prices not only in pounds but in German deutschemarks, Italian lire, Portuguese escudos, Spanish pesetas, Swedish krona, Danish krona, and French francs, among others. Thus, by the late 1980s metal magazines covered the globe.

Although all media can be either mass, specialized, or somewhere in between, depending on the character of their audience, the print media more easily cater to specialized interests and audiences than do the electronic media. Not only are magazines generally cheaper to produce, in terms of capital expenditures, than radio programs, television programs, and movies, but they provide the opportunity for enthusiasts to read and look at them at their own pace, selecting just what they want to attend to and how intensely and in what order they want to attend to it. The magazine is there for a member of a music-based subculture to pick up and put down at will, and often contains a wealth of detail absent from most radio or TV programs. Perhaps most importantly, magazines freeze the signifiers of a subculture, allowing them to be learned and absorbed. The reader finds out what's "in" in terms of style, fashion, and lingo. As a result of the distinctive way in which specialized magazines mediate, they tend to reinforce rather than to dilute the particularities of subcultures; that is, they project and objectify the subculture's standards.

Magazines perform a range of specific mediating functions. Reviews of recent record releases connect the audience to the music by letting its members know what recordings have recently been released and which ones they might like. These reviews also connect the audience to itself, expressing its musical standards and values. For a pop audience criticism is irrelevant, but for a subculture, such as metal's, the values expressed in the reviews are of great significance. Criticism also connects the musicians to their audience, affirming, clarifying, and applying the standards that they share. The reviews also mediate between the audience and the industry, giving the record companies qualitative feedback on their releases. Reviews, finally, serve to mediate the industry itself. They are included in press kits sent to programmers at radio stations; that is, they are used as promotional devices. They are even included in press kits sent to magazine reviewers.

Mainstream rock reviewers, like movie reviewers, have become more like entertainers and shills for the media they review than critics applying intelligible standards. Members of the metal subculture are far more self-consciously critical than are the members of the general rock audience. They want the reviewer to point out the strengths and weaknesses of a new release or of a concert, applying the standards that they share in common. Metal critics are and see themselves as specialists who are embedded within the subcultural audience. As such, they actively coconstitute the audience via criteria of aesthetic criticism.

The magazines underscore the centrality of concerts in the metal culture. Concert photos and reviews are staples, and so too are tour-date listings and personal ads seeking musicians for bands. Roughly one-third of all the pictures in these magazines depict bands playing before an audience.[99] Much space is also devoted to covering the metal festivals, such as the Monsters of Rock Festival in its British and German incarnations. Here there are fewer on-stage photos than there are backstage and audience shots. There are even pictures of the press passes and of the empty litter-strewn field.

Many of the biggest-selling magazines devote more space to photographs than to written text. All fan magazines, indeed all celebrity magazines, rely heavily upon photographs. Metal photography, however, is not mainly concerned with conveying the artist's personal appearance. The clothes, the stance, and the metal style are at least as important as the face. The photos show subculture members how they should look and comport themselves. Some of the best photographers, such as Ross Halfin, can get their work published in any number of magazines. Halfin finds it important "to develop a relationship, an element of trust with an artist, before you can get a shot that transcends the regular artificial, wax work dummy corpse impersonations that usually accompany record company releases."[100]

Metal photographers are highly specialized. They know, either explicitly or implicitly, the codes of the genre and of the subculture. Those codes involve the stances, accessories, gestures, and facial expressions that are appropriate for metal. Guitarists are shown in deep concentration, singers are displayed sweating and with mouths agape. Band members lean into one another, bathed in a halo of colored lights. There are posed shots of artists atop Harleys or a stack of Marshall amps. The photographers mediate the stars to the audience in a filtered way.

The performers recognize the importance of their appearance before the camera. Bands often impose rules about which songs the photographers can shoot at their concerts, and band members will be sure to pose for the cameras during the performances of those songs. Photographers tell stories of shoots: "The band members take turns pumping a twenty-pound barbell before doing a bare-armed pose. Sixx, who has been working out regularly, throws a mini-tantrum when he sees how chubby his arm photographs in the preliminary Polaroids."[101] The medium may not be *the* message, but it does impose a filtering form on the message it conveys. To some degree the magazines create a sense of intimacy between performers and audience, with the emphasis on the word "sense."[102]

A whole series of features in metal magazines serve to mediate interaction among fans. Letters from readers are omnipresent. Some publications print lists of the favorite albums of fans or ratings of albums by fans. These direct mediations are supplemented by penpal columns through which people in different countries can get together through their common devotion to metal. Classified ads from the audience to buy or sell records are also common. The British magazines in particular are likely to run personal columns, with entries such as this: "Female 18 living in Aberdeen, into heavy metal, like to meet males and females for gigs etc."[103] Lists of names and addresses of fan clubs are regular features. The magazines thus make it possible for loner metal fans to connect with the wider subculture. They are also the source of the information and evaluations that fans exchange with one another to express their solidarity and to prove their personal bona fides at metal concerts.

An important subset of metal magazines are not primarily commercial endeavors, but are extensions of the metal subculture(s), produced by members of the subculture(s) out of devotion. Metal fanzines began in earnest in the early 1980s, at the same time that the audience for metal was growing.[104] They proliferated in the following decade. Denisoff distinguishes commercial magazines, which he calls "prozines," from fanzines, which are produced by one person, working out of his or her home. Financial reward is neither the primary goal nor is it normally realized.[105] There are perks to the job, however, such as meeting the bands: "You get in free to all the shows [and also get] free records."[106]

Like fanzines in other youth subcultures, metal fanzines are characterized by a passionate, almost proselytizing, tone. Fanzine editors are fans in the true sense of that term's etymology. They adhere *fanatically* to the metal conventions, standards, and practices. Reviews of albums and concerts, and interviews and photographs appear in the fanzines. In a sense fanzines create a network that spans the globe, allowing for exchanges of "underground information."[107] They not only connect fans to one another and to bands, but also, in the words of a British prozine, "provide the training ground for many of the country's most sussed music journalists."[108]

The lack of radio play for metal and the hostility of the mainstream press to it made the fanzines an important part of the record companies' promotion activities. An executive of Music for Nations, a British metal "indie," states, "It was certainly through fanzines that Metallica were broken in this country."[109] The major rock magazines had ignored thrash metal, refusing to take the subgenre seriously.

Three basic types of metal fanzines can be distinguished: those based on a band, on a local area, and on a subgenre of metal. *Killing Yourself to Die*, an international Black Sabbath fanzine, is an example of the first type; its eighth volume, published in 1987, consisted of forty pages with photos. *Rock Brigade*, from Cambuci, Brazil, containing color posters and reviews, is an area-based fanzine. Another is *Metal Caos* from Italy, with a circulation of 5,000. Its seventy pages include interviews, reviews, photos, and posters. In Britain the major heavy metal magazines are located in London, but the fanzines are based up north, where the music originated, and cover their local scenes in detail.[110]

The fanzine that specializes in a specific subgenre has become the most widespread, following the fragmentation of metal as a cultural form. *White Throne* is a California-based journal interested in Christian metal. *Speed Corps* from British Columbia, Canada, and *Metallic Beast* from Denmark are concerned with thrash.

Like the metal show on college radio, the fanzine is a direct projection of the metal subculture(s) into the externalized mind of the media. In the Hegelian sense, it gives the subculture an objectivity, an ability to define itself to itself and, therefore, to gain control over its full range of expressivity. That is, the fanzine is the most specialized medium of all, in which gifted members of the audience take over the function of mediating between artists and audience without the help of external third parties with their own commercial interests. That these gifted members are also intensely committed devotees (fanatics) is the basic reason why the proliferation of specialized media in metal culture in the 1980s has heightened the splits in that culture that had always existed, but had, in the 1970s, been compromised and held in unreflective suspension.

Heavy metal existed and, in certain senses, thrived for much of its history without the offices of such media as radio, "music video television," and magazines. As these media have begun to mediate the cultural form intensively, they have diluted it when aiming for a mass audience and strengthened its particularity when they have expressed metal's subculture. On the whole, the more mass or general the media have been, the more they have favored and furthered the melodic side of the music and the interests of the peripheral audience (the younger, female, and middle-class components). The more specialized they have been, the more they have promoted the harder side of the music and the interests of the core audience. In terms of exposure and money, the more general media seem to have exerted a decisive influence on metal, but it is not clear that they have diminished the diversity of its musical expression or destroyed its unique subculture. Much more, the impact of radio, TV, and magazines has made the internal differences that always existed in metal more clearly defined and, indeed, extreme than they were in the years of exile.

Concerts

Two media, records and concerts, have been integral to the constitution of metal from its beginnings and are coextensive with its definition. The concert is a medium because artist and audience do not find one another: they must be brought together by an apparatus of promoters, venue owners, and technicians, who condition their direct encounter.

Heavy metal concerts, held in a variety of venues, were an integral part of the rock-concert business in the 1970s, in both the United States and Great Britain. They were lucrative, since they did not need much promotion to attract sell-out crowds. The promoters could accurately predict audience sizes and thus schedule the concert in an appropriate-sized venue. Predictability is essential to profitability, since empty seats cut into the promoter's, not the artist's, profits. The concert was also the primary technique for promoting record sales, due to the exile of heavy metal from the other media. But, most important, the concert had become the central ritual/experience of the heavy metal subculture.

The adolescent male audience, many of whose members were well-built and high on beer, pot, and other assorted drugs, did not pose a significant problem to concert promoters, who hired security staffs who looked equally tough. At a metal concert people on both sides of the security fence often look like they could audition for a role in a movie about the Hell's Angels. The security staff knew the audience well, since it saw metal audiences frequently. The security people knew what the general public did not know: the audience for a heavy metal concert is an easy bunch to handle. They are at a concert to experience the music and to affirm their subculture in solidarity with one another. They are not, despite their looks, a wild and violent group. Security details in Chicago repeatedly told me that they preferred the metal fans to audiences for country-music groups, such as Alabama or Charlie Daniels, because they found the latter more prone to fighting with one another and with the guards.

Promoters can and do handle a wide variety of popular music performers, since venues are not specialized according to genre. A site becomes dedicated to metal by moving in the band's stage set and attracting the fans with their fashions, styles, and symbols. Concert promoters need to coordinate a large number of specialists, from lighting, audio, and stage technicians, to venue owners, caterers, lawyers, and booking agents. It is connections rather than capital investment that make concert-promoting organizations successful. Promoters generally start out on a small and local scale. With luck, some talent for business, and lack of competition, they can grow dramatically. The late 1970s were good years for concert promoters. Metal was an important and growing part of their business, but not a differentiated one. The same technicians who worked on other concerts could be used for metal shows. The same kinds of booking arrangements could be made for the various genres of music.

By 1978, in the United States, groups such as Black Sabbath, Rainbow, Judas Priest, and UFO, among others, were playing at the larger venues. The rock-concert business, not merely its heavy metal component, was doing so well that more and larger venues were built, both indoor arenas and outdoor sites. Some of them could also be utilized by sporting events. In addition to capacity, two other considerations were relevant to where a heavy metal concert could be held. The sound system had to be powerful, with clarity or fidelity somewhat less important than a high decibel level. And the seating could not be upholstered, since upholstered seats could not withstand the pounding feet and the bath of beer that a metal audience delivers.

In the early 1980s heavy metal concerts were being held at a wider range and a larger number of venues. Heavy metal festivals, such as the one held at Donington in England, were introduced. The US Festival in 1983 was particularly significant for heavy metal. Backer and initiator Steve Wosniak planned the festival as a nostalgic homage to the Woodstock extravaganza of 1969. But he was forced to realize that changes in the audience over the years had made his model impossible to follow. The same audience would no longer sit to hear a wide variety of musical genres performed on the same stage. Fragmentation characterized the American rock audience in 1983, and the Wosniak festival reflected this by offering different musical styles on separate days. One whole day was set aside for heavy metal, showing that it had become by that time a significant part of the music scene. The size of the audience for that one day, as well as its enthusiasm, overshadowed the rest of the festival. The industry took notice.

Musicians were also influenced by the 1983 US Festival. Hearing a radio broadcast of the festival, the members of Poison heeded the call to "Go west young man." They were convinced that California groups like Quiet Riot and Van Halen heralded a strong metal scene on the West Coast. Poison packed up its gear in a used ambulance and moved to L.A. Once there, they pioneered the practice of bands passing out fliers for their own shows.[111]

During the last part of the 1980s, the concert business for all types of metal flourished. Many smaller clubs sprang up to cater exclusively to local and touring metal bands. The megapopular bands appear at summer outdoor arenas and European festivals, sites where they can reach thousands (sometimes over 100,000) of people on the same night. The profitability of the tours has been bolstered by two very commercial practices. Beer and cigarette companies now provide corporate sponsorship to concerts, and concert merchandising is a big business. By the late 1980s the cost of T-shirts was running from $15.00 to $20.00 each. In addition, a wide range of other band-related merchandise is sold at concerts, from hats and headbands, to pins and tour jackets. The profits from concert merchandising are controlled by the band rather than by the promoters. Rock bands no longer do concert tours in order to promote their latest album: "Now they tour for the big bucks—from concert tickets and merchandise."[112] The promoters add to their profits from ticket sales by taking part of the beer concessions.

The concert tour of a popular band has become rationalized along several lines. Booking agencies connect venue owners or promoters with potential bands or their managements. Tour buses, outfitted with complex stereo systems and refrigerators for beer, are easily rented from specialized companies. The media that promote heavy metal records also advertise concerts extensively. Major concerts are more regularized. With tour managers who are trained specialists and a broadening base of technologists, the venue is transformed into a combination movie set and recording studio—the imitation of a video. The tours of unknown groups, especially those in the speed/thrash subgenre, are, in contrast, rather haphazard and spontaneous affairs, reflecting the splits within metal as a cultural form.

But changes in the concert business have done little, if anything, to alter the encounter of artist and audience front-stage. Of all the media, the concert apparatus is the most faithful servant of the artist-audience relation, its core medium.

Records and the Recording Industry

The record has been inseparable from the concert in the constitution of metal from its beginnings. At the concert the artist and audience encounter each other directly, affirming each other and the symbols and values of the metal subculture. But the ritual-experience of the concert is transitory, an epiphany realized normally no more than once or twice a year for any given artist and audience member. The record is the most reliable access that the member of the subculture has to the music and the record is a prime means of support for the artist. For the audience the record comes alive at the concert, whereas for the artist the concert promotes the record. The two media, concerts and recordings, are fully reciprocal. The concert has priority as epiphany, but the record is privileged as the primary means through which the members of the subculture constitute that subculture in everyday life. One need only pass by a midsize American car that has seen better days, with the sound of metal blasting from its tape deck, to realize this truth. More than any other medium, the record is metal's lifeblood.

During the first eight years of the 1970s, heavy metal could be found only on the rosters of the major record labels. AC/DC was on Atlantic, Black Sabbath and Deep Purple were on Warner, and Judas Priest was on Columbia. These groups required very little in the way of promotional services because their music had been excluded by the mainstream press and radio. The labels promoted them by having them tour, which made the record/tour cycle the basis of the artist's connection to the audience. The tours sold very well, due to the loyalty of the core audience, whose members also bought the records. The majors especially liked their metal artists because fans were not only interested in the latest release, but bought their back catalogue too, a habit that increased corporate profits. Heavy metal albums had "commercial staying power"[113] because each new cohort of metal fans got turned on to established groups and bought their older records.

By the end of 1978 the record industry as a whole was changing. In terms of units shipped, the number of gold and platinum records created per year, and gross revenues, the 1970s had been a glorious triumph. In 1972 the industry's gross revenues were just under 2 billion dollars. In 1978 they had risen to over 4 billion dollars. But the worm had turned and the revenues for 1979 fell to about 3.6 billion dollars and stayed at that lower level through 1982.[114]

The causes for the reversal are complex, including the worldwide recession which finally caught up with the record business, the conservative policies of the oligopoly that the industry had become, the impact of increased list prices for records, alternative entertainment competing for youth's attention and money, the disappearance of the remnants of the "youth culture," and the tailing off of the baby boom generation. Between 1974 and 1980 the record industry became concentrated in a few firms. In 1974, 79 percent of the hits were on the top eight labels. By 1980 98 percent of the hits were on those eight labels.[115] Oligopolies tend to prize stability over the risks of innovation. The big record labels played it safe with music and, perhaps, began to lose touch with youth.

By the end of 1982 the slump was clearly over.[116] But the changes wrought in the industry had become fixed as standard operating procedure. Fewer records were released each year.[117] In an attempt to achieve predictable sales and hold down development costs, the companies became very selective in signing new artists. Record deals became far harder to get. The golden ears of company A&R staffs were augmented, if not fully dominated, by committees of accountants and marketing experts. In consequence, the companies took far fewer risks with new types of music. One estimate is that they signed about 50 percent fewer bands during the recession than in the years prior to it.[118]

Heavy metal survived the slump better than other musical genres. Newer metal bands were signed. As a record executive explains, "In a time of recession, the only people who will buy records are kids to whom music means more than money."[119] The loyal members of the heavy metal subculture fit that description perfectly. Companies, however, preferred to sign only bands that were already established rather than to develop and break new talent in-house. They evaluated bands not only in terms of their songwriting ability, but also in terms of their management, equipment, and financing. Further, they were no longer ready to give bands free rein to do "their own thing": "We don't have the time or money to deal with amateurs or egos," one record executive was quoted as saying.[120] Gone, too, were the once-common junkets for press and radio people, and the lavish after-concert parties. Tour support was cut back and farmed out to "corporate sponsors."

The impact of these changes was felt throughout the music industry. The majors wanted professionals and shifted the burden of training to others, much as the medical industry has always relied on the families of prospective doctors to finance their education. For example, Mötley Crüe's first album (1982) was self-financed and released on their own independent label, Leathür Records.[121]

The reluctance of the record companies to provide development costs posed a particular problem for heavy metal musicians. Traditionally they had come from working-class backgrounds, from the kinds of families that could not afford to bankroll them, even if they wanted to. After the recession hit the industry, metal artists increasingly came from middle-class backgrounds because members of the middle class could rely on their families for the financing required to buy instruments and costumes, to make demo recordings, to rent out practice space, and even to support them while they tried to achieve success. An alternative way to gain financing was provided by entrepreneurial managers. Not uncommon prior to 1979, they now proliferated. They provided the financing for a fledgling band in return for long, potentially lucrative contracts with it.

The rise of independent record labels was to some degree a response to the new policies of the majors.[122] Although the majors were signing bands, more groups with talent had sprung up than the majors were willing to take. A second generation of metal artists had arrived, who had learned from the classical bands but who were exploring the genre and not merely copying their predecessors. At the same time, the audience for heavy metal was growing, and had now matured sufficiently to want new music within the genre, not only music by the classic superstars who had forged the genre independently. That is, it could recognize the genre of heavy metal as a musical form that it desired to hear as long as it was performed well and presented according to the codes of the subculture. Unlike the classical heroes, who were like the outside lawgivers celebrated by ancient Greek cities, the new metal artists came from the audience itself and were drenched in its subculture. The "indies," along with the college radio stations and the prozines/fanzines, came along to mediate the new artists and the larger and more differentiated audience. The play-it-safe and cut-the-costs policies of the majors left the indies free to serve a neglected market.

The early 1980s were, for metal, the years of the indies. These small companies did not require vast outlays of capital to find and record artists. The requisite low-cost recording technology and the independent studios had been available before the economic slump. The main problem faced by the indies was distribution. The explosion of fanzines and prozines helped spread the word. The metal subculture, in which fanatics turn friends on to new stuff, did the rest. The indies initially emerged in Britain, where the network of fanzines and the metal subculture was strongest. Also, touring that compact country was a less expensive undertaking than mounting a nationwide tour of the sprawling United States. When the American metal indies came into being, they relied on college metal shows as well as on the local and imported magazines.

In the early 1980s American members of the heavy metal subculture were avid buyers of imported albums. There was a definite cachet attached to owning a record on an independent label, a whiff of underground culture consistent with the anticommercial bias of artists, audience, and the noncommercial, specialized media in the heavy metal culture.

The major record companies shifted the risk of finding and developing new metal talent to the indies. When that talent proved itself, the majors moved in, ready to skim off the cream with fat contracts. The indies made some money from this arrangement, but the big profits followed the old rule that the rich get richer. Rather than viewing them as competitors, the majors saw the indies as useful developers and testers of talent. Indeed, people who started the independents had often worked for the major companies. Music for Nations, an early and influential British indie metal label, was founded by Martin Hooker, who had worked for EMI. Hooker had gone from EMI to the punk indie Secret Records before starting his metal label. As in the case of the fanzines, punk led the way for the indies, demonstrating that alternative media could be created to serve a music-based subculture.

During the first half of the 1980s, indies in the United States began to relicense British imports for American distribution. One of the more successful American independents, Metal Blade, began in this manner in 1983, but soon was producing local bands. Its list focused heavily on the speed/thrash subgenre, with bands such as Slayer, Satan, Nasty Savage, Sodom, Malice, and Tyrant. Metal Blade's growth, both in terms of the number of bands it handled and the complexity of its organization, is somewhat typical. By 1986 Capitol Records, a major among the majors, began to handle Metal Blade's distribution arrangements, and Metal Blade started a specialized label, Death Records.[123] Music for Nations also started a specialized label, Under One Flag, to concentrate on speed and thrash.[124]

The independent metal record labels vary in size, organizational complexity, profitability, musical specialization, and ties to the majors. One of the more interesting indies is New Renaissance, which operates more like a collective than a company. The label does not provide financial support to groups but works to get other companies, majors or indies, to notice their bands.

The major difficulty for American independents is distributing their product. Distribution became highly organized and concentrated during the 1970s and early 1980s, in part as a consequence of the recession. The retail return policies of the majors became more strict, and they were able to demand that stores take their unproven records if they wanted to have access to the sure sellers. The independents had no such clout. The majority of records are now sold in chain record stores or in department stores, rather than in small retail operations. Thus, independents are cut off from their potential end-users unless they gain access to the distribution networks that the majors control. One solution, increasingly used in the United States by firms such as Mechanic Records and Roadrunner, is a distribution agreement with a major, in these two cases with MCA.[125]

The emergence of the indies in the 1980s did not so much detract from as supplement the influence of the majors. The newer metal bands that came into existence in the late 1970s found their way to the majors, directly or indirectly. Two prominent groups that were part of the new wave of British heavy metal, Iron Maiden and Angel Witch, were both initially signed by EMI. The older 1970s groups, such as the Scorpions, and their offshoots, such as Dio, remained on major labels, which also signed up large numbers of metal bands, many of them graduates of the indies. The majors concentrated on classical heavy metal and the lite metal subgenre, leaving the indies with the speed/thrash metal, especially that originating outside Britain and America. For example, Roadracer has cornered the market on Brazilian thrash metal, with releases from Sepultura and Ratos de Porâo. By contrast, lite metal is the province of the majors with Poison and Great White on Capitol, White Lion on Atlantic, Def Leppard on Polygram, and Ratt on Atlantic. Despite the attempts at rationalizing development and distribution that were inaugurated during the slump of 1979–82, 90 percent of the majors' releases in all genres still fail to recover their costs.[126]

Some of the majors have begun their own specialty metal labels. Others have used the marketing skills of the indies. Music for Nations finds "the major labels knocking at their door for help in breaking their latest rock bands."[127] Further, the independents are less reluctant to handle the more controversial records. EMI, for example, feared their shareholders' reactions to W.A.S.P.'s single, "Animal (F**k Like a Beast)," and made a deal with Music for Nations to put it out for them.[128] Specialized businesses, notably Concrete Marketing, were created in an effort to provide metal-marketing expertise to a wide variety of record companies.

The majors have not lost any of their power in the general rock industry. Their concentration, in terms of the proportion of top-selling records produced by the largest firms, is almost complete.[129]

In 1990 six conglomerates (WEA, CBS, Polygram, MCA, BMG, and CEMA) were responsible for 94 percent of all types of American recordings.[130] They gain and keep their standing primarily through their control of the distribution system. They are the distributors of all of the major labels, of boutique labels within the majors, and of a growing list of independents. Indeed, it is no longer clear that "independent" is a fully accurate term to describe companies that undertake the function of developing groups, but later funnel their talent to the majors either directly or through distribution agreements.

During the 1980s the number of metal records that became bestsellers vastly increased. (See Appendix C.) Yet of the 47 metal records making *Billboard's* "Top 100" pop albums from 1987 to 1989, only one was released on an independent label.[131] Pareles concludes, "Independent labels are still doing most of the legwork, and taking the risks, on . . . fringe styles—but the majors are getting quicker on the uptake."[132]

The pattern of change in the record industry's relation to metal falls into the same three periods that have been used to characterize the other media. During the 1970s heavy metal was one of the many types of music offered to a fragmented audience by the major record corporations. The market was well defined and relatively stable and predictable, comprising a subculture that lacked its own institutional expression. In the late 1970s and early 1980s the independent metal labels emerged along with the other specialized media, such as college radio and magazines, to give metal and its subculture objective expression. This period of incipient growth was also the time when the subgenres of metal became established and metal's audience began to overflow the core subculture. Finally, through the rest of the 1980s, when metal became a big business (in 1988 metal albums accounted for "about fifteen to twenty percent of the record industry's $6.5 billion revenues"[133]), the majors and the indies became coordinated by differentiating the functions of development and distribution. The new coordination is aided and abetted by the changes in the promotional media, such as radio, MTV, and magazines, which have taken advantage of the expansion in the audience for and the output of metal.

Throughout the history of its relation to metal, the record industry has played a relatively conservative and reactive role in constituting metal as a cultural form. During the 1970s it left well enough alone, allowing established artists to serve their subcultural audience as they saw fit. When new developments in the musical culture occurred in the late 1970s and early 1980s, the large record companies, faced with recessionary financial pressures, left the field open for independent record labels to develop new talent. Finally, as some forms of metal went mainstream in the 1980s, the large record companies tried to influence bands to conform to the mass codes of AOR and the somewhat less restrictive codes of MTV, and co-opted the indies into their distribution networks and used them like the major leagues in baseball use their farm teams. Through all of these changes the companies, especially the majors, did little or nothing to influence the inherent or delineated meanings of the music. They remained, like the concert promoters, mediators concerned with making profits from what they took up, rather than culture fabricators or culture creators. Though certainly without altruism, generosity, enthusiasm, or partisanship, the majors brought together artist and audience, serving more as a specialized than as a mass medium.

The expansion of metal in terms of the size, differentiation, and broader demographics of its audience has led to important changes in the way metal recordings are created, leading to the emergence of new mediators internal to the recording medium. These mediators, rather than the record companies, do exert a measure of control over the inherent and delineated meanings of the music.

Primary among the new mediators is the record producer, a quintessential generalist. The position of producers throughout all forms of popular music has become one of great power. Originally they were company salarymen, overseeing the taping of a full group of musicians. Two circumstances changed this modest role. The first was the development of multitrack recording technology, which took control of the recorded sound out of the hands of musicians. The editing and mixing of the tape allowed producers and engineers to manipulate the sounds made in the studio by the musicians. The musicians no longer needed to be present as a group during the recording phase of production. Different members could come to the studio on different days to lay down their tracks. In order to regain control of the sound, the wealthier bands began to hire their own producers. They also rejected company studios, seeking out those that had equipment and personnel that suited their tastes. Producers were now paid a fee, not a salary. By the 1980s the technology and politics of the recording process had caused further changes in power relations. Bands now were more likely to go to studios preferred by producers, who were in a stronger position than ever before. Their remuneration was now royalty-based, in recognition of their artistic input, rather than a fee for technical services. *Billboard* charts listing top-selling records started to include the producer's name, along with the artist's.

These changes characterized most of popular music, but were exaggerated in metal because of its aesthetic standards for records.[134] Despite the importance of the "live" album in metal, the standards for studio recordings do not reflect a live aesthetic. Unlike punk and blues, where capturing a more-or-less live sound is valued, metal records of all styles are supposed to be elegant and refined. Rather than seeking a diamond-in-the-rough rawness, metal wants a perfectly faceted, highly polished gem. Record reviewers frequently make mention of the "production values" of the record, denouncing "muddy" and praising "clean" sounds. Producers are explicitly praised or damned.[135] Producers who have had hits with other metal groups are avidly pursued because they are seen to have the ability to unite the artist's work with the audience's taste. Companies now have some veto power, at least with new groups, in the selection of a producer. The task of production not only mediates between the audience and the artist, but also directly negotiates the interests of the company with those of the band. Having a well-known producer gives credibility to a new band. Said one tyro about the impact of using a well-known producer, "it means that the industry will start to check us out."[136]

Many groups attempt to maintain control over their sound by producing their recordings themselves. Self-production also gives them additional royalties. Since the cost of production is borne by the band (most directly when the group is unsigned and making a demo, or when it is using its advance on royalties from the record company), it is in its own financial interest to keep costs down. But it is also in the group's artistic interest to spend as much as necessary to get a "great" sound. It is not unusual for metal groups working in the classical tradition to spend four months in the studio.

Can the group trust itself, or one of its members, to balance its

financial and artistic interests? Many top bands that have successfully produced records for other groups still want someone outside
their band to act as their producer in order to gain more objectivity
in reconciling conflicting interests. In addition, the producer can
objectively mediate within the band itself. Innumerable questions
of "artistic difference" need to be resolved. Which songs belong on
the album? If the songs are attributed to individual members rather
than to the group as a whole, this is not merely an ego issue, but
also a financial one: writers receive royalties. How long should the
guitar break be? Is this vocal good enough or should the singer do
another take? How should the edited tape be mixed—with the
vocals predominant or integrated into the musical parts? The number of possible differences is vast, and producers play the role of
adjudicators in such disputes. The producer, finally, can serve as a
cheerleader for the band, urging it on to greatness in the same way
as fans do at concerts.

More subtly, but perhaps more importantly, producers also mediate musical culture. Many producers specialize in one genre, and
this is particularly true in metal. They bring knowledge gleaned
from working with one band to their work with the next. Artists
remark that producers teach them how to improve their performance.[137] Since metal musicians rarely take music or voice lessons,
the producer is one of their few sources of instruction. Reviews and
press releases mention the prior band with which the producer of
the new album worked. A musician whose album was recently
done with producer Bill Metoyer remarks approvingly that he "has
produced so many bands, but he's gained a lot of experience in
doing so."[138]

Along with the producer comes a wide range of professionals
and craftsmen, such as manager, stage-set designer, and audio technician, all of whom are increasingly specialized by genre and, therefore, serve to mediate the musical culture, reinforcing certain of
its standards and, perhaps, shaping others. The more successful
managers have incorporated. The contacts they have developed with
metal groups in the past can be used to benefit their newer groups.
Managers can convince their well-known bands to use their new
bands as opening acts, giving the latter audience and industry
exposure.

As functional differentiation has proliferated in the recording medium, mediators of the medium have appeared. Concrete Foundation, starting as a specialized metal marketing firm, publishes an industry newsletter and sponsors an industry conference. CMJ, which serves college radio, does the same. These groups and others, such as independent record companies, also put out compilation albums and put on showcases. These allow unsigned bands to be seen and heard by A&R people from the major record companies.

The dense thicket of mediation might seem to de-center the artists from the recording process and even from their own creativity and their audience. As new and unproduced bands copy produced bands, the artist can become merely the shadow of a creator. This tendency is most pronounced in lite metal, which is the form of metal closest to pop music, in its sound, its audience, and the social constitution of its production. But it is not absent in the other variants of metal. In this sense, metal might become a victim of its own success, as technicians and media generalists strive to make its success formula fixed and repeatable. That would be a prescription for cultural suicide, but it is far from happening yet. Indeed, the more the mediators proliferate, the more the fate of the cultural form becomes indeterminate as incalculable factors enter into its constitution.

Conclusion

Throughout the history of their involvement with metal the media have been essentially true to their mediating function of bringing artist and audience together through conveying both the music made by artists and the styles, fashions, and symbols of the music-based subculture(s). That is, in the case of metal, the media have not fabricated genres and fashions by creating music and musicians, nor have they developed an audience for them through promotion. Neither the artists nor their audience(s) are creatures of the media in the manner of pop phenomena. The media did not contrive the metal subculture the way it contrives fads; it merely found that subculture and began to supply it. The media also found the bands and delivered them to the audience.

But that is only half the story. The media found the artists and the audience within itself, as their infrastructure. The two media that have always been part of the metal world—the concert and the record—are essential to its constitution. Only through recordings can metal subculture(s) be reproduced on a daily basis in the ordinary lives of members of the audience, whether they belong to the mainline, heavy metal subculture, the subgenre subculture of thrash, or the taste-public/subgenre subculture of lite metal. The concert, where audience and artist encounter one another directly in a ritual-experience, is itself the peak experience, the summum bonum, the fullest realization of the subculture. Records and concerts are integral constituents of metal culture, as essential to it as the music and the subculture(s), only weaker than them in the sense of being able to determine what the result of putting the three constitutors together will be. The media serve the artists and audience, for a price, but there is no way of removing them. The record producing and distributing systems, and the concert promoting and venue systems are a genuine infrastructure for metal culture(s).

The first period of metal's cultural history, the era of "heavy metal," was one in which the music and the related culture surrounding it were exiled from all media except records and concerts. Heavy metal existed, from the aspect of the media, as a specialized niche within mass-commercial entertainment corporations. The music had a loyal audience, the members of which would fill concert halls and buy the back catalogue of albums. But that audience was also limited in size. It wanted musical fare that was unacceptable to the mass media. Thus, the major recording companies and the concert promoters had the simple task of giving an identifiable and predictable audience the product that it wanted. The record companies and concert promoters had no incentive to change this situation. The metal fans were already sold and the product was waiting to be delivered. Metal was a cash cow.

The situation changed because metal proved to be an attractive product. Not only did the audience rapidly grow but its demographics slowly expanded, and parts of it became sophisticated. Growth in the audience showed the appeal of both the music and the subculture to young males around much of the world who experienced marginalization and found that the persona of the proud pariah expressed their identity. The more musically inclined members of the audience began to play the music themselves, in their own ways, carrying on the tradition of authenticity rather than becoming slavish imitators. The audience as a whole was ready to accept new metal, having gained a consciousness of the value of the genre beyond the works of its musical founders.

As the audience grew, it began to differentiate internally. Artists worked on different parts of the genre, preparing the way for the emergence of different groups of fans. Some fans created specialized media, bringing the subculture to greater self-consciousness and nurturing a partisan spirit of exclusiveness for the genre or one of its subgenres. Specialized commercial media entered the play and a network of college-radio programs, prozines, fanzines, independent labels, and specialized venues erupted.

At about the same time, in the early 1980s, the more mass or general media began to take notice of heavy metal's growing appeal and especially the presence within it of a strain of melodic music acceptable to a broader youth audience including, especially, females. MTV became the vehicle to serve that more general audience—a combination of a taste public and a subgenre subculture—with the subgenre of lite metal, which it in turn mediated to mass and general commercial radio. MTV became a genuine coconstitutor of lite metal, helping to shape a visual style and sensibility for the subgenre and thereby influencing the content of its subgenre subculture. In doing so, it diluted the social, cultural, and musical punch of what it took from heavy metal, creating a quasi-pop form of metal, still claiming roots in heavy metal music and the heavy metal subculture, but mixing in "sensitivity" (read pop sentimentality) with the traditional bad-boy image.

In its period of incipient growth heavy metal outgrew itself and began to fragment. No longer an exile, it was also no longer secure in a specialized niche in the media conglomerates. Artists differentiate subgenres and audiences differentiate subcultures based on them. The media perform their function of mediation, erupting from within and connecting from without. They do not create art or develop audiences, but work with what is there and bring the sides together. In doing so they change what is there by reinforcing and exaggerating it. The mass media made the pop features of lite metal more extreme, whereas the noncommercial, specialized media made the harder features of heavy metal more pronounced, fortifying in particular the subgenre of thrash and its uncompromising subculture. One might even argue that in a completely unplanned way the split between the mass/general and the specialized media caused the breakup of heavy metal into a classical tradition that continues the conventions of the genre, and two subgenres, neither of which can abide the other and both of which are classified under the same broader label because they claim lineal descent from heavy metal and its subculture. Thrash resides in the "alternative media" where lite metal must fear to tread. Lite metal is domiciled on MTV and commercial radio where the many varieties of thrash and speed are unwelcome. Classic metal mediates the two subgenres, welcome on the alternative media and acceptable on the general youth media. Without the exaggerating and reinforcing effects of the media would the split have been so pronounced?

In the third period of metal's history, continuing through this writing, the media have formed an infrastructure for the bricolage of metal, that structure of the tradition/trace of a genre mediating two irreconcilable and unassimilable subgenres. At one pole of the infrastructure is mass-commercial radio which takes the most pop items in lite metal, the power ballads, and mixes them into the rotation of pop sounds that it endlessly recycles for an undifferentiated audience. At the other pole are the noncommercial specialized media, catering to exclusivist subcultures that self-consciously reject the musical tastes and general value systems of mainstream society, especially the pop ethos and sensibility. Between them are the specialized commercial media and the general, youth-market, commercial media, welcoming all forms of metal in greater or less proportion, depending on how specialized their audience is. The more general a youth audience is sought, the less thrash, harder heavy metal, or exotic microgenres will be covered or carried. The more specialized an audience is served, the more the "underground," alternative, and exotic metal will be covered or carried.

The general and specialized commercial media mediate between the two poles of mass and hyperspecialized media, keeping the bricolage together by housing opposites under the same name. That is in their financial interest, but it is also what keeps the culture of metal from dissolving into its parts.

The Concert: Metal Epiphany

"Burning Up the Night"
—*Krokus*

At the concert the constitution of metal as a cultural form becomes concrete, as each of the actors in the constituting transaction meet. The concert is the event that epitomizes the cultural form and brings it to fulfillment. In the preceding chapters the constitution of metal as a cultural form has been interpreted through the perspectives of each of the constituting actors. Their order of appearance followed an order of cultural significance: the artist creates the music and is brought together with an audience through the offices of the media. The transaction can also be described in another way, which emphasizes social structure. In this case the artist stands between the two worlds of the audience and the media, and the transaction is one in which the audience pays the media to deliver an artist to it. Here the artist functions in two ways, as a commodity for the media to sell and as a culture hero for the audience to admire. That is the structure of the concert.

The great divide in the concert is between the backstage and the frontstage. Backstage is the world of the media, governed by functional specialization, calculations of financial interest, and instrumental rationality. Frontstage is the realm of the audience, ruled by a sense of community, adherence to the codes of a valued subculture, and expressive-emotional experience. The stage itself is the site of the mediation of these two worlds by the performing artist who binds them together with the music. Media and audience share two radically different interests in the same thing, the music. The artist, in bringing the media and the audience together, must belong to their different worlds; he is a trickster figure, combining opposites. The artist is the bricoleur of the bricolage that is the concert.

There are all manner of concerts. They differ in size of venue, type of crowd, numbers in the audience, solidarity of the audience, expense and elaborateness of production, and quality of the performance. In addition, there is a significant set of structural differences between thrash metal concerts, on the one hand, and classic and lite metal concerts, on the other. The paradigm for the following discussion is the classic metal concert presented in its most positive or fulfilled form. Comparisons with the thrash concert will be made along the way.

Backstage Story

The backstage/frontstage binary opposition that structures the concert is not unique to it. The Edwardian mansion, celebrated in the popular television series "Upstairs Downstairs," is another such social structure. Similar, too, is the bifurcated world imagined by H. G. Wells in *The Time Machine*, where the ugly Morlocks toiled underground and the attractive Eloi played in the sunshine. Erving Goffman's distinction between frontstage and backstage has an informed understanding of the vast array of organizations that deal with clients, customers, and the public. Backstage is defined by Goffman "as a place, relative to a given performance, where the impression fostered by the performance [frontstage] is knowingly contradicted as a matter of course."[1] At a heavy metal concert the two sides of the binary opposition are kept so separate that they define two different worlds of experience, opposite to each other along a range of essential dimensions.

The backstage is a microcosm of the modern world in its advanced stage of economy and technology. Primary and secondary economic activities are not in evidence. Only the tertiary, the so-called service economy, is present. The personnel vary from grunt laborers, whose major assets are their brawn, to highly skilled, sometimes formally trained, technicians. The division of labor is extensive and, for large tours, intensive. The backstage is uniform wherever it appears around the world. It is based on an invariant technological and social apparatus, which can bring forth the most different appearances on the frontstage.

Aside from possessing different kinds and levels of skill, the workers vary according to whether they travel with the band. The basic retinue of a group includes technicians in charge of the various instruments, roadies (often doubling as gofers), and a tour manager. Except for small tours, a host of others also accompany the band. There are people to work the sound and lighting boards, people to take care of the band's wardrobe, and a pyrotechnician to control the special effects. Even midsized tours begin to resemble a premodern royal retinue during its progress from the winter to the summer castle, except the metal tour's entourage includes personal trainers, bodyguards, chefs, photographers, accountants, and hairdressers. As one wag put it, a tour involves mobilizing as much "manpower and machinery [as] you are likely to encounter outside of a small war."[2]

Some concert workers are permanent employees of the venue, while others, such as electricians and Teamster-affiliated loaders, are hired wage workers. Others are employed by such suppliers as lighting companies and caterers. Security guards form another group of locals; when they are hired by the promoter on a per-concert basis, rather than being attached to the site, the security personnel for heavy metal concerts are the biggest and bulkiest guys around.

Backstage workers are further distinguished from one another by the rewards they receive. Some are on salary, others get paid hourly wages, some are paid a one-time fee, and others receive a percentage of the gate or of the merchandise sold. The amount of remuneration can vary dramatically, as it ordinarily does in a highly differentiated production apparatus. Those who ride the tour bus, however, no matter what their job, often get the same per-diem cash allowance for incidentals.[3]

Money, of course, is the basic compensation for service in the backstage world, but workers are also rewarded with other perquisites and pleasures that are regarded as valuable. Here, too, diversity is the rule. For example, some people enjoy easy access to the band, whereas others barely meet the performers. Some workers are given tour jackets or get to stay at hotels rather than sleep on the bus. Groupies are differentially available. Aside from the performers, security men have more access to them than others: "The name of the game became 'If you want to ball the star, you've got to ball me first.' "[4]

Georg Simmel's discussion of how time dominates the modern world applies pointedly to the backstage: "The relationships and affairs . . . are so varied and complex that without the strictest punctuality in promises and services the whole structure would break down into an inextricable chaos."[5] The workers, from such different backgrounds, specialties, and interests, are integrated by a "stable and impersonal time schedule." They are told when they may start and when they must complete their tasks. The overall schedule, such as dinner for the crew and stage times for each band, is prominently posted. When the concert is over, the tour buses do not leave until the set is loaded out. The musical instruments and the vast array of electronic and mechanical devices linked to them, the parts of the stage set, and all property of the band and its assistants must be put on the trucks. On small tours, everything and everyone is crammed into a van. Larger tours use one or more buses and one or more trucks. The roadies and sometimes the technicians who pack up the sophisticated equipment seem to make a sport out of seeing how fast they can load out. Roger and Martyn Dean, speaking about designing the stage sets, describe the impact of that game: "The effect of the finished stage was so impressive, the illusion of an alien technology so complete, that it is easy to overlook the practicalities of putting something so complex on tour at all. It is not only what the set looks like on the stage that matters, it is how it travels, how it fits into the back of a truck. The road crew are going to be moving it every day for several months, and anything that does not work is soon going to be smashed. Loading a truck after a gig is a high-speed art."[6]

Time differentiates the backstage personnel. Their peak work times do not coincide. Some of them work prior to the concert, such as the guy who sets up the drum kit and checks the miking for it, and the security manager who discusses the strategy for that evening with his crew and assigns them to different areas. Others work during the concert, such as those manning the sound and lighting boards. The roadies do most of their work well before and after the concert. Finally, when everyone else has completed his job, the bus driver begins his. The uneven distribution of tasks over time means that the people who are living together and sharing the same space for weeks, if not months, at a stretch, do not fully live together. The effect of differences in work schedules was observed when some drugs were passed around on a tour bus about an hour and a half before a concert was to begin. Three people refused them, saying that they would indulge after the concert. They were working during the concert and wanted to be as fully in control as possible. Those who did indulge were off, having performed their duties earlier, and could fully relax. People who work before or after the concert have the choice of viewing it or not. Here, too, there is no uniformity, but a continuum ranging from those who adore the band and never miss a performance, to those who are not at all keen about the music and tend to avoid it.

The individual concert falls into a wider temporal series of events. The whole series is called the tour. Bands name their tours to give them greater cohesion and to sell T-shirts with the tour's name on them. Long before the first date of the tour much "backstage" work is already done. The time-consuming process of designing and building stage sets has been completed. The lighting has been designed, sometimes by or with the aid of the lighting technicians who will work on-site at the concert. The sound-board technician also had to be present for concert rehearsals. The band's management, one or more members of whom accompany the tour, have had to plan its particulars, such as concert dates, transportation, securing equipment, and the like. Caterers have been booked. The record company and the band's management have usually worked together to co-ordinate press passes and interviews, and other promotional arrangements, such as in-store appearances. Members of the metal press, the interviewers and photographers, have been given backstage access. The local metal deejay, who invariably announces the group to the audience, will also be there.

The backstage complexity is not fully rationalized, since there is no single bureaucratic hierarchy of authority. Some workers are ultimately subordinate to the tour manager, others to the venue manager, and others to the promoter. In cities where some of the local workers, from grunts to electricians, belong to powerful unions, there are further independent power bases. The representatives of the communications media, the groupies, and assorted others with backstage access have no obvious superiors present, with the possible exception of the security force. The backstage area is polycentric, characterized by multiple centers of power rather than by a monocratic hierarchy of authority.

The backstage of a heavy metal concert is not unique in its complexity as a work site, but it surely ranks as one of the most complex. It shares features with a number of other settings that have been studied by sociologists. In his classic study of the restaurant, William Whyte detailed how this system of interdependence required that all the workers perform their tasks properly in order for each one to do his or her special task correctly.[7] The formal structure of the restaurant does not hint at the informal interactions and the attitudes necessary to make the whole function. The same holds true backstage, where the social organization is far more intricate than it is at a restaurant. The interdependence of the backstage crew is a source of frustration, bordering on panic, when someone fails to do an assigned task in an effective and timely manner. However, when everything functions smoothly on a tour, the acknowledgment of interdependence and the extended interactions create a sense of solidarity in the crew, a feeling of "family."

Whyte describes the devices that waitresses use to give orders to male cooks. The problems faced by the waitresses in 1949, when his study was done, are not so different from those encountered by female workers at heavy metal concerts. A female lighting technician from the local area had to negotiate with male union electricians and male light designers/technicians traveling with the tour. She had to prove her mettle physically and symbolically before they would accept that she had expertise and a legitimate sphere of competence.

The stage itself is the key site on which the backstage world converges, although many members of that world, bus drivers and caterers, for example, never set foot on it. The stage at an arena is much like the operating room of a hospital.[8] Both are the focal points of the larger sites. A series of differentiated workers coordinate shifts of activity to ready both of these "theaters" of operation. Nurses arrive on the surgical floor as maids are finishing the cleaning. Their aides bring in tables of sterilized implements and these are laid out for use by the surgical team. In like manner, at the concert, technicians set up the equipment, attaching wires and laying tape over them on the floor, after the roadies have brought in the boxes of equipment. Supplies and equipment are ready to hand, with provision made for emergencies. Only when everything is in position, including the prepped patient or audience, do the stars appear on the scene. Surgeons do not make grand entrances, accompanied by majestic music, lights, and wild cheering by the patient. But, in their respective worlds, the surgeon and the band are the necessary agents who set the prepared scenes in motion. Prior to their entrance all is prologue—preparation by the backstage workers and anticipation by the patient or audience.

The analogy of the audience to the patient does not work as well for heavy metal as it does for other forms of rock or for pop. The audience that greets the heavy metal band, and does so emphatically, is not a mass audience passively subject to transient excitements. The concert is more than a voyeuristic spectacle for the heavy metal audience, which is in great part self-prepared and participatory. It is prepared to have specific emotional experiences, to affirm itself as a subculture through ritual activity, and, finally, to celebrate the music and its bearers as a celebration of itself as a subculture. The audience is a coconstitutor of the events that will unfold in the concert.

The Audience Gets Ready

The metal audience has prepared for the concert with as much diligence as the backstage crew, though in radically different ways. When the band triumphantly appears on stage all three actors in the metal transaction—the media, the artists, and the audience— have prepared the way for the concert to approach its ideal form. The work done by the members of the audience can be summarized in the phrase "getting pumped up for the concert."

Prior to the day of the concert, the fans bought tickets, often spending hours in line before they went on sale so that they might get good seats or out of fear that the concert might sell out. They have talked with friends about the upcoming concert, speculating on what will be seen and heard there, and generating enthusiasm. They have listened to the band's albums, anticipating hearing the songs performed live. On the day of the concert they dress in their metal uniform, which is often a special variant of their everyday garb. "Dressing up" for a concert, the way people dress up for a wedding or some other formal occasion, is not proper here, but there is a special code for choosing concert clothes.

Thought must be given to the specific metal T-shirt to be worn. If one of the concert bands is a fan's favorite and he or she happens to own a shirt displaying that band's logo, that T-shirt will be the fan's first choice. If a certain favored band member had previously performed with another band, that former band's T-shirt would also be appropriate. Any other band's T-shirt or a shirt advertising Harleys or some brand of beer would also be acceptable. The point is to represent the primary symbols of the subculture on one's body. Until the mid-1980s all T-shirts were black, short-sleeved, and crew-necked. Modifications, such as ripping off the sleeves or the neck-band, enhance the look. Since then, the growth of merchandising as a significant generator of profits has spawned a wide array of colors and styles for the band's official clothing.

Travel to the concert, either by car or in the buses favored by British fans, is a celebratory experience. Tapes of the concert bands are played, and beer and pot are frequently consumed. Arriving at the site, one finds oneself amidst a sea of people who are playing similar tapes, imbibing similar substances, and looking not unlike oneself in clothing, hairstyle, and general demeanor. The accent is on identification with the others, on mechanical solidarity, in contrast to the organic solidarity of the work crews.

The contagion of excitement generated during travel to the concert is extended to others whom one has never met before, but who are obviously members of the subculture. Nor is everyone a stranger. Nodding to people one has seen before at other concerts, or looking for friends and acquaintances, is a usual preconcert pastime. When the tickets indicate assigned seats the parking-lot scene is characterized by leisurely excitement, but if the concert is general admission, getting on line enhances the anticipation. How close to the stage can one get? Serious fans have shown up at the venue hours earlier to position themselves for the best seats, or, more likely, the floor spaces closest to the stage. Metal fans do not follow the band caravan-style, camping out, the way Deadheads do. When a favorite band is playing more than one date in the vicinity, it is unusual, but not unknown, to see the same fans several nights in a row at different venues.

The economics of concerts in general and the particular importance of extravagant stage sets in heavy metal means that major bands play only at the larger venues. Fans who do not live close to such sites often travel long distances to reach them. British fans, in part because the core audience in Britain is larger, and in part because the excellent system of motor coaches reduces much of the onerousness of a long ride, are willing to endure longer travel than Americans. To get to the Monsters of Rock Festival held at Castle Donington some fans had to be on the bus by dawn: "We set out for Donny at 7:00 a.m. from Louth by coach. We arrived at Donny at 2:10 p.m., missing Helloween altogether and just catching the last couple of minutes of Guns N' Roses. A journey that would take just a couple of hours took seven hours (talk about traffic jams)."⁹

"Just" a couple of hours travel to and from a concert is not viewed as an unusual hardship. One of the major outdoor heavy metal venues in the Chicago area is located about ninety-five miles from the center of the city. The trip is not perceived as a bother. Since travel and waiting in line for the venue to open generate excitement, the longer it takes the better the audience is prepared for the concert. Once inside, the excitement grows. The density of people per square foot increases; if one is standing near the stage that density can approach its theoretical maximum. Beer and drugs are consumed. Music blares from the loudspeakers, not nearly as loud as the live music will be, but far from aural wallpaper.

The major requirement that the audience must fulfill to coconstitute a good concert is to mold itself together into an approximation of a community for the event. That requisite is achieved by its members' adherence to subcultural norms, including codes of visual style and commitment to the subculture's values.

The heavy metal subculture's rules of fashion are heeded, creating a uniform that encourages identification. The merchandise stands are situated at the entrance to the venue, and the enthusiasm for a given group can be gauged by the number of fans who buy and immediately put on the band's tour T-shirt. Decorated jackets with band logos are worn by fans with something resembling the pride in his medals of a veteran at a Memorial Day celebration. In the United States the jackets are created with purchased patches and buttons. In Great Britain, jackets may have had embroidery depicting logos or, more ambitiously, favorite album covers. Artistic creativity is also expressed through the drawing and painting of banners, which the creators proudly display for the rest of the audience long before the band or the radio deejay, who may have run a banner contest, can see them. The rest of the audience actively examines and evaluates these works.

Long hair that may have to be worn pulled back at work hangs free at the venue. Inside the site the fan's demeanor changes. A parallel but different phenomenon has been observed at classical symphony concerts: "From the moment of entering the building one's behavior changes, becoming more formal and inclined to be muted."[10] Elias Canetti is astonished by this behavior in which "all outward reactions are prohibited. People sit there motionless, as though they managed to hear *nothing*. It is obvious that a long and artificial training in stagnation has been necessary here. We have grown accustomed to its results, but, to an unprejudiced mind, there are few phenomena of our cultural life as astonishing as a [classical music] concert audience. People who allow music to affect them in a natural way behave quite differently."[11] Of course, the metal audience does not change toward formality and hushed tones, but in the opposite direction. As they enter the arena the fans move with a bit more of a lumbering swagger and bounce to their step, and their voices become louder.

During the time before the concert the aesthetic standards of heavy metal are expressed and represented. Conversation is almost exclusively concerned with the genre, and one can always hear judgments about which albums and which lineup are a group's best. Other discussions range from who is the best guitar player and why he is best, to why the sound quality of records pressed in Japan is better than the quality of recordings made elsewhere. The bands on the concert's bill are the center of attention, but they are compared and contrasted to others with similar styles. Taking part in these conversations establishes one's metal bona fides and reinforces and teaches the common standards of criticism.

Information (trivia from an outsider's perspective) is more highly valued than interpretation. Commitment is displayed by becoming a walking encyclopedia of metal lore, a fount of facts. It is perfectly acceptable to ask a nearby stranger a question about any of the bands on the bill. It is a way of making connection, not unlike the "What's your sign?" line used at a singles bar, although with the intention of identification, not of cathexis.

Aesthetic standards are also articulated in reactions to the recorded music played over the loudspeakers. Songs by favorite groups are greeted with much cheering. Nonmetal groups, especially pop or disco bands, are emphatically hooted and booed.[12] Bands often supply tapes of music that they wish to have played before they take the stage. Some metal groups play tapes of the music that has influenced them, which may include classical music from appropriate nineteenth-century romantic composers.[13] The recorded music, whatever else it is and evokes, is not the live music that the audience has come to hear. It makes the audience aware of waiting, increasing their anxious anticipation and excitement.

Indulging in the approved alcoholic beverages and drugs is another feature of the wait. Martinis or fancy mixed drinks with decorations are not to be found at heavy metal concerts. Some fans sneak in a pint of Jack Daniels or other hard stuff, but the drink of choice is beer. Quality is not the issue; only quantity matters. Fans delight in big containers. If only small cups are sold, people insert their full cup at the top of a growing column of empties. Beer has a Dionysian significance at the concert, aiding and representing release into ecstatic experience.

When drugs are used, the drug of choice is pot, whose smoke, especially before the "War on Drugs" in the United States, was thick enough in the air to provide those not directly indulging with a "contact high." But the antidrug war has even permeated heavy metal concerts. W.A.S.P., in 1989 concerts, showed a film and lectured the audience about the evils of crack, coke, and heroin. The crowd cheered when it was over.[14] W.A.S.P., however, made no mention of beer (or of any alcohol) or of pot. Quaaludes are also frequently consumed at concerts. Their effect is described as being similar to drinking a six-pack of beer, without the need to continually empty one's bladder. A visible side effect of ingesting 'ludes is the desire/need to spit constantly. Belying their slob image, most fans use an empty cup, placed on the floor between their legs, as a cuspidor. Other drugs are not unknown. Cocaine use became evident when cocaine became popular with older and more affluent adolescents. It was not snorted dramatically from mirrors with rolled-up bills, but was taken surreptitiously with small inhalers made for the purpose. Coke was usually not shared, except between very close friends.

Drugs, of course, are found at other rock concerts. At Grateful Dead concerts they are rather openly hawked in the parking lots: "Shrooms! Tabs!" yell the sellers. Pearson suggests that the Deadhead's "sacramental use of drugs dates back to the origins of . . . Acid Tests in the mid-1960s, and is inextricably linked to the scene's origins."[15] For the metal subculture drugs have no ritual significance; they are used simply to promote the experience of getting wasted. The behavior exhibited by those who indulge in drugs at concerts is not very different from that of those who "just say no." This observation was confirmed at Christian metal concerts, where the members of the audience do not "do" drugs or alcohol, but behave no differently than a secular group of headbangers.

The audience builds solidarity through its commitment to the concert. Travel times, waiting on line, and ticket and merchandise costs are burdens that are stoically, and sometimes proudly, borne. At outdoor and at crowded, smokey indoor venues the ambient climate is another ordeal. A British metal fan notes some of these inconveniences: "Donington for me, and for every other headbanger in this country, is the heavy metal event of the year. You might not go to any concerts in the year, but you just can't miss Donington. But Donny has to be the worst [outside] venue in England, because it's in the middle of nowhere, there's no proper parking for cars, bikes, coaches, etc. Everything is so badly disorganized. Of course when you get to it it's one big rip off. The cost of sweatshirts is around £20.00, tee shirts are around £8–£12.00 and programmes cost £5.00, plus you have to wait for ages in the queue, and being England, 9 out of 10 times it rains. This is the biggest pain in the arse, standing on the same spot for ten hours in the pouring rain, with mud up to your knees. . . . Don't get me wrong, I'm not having a moan, that's the way it is. You can have one hell of a good time. . . . it's a pity it's only once a year."[16] One bears these costs proudly, just as the member of the subculture bears the image of the proud pariah.

Finally, the audience must constitute itself as a community of comradeship, albeit a transient one. Using Tönnies's term, the members of the audience create a *gemeinschaft*. Far from being calculating and suspicious, as participants in a *gesellschaft* are, they behave in a manner closer to the ideal of *philia*, the "brotherly love" that was valued in the hippie counterculture. Goods are shared with others, including with those who are not known to one another except as members of the audience. Joints and cigarettes are passed around, and so is beer when it is hard to obtain otherwise. Those who bring binoculars not only share them with neighbors who ask to use them, but often proffer them to those nearby. Consideration for others, a basic politeness, is another characteristic of the *gemeinschaft* created by the heavy metal audience. Places on line, seats, and even undemarcated floor spots are saved, and not just for friends. For some time I thought that the amicable treatment I received was due to my demographics, my status as an adult female. I thought I was being indulged, sort of like a pet. But I started to notice that behavior toward me, or toward other females or older audience members, was no different from conduct toward the demographically modal seventeen-year-old males.

People make sure that they are not blocking the view of someone far shorter than they are. If asked to move slightly, they respond with alacrity. Walking around the concert area before or after the show, when the foot traffic is very dense, people try hard not to bump into one another. Similarly, even when standing packed in front of the stage, the proxemic rule of metal is observed: Do not touch. If you happen by accident to do so, you give a brief nod of apology.[17] People walking around on crutches or with canes are safer in a metal crowd than on a crowded city sidewalk.[18] That these standards of behavior exist is evidenced by the outrage expressed at growing signs of their violation. "More and more people don't give a damn about their fellow metal fans," complains one headbanger. More will be said about reactions such as this one when the rules of thrash concerts are discussed.

Every so often a beach ball, inflated condom, beer cup, glow-in-the-dark plastic novelty, roll of toilet paper, or some similar object is seen sailing around the waiting audience. This play symbolizes the relations among those in the arena. The object is a gift freely given to any member of the audience. It is not kept but reciprocated by giving it to someone else. The choice of the recipient is random, showing that all members of the audience are equal.

Frontstage Story

The audience has done its work. It is now a pumped-up, self-conscious, and unified metal community. The backstage workers have completed their preparations. The stage is ready, the mikes have been tested, the bottles of beer are strategically placed for easy reach, and the little red lights on the stacks of amplifiers are lit. Everything is at the ready, but nothing is happening. Someone starts chanting and immediately all join in the refrain: "We want Sabbath, we want Sabbath," or "Priest, Priest," or "Maiden, Maiden." Fans intone the familiar form of the band's name, rather than its official name, over and over. The duration of the chanting is a good indication of the esteem in which the band is held by the audience and of its own level of excitement. But sooner or later the voices die down, only to start up again some time later. Then, during the chants or between them, the wished-for signs occur. The recorded music stops and the house lights go out, leaving the audience in a primordial darkness. Everyone immediately rises, feet either planted on the floor or atop seats, and they produce a deafening roar. Cigarette lighters are held ablaze. A split second later (or was it a lifetime?) the audience is drowned out by the blasts of magisterial music preceded by the excited cry of a local deejay at the microphone yelling a brief introduction to the group, and the stage emerges from its blackness.

One cannot make sense of what one sees immediately. One blinks and stares; the effect is somewhat like emerging from a long, dark tunnel. But this is no ordinary vision, and eyes widen in amazement and disbelief at what they see. The band is simply there, emerging from nowhere, out of the dark and often out of flashpots or fog. Concentrating on the performers is made difficult by the stage set, which commands the center of visual attention. Before what the set represents can be understood, it is perceived as shapes and color.

What is it? Materially it is wood, cloth, metal, and paint; surfaces receiving and reflecting a myriad of moving lights of different colors and intensities. The stage set is hard to read because it is an illusion of something else. What is it supposed to be? One must look more closely because it is not a depiction of some ordinary, familiar scene. It is something like a castle, or maybe like a dungeon, or, most often, it is not specifically anything. What is seen and the way it comes into being is the stuff of fantasy, of dreams, not of this world.

The concert starts, following the order established in AC/DC's proclamation that there be sound, light, drums, and guitar. But that is not all. As a whole, a heavy metal concert encompasses a very dense and wide variety of communicative actions, which produce three distinctive results or consummations that define the concert as the epitome of the heavy metal culture and especially of the subculture of the core audience.

The first consummation is pleasure, experiencing an exciting entertainment, the perfection of which is ecstasy. The second consummation is the representation of the heavy metal subculture to itself in an idealized form, a form in which the members of the subculture can take pride. The third consummation is the bonding of the audience and the band with one another. These consummations of the frontstage stand in stark contrast to the backstage instrumental activity of the working man, even though their content is, in great part, a blue-collar romance. All of the consummations are for the audience, and each one reinforces the other two: the concert exists as a social, though not as a cultural or economic, form for the fulfillment of the audience. In describing what goes on at the concert, I will relate the typical communicative actions to their characteristic consummations for the audience.

Ecstasy

Ecstasy is the extreme form of pleasure and enjoyment, the attachment of heightened excitement to sources of delight. An ecstatic experience eliminates calculative rationality and circumspective concern. It removes the everyday-life world, with its remembrance of things past and its anticipation of things to come. It is the experience of falling into the moment; time stands still. When the excitement is not so strong, the experience can be characterized as having a good time, enjoying a pleasant diversion. But what the members of the core audience really seek is a true ecstatic experience. They refer to the experience as "awesome" and "wow," using terminology appropriately borrowed from hippies describing great acid trips.

Ecstasy at a heavy metal concert requires more than the music. There must also be a great deal of excitement generated by non-sonic means. There are many ways of creating excitement, and all three actors that constitute the concert—the band, the backstage crew, and the audience—do their part to raise the emotional pitch. Excitement does not just happen at a heavy metal concert. It is planned for, worked on, and strongly encouraged. Having multiple sources of excitement means that audience members with different sensibilities will all be reached. It also means that one source will reinforce and heighten others, ideally producing an upward spiral. As the concert gets underway the audience is immediately assaulted by a multitude of visual and aural stimuli. Rock concerts have evolved into prototypical multimedia events. A heavy metal concert is a multisensory experience, which can only be described by de-taching its components from the felt whole that they jointly create. Each of the senses is simultaneously receiving variegated but con-stant stimulation, with a mutually reinforcing impact. After a time the listener/viewer experiences a sense of sensory overload, which itself enhances emotionality and, indeed, produces the final con-summatory emotion, the experience of being totally relaxed and done in, "wasted."

Let there be sound! The sound is loud, the sound is music, and the sound is heavy metal. Each of these three aspects contribute to excitement. The volume is so loud that it startles. Small children cry and everyone else is called to attention. Heavy metal prides itself on being the loudest musical genre.[19] When Black Sabbath was starting out, the band supposedly blasted their music in an attempt to be noticed by somewhat indifferent audiences.[20] But whatever the origin of the practice, metal bands play in the danger range, risking sonic pain. Whether hearing is ultimately damaged by this exposure is debatable.[21] Loud sounds, however, are known to raise adrenalin levels, a major factor in stimulating excitement.

This physiological response is the natural reaction to danger; but here loudness is a play form, not the roar of a predator or the report of a gunshot signaling actual harm.

Sheer volume of sound, the critics of metal notwithstanding, is not the whole story. Metal is a form of music, and the impact of music on the emotions has been noted throughout history. Whether music is judged to be delightful, as Martin Luther judged it to be;[22] dangerous and, thus, demanding proper control by the state, after Plato's fashion; or the only thing that makes life worth living, as Schopenhauer argued, the emotional power of music has been widely understood. In contemporary communication theory, Lull, for example, contends, "Music can elicit feelings of mental and physical 'ecstasy' that can lead to 'peak experiences,' a kind of sensual stimulation that may be matched only by sex."[23] The ecstasy associated with music is not limited to the "more primitive" forms. Classical concert-pianist Glenn Gould identified ecstasy as an aim of his musical practices, "a matter of being lifted out, stepping away—as a musical goal."[24]

Explaining why music has such an emotional effect, John Dewey calls the ear "the emotional sense." Unlike sight, which initially needs to be interpreted, sound agitates directly.[25] A more sociological interpretation, which is especially pertinent to the adolescent, is that music relaxes because it contrasts with verbal communications, which are associated with repressive orders.[26] Physiologically, strongly rhythmic music, such as heavy metal, increases breath and blood-pressure rates.[27] Runners are familiar with the "runner's high," which kicks in after a certain level of activity has been reached. Despisers of rock music have used the metaphor of the drug experience for their own purposes. A Soviet writer stated that rock music is similar to a shot of morphine in that it heightens the emotions and reduces any feelings of pain. Soviet scientists specifically indicted heavy metal, reporting that its fans were found to have high pulse rates and "jangled nerves." The listeners were said to be hooked on the music, as if they had taken morphine. Indeed, when a machine factory no longer allowed heavy metal to be heard during work time, the workers were reported to have gone through a "withdrawal phase," during which their productivity was cut in half.[28]

Part of the impact of heavy metal music on the emotions is based on moving the body in time with its beat. The audience does not dance at heavy metal concerts, but is nonetheless engaged in continuous kinesthetic activity.[29] The metonymic term "headbanger" refers to keeping the beat by making up-and-down motions of the head.[30] Another popular gesture is thrusting an arm upward, at a 45° angle, in a punching motion. Many fans tap a foot in time to the music too. Psychologist James E. Fletcher claims that these movements "by increasing the neural flow synchronized with the music, should emphasize or make more prominent this 'transporting' effect of the music."[31] Fletcher's conclusion is particularly appropriate for headbangers: "If this druglike effect of popular music is the typical case in devotees of popular music, then it would not be surprising to see fans rearrange interpersonal loyalties in order to protect the source of such pleasure."[32]

Live performance itself is a contributor to heightened emotion due to the possibility that the performers will make errors.[33] In contrast to the recording studio, there are no retakes or splicing at a concert. The band is walking a tightrope without a net.

The emotional impact of the music is augmented in metal by the sound of the singer's voice. It is not flat, maintaining a studied lack of emotion, as in the punk genre, but goes to the opposite extreme, betraying the influence of the blues and its cri-de-coeur spirit. It is only by dint of much training or great repression that human beings fail to be touched by the strongly expressed emotions of others. At the metal concert the emphasis is on relaxing constraint and desublimating, on being open to the performer's emotions. The vocals are reinforced by the singer's facial expression, "a 'look' of transcendence—half open eyelids and mouth."[34]

Let there be light! Many of the visuals, which are particularly imposing in larger venues, are geared to provoke excitement. Stage sets are bigger than life and stand out in their illumination from the darkened auditorium. As in a movie theater, suspension of disbelief is encouraged. Credulity coupled with the fantastic sights of the stage set, the lighting, and the assorted special effects, from laser lights to giant monsters, make a formula for excitement that rock concerts did not invent. Designers of religious ceremonies and theatricals have been using such tricks for centuries. Aldous Huxley, in his book *Heaven and Hell* (which shares its title with a Black Sabbath album) assesses the impact of visual spectacle. He is talking about the theater, but his remarks also apply to any of the concerts on Sabbath's "Heaven and Hell" tour, and to heavy metal concerts in general. The lighting effects transfigure the backdrops, the props, and the costumes "so that they became capable of transporting the spectators toward that Other World, which lies at the back of every mind, however perfect its adaptation to the exigencies of social life. . . . [They] . . . project beams of preternatural light, and preternatural light evokes, in everything it touches, preternatural color and preternatural significance. Even the silliest spectacle can be rather wonderful."[35]

Heavy metal has a long tradition of concert spectacle, starting with its borrowings from psychedelic light shows. In the mid-1970s Judas Priest introduced a biker-from-hell look to the metal stage: "The members of Judas Priest wore leather and metal studs in abundance, giving heavy metal a visual image it previously lacked."[36] Priest's singer, Rob Halford, generally makes his stage entrance atop a Harley. One should note that prior to his musical career Halford was involved in theatrical lighting. He remarks, "In concert, heavy metal is larger than life, so we performers try to look larger than life ourselves, as a sort of visual representation of the music."[37] As Halford's comment indicates, many of the features of a concert that foster emotion are also expressions of the heavy metal subculture.

MTV has probably goaded bands to augment their spectacles, since the production values of the videos placed stage presentations in an unfavorable comparison with them.[38] Extremes of theatricality are seen in concerts by bands such as Mötley Crüe, whose extravaganzas are particularly extravagant. In their 1990 show drummer Tommy Lee traveled around on a monorail-cum-drum-kit, high above the audience, bashing his drums as the Disney-like ride brought him, revolving, toward the stage.

Representing the Subculture

At its best, as an emotional experience, the concert creates a heightened level of excitement, achieving the peak of ecstasy. But, as Rob Halford implied above, it is also something more, an opportunity to represent and affirm the heavy metal subculture's values and norms, to realize that subculture as a community. That is, the concert is a semiotic thicket.

As the band goes through its musical and theatrical routine, and the audience encourages and reacts to the performance, representations of the heavy metal subculture fill the venue. Reading a heavy metal concert involves decoding a complex array of communicative acts by using the heavy metal codebook.

There are myriad ways of signifying the subculture. Much of the burden, obviously, is carried by the music itself, both lyrically and sonically. Added to the music is the body language of the musicians, their facial expressions and individual and collective gestures. Band members also communicate by talking to, touching, and throwing things into the audience. Further, the backstage crew communicates via the lighting, sound system, stage sets, and the design of the venue.[39]

Any given communicative act may be overdetermined, that is, it may signify several themes rather than just one. Moreover, signifiers can also be overdetermined in the sense that they can function not only to represent the subculture to itself, but to elicit excitement and/or to bond the audience and the band.

The following discussion can only hint at how the subculture is represented at the concert. The signifiers are far too numerous and varied to catalogue here. They form a bricolage, not a system, and, as such, cannot be ranged under a single principle. An adequate ethnographic analysis of just one heavy metal concert would constitute a book by itself.

The songs performed by the band embody the values of the subculture. The ones that the band selects to play are not randomly chosen from its repertoire, particularly if it has released several albums. Concert favorites are those giving voice to subcultural themes by idealizing them. For example, the value of pot and beer are extolled, respectively, in Black Sabbath's "Sweet Leaf" and W.A.S.P.'s "Blind in Texas," which those bands are sure to include in their concert repertoires.

The visual spectacle of metal concerts, particularly the stage set and props, follow Halford's principle of representing and symbolizing the genre. Many of the items echo the gothic-horror or heroic-fantasy motifs that adorn so many heavy metal album covers. An elaborate example of the gothic aesthetic was the spectacle of Ronnie James Dio's mid-1980s Sacred Heart tour. The basic set consisted of a castle, with turrets, parapets, and a blazingly lighted entrance. Atop the castle was an elaborate drum kit. The drummer was almost twenty feet off the ground, at the same height as the head of a moving, smoke-emitting, red, laser-eyed dragon. The band shared the stage with two eight-foot-tall robots who fought alongside (or was it against?) Dio with laser beams. Iron Maiden's stage sets, and their twelve-foot-tall Frankensteinish "alter ego" Eddie, resonate the gothic element, as does the group's name.

The gothic motif represents and idealizes the proud-pariah self-image in complex ways. The heavy metal subculture identifies with, or at the least, is fascinated by the monster, who is feared by and excluded from society. But it also identifies with the hero, who defends goodness against evil forces, often those who control society. These opposite mythemes, often present in the same imagery, are objectifications of the bricolage-persona of the proud pariah.

More frequently, the heavy metal bands look like blue-collar rather than fantasy heroes. Tattooed, booted, sweating, with muscled arms and hairy chests exposed, heavy metal performers eschew all bourgeois and yuppie symbols. They are proud blue-collar laborers, loving and proficiently using the tools of their trade. Their instruments are not worn with use, like the guitars of blues musicians, which show longtime attachment to an alter ego; nor are they battered clunkers like punk guitars, which symbolize the no-future, destructive image of that genre. Heavy metal instruments must gleam, like polished metal. Guitars are finished in some vivid color or striking design. Their surfaces reflect the high-tech standards demanded for the music by the subculture, an idealization of blue-collar working life in a technological age. The elaborate drum kit, with myriad surfaces on which the drummer can make a wide array of sounds, also symbolizes the power of production.

The love of the tools of their trade—their instruments—and the appreciation of modern technology are values of the subculture. They go along with the value of virtuosity, the ability to use these tools in an exemplary manner. The hero is the guitar god. The projection of the lead guitarist as hero has become clichéd, but no metal concert can dispense with the symbol. The singer shares the spotlight, in alternation with the guitarist, on each song. The guitarist is given one or more long solos during which the singer and sometimes the other musicians leave him alone on the stage.

The guitarist does not just play very well: he dramatizes playing well. His spread-eagle stance and facial expression denote total absorption in a difficult task. The fact that he may not be playing a particularly difficult piece, especially since he has played it many times before, is not relevant. Many of the guitarists choose to play visually exciting pieces, going up and down the fretboard at break-neck speed. Showmanship, such as playing the guitar behind one's neck, with one's teeth, or while someone else is holding it, is a long-standing metal tradition, traceable to culture heroes such as Jimi Hendrix. During the guitar solos the fans focus their attention too. Their identification with the values of the guitar hero can be seen in their imitative air-guitar play. Only a fraction of those in the audience seriously aspire to be on stage. But they all feel at one with the idealized representative of their values.

The value of blue collar and the related behavior of *épater le bourgeois* (shocking the establishment) is expressed in the speech patterns of the performers when they talk directly to the audience. Their discourse is peppered with every curse word still capable of conveying shock value. In addition, British performers speak in an exaggerated lower-class accent, the antithesis of a refined accent.

The value of the blue-collar worker is shown by representing the exertion of work. Displays of energy are universally demanded of the singer and drummer. They serve to embody, literally and fig-uratively, the value of work. Angus Young, AC/DC's guitarist, con-stantly does "six-string wind sprints" from one side of the stage to the other; it has been estimated that in one decade he had traveled almost 3,000 miles on stage.[40] Sets have ramps, or at least a drum riser, permitting the singer to move up and down. The folkie astride a stool and the crooner planted all evening at the mike stand are excluded by the code of heavy metal. One key to a metal perfor-mance is the power of its passionate activity.

The movement and the heat of the lights cause the performers to sweat profusely. Honest sweat, the emblem of having worked, is another badge of labor. The clothing and hairstyles in metal (more so in classical and thrash metal than in lite metal) make the sweat easily visible to the audience. Long hair becomes matted and plastered to the sides of the face. Bare chests gleaming with sweat are on display, framed by leather vests. Going bare-chested altogether, after a few songs or on returning to the stage for an encore, is a common practice that emphasizes the masculine, blue-collar mystique. The stage costumes, whether T-shirts and jeans, or designer-spandex outfits, also contribute to the representation of blue-collar values. They permit the display of well-developed muscles.

The swearing and the sweating, the combination of master craftsmanship and high-tech, and the clothes represent not only a blue-collar romance but also an idealization of masculinity. The value of machismo is manifested in a variety of ways at the concert, most of them involving male bonding. Some analysts have called attention to these activities with the term "cock rock." Guitar playing, for example, is interpreted as a symbol of masturbation. Cock rock, which is specifically applied to designate such bands as Mötley Crüe, Twisted Sister, and Iron Maiden, is understood as "an explicit, crude and often aggressive expression of male sexuality."[41] The spandex costumes serve as showcases for the pumped-up body, including the muscle that gets pumped up by lust rather than by a workout at the gym. The familiar stage choreography, in which the singer and guitarist lean into one another, can be clearly read as male bonding, and it also assures the audience that the members of the band are united, providing the audience with a model of male bonding to emulate.[42]

The value of masculinism is also expressed in the band's attitudes toward females. Women, on stage or in the audience, are either sex objects to be used or abused, or must renounce their gender and pretend to be one of the boys. The few female metal performers must conform to the masculinist code, and have generally opted to appear as sex objects.

Some metal bands have developed an overtly sexist shtick as part of their performance. One such group is W.A.S.P. During the Chicago stop of its 1989 tour, Blackie Lawless, W.A.S.P.'s singer, introduced one of the band's most popular songs, "Animal (F**k Like a Beast)," which holds a place of honor near the top of the PMRC's hate list. In line with the code of heavy metal, the fans who were partial to the song, which in this case was most of the audience, stood up. A girl of about seventeen, sitting with another girl three rows in front of me, stood up and thrust out her hand in the classical appreciative salute during Blackie's introduction. This was one of her favorite songs. Then Blackie asked, as he leered and described a female figure with his hands: "Anyone here come to get some *pussy?*" As he said the last word very slowly and deliberately, the crowd roared its affirmative response. But before they did so, when the word was being uttered, the girl abruptly sat down. She obviously realized that it would be inappropriate for her to participate in this wild appreciation. It was fine to stand for the song itself, which did not exclude females from enjoying animal lust. It was the word "pussy" that labeled females as pure objects, not as pleasure-seeking or pleasure-obtaining subjects, that excluded her. The song then began and she stood up with the rest of the crowd to savor it.[43]

Dramatic enactions of or boastful stories about power over women are not only expressions of machismo, but of power, especially the vital power of youth to expend energy. If heavy metal concerts are about anything, they are about youthful power. Bulging biceps signify that power, as does frenzied playing of instruments. No particular strength is needed to play the electric guitar, but performers suggest the opposite through the use of facial grimaces and body stances that indicate a great deal of brawn is required to handle the instrument. The spectacle of the drummer, bashing away at the variety of percussion devices that surrounds him, is the embodiment of energy. The sound itself, its booming volume and emphasis on the lower registers, projects power. The sound is not only heard but felt. The physical properties of sound require the lower tones to be amplified many times more than the middle and upper registers, if they are to be equally audible.[44] The sound is powerful in concert, not only metaphorically, but in a literal, tactile sense—an assertion of the youthful capacity to tolerate large quanta of sensory stimuli.

The lighting, too, is an expression of power. Multicolored lighting is a rock-concert staple, filling the stage from above the performers and giving those toward the back of the venue a larger scene to enjoy. In metal the lights are not visual distractions, but signifiers of energy. Flashpots explode; strobes mesmerize. The changes in the overhead lighting from one set of colors to another are more abrupt and far less subtle than in concerts for other musical genres.[45] The changes punctuate the atmosphere much like the arm thrusts. The spectrum of colors shown at heavy metal concerts also signify power, with the emphasis on the hot reds rather than the cool blues. Blue tends to have a calming effect, whereas red, the color of blood, demands attention. Laboratory researchers have found that red enhances physical strength.[46] Rob Halford puts it bluntly, "First, heavy metal is power."[47]

The power of the performer, as the hero who idealizes the subculture, is made explicit by spot-lighting. It is symbolized by the fact that the audience must do the waiting.[48] Fans wait on line to buy tickets and to enter the venue, and they wait for the band to take the stage. Concerts rarely have one band. Usually, a new or less famous band opens for the major attraction. The power of the headline band is illustrated by its contrast with the opening act. Not only does the audience show the headliners more respect by refraining from coming in or walking around during its set, but the symbols of power are unequally distributed. The opening band is required to play at a lower volume, has the use of fewer lights, and is given only a portion of the stage on which to move around.

As a vehicle for idealizing the heavy metal subculture for its members, the concert creates a quasi-community among the members of the audience. One critic got it partly right when she observed that concerts provide fans with "the sense of belonging to a secret society, complete with codes and initiation rites."[49] But this comment makes it seem that the sense of belonging is created at the concert from an atomized aggregate, which is not true. Nor is the society meant to be secret. At the concert an already existing subculture becomes concretized in a transitory community through the projection of itself in an idealized form.

Creating the Community

The concert represents the heavy metal subculture to its members in an idealized form, but it also relates the members to the wider culture of heavy metal by bonding them with each other in a transitory community. That community is, to be sure, a semblance of a continuous community, but for the duration of a few hours it genuinely comes into being, with an apparent past and future. The performers employ many methods to create the community. Moreover, the members of the audience come prepared to participate in communion, looking and behaving in a manner that stresses shared values. Further, their responses to the music—moving to it and cheering their favorites—assist in forging solidarity. Social psychologist Carl Couch finds that "The display of affect with others—in unison—does not assure the formation of a solidary relationship, but displays of affect in unison are necessary if a solidary relationship is to mature."[50]

Getting the audience to behave in harmony with one another is the basic way of forming the concert community. Eliciting cheers, applause, and other signs of gratitude and enthusiasm is a feature of all concerts, but heavy metal bands employ a large number of devices to provoke a positive response. Solos, encores, announcing the name of the next song to be played, mentioning the name of the city, feats of derring-do, and special effects all get the members of the audience to express their delight together. Having the audience act as one by singing is another well-worn device. Words of encouragement to sing along—"Sing it! I can't hear you!"—are staples, as is having the singer stop while the rest of the band continues playing, allowing the audience to fill in the singer's part. He turns his microphone toward the audience with the assumption that they will know the words. When Helloween does this during their song "Future World," the singer stops at a telling phrase and the crowd continues the song, singing "We all live in future world,"[51] underscoring their sense of community in the special world of the concert. The audience is often broken into halves, such as balcony and main floor, or left and right sides, and goaded into a singing or shouting competition with one another. Sociologists, such as Durkheim and Simmel, have argued that competing moieties enhance the solidarity of the whole community.

It is important to note that heavy metal artists can use so many and such direct devices to involve the audience because that audience is already prepared to respond enthusiastically. For example, a popular band can count on the audience to sing along, making the exertions to get them to do so something of a ritual game in which the band pays obeisance to the audience by coaxing it. If the band cannot count on a favorable response, it will avoid the risk of trying to provoke one.

Bands are sure to play their anthemic metal songs, which proclaim and praise the community of heavy metal. Each group has at least one in its repertoire, noteworthy examples being Saxon's "Denim and Leather," and Running Wild's "Chains and Leather," UFO's "Lights Out," Judas Priest's "Living After Midnight," and Iron Maiden's "Two Minutes to Midnight." Music has always been used to celebrate and stimulate community. Religious groups incorporate music into their celebrations and nation states and Japanese corporations have followed their lead. George Lewis maintains that using music at gatherings enhances "feelings of communal belonging and social solidarity. Such social rituals, when they are effective, help to emotionally charge the interests members of these groups hold in common, elevating them to moral rights and surrounding them with a sort of symbolic 'halo of righteousness.' "[52]

Spoken words also function to create solidarity. Indeed, much of the singer's chatter between songs can be read as rhetorical appeals to a sense of community. These comments stress the fan's collective knowledge of metal's history, and allude to the past and future of the community. Remarks such as "See you next year" and "It's been a long time since we've been here" are examples of connecting the present to a wider communal time frame, as are allusions to songs that were first done with other bands: "We should like to do this one for you—a song that you've not heard from us in a long, long time, I'm sure. It is a song done . . . when we were in another band."[53]

The singer also binds the local audience to the general metal community. He usually makes some favorable comment about the city in which the concert is being performed, and speaks at least a few words in the audience's native tongue at concerts in countries where English is not spoken. Performers also make reference to the particular situation in the local area. For example, Dio introduced a song to a rain-soaked crowd at Castle Donington, by saying, "This is something that really applies to all of us here: 'Naked in the Rain.' "[54] At Christian metal concerts the singer shouts "Jesus loves you!" to the rousing cheers of the audience. Such devices are used at many concerts in various musical genres. But they are employed by heavy metal artists with greater frequency, in part because they can count on enthusiastic audience response.

Rallying the audience to the cause of heavy metal by calling attention to its foes is a special method that recalls the appeals of religious and national groups to an external enemy in order to foster internal unity. The mass media's rejection of metal was one popular rhetorical theme. At a Black Sabbath concert in 1982 the singer said to the audience, "It's a good feeling to know you are successful because of yourself, not for what critics say, or what they play on the radio, or don't play on the radio."[55] Mentioning the names of bands that clash with heavy metal's symbols and sensibility also unify the audience by negation. Blackie Lawless frequently makes digs at MTV and criticizes nonmetal bands, as he screams to the audience such remarks as "Television videos suck. Fine Young Cannibals. Fine Young Assholes. New Kids on the Block. New kids who suck my cock!"[56] Each remark was greeted with uniform booing, creating a strong we-feeling. But perhaps the most useful enemies of heavy metal have been Tipper Gore and the PMRC, the spearheads of the antimetal movement. Their names are ubiquitously mentioned at concerts, and their menace to metal generates a circle-the-wagons mentality. Blackie Lawless, this time at London's Hammersmith in 1986, told the audience, "I've been reading a lot in the newspapers and the magazines about what they have been saying about me and my boys. You know what they say about us? They say we are sexual perverts! They say that W.A.S.P. are every parent's worst nightmare!" Cheers greeted each sentence, giving voice to the pride of the pariahs.

Bonding and Gratitude between the Artist and the Audience

All of the devices by which the band involves the audience in the concert performance strengthens the bond of identity between the band and the audience. Metal's message is that "the bands and the fans were all in it together."[57] The singer, for example, identifies with the locale of the audience, and the audience identifies with the singer by completing his lines. Both identify with each other in a common disdain for a common enemy of their culture. The call and response patterns bring the audience closer to the band. The pattern is similar to the one used by a Baptist minister, who is both part of the church community and above it. The parishioners constantly interject words of assent. In contrast, in the Catholic church service or a classical-music concert, the communicants save their expressions of appreciation for a final "amen"/applause.

The artist, however, is not merely a member of the heavy metal culture on a par with the audience, but someone who is different from the audience, a culture hero who stands above it. The distance of artist from audience is maintained by all of the ways in which the artist represents the subculture to its members in an idealized form. But lest that distance become too great, rituals of compensation exist through which artist and audience constitute a community through their differences, by mutual acknowledgment.

The basic means of creating unity through difference is the act of appreciation, gratitude, and adoration.[58] Noisily cheering, screaming, whistling, clapping, and stomping, the members of the audience use a host of sound-producing parts of the body to express to the band, and to the rest of the audience and to themselves, their profound pleasure at the performance. They are not crying in the wilderness; the band acknowledges their tributes. In addition to the performers' smiles and nods of notice, they receive verbal responses such as "Thank you! Thank you so much!" and "I'm glad you like that one." Heavy metal performers are the antithesis of the "aloof and distant" jazz musicians.[59]

The audience also expresses its gratitude by gesture. Sitting primly may be an appropriate way to listen to a symphony orchestra, but for a heavy metal band such deportment could only be read as a thumbs-down sign of displeasure. Standing is a sign of admiration, and standing on the seats is a special gesture of praise. Head-banging and arm thrusting are other messages of approval. The arm thrust may be done with the fist closed or with the two-fingered "malocchio" form of salute.[60] If a band member uses one of these two options on stage, the audience tends to imitate that one.

Since the house lights are off, the band cannot see the audience. How can they read these noiseless communiqués? On rare occasions the singer may yell, as Black Sabbath's did, "Turn the lights on so that we can see everyone's face."[61] However, the usual method is to allow those closest to the stage to represent the entire group. The stage lighting is extended so that the first few rows are not in the shadows. They are lit so that both the band and the rest of the audience can see them. The fans in front are the mediators, expressing the full audience to the band. The performers interact directly with this subgroup, making eye contact or bending down to shake their hands, and tossing guitar picks and drum sticks to them. Gifts are exchanged. They range from banners—usually hand-decorated bed sheets—to cups of beer, joints, T-shirts, and bras and panties. The remainder of the audience, those up in the nose-bleed section of the balcony or way in the back, understand these interactions as symbolically including them. The front of the crowd is their proxy.[62]

In addition to those nearest the stage, there is another specialized subset of the audience that bonds with and expresses gratitude: the groupies. They provide sexual services to the members of the band, before and after the concert. Prior to the advent of MTV, females wearing micromini skirts, fishnet stockings, and spiked heels were likely to be groupies. Now that look is a popular option for female headbangers, so that only a small fraction of those who might look like groupies really are. Unlike the fans who are near the stage, groupies are not appreciated by the rest of the audience. Many of the males think that their access to the performers is "unfair," even if they can identify with the recipient of the groupie's favors. This ambivalence reflects the balance of nearness and distance, of the artist's unity with the subculture and his special role of being a culture hero for it.

Thrash metal concerts are characterized by two practices to demonstrate appreciation and bonding that are not shared with other genres of metal. "Moshing" and "stage diving" were imported, along with some other conventions, into thrash metal from the punk/hardcore subculture. Moshing is a circle dance, which is similar to numerous folk-dance patterns found around the world. There is one moshing circle, called a "pit," located close to center stage and equally visible to the band and the rest of the audience. Moshing is a hard skipping, more or less in time to the music, in a circular, counterclockwise pattern. Elbows are often extended and used as bumpers, along with the shoulders. The action is reminiscent of bumper-car rides found at amusement parks. The ideal is a friendly jostling among those in the pit and between those in the pit and those located at its circumference.

Moshing is a modification of punk-style slam-dancing. The latter is a form of individual, not of group, dancing, and violent contact between members of the audience is expected. Traditional heavy metal fans are somewhat outraged by the moshing pits. They violate several of their standards, such as refraining from dancing and from physical contact. In the past few years many hardcore bands have changed their styles and have crossed over to thrash. They bring with them their hardcore audience, whose standards of audience decorum clash sharply with those of the headbangers. These crossover fans make explicit the violence that is merely hinted at in moshing. A self-proclaimed headbanger complained, "When Suicidal Tendencies came out the scene changed drastically. Slam dancing was definitely the primary activity during this act. I got far away from the stage, where the slam dancing was taking place, so as not to get 'attacked' by one of the dancers. It was amazing to watch people practically beat the crap out of other people and have fun, both giving and receiving the 'punishment.' It seemed as though hardly anyone was paying attention to the band because they were too busy slam dancing. I found this very different, to say the least, from the type of concerts I usually attend."[63]

Despite the lack of overt signs of attention by the moshers to the musicians, thrash bands read an active moshing pit as a sign that their music is appreciated, reflecting the energy of the band's performance. Small clubs without seats easily accommodate moshing. Thrash bands whose popularity allows them to play larger venues, where the floor area is generally covered with seats, cannot receive this communication. Both they and their audience are frustrated by the blocked channel.

Another band-audience interaction that is specific to thrash is stage diving. This practice also comes from the punk/hardcore scene. As a kinesthetic signifier, it is a form of theatrical choreography, a fine example of Kenneth Burke's view that dramaturgy functions to secure identification.[64] Members of the audience climb up to the stage, touch or imitate the band members for a moment, and then dive back into the audience. The style of the dive is the belly flop, but instead of water the divers land on the outstretched hands of the audience. That they are caught, and prevented from crashing on the hard floor, is a sign of audience solidarity, although there are times when a diver painfully overestimates that solidarity. Punk singers tend to return the gesture, by diving into the audience. This practice is not unknown in thrash, but is less common there.

Except for thrash, touching or mingling between artists and fans is highly restricted at metal concerts. Philip Bashe comments, "Interestingly, unlike most rock fans, heavy metal fans are probably the least compelled to meet their heroes outside the confines of the stage show."[65] The encounter occurs during the concert, symbolically. The artists touch the fans in the first row and walk out on stage extensions that allow an artist to be both "on stage" and "in the audience" simultaneously. There are a few exceptions to the code of limiting contact, which tend to prove the rule. For example, AC/DC's guitarist Angus Young is noted for his forays into the audience, astride the shoulders of singer Bon Scott or a roadie, without interrupting his playing.

The contrast between the codes of appreciation in heavy metal and thrash metal highlight the significance of maintaining a distance between audience and artist in the former. In heavy metal the artist must finally be an idealized representative of the subculture, the transient incarnation of a culture hero. Therefore, certain taboos on contact must be respected. Further, in witnessing their subculture represented to them, the members of the audience must be more involved with the performance than with each other; that is, even their joint rituals must relate them to the performance. In thrash, the artist is much less a culture hero than a specialized member of the subculture, providing an element of the concert experience rather than being its raison d'être. Thus, thrash bands try to "hang out" with the fans before and after the show. Other metal musicians do not follow this practice, nor do their fans expect them to.

In their assessment of rock concerts, Montague and Morais assert, "The order of material in the concert is aimed at gradually heightening the performer-audience bond."[66] Heavy metal concerts radically emphasize this bond, but because of the solidarity of the core audience it remains at the same high intensity from the beginning to the end of the concert. The band does not have to convince the audience to be enthused. Indeed, the elaborate, highly ritualized encore at heavy metal concerts strongly resembles the initial appearance of the band. The band can count on the audience to express its desire to have the interaction continue. The members of the audience plead with the band to return to them, shouting their name and standing with flames in the dark. The religious overtones of holding Bics as simulacra of lighted candles are even more obvious if one believes that the practice originated at Led Zeppelin concerts when the band played "Stairway to Heaven."[67]

The Concert as Hierophany

As the idealization of the culture of heavy metal the concert is "the definitive moment."[68] It makes a transient community of some members of a music-based subculture and bonds them with artists in a greater and more complex whole. In performing these functions the heavy metal concert is similar to concerts for other music-based youth subcultures, such as Deadheads and punks.

When the show is merely good, it is a heavy metal entertainment. But that is the diminished form of a heavy metal concert. At its best, when it realizes its ideal, it is an ecstatic experience, a celebration of heavy metal where the metal gods rule from the stage as culture heroes. When the emotion reaches a peak and the representation of the subculture and the bonding of artist and audience reinforce one another, the concert becomes an awesome experience. At the point of perfection, time stands still and one feels that one belongs to a higher reality, far away from the gray, everyday world. To see the dazed and confused, happily exhausted, faces of the crowd as it files out of the venue into the night; to hear the terse, whispered reviews—"Awesome, man," "That was really something!"—is to understand that a great heavy metal concert is not, or is not merely, an entertaining diversion. The fans have been "wasted," have been taken on a physical and emotional journey that leaves them satiated, satisfied, spent. For the moment, they could desire nothing else.

From a sociological perspective, the ideal heavy metal concert bears a striking resemblance to the celebrations, festivals, and ceremonies that characterize religions around the world. For Emile Durkheim, the preeminent sociologist of religion, celebrations are "the bringing together of normally isolated groups to celebrate, and indeed create, their corporate existence. . . . For a society to become conscious of itself and maintain at the necessary degree of intensity the sentiments which it thus attains, it must assemble and concentrate itself."[69] If fans of heavy metal were merely a taste public, the dissemination of the music by the mass media would be sufficient. But they are members of a subculture, and the concert experience is crucial for them.

The ecstasy, representations of the community to itself, the strong solidarity felt within the audience, and the bonds of mutual appreciation expressed by band and audience resemble features of religious festivals. Using the terminology of Mircea Eliade, ideal metal concerts can be described as hierophanies in which something sacred is revealed.[70] They are experienced as sacred, in contrast to the profane, everyday world. The sacred takes place in its own sacred time ("reversible, indefinitely repeatable") and place, where the *ens realissimum,* the greatest reality, is found.

The Artists as Mediators of the Concert

When the band takes the stage, the backstage activity is suspended or hidden.[71] The stage now belongs to the world of the frontstage, a world that is the antithesis of the backstage. The focus is not on work but on celebration. The instrumental rationality of the mediators (media and technicians) is replaced by the consummatory expressive emotion of the audience. Time dominates the backstage; time stands still in the frontstage. The wide variety of backstage personnel are united by their interdependence, their workmanlike attitude toward their different tasks, and their blasé attitude toward the band. Visually, their unity is expressed by their ever-present backstage passes, laminated for the boys on the bus, stick-on for the locals. Frontstage unity is based on a felt similarity, a recognition of oneself in others. It is the unity of shared identity, which Durkheim described as the basis of mechanical solidarity. The backstage has organic solidarity, as befits the modern world. The cohesion of the frontstage is of the ancient and primordial sort. Performing on stage, the band is in a netherworld that serves to separate the frontstage and the backstage. It is the site of the boundary, and the band is the boundary between the sacred and the profane, the consummatory and the instrumental.

The band mediates the *gesellschaft* of the media and the *gemeinschaft* of the audience, but only by sacrificing any unity of its own, except for the music itself and the moments of Dionysian ecstasy that its members may experience. It must appeal to different forms of authority in linking itself to the two worlds. Toward the audience, the band exerts a complex form of authority combining charismatic, traditional, and value-rational elements. That is, the band has the charismatic "gift" of the music, but it must also perform it in ways that satisfy the codes of heavy metal and make it part of an event that fulfills the values of the core audience. Here the artist is the leader of a transient community rooted in persisting signifiers and practices. Toward the technical apparatus, in contrast, the band's authority is legal-rational, based on contracts exchanging specified labor for specified remuneration, and on the certified or demonstrated expertise of the workers. The band members are captains and captives of each world. Mediating the two, the band is native to neither. The band members are strangers in two strange lands, and must ingratiate themselves, prove their loyalty, in each.

Backstage, their legitimacy is bought with gifts of tour jackets and tour bonuses, and by tributes of lavishly catered preconcert meals. After the concert the band makes its transition to the backstage world by means of the postconcert party, where representatives of the subculture—adoring groupies and media interviewers—interact with the band apart from any musical performance. Members of the touring crew are also present at the postconcert party. Indeed, the members of the band become, in a sense, members of the crew, parts of a team. They level themselves to be just one of the boys, often participating in debasement rituals of overindulgence in alcohol or drugs. That is, they must forge a new community backstage that compensates for the strains of inequality in the organic solidarity of the *gesellschaft*. It is always the band's job to build community.

The heavy metal communities created by the artists are always tenuous. That is obvious backstage, where *gesellschaft* can be softened but never made secondary. But it is also true frontstage. There is also a cash nexus out front. Admittance to the concert is not free and the tour promotes the band's latest album. The antibourgeois and anticommercial ideology of the heavy metal subculture requires artists to demonstrate that they are not tainted by the backstage world. The backstage is kept hidden during the concert, symbolically separating the artist from it. The band cannot be judged to have sold out, to have become Judas-priests to their followers. The whole array of practices that pervade the performance can be read as a rhetoric of authenticity, a demonstration of loyalty to the frontstage world. Among the signifiers of authenticity are the facial expressions of concentration, the sweat, and the displays of energy. Before coming out for an encore, band members may change clothes or walk back on stage with towels draped around their necks, underscoring the fact that they had sweated a great deal. Their profuse declarations of love to the audience—"I love you!"—do not merely promote bonding, but proclaim allegiance to the frontstage world.

The concert is a bricolage of frontstage and backstage, held together by a bricoleur, the artist. As much as any form of music, heavy metal illustrates the fundamental separation in modern life between the instrumental and the consummatory, here brought to reification in two separate and radically opposed worlds, which must be kept scrupulously apart. A predominantly commercial apparatus caters to a subculture that holds as its highest virtue remaining a proud pariah from that apparatus and the incentives that sustain it.

Yet both the apparatus and the subculture need each other. Their relations are simple and distant: the subculture pays and the apparatus delivers. The significance of the transaction can be forgotten by both of the parties to it. But the artists cannot forget it, because they are between both worlds, commodities to one and culture heroes to the other, never what they are most to themselves: artists. Most deeply, frontstage and backstage can never be mixed because the artist can never be a culture hero to the backstage and must never allow himself to be seen as a commodity by the frontstage. Here the artist is a trickster figure, the mediator of a nonlogical synthesis. The artist clings to the music as the thread that connects the moieties and thus becomes the manifestation of the metal culture to the outside world and the target of its critics.

Maligning the Music:
Metal Detractors

"Am I Evil?"
—*Metallica*

Perhaps Newton's Second Law of Motion, which states that for every action there is an equal and opposite reaction, also applies to some sociocultural phenomena. It certainly seems to hold for heavy metal. The intense loyalty and devotion of its fans is matched by the contempt and loathing for the genre expressed by those who presume to pass judgment on cultural phenomena. Indeed, it is hard to think of other human phenomena, outside child torture and cannibalism, that evoke such intense abhorrence. Heavy metal polarizes people. Those who are aware of it either love it or hate it.

The cultured and no-so-cultured despisers of heavy metal form an unfamiliar, if not unholy, alliance. Heavy metal is one of the few sociocultural phenomena in the United States that evokes the same response from those normally bitter opponents, the politically correct progressive critics and the religious and populist right wing. What is so special about heavy metal that has made it one of the few things that unite Left and Right in a common cause?

The maligners of metal come to their positions for superficially different reasons. To summarize what will be presented in detail below, the progressives repudiate heavy metal because it substitutes hedonic ecstasy for the political commitment and social concern that they would like to see in popular music. They find it difficult to criticize heavy metal on any intellectual basis because their system of criticism is framed by a dichotomy between serious and politically committed rock music and mass popular music, which takes the edge off life and pacifies the subjects of a disciplinary/consumer society. Heavy metal, as has been shown in the preceding chapters, is not commercial pop, but neither is it politically progressive. Its spirit is that of Dionysian rebellion that challenges static order in the name of the freedom to exercise vital power. The progressive critics have no place in their ideology for something like metal, which is not pop, but which also does not meet their criteria for good music.[1] Thus, they try to reduce metal to nonsense, making no effort to grasp it as a cultural form, and dismissing it as a revolt against form, "noise," and "drivel."[2]

The cultural conservatives, in contrast, do not play on the binary opposition of hedonism-commitment, but instead focus on what they see as the anti-Christian symbolism of metal. For them, heavy metal, with its themes of evil and use of symbols associated with Christian religiosity, is a systematic temptation whose aim is to lead youth into the paths of sin. Whereas for the progressives metal is a competitor for the rebellious energies of youth, for the conservatives it is a competitor for their souls. The root of the complaint, however, is the same. In metal Dionysian rebellion often takes the form of transvaluing—changing the value signs—of the objects of the Judeo-Christian tradition. Heavy metal stresses the power of the world as a positive dynamism, whereas the religious right condemns "the world," along with "the flesh and the devil." When heavy metal appropriates Christian symbolism, it absorbs it into its Dionysian sensibility, giving "the world, the flesh, and the devil" new meaning as rebellious play, as in AC/DC's thought that "Hell Ain't a Bad Place to Be." Metal's reinterpretation of these symbols is lost on the cultural conservatives, who stick to their own "literal" reading of those symbols. Their dichotomy is between faith and sin. Lacking any conception of a positive affirmation of rebellious vitality, they must judge heavy metal to be sinful and a direct competitor to them.

Heavy metal, then, is the common enemy because it is the proud pariah. It sins by excess of ecstasy and of play with symbols that some segments of the society hold sacred. The left is repelled by its focus on present pleasure rather than the need for future change, and the right is offended by its substitution of symbolic play for belief in their code. Of course, neither of metal's adversaries appreciates metal for what it is, since neither values Dionysian experience. Metal's ecstasy is seen as mindless and gross sensation by the progressives. Its play is viewed as a malign will to corrupt by the conservatives. Thus, the two opponents of metal distort it in their own ways, according to how they can fit it into the categories of their ideologies. Their policy stances toward the "social problem" of heavy metal reflect their ideological constructions of heavy metal rather than what heavy metal is to its fans, the artists who create it, its mediators, or an ethnographer. The public criticism of metal is as clear a case as can be presented of the tendency of the discussion of public policy to mischaracterize its objects through the projection of ideological constructions.

Progressive Criticism

Rock criticism was already established by the time heavy metal came on the scene. Gossip columnists had been attracted to rock and roll from its inception, but rock critics, who were dedicated to evaluating rock as a serious creative expression, if not an art form, emerged with the counterculture of the 1960s. Influenced by and initially concerned with Bob Dylan and the Beatles of the psychedelic era, rock criticism came into its own in 1967.[3] When Led Zeppelin and Black Sabbath erupted at the start of the 1970s, the critics responded to those bands and to their fans as a personal affront.

Sabbath and Zeppelin were rejected as musically "primitive," and their lyrics were derided as mindless and sexist. Bashe describes how heavy metal musicians and their fans "have been ridiculed as living contradictions to the theory of evolution" by the rock critics.[4] Black Sabbath's bassist, Geezer Butler, recalls, "Right from the start the rock journalists almost unanimously condemned the band as simple-minded noise."[5]

In his 1972 analysis of Black Sabbath, Lester Bangs concurred with Butler, remarking that the critics reacted as one in damning the band.[6] Bangs was one of the few rock critics who, at least initially, did not join the metal-bashing bandwagon. He argued that

Sabbath were moralists, like Bob Dylan and the novelist William Burroughs. He upped his rhetorical comparisons by stating that the group was "the John Milton of rock 'n' roll."[7] Critics Robert Palmer and Jon Pareles of the *New York Times* have also been exceptions to the rule of metal bashing. Palmer has argued that the "darker" kinds of metal, like other horror genres in popular culture, simply reflect the anxieties and problems of the society at large.[8]

Criticism of heavy metal has not changed much since the early 1970s. In an assessment of the resurgence of the genre in 1984, heavy metal was referred to as "that bête noire of rock progressivism."[9] In 1988 a rock critic for a major newspaper scored heavy metal's boasts of substance when it only came up with a "manipulated aura of mindless hedonism in place of fun, and virulent sexism instead of love."[10] Even when trying to argue against the conservative critics of metal, who seek to ban the music on moral grounds, *Rolling Stone* journalist Anthony DeCurtis could not avoid disapproving of the genre, observing that frequently metal and rap musicians express the biases of their fans. He would prefer them to challenge these perspectives, "channeling righteous anger into intelligent political action."[11] Rock criticism has always defined the meaning of music "in only one way: the ability, or anyway the desire, to shake up the world."[12]

Progressive criticism of heavy metal also appears in academic writings on rock. In an article about youth subcultures in Britain in the late 1970s and early 1980s, Ellis Cashmore compared the heavy metal subculture unfavorably to other music-based subcultures such as the rastas and punks that had "posed trenchant critiques and, in their own sometimes eccentric ways, alternatives. Romantics and heavy metal kids continued more disguised critiques but opted for strategies of measures designed to enhance their own lives, to ensure their own health of mind as opposed to upgrading others."[13] Heavy metal, according to Cashmore, was "a dinosaur of youth culture, surviving its contemporaries and lasting seemingly without change into the 1980s. The dress remained the same, as did the political apathy and, of course, the music."[14]

The progressivist critics agree that heavy metal is musically simplistic, "primitive," and unsophisticated; and that its lyrical themes are sexist paeans to hedonism and militate against hope for the future. Metal is "the beast that refuses to die," maintaining its traditions as other music-based subcultures change or become extinct. The progressive critics assume that they are speaking to and for a community with shared standards. When rock criticism came into being that was a fair assumption; indeed, the critics helped to inform an audience that was willing to learn. After the 1960s, however, rock music began to diversify and fragment. The counterculture dissolved and was replaced by a multitude of taste publics and several music-based subcultures. It was no longer fair for critics to assume a community with shared standards to which they could contribute enlightenment. But they continued to make that assumption, which, in the case of heavy metal, made them systematically fail to appreciate the inherent structure of the music and, therefore, to mischaracterize it.

The charge that heavy metal is musically simplistic illustrates the bias of the progressive critics. Most forms of music tend to be relatively simple in some respects and more complex in others. In heavy metal, for example, the rhythm is often simple and the sound is dominated by a booming bass line that lacks subtlety. However, the essential guitar parts are anything but crude. One has only to look at the attempts to create metal-guitar notation systems to appreciate the complexity. A vast array of symbols are added to the standard notation in order to indicate "grace not being bent to the next note," "slide down string with pick," and "fast hand vibrato," among many others.[15] Certainly, when compared to punk or folk rock, two musical styles praised by many progressive rock critics, heavy metal cannot be described as musically primitive.

With regard to lyrics, the critics are more accurate, but their objections hold for most of rock music, from its beginnings. Hedonism, for example, was definitive of early rock and roll, the lyrical staple of its founders such as Chuck Berry, Jerry Lee Lewis, and Little Richard. It is still the mainstay of rock music, from Bruce Springsteen to Cyndi Lauper, and from the Beach Boys to 2 Live Crew. Sexism also has been inseparable from rock. The lyrics of the Rolling Stones and Bob Dylan, let alone 2 Live Crew, are more sexist than heavy metal lyrics. The subtext of progressive criticism is that lyrics should be serious and should relate to sociopolitical concerns, not to mere personal pleasure. Of course, heavy metal also addresses such concerns, but not in the radical or reformist ways that the critics favor. Thus, they ignore its messages.

Metal fixes on the nasty, brutal, "first you live, then you die," facts of life, though it carries on the tradition from the counterculture of concern for social justice, freedom, and peace. For the progressives metal's sin is that it does not hold out much hope for the future. Anthony DeCurtis, in *Rolling Stone*, reproached metal (and rap) for failing to encourage "intelligent political action."[16] Beneath the repudiation of hedonism lurks left-wing interests in having youth use their vitality to "fight the good fight" rather than "party 'til you puke." The critics are galled by such postures as Guns N' Roses repudiation of politics as a senseless civil war.

At the root of the progressive critic's special contempt for heavy metal is the fact that it broke the faith of the counterculture. Black Sabbath, in particular, self-consciously inverted the counterculture's central symbol of love. Instead of focusing on love, they sang about evil, pointing out its pervasiveness and playing with its value sign. Heavy metal does not celebrate "love," either as something that is or should be the basis of sociopolitical relationships, although the spirit of community and sharing does inform many of the practices of the heavy metal subculture. Until recently, and then only in punk-influenced thrash, political reformism was alien to metal lyrics. The audience for metal is unhip. The notion of being politically correct is completely alien to its members. They are rock-and-roll rebels with a taste for Dionysian pleasure. They have judgments on politics, but those judgments do not involve programs of collective action.

The relative lack of attention to political protest in heavy metal is counterbalanced by its sensitivity to what were called themes of chaos in chapter 2. Heavy metal's tendency is to hold that the deepest conflicts and frustrations in life cannot be resolved by political reform or revolution. These difficulties must be met squarely by the individual and overcome through personal effort. By stressing the boundaries of ordinary life and the pervasiveness of disorder and meaninglessness beyond those margins, heavy metal resembles the philosophical movement existentialism. Just as political progressives excoriated the existentialist for lacking confidence in collective action, they attack heavy metal for its failure to be committed to radical or reformist programs.

Heavy metal fans and bands are also castigated for refusing to change, for their disdain for innovation. In terms of clothing and hairstyles this observation is accurate. That many of the critics wore jeans and long hair in their youth probably has something to do with their contempt for the appropriation of these styles by the heavy metal subculture. The styles do not signify in the metal subculture what they did in the counterculture. Heavy metal forces the critics to confront a legacy of their youth that they might prefer to ignore. In the meantime, the critics have aged and have abandoned their youthful styles. The metal subculture reminds them of the loss of their own youth.

The charge that heavy metal music has remained the same has much less truth and results from a failure to attend to the music carefully. Yet heavy metal does retain greater continuity than other forms of rock music. Fans still adore the older heavy metal material, buying albums that were released years ago. Bands oblige them by playing their early work in concert. Further, the music made by a band when it first started out is normally not radically different from what it makes years later. The band is compelled, mainly by the expectations of its fans, but also by the norm of expressing its authentic sound, to keep within the bounds of its "signature sound." Such consistency and adherence to tradition is highly valued by critics of such musical forms as the blues. Progressivist critics, however, reject continuity when they judge rock music. They evaluate each new album in part by comparing it to its predecessors, judging it good if it demonstrates the band's "artistic development." If a band produces a critically esteemed album and the next album is no different, the latter is downgraded for not showing the band's "growth." Beyond expecting rock music to further their agenda of sociopolitical change, progressive critics also want it to keep changing internally. Applying the latter criterion to heavy metal fails to grasp the connection of the music to a subculture and is a prescription, intended or not, for weakening that subculture.

The charge, however, that heavy metal as a genre has not changed musically is simply inaccurate. Earlier chapters have described the genre changes in some detail. Here I need only repeat that the genre has undergone a number of innovations and transformations since its inception. That these modifications have not been noticed by the critics only means that they have been unwilling or unable to give the music an attentive hearing. Having an animus against it for ideological reasons, they have preferred to treat it as undifferentiated "noise." Any heavy metal fan can detail the changes in the genre, and debates about those changes form a major portion of their musical discussions.

The mischaracterization of heavy metal by progressive critics has been noted by fans and artists working within the genre, who have responded in kind. Bon Scott, the late singer for AC/DC proclaimed, "We don't listen to critics. We play for the public."[17] In their book on major heavy metal bands, Ross Halfin and Pete Makowski indicate that the critics are "self-ordained guardians of taste" with "the perception and depth of a shallow puddle," who have "utter disdain" for heavy metal. They treat the genre "like some neanderthal subculture, and its audience as brainless, immature juveniles."[18] Indeed, the proud pariahs rejoice in the establishment's (and these counterculture holdovers and their younger brethren are now the establishment) rejection of them. Heavy metal journalists, especially Philip Bashe, have countered the attacks by bringing to light their inaccuracies and prejudices.[19] Indeed, the progressive critics contribute to the heavy metal community's solidarity. The course of action implied by their criticisms has no negative impact on headbangers since it is recommended to everyone else but them. Although the policy of the progressive critics toward heavy metal is never made explicit in their critiques, its directive is never far from the surface: avoid it like the plague, lest you be tagged unhip.

For the most part, however, the progressives ignore heavy metal since it does not fit conveniently into their categories, which dichotomize commercialized pop and committed rock. Since heavy metal is rebellious and therefore not a simple agent contributing to the conformity characteristic of a disciplinary/consumer society, and is also not politically radical or reformist, it is an anomaly, the kind of object that, according to a structuralist analysis is "dangerous" and likely to be made a taboo.[20] Progressives must never get close enough to heavy metal to let it contaminate their purity of commitment with ecstatic pleasure.

Conservative Criticism

The Fundamentalist Strain

The conservative detractors of heavy metal, in contrast to the progressives, are obsessed with the music, making it a prime symbol of everything that they find wrong with contemporary culture. Heavy metal, indeed, is just the latest object of denunciation in a long tradition of conservative opposition to popular music.[21] Since its origins in the 1950s, rock music has been plagued by, and has delighted in and often profited from, its critics. During the 1950s rock and roll emerged in the wake of McCarthyism and the whole postwar attempt to have a "great celebration" of American power. Rock and roll was maligned at that time for the danger it posed of inflaming the sexual passions of the nation's youth. This surface criticism masked widespread racism and fear of miscegenation. Rock and roll was believed to be infecting white youth with the supposed moral laxity of blacks. The mass media responded to that fear with the compromise of presenting white cover versions of rock-and-roll songs that had been originally recorded by blacks. Posters circulated by the Ku Klux Klan in 1955 directly express what other critics of rock and roll were suggesting more circumspectly: "Help save the youth of America: Don't buy Negro records. The screaming, idiotic words and savage music of these records are undermining the morals of our white youth in America."[22]

The reaction to rock and roll by cultural conservatives was to a large extent a replication of the conservative response to jazz after World War I. In his excellent analysis of the reaction to jazz by the "spiritual descendants of the 'know-nothing' party," Richard Peterson cites an Illinois Vigilance Association report, written by a Reverend Yarrow, which "found that in 1921–1922 jazz had 'caused the downfall' of one thousand girls in Chicago alone."[23] Jazz and its descendent at several removes, rock and roll, were denounced for their sound, which caused a relaxation of sexual control and a descent to the sexual primitivism attributed to blacks. Not coincidentally, both the 1920s and the 1950s were characterized by an increase in racial mixing that resulted from migrations of southern blacks to the North during and following each of the world wars. Both eras were also marked by the growth of new and very public youth cultures—the flappers and the teenagers, respectively—that seemed to reject strict parental supervision and adherence to parental standards.

The situation was more problematic for conservatives in the 1950s. The general public mood was one of anxiety, demonstrated and exacerbated by McCarthyism, fear of the atomic bomb, and the cold war. Adding to the tension was the decision by the Supreme Court in the *Brown* case of 1954 to find the racial segregation of public schools to be unconstitutional. In addition, general prosperity had created a leisure class of teenagers who had the free time and space (a car) to partake of hedonistic enjoyments, including sexual relations. Conservative critics were partially right: rock and roll's sexual overtones and its "blackness" did contribute to its popularity. But the conservatives erred in making the music a metonym for all of the complex causes of their discontent, just as music-based subcultures make music a metonym for their entire life-styles. In a sense, the cultural conservatives became an anti-music subculture.

Academic cultural conservatives made their complaints against rock and roll from the theoretical position of mass-culture criticism. Here the music was not singled out, but was lumped with the rest of popular culture. Rock and roll was one expression of what these authors termed "masscult," "lowbrow," or "brutal" culture.[24] It all was seen to lack any redeeming artistic virtues and to be made for the lowest common denominator of a heterogeneous, unschooled audience.

In the early 1960s young people, mainly college students, championed folk and folk-rock music. They also began to help with the civil rights movement and, more generally, to question the practices of big business and government. The political music of the Great Depression was rediscovered and refurbished for a new age by such artists as Bob Dylan and Joan Baez. The conservative cultural critics attacked folk music as being communist-inspired. This time they did not assail the sound but the lyrics and even more the "pinko" artists, who were causing youth to think and behave so badly.

The outcry against youth music reached another crescendo in the late 1960s and early 1970s. The music, again the critical target was lyrics, not the sound, was causing kids to opt out of the "system," to "turn on, tune in, and drop out." Rock was blamed for the antiwar stance of the young and especially for their fondness for marijuana and LSD. Vice President Spiro Agnew was the point man best known for making accusations against rock, charging that the lyrics caused the youthful audience to take drugs and that the music was sapping the nation's power.[25] At that time, Charles Fowler, a music educator, wrote that cause and effect should not be confused: "Rock lyrics have not been responsible for the use of drugs."[26] Admonitions such as Fowler's obviously had little impact then, and have little impact today, on conservative criticism. Music, as a compact and readily discernible expression of emotion and attitude, is a compelling metonym for more complex sociocultural phenomena. It is easy and tempting to make the metonym into the cause of the supposed problem.

The disgrace of Richard Nixon's forced resignation from the presidency and the even more disgraceful end to the Vietnam War encouraged the conservatives to keep a low profile during the early 1970s. But by the end of the decade, stimulated by the perceived failures of the Carter presidency, they rose to greater prominence than ever before. Their leadership was crystallized in the fundamentalist Protestant church groups, but they also gained support in the mass media and from the general public. The new legitimacy and pervasiveness of cultural conservative criticism in the 1980s coincided with the spurt in popularity of heavy metal in the United States. In the context of greater permissiveness in the mass media and the appearance of MTV, the stage was set for a major attack on heavy metal from the right.

Since the late 1960s there has been a progressive relaxation of "moral" standards throughout the mass media. The "twin beds" rule of early television was replaced by steamy soap operas and leering double-entendre sitcoms. Movies that once would have been banned in Boston or shown in porno theaters on Times Square became box-office hits. Ironically, the Reagan administration's policy of deregulation, including major policy changes regarding the FCC's monitoring of radio and television, can be held partially responsible for the trend. Raunch and violence, always attractive to large segments of the mass audience, could grow unfettered. The combat zone came to the small cities in heartland America and into the living rooms of the respectable middle class via the television, especially cable TV. Groups that had been insulated from the more raw forms of popular culture were now exposed to them, and they reacted against the assault on their sensibilities.

The combination of the relaxation of restraint in entertainment and the rise of the fundamentalist right inevitably led to confrontations. Skirmishes and battles were mainly, although not exclusively, focused on youth. Young people were seen to be especially vulnerable to the suasion of the mass media. They were also regarded as the hope for the future. Church groups held more record-burning and record-smashing rallies. "Satanic rock albums" were burned in an Iowa rally in 1980.[27] Jesus People ministers, Steve and Jim Peters, organized a bonfire and album-smashing event in St. Paul in 1981.[28] Other such events also took place.

A student at a Florida school run by Southern Baptists described a record-burning rally held in 1982: "One Thursday we were taken to where a man gave a sermon on the evils that were assaulting our youth. He spoke mainly about rock music. After several minutes of whipping the crowd into a frenzy, he said we should 'purge' our lives of this evil, just as he was about to do. He then began to hold up record albums, say a few things about each one—either a line from the lyrics or a statement of condemnation—and break it, throwing the album into a raging fire. . . . Many albums later, he held up the Pat Benatar single, 'Hell Is for Children.' He said, 'This song openly promotes devil-worship among our youth!' He had lied about many records, but this was the worst. We started shouting things like 'that's bullshit!' and 'you never even read the lyrics!' Without a moment's hesitation he said, 'See how the Devil despises His work! His evil is deeply ingrained. Don't be surprised if your children are as intolerant!' One of the old men beside him asked, 'Are they possessed?' I couldn't hear what he replied. The crowd went wild."[29] Benatar, a hard-rock singer, had written the condemned song as a denunciation of child abuse. The leaders of the rally had taken her figurative use of the term "hell" literally.

By the mid-1980s a concerted assault on rock was underway. Heavy metal became a metonym for rock as a whole. There was some poetic justice in this oversimplification, for metal continues with more purity than other forms of youth music the original ethos of rock and roll described by Charles Hamm: "Derived from the music of several subcultures (black, poor, and rural white), it incorporated from the start an aura of rebellion, of rejection of the patterns and life-styles of white Middle America."[30] Heavy metal is loud and its strong bottom sound booms through walls and floors in houses. Its themes are replete with rebellion and general revulsion against the standards of polite society, and they emphasize the chaos which society seeks to keep at bay. Its audience is composed almost exclusively of adolescents. They form the group that is the focus of fear and hope in the West, especially since the rise of "teenagers" as a social category, which made youth a group "in itself and for itself" in the late 1960s. Most importantly, heavy metal was, by the mid-1980s, no longer an obscure musical genre known only to the members of its subculture. Through the good offices of MTV heavy metal could be seen and heard in any cabled house in America. Greeson and Williams appropriately contend that "MTV may be viewed as crossing over from traditional middle-class values transmitted by TV to youth culture values traditionally associated with rock music themes."[31]

The battle was joined on all fronts: church, academia, courts of law, public schools, concert venues, mass media, and homes. The dual sources of Western values, Athens and Jerusalem, were culled for denunciations of rock. The most significant battle in the campaign was fought at a United States Senate hearing held in Washington, D.C., during September 1985. Formally titled Record Labeling, Senate Hearing 99–259, it is popularly known as the PMRC hearing. It provided a platform for, and bestowed a legitimacy on, the fundamentalist positions against rock and especially against heavy metal.[32]

The cultural conservative case was broadcast to the general public by the mass media, which found the circus atmosphere of the hearings to be congenial. The general public learned from these hearings that heavy metal was, if not diabolical, at least in very bad taste.

The Parents Music Resource Center (PMRC), which was founded, in part, by the wives of several United States senators, was only concerned with the lyrical content of rock music. No objections were made to its sound. Senator Ernest Hollings (South Carolina) opened the hearings by decrying "this outrageous filth, suggestive violence, suicide, and everything else in the Lord's world that you would not think of."[33] Senator Paul Trible (Virginia) objected to "song lyrics describing rape, incest, sexual violence, and perversion."[34] Susan Baker, wife of James Baker, then treasury secretary, led off for the PMRC, denouncing lyrics that were "sexually explicit, excessively violent, or glorify the use of drugs and alcohol."[35] Her testimony described lyrics of songs by the heavy metal artists Quiet Riot, Judas Priest, W.A.S.P., Ozzy Osbourne, Blue Oyster Cult, and AC/DC, and by the black-contemporary artists Prince and Morris Day. Ms. Baker and the PMRC "experts" who gave testimony after her specified three areas of concern with lyrical themes. They can be summarized by the triad suicide and aggression, sexual perversion, and satanism.

SUICIDE AND AGGRESSION. Baker's testimony put forward the standard line of cultural conservatives about heavy metal's influence on suicide: "Some rock artists actually seem to encourage teen suicide. Ozzy Osbourne sings 'Suicide Solution.' Blue Oyster Cult sings 'Don't Fear the Reaper,' AC/DC sings 'Shoot to Thrill.' Just last week in Centerpoint, a small Texas town, a young man took his life while listening to the music of AC/DC. He was not the first."[36] Two points should be noted about Baker's claims. First, she grossly misinterprets the lyrics in ways that fans of heavy metal find astonishing. Second, she implies a causal connection between being a heavy metal fan and doing violence to oneself or others.

"Suicide Solution" was a cut on the first album that Ozzy Osbourne made after he left Black Sabbath, *Blizzard of Ozz*. The name of the album is relevant here. It is a clever word play on *The Wizard of Oz*. Dorothy's tornado is converted into another turbulent weather phenomenon, which has the same two consonants as Osbourne's first name. Oz is the place ruled by a wizard, who is rather a fraud, and some of Ozzy's songs, such as "I Don't Know" are reflections on the discomfort he feels when fans see him as a miracle worker or a seer, which, he admits, he is not.

The title "Suicide Solution" is another play on words. "Solution" refers both to the resolution of a problem and to a liquid in which other substances are dissolved. The song starts out with the lyrics "Wine is fine but whiskey's quicker / Suicide is slow with liquor." The song is a denunciation of alcoholism, arguing that it is a slow form of suicide. Alcohol is the "suicide solution" in both senses of the word *solution*. Alcohol should be rejected because it is a way of killing oneself. Indeed, at the time he wrote the song, Ozzy was thinking both of his own constant battles with the bottle and of the recent deaths of heavy metal boozers, especially Bon Scott of AC/DC. Alcoholics, himself included, he argues, are killing themselves: "The reaper is you and the reaper is me."

"Suicide Solution" is a poignant antialcoholism song. The interpretation of it given here is obvious. All that one needs to do to understand the lyrics is to listen to them or read them, and to grasp a simple pun. But the fundamentalist critics, who originated the misinterpretation of the song as an advocacy of suicide, are trained to give texts literal interpretations. They are blind to puns. When they see "Suicide Solution" they read, "Suicide is the solution to your problems." Other critics then take up that "literal" interpretation, apparently without taking the trouble to listen to or read the lyrics themselves.

The misinterpretation of "Suicide Solution" has, indeed, become conventional wisdom in public discourse. The song is always referred to by the moral critics of heavy metal. Five years after the hearings, the Catholic archbishop of New York, John Cardinal O'Connor, cited "Suicide Solution" as an example of "heavy metal music spiked with satanic lyrics" that disposed listeners to "devilworship and demonic possession."[37] It was the only song mentioned by name in the archbishop's statement. The mass media, adopting its usual credulous posture toward authority figures, perpetuated the misinterpretation. *Time,* for example, reported that the Roman Catholic archbishop of New York had targeted Ozzy Osbourne for a song he had recorded with the theme of suicide.[38] The public relations office of the archdiocese revealed that the archbishop's information about heavy metal came from Tipper Gore's 1987 book.[39] Tipper Gore, wife of Senator Albert Gore (Tennessee), is a founder of the PMRC and its leading spokesperson.

The distance between what the lyrics say and how the cultural conservatives interpret them is partly explained by the emphasis of the conservatives on the visual side of heavy metal culture. Much of the evidence presented at the Senate hearings was pictorial. Dozens of album covers were displayed and constant references were made to music-video images. Thus, in support of their interpretation of "Suicide Solution," the PMRC entered as evidence a magazine picture of Ozzy "with a gun barrel stuck into his mouth."[40] A newspaper story confirms that the group was upset by "What they heard in the lyrics, saw on album covers, and watched on rock videos."[41]

The conflation of visual and lyrical material is evidenced by Senator Albert Gore's interrogation of soft-rocker John Denver, who argued against the imposition of record labeling. Gore posed a rhetorical question to Denver: "Let me come back to the question about suicide. Let us say you have a popular rock star who has a lot of fans, who sings a song that says suicide is the solution, and appears in fan magazines with a gun barrel pointed in his mouth and promotes material that seems to glorify suicide. Do you think it is a responsible act for a record company to put out a song glorifying suicide?"[42]

"Suicide Solution" was not the only song that was grossly misinterpreted at the senate hearings. A song by AC/DC, "Shoot to Thrill," was brought up by several PMRC witnesses. Any AC/DC fan knows that the song's title has nothing to do with killing or shooting guns. The bulk of AC/DC's songs are about sex and, despite the group's name their view of the subject is quite straight. Their trademark is to use and build on traditional blues terminology, in which sexual terms are coyly, often cutely, transformed into puns and suggested by metaphors. One of their best-loved cuts is called "Big Balls." On the surface "Big Balls" is a celebration of formal dances, but the obvious subtext refers to male genitalia. This blues tradition was appropriated by rock and roll at its inception. When Georgia Gibbs covered a black R&B hit about making love, "Work with Me Annie," the word "work" was judged to be too suggestive and was transformed to the word "dance." Indeed, the word "dance" has maintained its double reference to patterned movement and to sexual coupling in rock lyrics through the present. The very term "rock and roll" was a common R&B term for sexual intercourse. "Shoot to Thrill" is about sex.[43] "Shooting" refers not to guns, but to male ejaculation. It is hardly an obscure metaphor.

Building upon their misinterpretation of lyrics, the PMRC witnesses claimed that the songs they had identified were responsible for teen suicides. Taking up Susan Baker's story of the boy who committed suicide in Centerpoint, Texas, while listening to AC/DC, PMRC consultant Jeff Ling repeated the claim of a causal link: "Steve died while listening to AC/DC's 'Shoot to Thrill.' Steve fired his father's gun into his mouth."[44] Ling added a second example of a San Antonio high school student who "hung himself while listening to AC/DC's 'Shoot to Thrill.' "[45] Ling then said, "Suicide has become epidemic in our country among teenagers. Some 6,000 will take their lives this year. Many of these young people find encouragement from some rock stars who present death as a positive, almost attractive alternative."[46] Senator Gore also glided from referring to "Suicide Solution" as "material that seems to glorify suicide" to noting that "the United States has one of the highest rates of teen suicide of any country in the world. The rate has gone up 300 percent in the last decade among young people, while it has remained constant among adults."[47] Thus, heavy metal becomes identified as a cause of suicide by unsubstantiated inference.

The inference that heavy metal causes teen suicide is as implausible as are the conservative's interpretations of heavy metal lyrics. Rates of suicide have, indeed, been increasing for those who listen to metal music. But they have also been increasing for youth as a whole, including those groups whose members are least likely to be fans of heavy metal. Moreover, this upward trend began before heavy metal erupted. Simple logic rules out metal as a cause of suicide.

Indeed, for each heavy metal fan who commits suicide there are hundreds who feel that the music actually saved them from killing themselves. For example, a letter published in *Hit Parader* describes the use of music "to forget my problems! Judas Priest's music makes me feel happy and alive. It's one of the real joys in my life. And I'd like to thank Judas Priest for saving my life many times!"[48] But citing such letters to show that metal prevents suicide is no more conclusive than arguing that heavy metal causes suicide by appealing to specific cases. The logical error in both cases is the fallacy of composition. It involves taking an example and arguing that its characteristics are those of the whole group. Prejudiced ideologues of all stripes have always resorted to this tactic. The cultural conservatives have made it a staple of their method of attack. For example, the "Willie Horton" ads in George Bush's successful presidential campaign spotlighted the mayhem that one prisoner in an early release program had committed, implying that his opponent would impose this program nationwide, and that all prisoners released early would behave in the same way. Bush's opponent, Michael Dukakis, governor of the state in which the prisoner had been released, was made to appear a dim-witted accomplice to mayhem. Similarly, associating particular cases of suicide with heavy metal makes all heavy metal fans appear to be suicidal.

Misinterpretation and illogic aside, it is not clear that lyrical meanings have much of an effect on listeners to heavy metal. "The PMRC seems to assume that adolescents listen attentively to music, pay special attention to the lyrics, and interpret both the explicit and implicit meanings of their favorite songs. Young people then apparently take these meanings and apply them to their daily lives in the form of behavioral guidelines."[49] As Verden and others indicate, there is good evidence that the lyrics are not taken at face value. Listeners, as was noted in chapter 4, tend not to concern themselves with the lyrics, but when they do, they interpret them within the context of the heavy metal subculture and not the discourse of fundamentalist theology.

Nonetheless, the causal link between heavy metal and suicide became fixed in public discourse. Parents of some heavy metal fans who had committed suicide began to blame the music. Ozzy Osbourne and his record company were sued by parents of a nineteen year old who had killed himself.[50] The court dismissed the case. But a Reno, Nevada, court allowed a similar suit against Judas Priest to proceed.[51] It was brought by the parents of two youths who carried out a suicide pact in which one died immediately and the other was seriously disabled and died later.

Nothing is quite so horrible for parents than the suicide of their child. Not only is their offspring dead, but society points a finger of blame at the parents: they did not love the child enough. The parents are therefore vulnerable to guilt in addition to their grief. They recall all of the abuse they piled on the child, all of the times they did not display love. No parent is free of such sins. In order to escape from guilt, people tend to displace blame onto something or someone outside themselves, desperately trying to convince themselves and others that they are not responsible. Shakespeare criticized this all-too-human tendency, "The fault, dear Brutus, is not in our stars but in ourselves." But people are still blaming the "stars," in this case the luminaries of heavy metal.

The Priest trial was a test of the claims of the cultural conservatives that heavy metal songs can and do make young people commit suicide. The parents sought to absolve themselves from blame and to receive financial compensation from the band and its record company. The initial strategy of their lawyers, which was avidly taken up by the media, was to try heavy metal.[52]

The suit as originally filed claimed that the lyrics of "Beyond the Realms of Death," from the band's *Stained Class* album, were a call to suicide. The lawyers changed their strategy when they discovered that courts had disallowed similar suits on First Amendment grounds. Switching field, they engaged engineers to seek "subliminal messages" on that album, which was found on the record player of one of the youths the day the suicide pact was carried out.[53] This new tactic narrowed the significance of the trial and the media began to lose interest. Anthony Pratkanis, a professor of psychology and expert witness for the defense, recalls that attention was focused on how many "subliminal demons . . . can dance on the end of a pin."[54]

The focus on subliminal messages turned the issue away from heavy metal to the effect of such messages on behavior. There was no academic opinion supporting the claim that subliminal messages caused behavioral changes. Indeed, researchers had found no such effects. A professor of psychology at York University in Ontario, who had spent a decade investigating the effectiveness of subliminal audio messages stated, "There's good evidence [they] don't work."[55] A psychology professor from the University of Washington in Seattle concurs with this opinion. The results of his study on subliminal suggestion, presented to the American Psychological Association, found no difference in mental function between subjects who had listened to a tape with subliminal messages and those who had not.[56] Other psychologists studied the role of suggestion in the belief that satanic messages had been heard on rock records and concluded that those who were told that satanic messages could be heard were far more likely to say that they had discerned such messages than those who had not been told that the records contained satanic messages.[57]

In August 1990 the case was decided by Judge Jerry Whitehead in favor of Judas Priest and CBS Records. Whitehead explained that the plaintiffs were not successful because they were unable to prove that subliminal messages were placed in the album "intentionally," or to prove that the messages caused the suicide and the attempted suicide.[58] The defense had claimed that the words "Do It" (implying encouragement of suicide) had been hidden on the record, but Whitehead found that the sounds in question were simply a "chance combination." The "do it" sound had been produced by the singer's audible breathing in combination with a guitarist's strum.[59] Yet he also said that they were a subliminal message, leaving open the possibility of future cases that would attempt to demonstrate a causal linkage between subliminal messages and suicidal or any other proscribed behavior. A lawyer for the plaintiffs commented that this would not be the last such case, adding that eventually one of them would be won.[60] Whether that prediction comes true, the narrowness of the case takes a good deal of pressure off heavy metal in the legal system.

The PMRC hearings not only spread the misconception that heavy metal causes suicide, but it also linked the music to mayhem in general. Here again lyrics were interpreted in a maximally incompetent way, logical fallacies were committed, and the distortions were tirelessly repeated and taken up by the media without reflection. Ms. Gore, for example, in an article printed in several newspapers, claimed that the lyrics of the song "Under the Blade" by Twisted Sister were sadomasochistic. Dee Snider, Twisted Sister's singer, was indignant when he testified at the senate hearings. He exposed Gore's gross misreading of the lyrics, which were not about sadomasochism but "about surgery and the fear that it instills in people."[61] It had been written for a friend who had faced surgery. Snider continued, "I can say categorically that the only sadomasochism, bondage, and rape in this song is in the mind of Ms. Gore."[62] Snider suggested that her misinterpretation might have been a result of confusing the video presentation of the song with the song's lyrics. He went on to point out that the videos for his group were based on Roadrunner cartoons, a staple of children's television.[63]

The fallacy of composition was committed to underscore the contention that heavy metal was responsible not only for suicide, but for mayhem in general. The Nightstalker murderer was cited by Jeff Ling at the senate hearings: "Of course, AC/DC is no stranger to violent material. . . . one of their fans I know you are aware of is the accused Nightstalker."[64] The newspapers, too, had repeatedly noted that the indicted murderer wore clothing that identified him as an AC/DC fan. The implication was that all AC/DC fans are potential murderers.

The same fallacy is committed by a few adolescent psychologists who have gained attention in the media and have even been accorded credibility in the medical community.[65] The most widely cited of these is Dr. Paul King. Studying the patients admitted to his hospital, he has published research that correlates drug use and musical preference with mental problems. It does not require a course in research methods to recognize that his generalizations are based on a highly skewed sample of heavy metal fans—those incarcerated in mental hospitals. In one publication King reported that heavy metal was chosen as their favorite form of music by 59.1 percent of patients treated for chemical dependency at his facility. Of these patients, 74.4 percent were involved in violence, 71.9 percent in sexual activity, and 49.8 percent in stealing.[66] What is one to make of such figures? To those already convinced of the menace of heavy metal, these findings reinforce prior prejudices. However, from a scientific viewpoint such conclusions cannot substantiate claims about the impact of heavy metal music. To use them to infer cause is like using the smoking habits of a prison population to argue that cigarette smoking causes violent crime. Indeed, one might just as well argue that heavy metal is used therapeutically by some young people to relax them and make them less aggressive. In that case, the violence would have been done not because of heavy metal but in spite of it. Kotarba argues that heavy metal music may be the "last attempt" of some disturbed children "to make sense of feelings of meaninglessness."[67] Suicide or aggression would then indicate the failure of that last attempt.

The sample used by King in his research might itself be unreliable. Adolescent commitment to private psychiatric hospitals has become a growth sector of the hospital industry.[68] Some of those committed to these hospitals are not seriously disturbed but are "simply rebellious teenagers struggling with their parents over anything [such as] the music they play."[69] Because heavy metal demands to be played loudly and is regarded in such a negative light by the general public, adolescents sent to psychiatric hospitals because of "the music they play" are very likely to play heavy metal.

SEXUAL PERVERSION. The cultural conservatives also accused heavy metal of fostering sexual perversion. Columnist Ellen Goodman's denunciation of the song "Eat Me Alive" by Judas Priest was brought up several times during the senate hearings by members of the PMRC, and has been repeated innumerable times since. Taking the song's title as a literal command is bizarre; such literalness fails to acknowledge the pervasive use of sexual imagery and metaphor in common speech. Again, the literal interpretation becomes absurd when the lyrics are exposed to closer examination.

A major theme in Judas Priest's work is the expression of hostility and vengeance against a society that is viewed as unjust. This theme occurs in many of their most popular songs, such as "Screaming for Vengeance," "Some Heads Are Gonna Roll," and "Breaking the Law." Within the context of the genre and, more specifically, within the context of the band's work, the cultural conservative's interpretation of "Eat Me Alive" as advocating sexual perversion is clearly mistaken.

Mötley Crüe is another band that is accused of championing sexual perversion. Comparing some of their work to the writings of Edgar Allen Poe and William Burroughs, Richard Corliss in *Time* wondered whether anybody but Tipper Gore fails to realize "it's a joke?"[70]

One of the PMRC's major consultants, Dr. Joe Stuessy, a professor of music from San Antonio, concludes that one of the basic themes in successful heavy metal music projects is "sexual promiscuity/perversion (including homosexuality, bisexuality, sadomasochism, necrophilia etc.)."[71] His opinion is based on gross misinterpretations of lyrics and more often simply of song titles, such as "Eat Me Alive." Since the heavy metal subculture is as homophobic as Dr. Stuessy seems to be, his idea that some heavy metal songs favor homosexuality testifies to his incompetence as a reader.

SATANISM. From the viewpoint of the fundamentalist right wing, the most offensive and ominous characteristic of heavy metal is its supposed promotion of satanism. "Satan has gotten a real foothold in rock," asserts Richard Peck in his fundamentalist diatribe against the music.[72] Peck further argues that "Whenever possible Satan will use this dark side of rock to lead Christians into sin."[73] Dr. King, the psychologist and consultant to the PMRC, finds satanism to be at the core of heavy metal: "The attraction of heavy metal music is its message that a higher power controls the world, and that power is hate—often personified by Satan."[74] This claim is echoed by Carl Raschke, who remarks that "In rock music, the symbols and paraphernalia of hate movements, particularly Naziism, have been the staple diet of so-called metalheads for more than a decade."[75] Phyllis Polack, a journalist who writes for heavy metal magazines, reported that the Right has accused record companies of hiring "satan-worshipping witches to put spells on albums to make sure they sell."[76]

In *The Triumph of Vulgarity: Rock Music in the Mirror of Romanticism*, Robert Pattison maintained that "Any number of religious fundamentalists have asserted that rock is the devil's work and some, with the hearing of dogs, have discovered subliminal messages on albums by Kiss and Led Zeppelin, more often than not audible only when the records are played backward—Satan's technological adaptation of the black mass."[77] One of the consultants for the plaintiffs in the Judas Priest trial is Wilson Bryan Key, who is a self-styled expert on satanic messages. Key has been used as a consultant in almost two dozen cases. He now specializes in heavy metal, but he also says that he has discovered "satanic or sexual messages on five-dollar bills, Howard Johnson's place mats and Ritz crackers."[78]

The fascination with appeals to satanism that are supposedly present in backward masking or other hidden messages on records resonates with the paranoid strain in American politics. An author of a scholarly analysis of the devil believes that "backmasking is an unnecessary game, since the overt lyrics are often diabolical enough."[79] The few instances of such recording trickery were done for fun and are searched for as treats by a few fans. More cynical headbangers have judged these manipulations to be pathetic commercial ploys. But the despisers of metal are convinced that they are pervasive and efficacious.[80]

The use of symbols of the underworld in heavy metal is an essential ground for the cultural conservative's opposition to the music. Stuart Goldman, writing in the conservative *National Review*, comments that the devil, if confronted with "the average heavy-metaler, might well claim to be a relatively innocent bystander."[81] Such critics as Goldman are updating the traditional conservative diatribe against rock music. Denisoff cites books with titles such as *Rock and Roll: The Devil's Diversion* and statements such as "rock music is the devil's masterpiece."[82] The charges that heavy metal is satanic simply continue an old battle, but, whereas the Rolling Stones's "Sympathy for the Devil" attracted much fire because it was one of the few songs of its time making use of satanic themes, the symbols of the underworld abound in heavy metal.

To single out metal as an expression or cause of satanism is absurd on the face of it. Symbols of satan are found in nonreligious cultural forms and artifacts throughout the West, from plays and short stories to Mardi Gras and Halloween celebrations. Moreover, most of the use of the imagery of the underworld in heavy metal is underscored by a tone that ranges from irony to burlesque. In the world of metal hell is the place where bad boys boogie, and, according to AC/DC, it "ain't a bad place to be." Metal artists are less likely than members of the general public to be true believers in the devil. For example, a member of Slayer, a band that is maligned by conservative critics, states, "I'm interested in it. . . . I'm not religious in any way."[83] Corliss agrees that Slayer is not satanistic. He compares their live shows to a Broadway musical—"*CATS* with a nasty yowl."[84] Metal insider Dante Bonutto, who hosts the British Friday Rock Show, states, "I mean Slayer aren't actually in league with the devil or anything. But they do give the impression that if they were to go to anyone's house for a scone and a sandwich it would be his."[85]

Heavy metal's embrace of deviltry is not a religious statement. It is a criticism of the phoney heaven of respectable society where no one boogies and everyone goes to ice cream socials. It is not a countertheology. Metal lyrics do not attack God and certainly do not malign Jesus. They just appeal to the devil as a principle of chaos. Heavy metal is a lineal descendent of the blues, using that style's musical and lyrical conventions. And just as blues transformed gospel into worldly music, despair into song, and repressed sensuality into the grit of everyday life, so metal deploys Satan and suicide as symbols of freedom from and resistance against organized constraints. It is a form of life, not of decadence.

Interviews with heavy metal artists underscore their rejection of destructive activity. In a very early (1972) article on Ozzy Osbourne, Lester Bangs quoted his expression of revulsion at people slowly killing themselves with drugs. Ozzy mentioned a concert where after the show innumerable syringes were found on the floor. "I felt sick, I really felt ill," he said when he realized that he had just played to people who were a "step nearer to the hole."[86]

Pattison suggests that fear of competition serves as one cause for the misreading of heavy metal by cultural conservatives: "Protestant fundamentalists have been quick to identify rock as 'the Devil's diversion' because it encroaches on the emotional territory where charismatic religion does its business."[87] A letter published in *Hit Parader* demonstrates Pattison's point: "Why can't you see the damage that your so-called heavy-metal music is having on the youth of America? All the music does is preach hate and anti-religious notions. If the children of America had a picture of God on their walls instead of photos of disgusting individuals like Ozzy Osbourne, our country would be in a much healthier state."[88]

The argument that heavy metal is so despised by the fundamentalists because it competes with them for the allegiance of a segment of youth also applies to the progressives. That does not mean that heavy metal is either a religion or a political ideology, but that it is an alternative to those forms of thinking. Especially in the case of the fundamentalists, the white, male, and blue-collar core of the heavy metal subculture is a target group for recruiting. Heavy metal, by transvaluing many of the symbols of fundamentalist belief, appears to be a direct adversary. But heavy metal is not a counter-religion. It appropriates religious symbols for its own Dionysian and rebellious uses. Rather than enlist in service to interests on the left or the right, the metal audience sings "Kill the King" and "Animal (F**k Like a Beast)."

For the fundamentalists, however, heavy metal's appropriation of Christian symbols represents the very worst kind of blasphemy. They take the use of these symbols literally and are convinced that the music is a tool of the Anti-Christ. Satanism, along with suicide, sexual perversion, and mayhem form a unity in the fundamentalist mind. Suicide, for them, is the denial of God's gift of life. In terms of the belief that we are all made in God's image, killing oneself is akin to deicide. Sexual perversion makes one a citizen of the fallen world, of Sodom and Gomorrah. Violence against others and the symbolization of Satan indicate affiliation with the Anti-Christ. Yet this reading of heavy metal is not carried out in terms of metal's own code. For the metal subculture these symbols are not used to denote rebellion against God and the embrace of evil, but to signal youthful rebellion against authority. Admittedly, they do speak obliquely to that part of the Christian tradition that identifies vital power with the power of an evil world, that is, with the aspect of Christianity criticized by Friedrich Nietzsche. In a sense what heavy metal is saying is that if society chooses to place the power of ecstatic experience in the realm of evil, then I will call myself evil. Such a rhetorical move is made commonly in the culture at large. The symbol of the devil is used throughout the popular culture, in the names given to muscle cars and the names and mascots of sports teams—in other words, wherever worldly power is involved. Heavy metal's viewpoint is Dionysian and rebellious, not directly anti-Christian. Despite the few sociopathic individuals who attach themselves to heavy metal, its core appeal is to a marginalized social group whose members feel the strains of marginalization, and not to deviant or disturbed individuals.

The playful, not sinister, use of the term "evil" and its symbols in heavy metal is not a call to act out evil deeds, but a transvaluation of the values of respectable culture. Evil is a metonym for the proud pariah's rejection of respectable society. It is also, in part, an introjection of the respectable society's judgment of the marginalized youth, a way of both turning that judgment on the judged and against the judge. That is, the use of satanic symbols reflects the ambivalence of the proud pariah: it is a compromise formation, in Sigmund Freud's sense of that term: a way of reconciling the emotional strain between grasping the goodness of vitality and not being able to escape, within oneself, from society's judgment of one as a failure. Heavy metal is a cultural coping mechanism.

"Am I Evil?" One can introject a poor self-image or choose a strategy of transvaluing values. The strategy of transvaluation has been adopted throughout history and is present in contemporary social movements such as gay rights, feminism, and Afro-centrism. At its best it is a rebellion against inauthentic culture, an attempt of life to raise itself above the herd. In heavy metal the transvaluation of religious symbols joins with the sound of the music, which is inherently vitalizing, to tweak a devitalizing, bureaucratic, in-authentic, iron-caged, and unfair world.

The Secular Strain

Conservatism is not exhausted by its fundamentalist strain, but contains a secular tendency that draws its inspiration from classical reason rather than revelation, from Athens, not Jerusalem. The most famous secular conservative critic of rock is Alan Bloom, a political theorist at the University of Chicago. The fact that his 1987 book *The Closing of the American Mind* made the best-seller list reflected a widely shared sense that the contemporary social order was in great need of repair. Bloom devotes more than a dozen pages of his work to a diatribe against rock music. He contends that it "is not only not reasonable, it is hostile to reason."[89] Bloom's knowledge of rock is abysmal but he does grasp its essence. He recognizes that rock represents a retrieval of the Dionysian, but he condemns this retrieval as irrational. Thus, Bloom does not distort the meaning of those sorts of rock music, like heavy metal, that make the power of the world a supreme value, but he does claim that such a valuation is anti-rational.

Bloom recurs to Plato's discussion of music as the basis for his argument. In book 3 of *The Republic* Plato is concerned with influencing the young to have self-control and to observe moderation in all things. He discusses what kinds of music would serve those ends, and what types would thwart them. He argues against "multi-stringed and panharmonic instruments."[90] Thus, Plato would ban use of the guitar. He cautions that the words, not the music, should be primary: "rhythm and harmony should conform to the words and not the other way around."[91] Music should foster reason. Plato insists that "extreme pleasure drives a man out of his mind no less than extreme pain."[92] Writing more than two thousand years before its eruption, Plato has denounced heavy metal. Those familiar with Rush's epic *2112* will recognize that Plato's arguments are the same as those offered by the priests of the Temple of Syrinx.[93] They banned guitars and when an old one was found hidden behind a waterfall they smashed it. The instrument was capable of producing a highly emotional music that they felt was inimical to the society that they ruled.

From Plato to Bloom, the assumption of classical rationalists has been that reason and emotion are in conflict, that the Dionysian spirit of life is counter to the Apollonian spirit of form. Philosopher Steve Crockett contends that in truth "music is not hostile to reason."[94] Indeed, emotion is permitted to expand in particular directions by musical form and practices of appreciating music. The recognition of the musical form, its beat, and its parts is necessary to appreciate any music and is an exercise of reason. Bloom, says Crockett, speaks as if "the music is active and the listener is passive."[95] Heavy metal fans, caught up in the Dionysian ecstasy of a concert or jamming on the recorded music, do exercise reason, are active listeners.

The issue, then, is not between reason and blind emotion, but between an interpretation of reason that excludes emotion and one that includes it. The latter view of reason is the romantic one. The band Rush, in its epic, *Hemispheres,* presents the romantic rationalist vision. Promoting the mutuality of reason and emotion, they appeal to Cygnus, the god of balance, to produce harmony.[96]

William Greider suggests that Bloom's attack on rock is based on his "detesting the young."[97] Greider sums up the intent and appeal of Bloom: "he is peddling fundamentalism for high-brows. It is the same bilious blend of prejudice, regret and resentment, the same simplistic appeal to the 'golden days' of memory, and it bashes the same targets."[98] Although Bloom did not single out heavy metal for special abuse, his polemic was read as an attack on it—as it was, by implication—by fellow cultural conservatives.

By 1990 much of the general public believed that heavy metal was disgusting and dangerous, if not downright evil. The conservative's understanding of the genre, rather than the progressive's or the metal subculture's has permeated the society. Commentator Bob Greene, for example, expressed surprise in his newspaper column that someone who was an Eagle Scout was also a "metalhead" and noted that "Occasionally you'll meet someone whose self-description seems to be a contradiction in terms."[99] Similarly, *Newsweek* advertised a special issue on teenagers by placing them "in the age of AIDS, crack and heavy metal."[100] In the mass mind, what AIDS had become to sex and crack to drugs, heavy metal had become to rock and roll.

Policing Heavy Metal

The condemnations of heavy metal in the 1980s were often linked to policies for controlling or eliminating the music. Some of the proposed courses of action were merely debated or threatened, but others were implemented.

The spokespersons for the PMRC stated that their intention was not to censor. Their proposed policy, they claimed, was "voluntary labeling." Ms. Gore's testimony at the senate hearings stated the group's position: "We have asked the record companies to voluntarily label their own products and assume responsibility for making those judgments."[101] She indicated that the policy should be implemented by the industry as a whole, which would create a panel that would "recommend a uniform set of criteria" and that would leave it up to the individual recording companies to label their own records according to the standards that were established. In addition, lyric sheets were to be made available to the consumer before purchase, but only for labeled recordings.[102] The PMRC's activities, however, extended far beyond this recommendation. The group also requested that record companies exert pressure on broadcasters not to air explicit music videos and records, and to reassess their contracts with stars who represented violence or sexual behavior in concert.[103] Obviously something more than just a call for labeling is at work here. Protestations that the PMRC is not suggesting censorship must be understood as a rhetorical smoke screen.

The Parent-Teachers Association (PTA) also called for a record-labeling policy. Testifying at the 1985 hearings, the vice president of legislative activity for the National PTA, Ms. Waterman, complained about the "many songs which include lyrics that may not be appropriate for young children or that send messages that may be dangerous to individuals or society."[104] Ms. Waterman was concerned both to "protect consumers from exposure to materials they feel may be harmful to themselves or children" and to avoid censorship.[105] The PTA's resolution called on "recording companies to consider the explicit contents of some songs and their responsibility to an unsuspecting public." It also called for recording companies to label record, tape, and cassette covers and "indicate the nature of the questionable content."[106]

Is it fair to call the PMRC's and PTA's policies censorship? The groups have not explicitly advocated laws to restrict what they consider to be offensive material, but perhaps only because they or their advisors know that recordings are protected by the Constitution, specifically by the First Amendment to the Bill of Rights. They hope that a labeling policy will cut off heavy metal at the point of distribution. Their idea is that chain stores will not stock labeled records if they face pressure and loss of patronage from the members of conservative groups and their sympathizers, and from concerned parents. Labeling, then, is a form of censorship through economic pressure, tilting the balance between heavy metal and its despisers in favor of the latter. Mass retailers, like all mass institutions, do not want to be "objectionable" to any compact minority. Labeling is a form of tyranny of the minority.

Throughout the hearings, an undercurrent of support for censorship became apparent. The senators kept repeating that the PMRC was not asking for any legislation. Yet Senator Hollings, in his opening statement, blustered, "if I could find some way constitutionally to do away with it, I would."[107] Senator James Exon (Nebraska) admitted to Frank Zappa, "This is one Senator that might be interested in legislation and/or regulation to some extent, recognizing the problems with the right of free expression."[108]

The efforts of the cultural conservatives to censor heavy metal by interest-group pressure have had a measure of success. As early as 1985 MTV announced that it would significantly reduce its programming of heavy metal videos. The network gave as the reason for this policy change the desire to air more "cutting-edge" material. Analysts indicate, however, that the gap was filled by older and top-forty videos. The real reason for the metal cutbacks, as most of the industry saw it, was that MTV was bowing to the pressure of various conservative watchdog groups.[109]

More recently, in response to the senate hearings and the attendant media buildup, the Record Industry Association of America (RIAA), the industry's trade association, agreed to encourage its members to place labels on albums with "explicit lyrics," acquiescing in great part to the demands of the PMRC and PTA. Frank Zappa surmises that the RIAA made such a quick and willing response because it wanted favorable legislation on blank tapes.[110] The same senate committee that conducted the labeling hearings was in charge of the tape legislation.

The impact of labeling has been similar to censorship. In a letter responding to a *Chicago Tribune* editorial endorsing labeling, Bruce Iglauer, the president of Alligator Records, described the repercussions. On the retail level chain stores have announced that they will not stock the "stickered" recordings. As a result, the record companies try to avoid releasing any work requiring a sticker. Musicians who insist on doing material that will be labeled will find that their contracts are not renewed. Iglauer concludes, "If this isn't censorship by fear, what is?"[111]

The pressure of right-wing groups on the record industry extends to the attempt to undermine the careers of individuals. A letter-writing campaign, launched by a group called Focus on Family, sought to have Peter Paterno fired as a head of Disney's new record label. Paterno was judged to be unsuitable for that position because he was once a lawyer for Guns N' Roses and Metallica.[112]

An indication that censorship is the real aim of the conservative antimetal movement is the appearance of legislative proposals at the state level to control objectionable music. Jean Dixon, a state representative from Missouri, was the author of a proposal for album labeling that served as the basis for similar bills in eighteen other states in 1990. Dixon complained that the movement to enforce record labeling would be larger if people could "stand the music long enough to understand the lyrics."[113]

In 1990 a bill was proposed in the Louisiana legislature to prohibit "the sale, exhibition, or distribution of lyrics harmful to minors."[114] Harm was defined as "advocation or encouragement of rape, incest, bestiality, sadomasochism, prostitution, homicide, unlawful ritualistic acts, suicide, the commission of a crime upon the person or property of another because of his sex, race, color, religion, or national origin, the use of any controlled and dangerous substance scheduled in the Louisiana Uniform Controlled Dangerous Substances Law, or the unlawful use of alcohol." Albums with harmful lyrics were required to be labeled by the record companies with the warning: "Explicit Lyrics—Parental Advisory." Selling a record with harmful lyrics to a minor was to carry a penalty of $5,000.

The Louisiana bill is consistent with the policies of the PMRC and the PTA, going beyond what those groups advocated in the senate hearings only in its use of the police powers of the state to enforce labeling and to prohibit the sale of labeled albums to minors. The definition of harm as "advocation or encouragement" of certain behaviors left open the possibility that metaphorical or figurative discourse might be punishable under the law, if it was interpreted by literalist prosecutors, juries, and judges. The introduction of this bill was met by threats from artists representing a wide spectrum of the arts to boycott the state if it was passed. The governor, citing constitutional concerns, eventually vetoed the bill. Thus, the first direct confrontation between the censorship movement and the artists was won by the latter. Other states dropped their pending legislation when the record industry agreed to use a uniform warning label. It reads: "Parental Advisory Explicit Lyrics." Retailers are left to decide whether to sell the stickered recordings.

In addition to the pressure placed upon the record companies and networks the conservative antimetal movement has engaged in a host of harassment tactics that put heavy metal and its subculture perpetually on the defensive. Communities have banned heavy metal concerts or have placed obstacles in the way of performing. In Johnstown, Pennsylvania, and in Salt Lake City, Utah, Sebastian Bach, Skid Row's vocalist, was arrested onstage. The crime was "thrusting his pelvis toward the crowd."[115] Metallica's scheduled concert at Notre Dame University in April 1989 was canceled on account of "bad publicity," according to the school. Only 2,800 people attended Metallica's Ames, Iowa, show that year because the local radio stations refused to carry ads publicizing it.[116]

The parents of fans have prohibited them from listening to the music or decorating their rooms or bodies with heavy metal paraphernalia. School officials have banned T-shirts with heavy metal logos and some ministers and mental health practitioners have tried to "help" metal fans by "demetalizing" them, much as "deprogrammers" worked on youths who joined religious "cults" during the 1970s. Several California police departments use the training manual *Punk Rock & Heavy Metal: The Problem/One Solution*, which lists dangerous bands, including Ozzy, Slayer, and Van Halen, and advocates that magazines such as *Creem, Hit Parader,* and *Circus* be censored.[117] Lawsuits, couched in terms of consumer safety issues, particularly the Nevada suit against Judas Priest, are extreme examples of such harassment.

More imaginative tactics in the crusade against heavy metal have been devised by a few fundamentalist leaders who have created an antimetal metal with the inherent musical meanings of the original but an evangelical message. The members of the Christian metal bands that are tied to fundamentalist churches are all well-versed in the Bible.[118] Between songs and after the concert they engage in pastoral and evangelical interactions with their fans. One evangelical minister, Bob Beeman, even claims that he created a Christian thrash metal group, Vengeance: "I handpicked the people to infiltrate the underground thrash metal scene," exults Beeman.[119] The group's singer is the pastor of the Southern California Sanctuary Church. Beeman praises the group's knowledge of the Bible and its study of apologetics and homiletics. However, Christian metal also has its detractors. In a Christian music magazine, a critic complained, "I don't believe that Christianity and moshing are real compatible."[120]

The response to censorship and harassment by heavy metal artists, the members of the subculture, and the media most closely tied to the music has been slow and not concerted. A Dionysian culture finds it difficult to fight civil wars. But as rap has joined metal as an object of intense moral criticism, parts of the wider rock community have mobilized to stave off attempts at censorship and harassment. The editors of the monthly newsletter *Rock & Roll Confidential* have written a pamphlet describing the various censorship efforts and identifying groups seeking to prevent them. Its title, *You've Got a Right to Rock: Don't Let Them Take it Away,* leaves no question as to their position. A clearinghouse, the Coalition against Lyric Legislation, based in Washington, D.C., monitors proposed legislation aimed at censoring music. A metal-oriented Chicago radio station is promoting an anticensorship organization. The most frequent response within metal has been expressive. Artists have written songs against the censors. Judas Priest's song "Parental Guidance" has become a concert sing-along staple.

The lack of a concerted response by the metal community to its detractors and its outright enemies would be explained by progressives by the supposed "escapist" nature of the heavy metal subculture. If the raison d'être of the subculture is enclosure in a rock-and-roll fantasy, political action, even of a defensive sort, is unthinkable. Indeed, the seeming inability or unwillingness of heavy metal to mount a defense against real threats to its existence would seem to substantiate the general progressive objection that heavy metal cuts the political nerve. A closer scrutiny of the situation in which the weak defensive response occurs reveals, however, structural rather than psychological grounds for that response. The structural position in which heavy metal functions as a cultural expression makes any vigorous public defense of it counterproductive for its own interests. The viewpoint of heavy metal is not legitimate or credible in the society in general, which meets it with a negative prejudice.

Discursive Terror

The prejudice against heavy metal, which is epitomized by *Newsweek*'s slogan linking it with the threats of AIDS and crack, is not random. The structural conflict underlying that rhetoric is the struggle between generations and between parents and children. It is no accident that the groups leading the attack on heavy metal are parent interest groups, the PMRC and the PTA. They identify in the music and its subculture a challenge to parental authority, even if they systematically mischaracterize and distort the nature of that challenge. That is, they have a genuine interest in inhibiting or eliminating a cultural form that has, as Pierre Bourdieu says of youth culture more generally, become "symbolically and materially active" as a defense against conformity to parental directives.[121] The attack on heavy metal is a middle-class reaction to a blue-collar romance that threatens their control over their children.

In the battle between parents and children the parents always have the advantage. The people who make the political decisions are adults (and often parents), and they give much more credence to the views of their peers than they do to young people. Youth is generally viewed by adults as being in a state of incomplete maturation. Parents and other adult authorities believe that they understand the interests of the youth in their charge better than the youth themselves understand those interests. Adults who speak for rebellious adolescents are viewed as exploiters or deviants, and are held to be no more credible than the kids.

The monopoly of adult opinion over the public discourse reflecting the parent-child conflict is enough to make the public defense of a youth culture from adult attack difficult and perhaps counterproductive, because any such defense will be interpreted by the respectable world in terms of its prejudices. However, in the case of heavy metal, the problems of defense are exacerbated by the content of the subculture and its distinctive social type or persona.

As was suggested in chapter 4, central to the heavy metal subculture is the figure of the proud pariah. The term "proud pariah" refers to a social "form," in Georg Simmel's sense, which appears in the musical subcultures of groups whose members have been marginalized by the dominant social hierarchy. Perhaps the native homeland of the proud pariah is the blues. Marginalized in many ways—by being black, rural in origin, from the South, and poor—the great blues singers made fortitude in the face of pain and hedonism as a reaction to deprivation into a badge of honor, affirming life even at its sorriest moments. The blues transvalued the singers' pain into pleasure through the inherent pleasure of the music itself and through allowing them to express their lives lyrically within the spirit of that music. They celebrated the aspects of the life-style of their group that made them pariahs to polite society, black and white: free-and-easy hedonism, vagrancy, and sexual appetite. They sang freely of "devilish" things, inverting, just as heavy metal does, the value signs of religious symbols. Their art and the appreciation of it by their audience redeemed, at least partly, a whole way of living. Its artists and core audience remained pariahs, but now had reason to take pride in their lot. They had a music of their own that expressed a spectrum of attitudes and a worldly wisdom.

Proud pariahs wear the grounds for their rejection from society as a badge of honor. Dominant society looks unfavorably enough on the groups that it marginalizes; it becomes militantly hostile against groups that flaunt the grounds for their rejection as marks of virtue. The proud pariah invites cultural warfare. Such has been the case for the blues. The music, its artists, and its audience were denounced as devil worshippers by the black churches. Then, in the 1960s, the blues came under attack from black-power radicals for being a music of resignation that fostered acquiescence in an unjust society and lowered black self-esteem. Neither attacker understood the blues as it was understood by its artists and audience. The blues did not respond in public debate, but only in song.

Heavy metal is another home of proud pariahs. Indeed, it might be usefully thought of as white-boy blues, a music appealing to the ethos of the marginalized group of male, white, blue-collar youth. The members of that group vary in their ability to become proud pariahs. Some of them have introjected the unfavorable judgment of the society on them so deeply that they suffer from self-hatred. They are the real "downers" who drop out irredeemably and often destroy themselves. They cannot be proud. At the other end of the spectrum are the youths who have found in heavy metal the way of being loud and proud, and who would not trade their life-style for any other. They have passed beyond self-hatred, enjoy Dionysian ecstasy, and affirm their pariah status against the respectable society, as a superior alternative. Between the "downers" and the complete "headbangers" is a spectrum of types that includes different mixes of self-hatred and affirmation of marginalization, grounding much of the temperamental diversity of the music.

The specific way in which heavy metal affirms the proud pariah is Dionysian rebellion. The inherent meaning of the music is basically youthful power, brought to a volume and resonance at which ecstasy through the power of sound becomes possible. That would be enough to make respectable society suspicious of heavy metal. But added to the sonic values is a set of delineated meanings that invert the values of respectable society. Long hair, tattoos, and "denim and leather" are all visible proof of one's self-willed rejection of middle-class values. Appropriation of religious symbolism for Dionysian play is blasphemy to some groups in the dominant society. The proud pariahs of heavy metal make themselves symbolically unacceptable to respectable society. By doing so they earn the frightened contempt of that society, which refuses to take them seriously.

By being proud pariahs the members of the heavy metal subculture—artists and audience—exclude themselves from dominant political discourse. The Dionysian spirit does not, in the first place, lend itself to political engagement, since it values present ecstasy over hope for the future and deferred gratification. But, beyond that, advocates for heavy metal would not get a fair hearing if they attempted to enter dominant public discourse. In a general culture that associates heavy metal with AIDS and crack cocaine any public defense of metal would be met with scorn. The subculture rejects "selling out," so artists could not cut their long hair and dress in a suit and tie to appear respectable in debate. They could not soften their message. From the viewpoint of prudence, it is counterproductive for the members of the heavy metal subculture to engage in public debate or even to start a defense movement. Opinion is already decided against them by virtue of the symbolic behavior that they cannot renounce because it defines their subculture. To call attention to themselves would only make matters worse. The real conflict regarding heavy metal, then, is symbolic: it is cultural politics, a war of icons.

Being excluded from serious consideration as a participant in public discourse, heavy metal is vulnerable to ideological terrorism. When an interest is not granted serious consideration, when it is discredited by prejudice in advance of being heard, it can be characterized in any way by the dominant discourse and that discourse will meet no resistance, even if it systematically mischaracterizes the interest. That is exactly what has happened to heavy metal in the policy process that has arisen over it. Rather than acknowledging that heavy metal is simply a symbolic threat to their authority, the parental, religious, and progressive interests ranged against heavy metal have redefined it into something that it is not in order to thoroughly discredit it. They get away with their mischaracterizations because heavy metal already has no credibility on account of its symbolic unacceptability.

The progressive critics call the music "noise" and the lyrics "drivel," listening carefully to neither and failing to note the complexity of certain aspects of the music and the pains involved in creating a good album or generating a successful concert. They are, perhaps, angry at the way that metal has appropriated and sometimes inverted the legacy of the 1960s. They believe that they are the only people authorized to appropriate that legacy, so they try to reduce their competitor to insensate meaninglessness. The conservative critics are simply maximally incompetent readers of heavy metal. They grossly misinterpret lyrics in terms of the projections of their own ideologies and they make fanciful and specious causal arguments about the contributions of heavy metal to suicidal behavior and moral laxity, and even about the power of nonexistent subliminal messages. Both the progressives and the cultural conservatives are discursive terrorists, redefining their adversary in false terms that suit their own interests, agendas, and worldviews.

In light of the public discourse about heavy metal, advocates for the music and its subculture might claim a common bond with such postmodernist perspectives as radical feminism, Afro-centrism, and gay rights. Patriarchy, racism, and homophobia all mischaracterize their enemies and, in doing so, discredit them and exclude them from serious consideration in public discourse. Heavy metal is terrorized in just the same way by hierarchical and centric discourses. But it has even less of a chance than the other marginals to have its own discourse given attention. The proud pariah, by self-definition, must always make it a point to remain marginal.

In evaluating the proposals to inhibit or censor heavy metal, it is crucial to keep in mind that none of them are based on an adequate description of what they are trying to limit. Their characterizations of heavy metal, which are artifacts of their ideological prejudices, do not square with the sociological and ethnographic evidence presented here. That evidence shows that heavy metal artists are serious creators, that the heavy metal audience gravitates around a subculture with its own intrinsic values and customary and ritual forms, and that its media have encouraged an internal tradition of criticism with self-conscious standards.

I would suggest as a norm of public policy that arguments based on the application of discursive terror (mischaracterization of one's opponent) should never guide or justify policy or institutional pressure aimed at inhibiting or eliminating a form of cultural expression. Until the despisers and detractors of metal offer more than projections, their policy proposals should not be considered and metal should simply be allowed to go its way undisturbed. If metal's opponents ever come up with some genuine arguments, which acknowledge what heavy metal is in its own right, and what effects it actually has, those arguments will have to be taken seriously. A critic internal to the metal subculture will engage those arguments, if there are any, with confidence, as a full participant in public discourse, who is respected for a legitimate point of view. But then the headbanger would no longer be a pariah.

The question, when the criticisms of heavy metal have been analyzed, comes down to whether public action should be taken or institutional pressure exerted to inhibit or suppress a symbolic rebellion against regions of the dominant culture. None of metal's opponents will put the question this way because to do so runs up directly against First Amendment protection of speech. But that is the only question left after their distortions have been corrected and their projections withdrawn. Its answer depends on the broader judgments that one makes about contemporary social life.

For those who seek to preserve their social power by means of cultural hegemony, symbolic rebellion is a clear-and-present danger. In contrast, for a lover of cultural freedom, the symbolic rebel, by profaning the sacred, prevents the triumph of bids for hegemony. The symbolic rebel makes sure that dominant values and symbols are never mistaken for the way that things must be. At its interface with society at large, heavy metal keeps culture honest by showing that its values and symbols have multiple, ambiguous, and undecidable interpretations.

8

Metal in the '90s

"Metal Meltdown"

—Judas Priest[1]

"The beast that refuses to die," a phrase used to describe heavy metal in the late 1970s and several more times in the following decade,[2] remains an apt description of the genre at the end of the twentieth century. Indeed, it is more than apt, given the death certificate issued for metal in the mid–1990s. The cause of death was listed as suspicious and fingers were pointed at several likely suspects.

Die-hard headbangers thought it was a knife-in-the-back murder and accused Metallica. The masters of headbanging metal seemed to have become puppets of mass-media masters. Metallica's 1991 eponymous release, full of pretty, radio-friendly ballads, went platinum. The band became the heavy-rotation darling of MTV. The music on their next two releases, *Load* and *Re-Load*, alloyed their pop metal with mainstream alternative. Long gone were their pledges of integrity to and proclamations of solidarity with metal's subculture. Metallica garnered the headline slot at alternative's touring festival, Lollapalooza, and the band members posed for the cover of *Rolling Stone* stylishly attired and sporting short greasy hair, eyeliner, goatees, and piercings. But one band alone can't kill a genre.

Cooler heads pinned metal's demise on the rise of the Seattle-spawned style, grunge. Metal's major market had mainly been in lite metal (what was called hard rock in the 1970s). In 1991, lite metal had a banner year. With a massive fan base and the new SoundScan technology (making retail sales figures less biased by prejudice and wishful thinking), albums by Skid Row, Motley Crüe, Van Halen, and Guns N' Roses[3] each debuted at number one on Billboard's 1991 charts. But Seattle-based Nirvana ended lite metal's reign; its major-label debut, Nevermind, released in November of that year, climbed to the top of the chart on January 11, 1992. A flock of other grunge bands followed in their wake.

The mainstream media embraced the new music and celebrated its charismatic frontmen, especially Nirvana's Kurt Cobain and Eddie Vedder of Pearl Jam. Major market radio stations developed new formats to feature the newly named alternative style, which combined grunge with a wide variety of what had been called indie and college rock in the '80s. Major metal station KNAC[4] in Los Angeles was sold and began a non-rock format in 1995. MTV put alternative's videos into heavy rotation and canceled the weekly late-night metal program, "Headbanger's Ball," in 1996. Rock magazines published tons of interviews, pictures, and reviews of grunge bands. Even the glossy metal magazines, including Kerrang!, opened their pages to the new fashion. In a feeding frenzy, major record labels signed newly-minted clones as well as older bands whose music fit the new mass-media format. Rock critics across the country, most of whom came of age championing obscure indie/college rock bands, were ecstatic; the mass public had validated their critical taste, something that hadn't happened since the heady late 1960s when rock criticism began.

Grunge was not metal, but it shared metal's guitar focus and strong lead singer. The styles had different song structures; grunge tended toward alternating hard and soft parts. Its hurt-and-despair lyrical focus didn't particularly overlap with metal's either. "We're heavy, but we're not heavy metal," Nirvana's Chris Novoselic said.[5] "Yet another misunderstanding surrounding Nirvana," a Rolling Stone writer opined, "is that the band plays, or even embraces, heavy metal—a myth perpetuated by reams of rave reviews from metal mags and an appearance on MTV's Headbanger's Ball. . . . "[6] Novoselic emphasized the desire to distance grunge from that uncool genre: "Metal's searching for an identity because it's exhausted itself, so they're going to latch onto us."[7]

Another type of popular music, rap, also began to attract a large white adolescent male audience, just the one whose demographics were once solidly behind lite metal. As grunge began its self-destruction, rap, especially gangsta rap, climbed up the charts. Over-the-top personalities delivered ghettoized potty-mouth rhythmic rhymes replete with sex and violence braggadoccio. Gangsta rap was a functional alternative to lite metal, with catchy rhythms instead of melody and phat flow replacing guitar proficiency.

Calling itself the "CNN of the ghetto," the sense of authenticity of rap's gangbanger origins was underscored by the thuggish murders of some of its major celebrities like Tupac Shakur. Senate hearings replayed the denunciations of heavy metal that were made in the Senate a decade earlier, this time targeting rap.[8] Chairing the proceedings was the senator from Illinois, Carole Mosely Braun, and replacing Tipper Gore and the PMRC was businesswoman C. Delores Tucker, both African-American. Pressure was put on major record labels to "self-censor." The charges leveled against rap had nothing to do with recruiting youth to Satan or causing them to commit suicide, but focused on allegations that the genre fostered disrespect for and violence against women (misogyny and rape). Just as the PMRC's reign of symbolic terror had enlivened the market for metal,[9] the antirap forces raised the profile, popularity, and profits of the music that they denounced.

The rise of grunge and rap can be understood as a resurgence of youth music for a new generation, dubbed by the media Generation X.[10] It was a return to authenticity in youth culture—the desire to "make it real." In terms of the emerging sensibility, lite-metal groups like Poison and Motley Crüe were into decadence, not authenticity.

Grunge's mass emergence coincided with the new post-Reagan/ Bush youth generation, which identified not with the rich (yuppies), but with the weak, maimed, and homeless—a return to rock's traditional prestige from below. In contrast, metal's messages stressed power and pleasure. Discussing the success of Nirvana's *Nevermind*, the band's biographer Michael Azerrad argued that "it coincided with a general yen for 'reality,' encompassing things like MTV's 'Unplugged' show, renewed interest in additive-free foods, the advent of network news segments that punctured the artifice of political advertising."[11] Nirvana's manager Danny Goldberg said that "Nirvana embodied the yearning for a moral universe that was more real and more sincere than what was going on in the conventional rock world at the time, and I think that resonates with a yearning in the culture for the post-Reagan set of values. There is a connection between their desire for authenticity and sincerity and ethics. . . ."[12]

Both grunge and rap were hard music with fashion and lyrics identifying with the white and black underclass, respectively. Grunge sport-ed thrift-store ripped jeans and well-worn shirts, and made heroin the drug of choice; gangsta rap preferred the gold-chain pimp-daddy look and, for gansta rappers, death by gunshot was the way to go.

Not fingered by those looking for the cause of metal's demise, but certainly deserving serious scrutiny for aiding and abetting the crime, was the serious disarray of heavy metal's mainstay bands. Metal in the first part of the 1990s was rusting out.

The initiators of the genre, Black Sabbath, were absent. Their original creative lineup lasted until 1978, when they jettisoned their out-of-control frontman, Ozzy Osbourne. At the start of the 1980s, with a new singer and songwriter, Ronnie James Dio, Sabbath released and toured in support of two strong studio albums. But the San Andreas fault line of so many metal bands, the tension between the creative visions and egos of the singer and lead guitarist, split Sabbath. For the next decade and a half, the band underwent a series of head transplants, each in turn rejected by the body. The revolving-door policy continued, including a reunion with Dio in 1992, which resulted in a rather good album, *Dehumanizer*. But the band's abortive flirtation with Ozzy Osbourne sent Dio packing. By 1995, guitarist Tony Iommi was the sole remaining link to the seminal Sabbath. Bassist Geezer Butler, the originator of that signature metal move, headbanging, recorded and toured with his modern metal project.

Ozzy, rescued and reshaped by his former manager's daughter and creatively helped by a series of strong guitarists (the first and best, Randy Rhoads, died in an unfortunate and stupid accident while on tour), was very successful. But in the early 1990s, Ozzy announced his retirement. After some months he then decided to "unretire." His 1990s output was far closer to lite metal than his earlier work and some of his mass audience was not even aware of his previous band.

Sabbath wasn't the only major metal band in disarray. Judas Priest was heavy metal's St. Paul, defining the genre's look and sound more than any other band. After the release of one of their best albums, *Painkiller*, in 1990, they became so moribund that it was assumed that they were no longer a band. Charismatic singer Rob Halford wanted to work in a more modern style of metal and initially believed that he could keep his new band, Fight, as a side project to his work in Priest.[13] He wasn't given that option and left Priest in a headless state of inaction. "There is a portion of people who just feel that I've been something of a traitor and that I walked out on something that I should have stayed with," Halford told me[14] with a tone of resignation. The High

Priest of Heavy Metal felt that he was being seen as a Judas, held responsible for the death of a major metal god.

Iron Maiden, the most significant of the New Wave of British Heavy Metal bands, was also falling apart owing to that same fault line between singer and lead guitarist. Energetic frontman Bruce Dickinson left to do his own musical project in 1993. Maiden released two live albums that year, and live albums are a sign of a band's stagnation. Maiden quickly found a replacement for Dickinson, but its subsequent releases and tours showed that the band had lost much of its once-massive American audience.

Decapitation, inactivity, and disarray also characterized other bands, including classic-metal UFO, thrash-initiators Anthrax, power-metal pioneers Helloween, and lite-metal bad-boys Motley Crüe.

Besides Ozzy's mega-popularity and the embrace by the mass media and audience of the new version of Metallica, there were a few other exceptions to metal's demise, or at least to its disappearance from the U.S. radar screen.[15] These bands were definitely and defiantly *not* lite metal, substituting aggression for heavy metal's embrace of power. Pantera's 1990 major-label debut, *Cowboys from Hell,* never made the top 200. But with no radio play and only some exposure on the still existing "Headbanger's Ball," the hard-touring band's early 1994 release, *Far Beyond Driven,* reached number one on *Billboard's* album sales chart. Also in that year, Slayer, Metallica's one time rival for most respected underground metal band, released their uncompromising *Divine Intervention,* which debuted in the top ten. Other bands working the aggro end of metal came out with powerful, no-holds-barred releases, including Machine Head and Biohazard.

Die-hard headbangers dealt with the drought of touring classic metal bands with a methadone fix of tribute bands. These club clones allow fans to see their ersatz gods up-close and personal and to hear their favorite songs played live with note-for-note perfection. Metal tribute bands abound, creating simulacra of Black Sabbath, Iron Maiden, Metallica, Ozzy, Dio, Queensrÿche, Rush, and AC/DC, among others. The commercial success of such projects indicates the tenacity of metal fandom.

A raft of tribute albums to metal's masters, beginning with the 1994 release of *Nativity in Black: A Tribute to Black Sabbath* and continuing with tributes to Judas Priest and Iron Maiden, among others, seemed to certify the genre's death. The last nail in the coffin was the 1996 release of Pat Boone's *In a Metal Mood,* a Tin Pan Alley tribute to metal featuring crooning and up-tempo wedding-band arrangements of well-known metal songs.

The Beast Is Alive and Well, Below *Billboard*'s Radar

There was no agreement about the cause of metal's death and no one ever did find the body; its existence was inferred from the absence of metal on the U.S. *Billboard* charts (see Appendix C). It turned out that the rumors of metal's death were greatly exaggerated; metal is alive and well, thriving as a creative art form with an enthusiastic fan base outside the U.S. mainstream market. Metal flourishes throughout the rest of the world and in the aptly named underground.

There are several causes for the globalization of metal. Probably the most important is the rise of pan-capitalism, which creates an industrial working class in which youth are in rebellion against their more traditional parents and invest their identity in neither the nation state nor religious groups. Popular culture, spread by the forces of capitalism, teaches that one should be true to oneself and that this can only be done by identifying with some part of popular culture.

The worldwide taste for heavy metal, from its classical incarnation in Black Sabbath and Judas Priest to newer forms, grew enormously in the 1990s. Heavy metal had spread throughout western Europe by the end of the 1970s and by the following decade throughout eastern Europe,[16] quickening after the downfall of the Soviet Union. Japan had a large, rabid following for metal. The music also penetrated major urban areas in Latin America. In the 1990s, metal extended its reach into all countries with industrial economies.

Beyond Japan, hotbeds of metal fans arose in some of the newly industrialized Pacific Rim countries. In the mid-'90s Asian MTV gave heavy airplay to Tang Dynasty, a mainland Chinese heavy-metal band.[17] Young men in Malaysia, Indonesia, and Singapore started their own musical careers. Modar, a death-metal band, comes from one of Malaysia's most conservative areas. In 1993, the Malaysian government banned live performances and airplay of heavy metal. A journalist reported that the genre "has a strong following in Malaysia" and indicated that conservative Islamic parties were responsible for the ban.[18] Another journalist concluded:

Heavy metal subculture becomes a home, a refuge for those dislocated in urban migration, caught between stereotypical racial politics and often fluid urban space divisions brought on by rapacious property development. . . . this internationalized language of stock rebellion and theatrical posturing clearly resonates for youth in Indonesia, Malaysia or Singapore, and offers comfort and identity to those still ambivalent about buying into the post-feudal/colonial capitalist environment that's being rapidly constructed around them.[19]

Similar transformations were occurring in Latin America. Heavy-metal audiences in urban areas of Brazil, Chile, Argentina, and Mexico shared the Asian dislocations and, owing to their Catholic upbringing, also responded to the religious symbols that are part of metal's stock in trade. Black Sabbath, Iron Maiden, Slayer, and Manowar, among others, have toured Latin America or have come down for the annual Monsters of Rock Festivals, playing to large and well-informed audiences.

Even Malta, a tiny Mediterranean island north of Libya and south of Italy, has professional metal bands, as do Israel, Iceland, and Egypt. There are still holdouts; at least I've not heard of metal concerts in countries like Saudi Arabia and Somalia.

A worldwide audience helped to preserve metal for U.S. fans, much like the Islamic world and medieval monasteries preserved the intellectual wisdom of ancient Greece and Rome for the European Renaissance. Metal's global audience made it worthwhile for bands to continue to make new records (even if they could only be had in America as expensive imports) and to tour (even if they didn't play in the States).

Besides flourishing globally, metal was creatively thriving in an underground that transcended geography. In musical discourse, the term *underground* has two meanings. Dante's fourteenth-century vision of the world beyond, *The Divine Comedy*, neatly reflects the distinction. Dante divided the underground into Hell (Inferno) and its outer reaches, Purgatory. In Purgatory, one has the possibility of redemption, of working off earthly sins and achieving entrance into Heaven (here the paradise of commercial mainstream popularity). Underground, in the sense of Purgatory, is a term for bands and styles that are not currently, but once were or might some day be popular. Underground, in the sense of Hell, refers to music that is too extreme, sonically, lyrically, or both, ever to attract a mainstream audience.

Bands playing underground metal of an infernal sort have no hope or desire (if they are rational) to break through to the other side, to that Heaven of pop stardom. Like any of the elite arts, underground metal is appreciated by a discerning audience.

Underground metal began when MTV did, as its evil twin, embodying everything MTV metal was not. It is devoid of pop tropes like ballads and star posturing. Its lyrics lack romantic fluff, hippie hopefulness, or Gen-X self-pity. The music is anything but simplistic, with complex time changes and chord progressions. The underground continues metal's original obsession with good and evil, verbally depicted in ways that would defrost Walt Disney's cryogenic tomb. Not that the words can be easily understood; in some styles, singing is best described as growling or screeching.

A metal underground could thrive in the '90s because of the wide array of mediators providing a rich infrastructure for producing and promoting bands. In the United States, the important indie labels include Century Media, Earache, Nuclear Blast, Roadrunner, and Relapse, each a branch of a European-based company.[20] Some labels have significant mail-order departments. The proliferation of used record stores, owing in part to the "indestructibility" of CDs, allows metal fans to indulge their penchant for seeking out bands' back catalogs.[21]

Commercial radio never did play underground metal, but hundreds of college radio stations have weekly metal shows that focus on extreme metal styles.[22] Reminiscent of the underground FM of the late 1960s, metal DJs expose their listeners to music and provide critical commentary, serving to create an educated underground. An informed audience is aided and abetted by a plethora of new and older metal magazines, ranging from commercially successful colorful glossies to one-person penned 'zines. Magazines like *Terrorizer, Rock Hard, Brave Words and Bloody Knuckles, Metal Maniacs, Pit, Midwest Metal, Ill Literature, Sounds of Death, Kerrang!, Metal Hammer, Burrn!, Rock Brigade, Scream,* and *Madhouse,* constituting a united nations of metal, provide interviews with musicians and reviews of shows and new releases.

Videos for underground metal bands had only the most limited exposure on MTV[23] in the United States before the demise of Headbanger's Ball and afterward had none. Few underground bands make videos and those are sold through retail channels or in metal video magazines.[24] (Metal videos and Headbanger's Ball are shown on European MTV, MTV Latino, and MTV Asia.)

The metal underground has been increasingly well represented in the 1990s at the metal festivals in Europe, the United States, and Latin America. These mega-band affairs bring together subcultural fans, label personnel, and metal journalists, and give exposure to newer as well as more well-known bands. In the United States, the major confab is Milwaukee's Metalfest. In its thirteenth year in 1999, 165 bands performed over a two-day period on four stages. Fans from around the country came to hear bands from Mexico, Norway, Sweden, Greece, Japan, Brazil, and from almost half the American states. European festivals, such as the annual Dynamo Festival in Holland and the Latin American Monsters of Rock, gather far larger audiences, numbering in the tens of thousands.

The metal underground has been flourishing since the mid–1990s in large measure through the internet. Whether the sites are made by fans, band members, or indie labels, they provide a wealth of information, including band histories, reviews and interviews, lyrics, pictures, sound clips, and links to related sites. The internet also allows indie labels to promote their new releases at little cost. With worldwide distribution and no printing or mailing expenses, magazines on the net (e-'zines) abound. Opinions on underground metal are also found on dozens of news groups (like alt.rock-n-roll.metal.heavy or alt.rock-n-roll.metal.black) where a wide variety of issues are discussed, albums and bootlegs are traded, and information on new releases, tour dates, set lists, and new web sites are posted. In some sense, the internet helps to form a virtual community of fans.

Internet technology also creates the opportunity to hear metal radio. A former DJ on the defunct satellite-based metal radio network, Z-Rock, Tracy Barnes runs Hardrock Radio (www.hardradio.com). Los Angeles lost its mainly lite-metal station KNAC, but it now exists on the web (www.knaclive.com). Rebel Radio, whose broadcasts can be heard only in the Chicago area, finds listeners worldwide via its site (www.rebelradio.com). The metal programs of college radio stations are also making their way onto the net. These internet meditations serve the interests of metal in general, enhancing the global reach of the genre.

The underground metal scene is far larger outside the United States, especially in Europe, for a variety of reasons. One is that the liquor laws in the United States restrict people under twenty-one years of age from buying alcohol, and alcohol sales are an important means by which venues, especially smaller ones, help pay for live music. Because underground metal, with its speed, volume, and over-the-top lyrics, particularly appeals to teenagers, venues cannot afford to put on shows featuring extreme music. Also, the policies of mass-market U.S. retailers Wal-mart and K-Mart exclude most underground metal albums; these mass retailers refuse to stock material with cover art and/or lyrics that they consider to be "unwholesome."

There are other reasons for the larger European metal audience. Many northern European countries have government grants, the dole if you will, providing money to older adolescents who do not hold full-time jobs. They can use their leisure to indulge musical proclivities as creators and appreciators. Some countries or municipalities provide young people with music lessons, practice spaces, and even musical instruments.[25]

Also, metal exudes a decidedly working-class attitude and Europeans have a larger and stronger working-class identity than Americans. European high schools often have separate blue-collar career tracks. Fewer adolescents go to college in Europe and college students tend to affiliate themselves with a distinctive middle-class perspective. Also, the college dorm experience works to broaden musical tastes,[26] making it less likely that individuals will maintain the subcultural affiliations of their high school cliques.

The Hydra-Headed Beast

Off the radar screen of mass media gatekeepers in the mammoth American market for much of the 1990s, metal expanded in many directions. The genre's development is analogous to the way plants and animals in isolated areas evolve to produce wildly extreme forms.

Mapping metal's myriad styles at the end of the twentieth century is a messy task at best. Style categories are not watertight containers— they leak, bleed into others, and mix with elements from anywhere. Take, for example, the categories of white and black metal. In the 1980s, this division, based on lyrics alone, applied only to religiously oriented bands. Bands with evangelical Christian messages were labeled white metal; those proclaiming allegiance to Satan were called black metal. White metal, with its original meaning, still exists, main-ly in thrash- and death-metal bands like Tourniquet and Living Sacrifice. But black metal has a far different meaning than it had in the 1980s. The term, taken from an early song by Venom, now refers to a sonic style begun in Norway by Mayhem and Burzum.[27] Many of the lyrics of these bands express an anti-Christian or pro-satanic position, but other themes have been added.

Mapping metal or any other musical genre is made messier still by the absence of sharp-shooting border guards who would make musi-cians stay within one style over the course of their careers or even through one album. Adding to the classification problem is the absence of some nocturnal council or respected dictionary that could standardize the names or boundary lines demarcating one style from another.[28] Even if there was agreement on terms, there are no umpires or thought police to enforce rules of assigning a given band's work to one or another category. Retail stores can place a record into any bin they like and fans, publicists, and rock journalists have the same free-dom to be arbitrary, inconsistent, or merely perverse. Chuck Eddy, for example, in his book listing his take on the best heavy metal albums, includes in his top ten choices the proto-punk New York Dolls, south-ern rockers Lynyrd Skynyrd and funk-diva Teena Marie, and, in his '90s-era top ten, Rancid, Sublime, and Hole appear.[29] Lewis Carroll sums up the way rock critics, not just Eddy, bandy about genre terms: "'When I use a word,' Humpty Dumpty said in a rather scornful tone, 'it means just what I choose it to mean, neither more nor less.'"[30]

Recall these caveats while reading the following overview; supple-ment it with visits to some of the innumerable metal web sites[31] where one can read more extensive descriptions as well as hear examples of the music.

Metal subgenres have come into being through processes of inten-sification and hybridization. Styles, as our retro times make all too clear, are infinitely resurrectable and revisable. In culture, as opposed to life, nothing ever dies permanently.

Bands long dead and gone can rise from the grave for reunions and the actual demise of musicians can be overcome with suitable replacements. Classic or traditional[32] heavy-metal bands (and they tend to be the same ones who constructed the style decades ago) are global troubadours making new records and, as they say, still kicking ass. Black Sabbath, Judas Priest, and Iron Maiden, among others, have revived (if only for a while).

Doom metal, a sludgy slow and heavy style that can be traced to some of Black Sabbath's 1970s songs, categorizes 1980s bands St.Vitus, Candlemass, and Trouble. It continued with bands like Crowbar and the psychedelic-tinged Sleep. A hybrid of doom and goth music describes other '90s bands like My Dying Bride and Avernus.

Thrash metal, a punked-up, American-made response to the New Wave of British Heavy Metal, is still out there too, both with older originators like Anthrax, Megadeth, and Slayer, and a few newer models. Metallica, another thrash originator, now saves that side of themselves for part of their concerts, choosing to record in a different style.

Thrash metal promiscuously sired several subgenres. The miscegenation of thrash and hardcore punk spawned a style that is sometimes called metalcore, which accentuates hardcore's staccato vocals and limited melody. Several metalcore bands have attracted widespread attention in the '90s, particularly Pantera, Biohazard, and Machine Head.

Another 1990s hybridization is rapcore. Body Count, led by rapper Ice-T, addressed themes that had crossover appeal to young males of all races.[33] The use of rapped vocals became rather popular later in the decade, although few bands that used them could be called metal.

Melding thrash with industrial dance music is the way bands as diverse as Godflesh, Fear Factory, and Rammstein create their sound. On the border of this industrial metal subgenre are bands like Ministry and Nine Inch Nails, more accurately understood, perhaps, as metallized industrial music.

The intensification of thrash in the 1980s, rather than its amalgamation with other styles, led to death metal. Influenced by bands like Bathory, Celtic Frost, and early Slayer, death metal has the lowest pitch of any form of music. Its standard features are down-tuned guitars, double-kick drums, and electronically transfigured vocals that require phrases like "gargling with acid laced with razor blades" to give some idea of their sound.[34] The largest contingent of underground metal bands play death metal; the subgenre's extensive worldwide reach is as ubiquitous as McDonald's. Death metal would work as the sound track to the movie version of Dante's *Inferno* or at least as Hell's Muzak. Its lyrics are fixated on death, decay, and the diabolical. Bands' names reflect these concerns: Deicide, Morbid Angel, Malevolent Creation, Cannibal Corpse, Death, Entombed, Six Feet Under, Dismember, Obituary, and hundreds of others in that vein. Death metal today is more than just the continuation of the original style. With so many bands, death metal itself diversified; for example, through amalgamation to form the doom-death and grindcore styles.

In contrast to the aggression and heavy sound of thrash and its off-shoots, power metal derives mainly from classic New Wave of British Heavy Metal bands like Iron Maiden. The subgenre, famous for epic songs with spiritual themes and strong tenor vocalists, often borrows from nineteenth-century symphonic music. Helloween, from Germany, was an early exponent. Among the better-known groups are Gamma Ray, Blind Guardian, Hammerfall, Iced Earth, Jag Panzer, Stratovarious, and Angra. Some combine power metal with progmetal, a term used for bands like Dream Theater, whose work incorporates musical elements from jazz and echoes the art rock of the 1970s.

Black metal erupted in Norway in the early '90s with Burzum and Mayhem. To a death-metal base, black metal added swirling layers of cosmic keyboard soundscapes, rasped screeching vocals, and musicians daubed in corpse paint. Members of the originating bands were deadly serious about their demonic posturing. Their cemetery desecrations, church burnings, and murders didn't kill the subgenre; like gangsta rappers' rap sheets, their deeds probably helped black metal's popularity by adding a semblance of authenticity. The number of bands playing black metal, especially in northern Europe, is growing exponentially, along with the number of fans for the style. Bands like Emperor and Dimmu Borgir are important enough to cross the Atlantic and play in the United States. The style itself is undergoing fragmentation, as some bands turn to a more New Age sound (Tiamat, Burzum) and others, like Cradle of Filth and Theater of Tragedy, meld black metal with doses of goth.

The continual innovations, schisms, and borrowings by musicians, plus the Humpty-Dumpty approach of critics, publicists, and fans, provide many openings to add to or disagree with the mapping of metal presented here.[35] Does Rage Against the Machine qualify as metal? Should the metallic funk of Sevendust or the hard rock hip-hop of Limp Bizkit be classed as metal? Unlike the cartography of the earth, cultural maps are always up for grabs.

The diversity of metal is a concern for editors and fans. Internet news groups burst with "flames" against one or another form of metal. A debate in the British magazine *Terrorizer* in 1998, for example, revolved around the inclusion of coverage of traditional metal bands. Many readers wanted the magazine's policy to exclude all but "extreme" styles. Others disagreed. One called for panmetallic unity:

"Why fight among one another when we have a huge battle on our hands with the hordes of brainless trend followers, ravers, wussy poppers and above all the obscene techno infiltration into Metal?" Another reader defended a latitudinarian approach as a good recruiting tactic: "Tolerance of the occasional slip into what we call lighter territory helps get more people into extreme metal who would otherwise no[t] know about it."[36]

Metal's diversity was made palpable during one week in the summer of 1998. In three very different venues in and around Milwaukee, Wisconsin, metalheads of all persuasions could find the whole panoply of Black Sabbath's spawn. At Marcus Amphitheater, Metallica's sell-out show included their pop lite-metal ballads, some performed in an acoustical set, as well as their ferocious thrash metal. Several days earlier, at the rural Alpine Valley shed, OzzFest held sway. The current version of Ozzy Osbourne no longer bedevils small flying animals or pees on the Alamo. His ballads get radio play and his albums go gold, but on stage he sings some of his decades-old Sabbath hits, like "Iron Man." Among the bands in 1998's OzzFest were the Melvins (the band behind grunge's heaviness) and Motörhead, the original integrator of punk and metal in 1975, who've probably played more gigs and been signed to more labels than any other band. A big tour draw was Limp Bizkit, whose best-selling mongrel style might earn it any number of classifications.

Between these two shows was Milwaukee's Metalfest's two-day extravaganza held in the grungy Eagles Auditorium. Bands and fans came from all over the United States and Canada, with some of the 115 bands flying in from Europe. Thrash metal (for example, Sodom from Germany), black metal in the older sense of the term (for example, Mercyful Fate from Denmark), and black metal as the term is used today (for example, Emperor from Norway) were well represented. Death-metal bands of all types and from many countries came in droves, including white-metal bands, an all-female group, and a band in which the singer-guitarist was not yet a teenager.

The Beast Is Back

At the century's end, despite or because of its radical diversity, metal's demise seems even less likely than it had been in the past. Beyond its densely flowering underground and its global reach, metal has recently erupted into the U.S. mainstream. The beast is back and there are a variety of reasons for its resurgence.

The mainstream rock press, like *Rolling Stone*, always did their darnedest to ignore metal,[37] hoping, I suppose, that it would go away. When it was mentioned at all, it was mainly with deprecation, as a synonym for and the best example of obviously inferior music. The tide, for the time being at least, has turned. *Spin* ran a major feature on New Metal in their August 1998 issue. The cover of *Rolling Stone* in February 1999,[38] adorned with a picture of the heavily tattooed, long-haired, and unsmiling visage of Rob Zombie, touted an article about the "10 Best Metal Bands." Titled "Metal: the Next Generation," the piece consisted of brief desriptions of bands representing a wide spectrum of styles. Many, like Black Sabbath, Pantera, and Morbid Angel, have been around for ages. Fans of these bands might not even consider some of the others on the list, like Korn and stoner rockers Queens of the Stone Age, as metal.

Black Sabbath, except for a few pieces in *Creem* when they began in the early 1970s, was hardly ever acknowledged by the mainstream rock press. But their 1999 reunion tour garnered full coverage in all the music media, including the daily newspapers. That tickets to their concerts quickly sold out and their *Reunion* album went gold are partly responsible for the attention, but the press is also a reflection of metal's resurgence. Yet old habits die hard; the snide put-downs that rock critics always reserved for metal have not disappeared. Typical was the *Rolling Stone* concert review, replete with digs: The band had "shaky chops," guitarist Iommi "hasn't mastered any new licks in decades," Ozzy didn't sing (he "croaked"), and audiences were "heathen hordes." The piece concluded that the band's success was owing to sticking with a "somewhat dunderheaded musical template."[39]

Spin's 1998 feature on "New Metal," which focused on bands like Korn and Limp Bizkit, was not free of denigration either: Their music offered "traditional metal ferocity minus the corny hail-Satanism, Tawny Kitean videos, and big hair of the '80s. . . . "[40] "New Metal" is defined by *Spin* as "a forward-looking hybrid that takes as many cues from alternative rock, hip-hop, and SoCal hardcore skate culture as it does from Black Sabbath and Slayer. For instance, Limp Bizkit, with their rapped vocals and full-time DJ, are New Metal."[41] Recognizing the style's myriad ancestors, why call it metal rather than hip-hop, alternative, or some other term that doesn't mention any of its constituent genres? Why label it metal, when members of these bands have stated that they are not at all desirous to be tagged with that term?[42] One answer is that calling it metal gives the hybrid a more familiar, and perhaps a more white and more rock, image. The promiscuous use of "metal" is itself a demonstration that metal is back, as well as a cause of that comeback.

The absence of any other "happening" style is one reason for metal's rising status. By 1998, alternative was on its deathbed; the new releases from standardbearers Pearl Jam and the Smashing Pumpkins were poorly received. The industry-pushed "next new thing," "electronica," had not taken off. Hip-hop was selling well but without any creative advances. Metal's faithful, self-sustaining, and unfashionable fan base[43] was still there, listening to their music, talking about it with friends, buying old and new releases, and coming out to see unhyped shows. When Black Sabbath's CD signing tour made a stop at a suburban Chicago shopping center in September 1998, about three thousand people waited in line for five or more hours for the chance to get the band members' autographs. The fans ranged in age from unrepentent forty-something headbangers, some with their own kids in tow, to fifteen-year-old death-metal fans wanting to pay homage to the genre's originator. Two years earlier Manowar, which hadn't played in the area in almost a decade, did a Chicago in-store signing; hundreds of fans, many of whom had never seen the band play live, stood in line for hours, animatedly chatting and holding their vinyls and CDs, waiting to meet the band.

If there was one specific event that began metal's resurgence, it was the industry's reaction to the huge success of OzzFest in 1997. The music industry, pundits, and powers that be perk up their collective ears when some untouted style attracts a large audience. The huge success of metal day at the 1983 US Festival was, in part, responsible for heavy metal's major invasion of the United States. After the 1997 concert season, when the score was totted up, the OzzFest tour, put together by the manager of, named after, and headlining Ozzy Osbourne, was a smashing financial success. It sold out shows along the way, but more significant, it outsold Lollapalooza, alternative music's annual touring fest.[44] It was, to quote Yogi Berra, "déjà vu all over again."

OzzFest[45] displayed metal's miscegenated spectrum, featuring Pantera, Machine Head, Fear Factory, Type-O Negative, Vision of Disorder, Neurosis, and three of the four original members of Black Sabbath. But it was the inclusion of Marilyn Manson (Alice Cooper meets Nine Inch Nails with an over-the-top sex-and-Satan shtick) that drew attention to the tour. Marilyn Manson riled right-wing Christians who posted denunciations of the band on the internet (many scurrilous), pressured local authorities to ban the concert, and protested in front of venues where the show went on. The main impact of their actions, beyond providing lawyers with work, was to keep the tour in the newspaper headlines.

Metal's high profile can also be traced to Metallica's mega-mainstream success. The band's music was played with increasing frequency around the country on major radio stations with a number of different formats. During the day they played Metallica's radio-friendly 1990s output, but at night they would also air their '80s thrash metal along with songs by other metal acts. In concert, the band performs their earlier songs, exposing a new generation to thrash metal. In late 1998, Metallica released a double CD of cover songs, including a raft of their well-known thrash hits. The package and the band's supporting tour, where they played their underground thrash, sold very well. Beyond Metallica, the major classic metal bands that had been in disarray during the first part of the decade have gained new life. Through reunions and head transplants, the definers of heavy metal's styles seem to rise from the dead to reclaim their own and the genre's vitality.

Judas Priest, the originators of the studded black leather look, lost their charismatic frontman, Rob Halford, in 1991 and were given up for dead. But they hadn't hung up their motorcycle boots. The self-pro-claimed "Defenders of the Faith" of heavy metal, who had triumphed in an infamous Nevada trial where their music was accused of causing two suicides, pulled off a resurrection. They found a simulacrum of Halford, Tim Owens, in a Judas Priest tribute band. "My first concert ever was the 'Defenders of the Faith' tour," Owens said. "I still remember that to this day. I've been to every one of their concerts."[46] How many thousands of Judas Priest fans have said the same thing? But Owens followed in his idol's footsteps. He was the singer in a heavy-metal band called Winter's Bane. He described their sound as "sort of Judas Priest mixed with Savatage." To gain exposure, an agent suggest-ed that they start a Judas Priest tribute band and have Winter's Bane open for them.[47] British Steel, its name taken from a Priest album, filled the clubs in and around Ohio with a satisfying spot-on pseudo-Priest show. Members of Judas Priest saw a video of the tribute band and hired Owens, bestowing on him the Priestly moniker "Ripper."

Lite-metal bands were also coming out of the woodwork. Motley Crüe, after more than a decade of decadence (making tabloid headlines rather than bagging critical reviews by the rock press), reunited with former frontman Vince Neil, released a greatest hits album, and played some shows. Replete with makeup, platform heels, fire, and other assorted bedazzlements, Kiss[48] mounted a highly successful reunion tour in 1998.

Bruce Dickinson returned to Iron Maiden and many lesser-known bands like S.O.D., Venom, and Exodus also reunited for new projects or one-off shows.

Reunions and new product from musicians well into middle age are not unique to metal. At the end of the twentieth century, it seems that nothing in popular culture is allowed to die—witness Hollywood remakes, fashion rehashes, TV reruns, and the Rolling Stones. We are mired in recycling and what postmodernists call archivalism (packaged by marketers as box sets) of pop culture that had been given up for dead. Most of retro culture is devoid of referentiality, but metal's current rise speaks to current tendencies in society.

Metal fits into the "prole" leanings of popular culture today, ranging from tabloid news, the mass popularity of pro wrestling, and the trash talk of the Jerry Springers and radio shock-jocks. Despite the virtuosity of metal musicians, the genre, like other "prole" entertainments, is free of subtlety and understatement. Metal's current popularity can also be understood as a counterweight or resistence to the feminization of popular music and its turn toward smooth (urban) black pop. Rock bands like Sublime and Garbage, country artists like Shania Twain and the Dixie Chicks, pop divas like Celine Dion and Sheryl Crow, and the kiddie-rock Spice Girls find their polar opposite in metal's hard, heavy power/aggression, which is equated with masculinity. In rock critic parlance, "metal" is used as the equivalent of "testosterone-fueled." Metal's traditional concerns with good and evil and its use of religious metaphors also connect with the millennial anxiety and moral discourse permeating the mass media.

Despite both the diversity within the meta-genre of metal and the way the term is promiscuously bandied about in the mainstream media, metal has not become an empty signifier floating untethered in the sea of popular culture. The metal subculture still knows what metal is; fans are attending metal concerts, buying new albums, putting up metal web sites, and endlessly talking and posting views and news on the net. As the century ends, metal does not; that beast refuses to go gently into any damn night.

Appendix A: Suggested Hearings

100 Definitive Metal Albums

That old saw about the inadequacy of words to describe music—writing about music is like dancing about architecture—is, of course, true. To really know the subject of this book, you need to hear it. In metal, the album rather than the individual song is the main unit of appreciation. The albums listed here are generally agreed upon by fans and critics to be definitive metal as well as excellent albums that represent the genre over its various styles and eras.

AC/DC	*Back in Black*	1980
Accept	*Restless and Wild*	1983
Amorphis	*Tales from the Thousand Lakes*	1994
Angel Witch	*Angel Witch*	1980
Annihilator	*Alice in Hell*	1989
Anthrax	*Spreading the Disease*	1985
Arcturus	*La Masquerade Infernale*	1997
Armored Saint	*March of the Saint*	1984
At the Gates	*Slaughter of the Soul*	1995
Bathory	*Under the Sign of the Black Mark*	1987
Benediction	*Dreams You Dread*	1995
Biohazard	*State of the World Address*	1994
Black Sabbath	*Mob Rules*	1981
Black Sabbath	*Paranoid*	1970
Blind Guardian	*Nightfall in Middle-Earth*	1998
Body Count	*Body Count*	1992
Broken Hope	*Loathing*	1997
Brujeria	*Matando Gueros*	1993
Candlemass	*Epicus Doomicus Metallicus*	1986
Cannibal Corpse	*Butchered at Birth*	1991
Carcass	*Heartwork*	1993
Celtic Frost	*Into the Pandemonium*	1987
Cradle of Filth	*Cruelty and the Beast*	1998
Crowbar	*Obedience Through Suffering*	1992

Death	*Leprosy*	1988
Deep Purple	*Machine Head*	1972
Deicide	*When Satan Lives*	1998
Diamond Head	*Lightning to the Nations*	1981
Dimmu Borgir	*Enthrone Darkness Triumphant*	1997
Dio	*Holy Diver*	1983
Down	*Nola*	1995
Dream Theater	*Images and Words*	1992
Edge of Sanity	*Spectral Sorrows*	1994
Einherjer	*Odin Owns Ye All*	1998
Emperor	*Anthems to the Welkin at Dusk*	1997
Entombed	*Wolverine Blues*	1994
Exciter	*Long Live the Loud*	1986
Exodus	*Bonded by Blood*	1985
Fear Factory	*Demanufacture*	1995
Flotsam & Jetsam	*Doomsday for the Deceiver*	1986
Forbidden	*Forbidden Evil*	1988
Gamma Ray	*Somewhere Out in Space*	1997
Godflesh	*Slavestate*	1991
Grim Reaper	*See You in Hell*	1984
Guns N'Roses	*Appetite for Destruction*	1987
Hammerfall	*Glory to the Brave*	1997
Helloween	*Keeper of the Seven Keys, Part II*	1989
Hypocrisy	*Osculum Obscenum*	1993
Iced Earth	*Iced Earth*	1991
In Flames	*Whoracle*	1997
Iron Maiden	*The Number of the Beast*	1982
Judas Priest	*Painkiller*	1990
Judas Priest	*Stained Class*	1978
King Diamond	*Abigail*	1987
Krokus	*Headhunter*	1983
Living Sacrifice	*Reborn*	1997
Macabre	*Sinister Slaughter*	1993
Manowar	*Into Glory Ride*	1983
Megadeth	*Peace Sells . . . But Who's Buying?*	1986
Mercyful Fate	*Don't Break the Oath*	1984
Meshuggah	*Destroy Erase Improve*	1995
Metallica	*Kill'em All*	1983
Michael Schenker Group	*Assault Attack*	1982

Ministry	*Psalm 69*	1992
Montrose	*Montrose*	1973
Morbid Angel	*Altars of Madness*	1989
Mötley Crüe	*Shout at the Devil*	1983
Motörhead	*Ace of Spades*	1980
Napalm Death	*Fear, Emptiness, Despair*	1994
Neurosis	*Through Silver in Blood*	1996
Nuclear Assault	*Game Over*	1986
Nugent, Ted	*Double Live Gonzo*	1978
Obituary	*The End Complete*	1992
Old Man's Child	*The Pagan Prosperity*	1997
Overkill	*Horrorscope*	1991
Ozzy Osbourne	*Blizzard of Ozz*	1980
Pantera	*Vulgar Display of Power*	1992
Possessed	*Seven Churches*	1985
Queensrÿche	*Operation: Mindcrime*	1988
Rainbow	*On Stage*	1977
Raven	*All for One*	1983
Sacred Reich	*The American Way*	1990
Savatage	*Hall of the Mountain King*	1987
Saxon	*Wheels of Steel*	1980
Scorpions	*Virgin Killer*	1976
Sepultura	*Chaos A.D.*	1993
Six Feet Under	*Haunted*	1995
Slayer	*Reign in Blood*	1986
S.O.D.	*Speak English or Die*	1985
Suicidal Tendencies	*How Will I Laugh Tomorrow When I Can't Even Smile Today*	1988
Sword	*Metalized*	1986
Thin Lizzy	*Jailbreak*	1976
Trouble	*Manic Frustration*	1992
Tygers of Pan Tang	*Crazy Nights*	1981
UFO	*Strangers in the Night*	1979
Vader	*Live in Japan*	1999
Venom	*Black Metal*	1982
Voivod	*Killing Technology*	1987
Witchery	*Dead, Hot and Ready*	1999
Yngwie J. Malmsteen's Rising Force	*Marching Out*	1985

Appendix B: Gender Preferences for Metal Subgenres

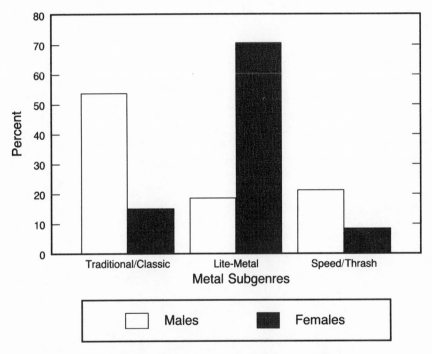

Source: Z-Rock requests for July 16–23, 1990

Classic/Traditional Metal is defined as requests for Black Sabbath (& Ozzy Osbourne), Judas Priest, or Iron Maiden. **Lite-Metal** is defined as requests for Poison, Bon Jovi, or Mötley Crüe. **Speed/Thrash Metal** is defined as requests for Suicidal Tendencies, Slayer, or Nuclear Assault.

Appendix C: Proportion of Heavy Metal Albums in Billboard's Top 100

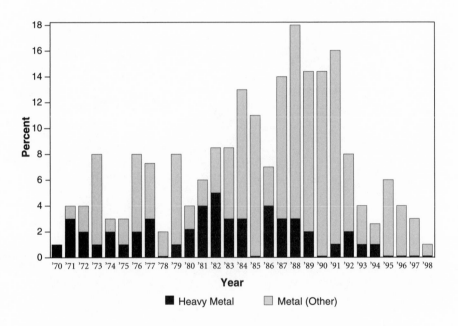

Albums designated "Heavy Metal" have been universally classified as heavy metal, including those by Black Sabbath, Judas Priest, and Iron Maiden. Those in the residual category, "Metal (Other)," include bands called "hard rock" in the '70s and relabeled "metal" in the '80s, like Kiss, lite-metal bands like Poison and Bon Jovi, and the post-thrash metal releases of Metallica in the '90s.

Notes

Chapter 1

1. John Milton, *"Paradise Lost" and Other Poems*, p. 52, lines 540–43.
2. Robert Duncan, *The Noise*, 36–37.
3. Cited in Linda Martin and Kerry Segrave, *Anti-Rock*, 233.
4. Testimony of Dr. Joe Stuessy, U.S. Congress, *Record Labeling (Senate Hearing 99–529)*, 117.
5. Ibid., 119.
6. Paul Battiste *(Creem*, 1972), cited in Philip Bashe, *Heavy Metal Thunder*, 24.
7. J. D. Considine, "Purity and Power," 46.
8. David Fricke, "The Year in Records," 218.
9. Cited by Mike Clifford, *The Harmony Illustrated Encyclopedia of Rock*, 57.
10. Lester Bangs, "Heavy Metal," 332.
11. Jeffrey Burton Russell, *Mephistopheles*, 256.
12. Loyd Grossman, *Social History of Rock Music*, 93–94.
13. His question was directed, incongruously, to John Denver; U.S. Congress, *Record Labeling (Senate Hearing 99–529)*, 70.
14. Advertisement for *Newsweek* special issue on youth, *Newsweek*, 14 May 1990, 71.
15. The term "bricolage" is used by the anthropologist Claude Lévi-Strauss to describe a wide range of systems of culture, ranging from myths to classifications of nature. In the present discussion the term is broadly defined, but it remains true to the spirit of Lévi-Strauss's usage by stressing the basically aesthetic structure of the bricolage. For Lévi-Strauss's discussion of bricolage, see *The Savage Mind*, 16–22.
16. The author has previously applied the concept of the bricolage to the study of rock music; see Deena Weinstein, "The Amnesty International Concert Tour."
17. Each of the features—sonic, visual, and verbal—is coded and, in terms of Culler's notion of genre, gives directions for what to look for and how to read sequences; see Ralph Cohen, "Do Postmodern Genres Exist?," 255.
18. Ronald Byrnside, "Formation of a Musical Style," 161.
19. "Genre" is not a precise term. As Ralph Cohen notes about genres of writing, "If writing were always identical, there would be . . . no need for generic

distinctions about whole works. And if each piece of writing were different from all others there would be no basis for theorizing or even for communication" (see Ralph Cohen, "Do Postmodern Genres Exist?," 244). Genres arise in the zone between monotony and uniqueness. Similarities of style, common influences, imitation, a tradition of criticism, commercial promotion, and audience preferences all come together to define a code, some of the elements of which become reflexively applied and others of which are implicit.

20. Lucy Green distinguishes between the sonic and other meanings of a musical "style." According to her, music consists fundamentally of "inherent sonic qualities," which communicate through channels of experience independent of language. But music also contains meanings that are "delineated" by its context of social use and that need not have any direct connection with its "inherent" meanings. In experiencing music, Green points out, inherent and delineated meanings are "inseparable" (see Lucy Green, *Music on Deaf Ears*, 33). They can and must, however, be distinguished for purposes of analysis. In order to describe a musical genre adequately, one must study both its inherent and its delineated meanings. The genre is a bricolage of sonic, visual, and verbal elements.

21. Byrnside, "Formation of a Musical Style," 161.

22. The metaphor of "family resemblance" comes from Ludwig Wittgenstein's philosophy of language. As Cohen says in relation to writing, "But since one piece of writing tends to be based on other pieces some theorists refer to genres as families of texts with close or distant relatives" (Cohen, "Do Postmodern Genres Exist?," 244). The same point can be made at the level of genres and subgenres of music, which have affinities for and traces of one another.

23. Having no center of its own, the transaction could only be described in an absolute way by imposing a center on it from the outside in the form of what Jean-François Lyotard calls a "meta-narrative" (see Jean-François Lyotard, *The Postmodern Condition*). Any of the competing "macrotheories" in sociology, such as classical functionalism and Marxism, could have served that purpose, but they would privilege some centers of the transaction over others, duplicating the original problem. Heavy metal has, indeed, not yet been given a comprehensive sociological description because schools of analysis have given priority to one of the participants in the transaction over the others. The two main centers of sociological literature on the genre, British cultural studies and American popular music studies, have been devoted, respectively, to scrutinizing the subculture of the audience and the workings of the rock industry. This study will include their contributions in the appropriate places and will add a third emphasis, on the artists, who have been relatively ignored. The result will not be a single narrative, but a series of perspectives, each one interpreting the entire transaction from its own viewpoint and each one containing its own history of how its function has been performed.

24. The triad lacks a version in which the audience mediates between mediator and artist. Although the audience is far from passive, it is basically receptive, the repository of a subculture that places limits on both artists and mediators.

Don't audience preferences in terms of concert attendance and record buying, for example, mediate between artist and the media? The audience determines who is successful and who isn't, thereby helping to establish contract terms, endorsements and commercials, etc.

Chapter 2

1. There is no standard history of popular music, especially of rock. Among the more interesting histories are Charlie Gillett's *The Sound of the City,* and Ronald Byrnside's "The Formation of a Musical Style."
2. The distinction between rock 'n' roll and rock and roll will not be used here, and both styles will be called rock and roll. For a discussion of these terms, see Gillett, *The Sound of the City,* 9.
3. AC/DC, "Let There Be Rock," *Let There Be Rock* (Atco [Atlantic], 1977).
4. Chuck Berry, "Roll Over Beethoven" (Chess Records, 1956).
5. It is no coincidence that the growth of individual music preferences for what might be called hyphenated rock (art-rock, southern-rock, psychedelic-rock, heavy-metal rock) occurred as Americans began to rehyphenate their identifications. What was called the ethnic revival and the *Roots* phenomenon, in which people focused on their racial and ethnic origins, led to all manner of hyphenated Americans. Spurred by the black power movement, but influenced by the OPEC-induced recession, the horror and dishonor of the Vietnam War, and Watergate, the post–World War II great consensus came to its end.
6. Ross Halfin and Pete Makowski, *Heavy Metal,* 5.
7. Pete Fornatale, *The Story of Rock 'N' Roll,* 143.
8. David Hatch and Stephen Millward, *From Blues to Rock,* 167.
9. Dan Hedges, "Metallica's Sonic Assault Makes Believers of Ozzy Fans," 28.
10. NA, "Fist/Thunder in Rock."
11. Byrnside, "Formation of a Musical Style," 161.
12. For a discussion of this style, see Roy F. Baumeister's "Acid Rock."
13. Gull Records, 1974.
14. Mike Saunders, review of *Demons and Wizards,* by Uriah Heep.
15. Blue Cheer's Dick Peterson acknowledges his band's impact on the development of heavy metal's sound. "All we knew was we wanted more power" (cited in David Fricke, "Metal Forefathers," 56).
16. Pete Townshend, cited in Steve Pond, "The Who Reboards the Magic Bus," 94.
17. When the genre was in its formative phase the term "downer rock" was a competitor with "heavy rock" and "heavy metal" for designating the erupting form of music. The term "downer" refers to the use of downer drugs by fans at concerts where the music was played. Use of downer assimilated the music to the drug culture of the 1960s. "Heavy metal," a musical designation of the genre, was a more appropriate designation for a form that had transcended the drug culture, and was not viewed as an accompaniment to a drug experience.

18. Quoted on "Metal Shop: Black Sabbath 20th Anniversary Special," broadcast on WVVX, 7 April 1990.
19. See, for example, Liam Lacey, "Heavy Metal: A Bluffer's Guide," and "Heavy Metal" in Jon Pareles, ed., *The Rolling Stone Encyclopedia of Rock & Roll,* 248.
20. Lester Bangs, "Bring Your Mother to the Gas Chamber, Part 1," and "Bring Your Mother to the Gas Chamber, Part 2."
21. "Heavy metal apparently got its name from William Burroughs, who used the expression as a synonym for torture in his apocalyptic 1959 novel, *Naked Lunch.* Rock critics borrowed it to apply to such groups as Grand Funk Railroad and Black Sabbath" (Cathleen McGuigan, "Not the Sound of Silence," 102). Others mention this origin, too, including Bashe, *Heavy Metal Thunder,* 4; J. D. Considine, "Good, Bad, & Ugly," 52; and Lacey, "Heavy Metal," 1.
22. William S. Burroughs, *The Soft Machine, Nova Express, The Wild Boys,* 56. The notion that Burroughs is the source of the term "heavy metal" has been proffered by Kim Neely who traces a trail from *Nova Express* through Steppenwolf's "Born to Be Wild" to Lester Bangs; see Kim Neely, "Wrap Up," 162. The connection of Burroughs with "Born to Be Wild" is not confirmed by the song's composer, Mars Bonfire. The author has not been able to confirm the connection with Bangs.
23. Mars Bonfire, private correspondence with author, 1 November 1990.
24. Mars Bonfire, private correspondence with author, 14 November 1990.
25. Mike Saunders, review of *Kingdom Come,* by Sir Lord Baltimore.
26. Ozzy Osbourne, "Ozzy Osbourne's Favorite Hard Rock of the Seventies."
27. George Lipsitz, *Time Passages,* 99.
28. A detailed history of the genre, which is outside the scope of this sociocultural analysis, would list the recordings of significant heavy metal groups in each of these eras. Consult books such as Halfin and Makowski, *Heavy Metal;* Bashe, *Heavy Metal Thunder;* Brian Harrigan and Malcolm Dome, *Encyclopedia Metallica;* Brian Harrigan, *HM A–Z: The Definitive Encyclopedia of Heavy Metal from AC/DC through Led Zeppelin to ZZ Top;* and Tony Jasper and Derek Oliver, *The International Encyclopedia of Hard Rock & Heavy Metal.*
29. If the term "classic metal" was not reserved here for the continuation of the styles perfected in the era of crystallization into the fragmentation of the genre in the later 1980s, this era would be called the "classic" period.
30. Bangs, "Bring Your Mother to the Gas Chamber, Part 1," 41.
31. Quoted during "Clapton Special," broadcast on WLUP, 3 April 1988.
32. Stith Bennett indicates that to be heard at an equal volume with other instruments in actual playing conditions, the bass may have to be as much as 100,000 times as intense as a middle-range frequency (Bennett, *On Becoming a Rock Musician,* 225).
33. Simon Frith, "Towards an Aesthetic of Popular Music," 145.
34. Considine, in his analysis of the genre, cautions his readers "never" to take the lyrics in a literal sense; see J. D. Considine, "Purity and Power," 50.

35. John Street, *Rebel Rock,* 7.

36. Teutonic lettering is appropriate to the pre-Christian, Northern European mythology, or at least the traces of it, that find their way into heavy metal themes and artwork.

37. Many of the earliest heavy metal album covers borrowed from the aesthetics of psychedelic music. For example, the *Led Zeppelin III* album (Atlantic, 1970) featured a movable wheel behind a cutout front, strewn with psychedelic images of flowers, butterflies, hummingbirds, dragonflies, and walnuts on a white background. The band's name is written in the typical puffy and curvaceous lettering associated with the graphics of the counterculture. Further, designers Hipgnosis, responsible for most of Pink Floyd's album covers, also did Black Sabbath's *Technical Ecstasy* (1976) and *Never Say Die* (1978), Led Zeppelin's *Houses of the Holy* (1973) and *Presence* (1976), and UFO's *Phenomenon* (1974) and *Force It* (1975). Prior to that time album covers were as likely to have an art-rock style as to conform to the code of heavy metal.

38. Norm Nite, *Rock On,* 169, and Bill Wyman, "Terms of Interment," 12.

39. Halford is credited with stylizing a "look that devotees of S&M had already distilled from the power merchants of past wars" (Chris Marlowe, "Full Metal Jackets," 39).

40. Jon Young, "Mean Duds," 54.

41. Bangs, "Bring Your Mother to the Gas Chamber, Part 1," 78.

42. Harrigan and Dome, *Encyclopedia Metallica,* 13.

43. The comparison of heavy metal with punk names is interesting. There is some overlap, especially of terms pertaining to death and violence. Missing from metal is the theme of loathesomeness for which punk is noted. For a description of punk band names, see Harold Levine and Steven H. Stumpf, "Statements of Fear through Cultural Symbols."

44. Joseph A. Kotarba and Laura Wells, "Styles of Adolescent Participation," 404.

45. Robert Gross notes, "A substantial amount of metal songs seem to concentrate on the concept of power. There are songs that discuss occult power, tracks that mention the power struggle between parents and teens, medieval power fantasies. . . . the key element in the majority of heavy metal songs is the concept of power" (see Robert L. Gross, "Heavy Metal Music," 124).

46. Judas Priest's first album, released in 1974, has a drug-related song, at least according to its title. "Caviar and Meths" is a psychedelic instrumental. Since the whole album would not be classified as metal, "Caviar and Meths" cannot be counted as a heavy metal drug song.

47. Will Straw, "Characterizing Rock Music Cultures," 113.

48. Metal is a substitute term, less frequently used to refer to the music, for example, Accept's "Metal Heart," and Helloween's "Metal Invaders" and "Heavy Metal (Is the Law)." Many songs use the term "metal," but it is not as frequently employed as "rock" and "rock and roll."

49. Robert G. Pielke, *You Say You Want a Revolution,* 202.

50. S. I. Hayakawa, "Popular Songs vs. the Facts of Life," 399.

51. Paul Oliver, *The Meaning of the Blues*, 329.
52. Richard Stivers, *Evil in Modern Myth and Ritual*.
53. This title was a self-conscious parody of the megahit by Led Zeppelin, "Stairway to Heaven" (Jay Allen Sanford, *AC/DC*, 13).
54. Authorial intention is another question altogether. One group, Slayer, a thrash metal band that specializes in the most extreme types of chaotic lyrics, indicates their intention: "The lyrics aren't meant to be taken as a serious message. . . . They're only songs." They compare their work with movies such as *Nightmare on Elm Street* (Oliver Klemm, "Slayer," 31).
55. Byrnside, "Formation of a Musical Style," 159–92.
56. For a description by a fan and a professional influenced by this era, see Lars Ulrich and Malcolm Dome, "Encyclopedia Metallica."
57. Cited in Chuck Eddy, "Heavy Metal," 184.
58. Bashe, *Heavy Metal Thunder*, 34.
59. Punk also underwent a remarkable fragmentation, starting about a year or two before metal's and continuing through much of the 1980s. Among other factions, it split into "Marxist avant-funk to revivalist rockabilly to power pop and techno-disco" (Chuck Eddy, "The Ramones," 80).
60. Philip Bashe, "Heavy Metal Comes of Age," 26.
61. According to deejay Matt Cotinni, the term was first used in 1983 in *Circus* with reference to Def Leppard. The term referred to the observation that the guitarist always seemed to be making poses and looking for the camera while performing on stage (WZRD, 26 December 1990).
62. Chuck Eddy, "Boogie Blunderland," 79.
63. Chuck Eddy, "Heavy Metal," 186.
64. Byrnside, "Formation of a Musical Style," 184.
65. Joli Jensen, "Genre and Recalcitrance," 33.
66. For a discussion of hardcore, see John Duke, "Intense Innovation."
67. Greg Kot, "Nuclear Assault," 10.
68. Street, *Rebel Rock*, 63.
69. Of course, Ozzy's "Suicide Solution" is also a plea against drinking too much.
70. Atrophy's "Puppies and Friends."
71. Thrash now includes crossover, which was begun in the mid-1980s by groups such as Suicidal Tendencies, which came from the punk-derived hardcore scene. Their tempo tends to be continuously fast, eschewing the tempo-changing convention of speed metal.
72. Chris Welch, "The British (Rock) Empire Strikes Back," 82.
73. For an example of this, see Doug Van Pelt, "Mosh for the Master?"
74. For a discussion of Christian thrash, see Al Menconi, "A Serious Look at Christian Heavy Metal," and Van Pelt, "Mosh for the Master?"
75. Vengeance, "Human Sacrifice" (Intense Records, 1988).
76. Steve Rabey, "Heavy Metal Mania," 10.

Chapter 3

1. Roger Karshner, *The Music Machine*, 75.
2. Rick Evans, "Lita Ford Trial By Fire."

3. Anthony DeCurtis, "Rock & Roll Photo Album."

4. NA, "Women in Metal."

5. The black community kept their artists within the confines of what was euphemistically called "urban contemporary" music, a bricolage of black musical styles derived from soul and disco. Hall and Oates, a white duo whose musical style fell within the parameters of "urban contemporary," kept their faces off their record covers so that casual listeners would not be turned off. The music industry, of course, aided and abetted this segregation of musical styles because it was a highly useful marketing device.

6. Richard C. Vincent et al., "Sexism on MTV," 941.

7. Alan Wells, "Women and Popular Music," 2.

8. This influence has been noted widely. An unlikely but highly credible reference to both Poison and the New York Dolls is a comic book, *Poison,* created by Todd Loren and associates.

9. Matt Snow, "Every Man for Herself," 8.

10. Ibid., 10.

11. Ibid., 9.

12. Deborah Frost, "Heavy Metal Rears its Ugly Head Again," 84.

13. Brian Slagel, "Bitch," 8.

14. NA, "Women in Metal," 33.

15. Charles Horton Cooley, *Social Organization,* 23.

16. Stith Bennett, *On Becoming a Rock Musician,* 18.

17. Ibid., 179.

18. For a fuller discussion of the merits of this form of organization, see Georg Simmel, "Super-Subordination without Degradation," in *The Sociology of Georg Simmel,* 283–85.

19. Bennett, *On Becoming a Rock Musician,* 147.

20. Ibid., 177.

21. Laura Canyon, "Kill with Power!," 21.

22. Howard Johnson, "Hard Nuts," 15.

23. Jennifer Foote, "Making It in Metal Mecca."

24. Ibid.

25. Leigh Silverman, "Finding Fame without Fortune," 33.

26. Winston Cummings, "Krokus," 54.

27. For a discussion of the types and reasons for "covers" in metal, see Deena Dasein, "Metal Covers."

28. Street, *Rebel Rock,* 5.

29. Hamm, "Acculturation of Musical Styles," 142.

30. Street, *Rebel Rock,* 134.

31. Metal Mike, "Scorpions," 16.

32. David Fricke, "Heavy Metal Justice," 46.

33. Jon Pareles, "Rewards of Rock Before the Gloss."

34. James Coffman, "Everybody Knows This Is Nowhere," 22.

35. Gary Graff, "Sophomore Slump."

36. Ozzy Osbourne, "Ozzy Osbourne's Favorite Hard Rock of the Seventies."

37. Toby Goldstein, "Who Among the Living Is Immune to Anthrax?," 67.

38. Dean Kuipers, "Chasing the Dragon," 36.

39. Lester Bangs, "Transcendence of the Orgasm," 37.
40. Geoff Wills and Cary L. Cooper, *Pressure Sensitive.*
41. Rick Evans, "Poison," 23.
42. Interview with Ozzy Osbourne, "The Friday Rock Show," broadcast on BBC One, 8 May 1987.
43. Leigh Silverman, "Finding Fame without Fortune," 33.
44. Max Weber, "Sociology of Charismatic Authority," in *From Max Weber,* 245–52.
45. Dennis Hunt, "Heavy-Metal Hit Wins New Respect for Iron Maiden."
46. Musicians plying their trade in the Christian metal subgenre are in a different situation. They are supposed to create a "holy noise" on stage but must renounce the wild life-style off stage. Unlike their secular brothers in metal, they are supposed to eschew the bacchanalian pursuits.
47. Punk and its hardcore progeny are notable exceptions here.
48. Gary Graff, "Crüe Change."
49. Interview with Ronnie James Dio, broadcast on WZRD, 26 September 1990.

Chapter 4

1. Bill Barich, "A Reporter At Large," 102.
2. Kotarba and Wells, "Styles of Adolescent Participation," 399.
3. Alan Bloom, *The Closing of the American Mind.*
4. Don Dodson ably argues that different types/eras of rock can be understood as primarily folk, popular, elite, or mass cultures (see Don Dodson, "Differentiating Popular Culture and Mass Culture").
5. Herbert Blumer, "The Mass, the Public, and Public Opinion," 43.
6. Straw, "Characterizing Rock Music Cultures," 115.
7. Lawrence Grossberg, "Rock and Roll in Search of an Audience," 177.
8. "Artistic productions must be seen as *interactional* creations, the meanings of which arise out of the interactions directed to them by the artist and his audience" (Norman K. Denzin, "Problems in Analyzing Elements of Mass Culture," 1035).
9. Grossberg, "Rock and Roll in Search of an Audience," 178.
10. Paul E. Willis, *Profane Culture,* 192–93.
11. Kotarba and Wells, "Styles of Adolescent Participation," 405.
12. Herbert J. Gans, *Popular Culture and High Culture,* 10.
13. Ibid., 11.
14. Ibid., 12.
15. Gans sees taste publics as subcultures, but not in the same sense as the British authors. Gans says, "In addition, taste culture is a *partial* culture, for it provides values and products for only a part of life, and except for a handful of high and popular culture addicts, and some of the professionals who create culture, it is not a *total* way of life. Even though taste culture is partial, it is tied to the rest of culture, because the values of taste culture

are often similar to other values people hold, for example, about work or family life" (*Popular Culture and High Culture*, 13).

16. E. Ellis Cashmore, "Shades of Black, Shades of White," 247.
17. Michael Brake, *Comparative Youth Culture*, 72.
18. Ibid.
19. Grossberg, "Rock and Roll in Search of an Audience," 186.
20. Pete Fornatale, *The Story of Rock 'N' Roll*, 143. Also see Bruce K. Friesen, "Functional Aspects of Adolescent Socialization through Deviant Subcultures."
21. Lacey, "Heavy Metal."
22. Editors of FLIP Magazine, *FLIP's Groovy Guide to the Groups!*, 173.
23. The person who signed both Bon Jovi and Cinderella to PolyGram Records says of the audience, "That core is seventy-five-percent males, who really get off on rock guitars" (quoted in David Handelman, "Money for Nothing," 58). See also John Shepherd, "Music and Male Hegemony"; Street, *Rebel Rock;* and Straw, "Characterizing Rock Music Cultures."
24. Street, *Rebel Rock*, 4.
25. Simon Frith and Howard Horne, *Art into Pop*, 90.
26. Brake, *Comparative Youth Culture*, 29.
27. P. G. Christenson and J. B. Peterson, "Genre and Gender in the Structure of Music Preferences," 287.
28. Jules Henry, *Culture Against Man*, 150.
29. Ibid.
30. Straw, "Characterizing Rock Music Cultures," 115.
31. David Wild, "The Band that Wouldn't Die," 46.
32. See, for example, Stephen Buff's discussion of greasers in the Chicago area in "Greasers, Dupers, and Hippies."
33. Willis, *Profane Culture*, 20.
34. J. Stoltenberg, "Towards Gender Justice," 35.
35. Deena Weinstein, "Rock," 6–9.
36. Bashe, *Heavy Metal Thunder*, 7.
37. John Clarke, "The Skinheads & the Magical Recovery of Community," 102.
38. If the legend is true, it is ironic that much of the studded-leather gear used by heavy metal performers and worn by fans came originally not from biker-shops but from stores catering to the S&M gay community (see Chris Marlowe, "Full Metal Jackets," 39).
39. James S. Leming, "Rock Music and the Socialization of Moral Values in Early Adolescence," 364.
40. Weinstein, "Rock," 8.
41. Stuart Hall and Paddy Whannel, *Popular Arts*, 273.
42. Brake, *Comparative Youth Culture*, 22.
43. George Lipsitz, *Time Passages*, 130.
44. Loyd Grossman, *Social History of Rock Music*, 93.
45. Cashmore, "Shades of Black," 247.
46. Mike Cobley, "Again & Again," 37.
47. Ed Ward, Geoffrey Stokes, and Ken Tucker, *Rock of Ages*, 486.

48. This acceptance contrasts sharply with the reception given to "older people" at hardcore concerts, who are at times ridiculed and jeered.

49. Dick Hebdige, *Subculture*, 44.

50. Harry Christian, "Convention and Constraint among British Semi-Professional Jazz Musicians," 222.

51. Clarke, "Skinheads," 102.

52. Jonathon S. Epstein et al., "Teenagers, Behavioral Problems and Preferences for Heavy Metal and Rap Music," 388.

53. Brake, *Comparative Youth Culture*.

54. Ibid., 79.

55. John Clarke et al., "Subcultures, Cultures, and Class," 26.

56. Cashmore, "Shades of Black," 249.

57. Brake, *Comparative Youth Culture*, 67.

58. Ibid., 22.

59. Hebdige describes the class basis of the genre in Britain in the late seventies, indicating that heavy metal "has fans amongst the student population, but it also has a large working-class following" (see Hebdige, *Subculture*, 155).

60. Hebdige, *Subculture*, 155.

61. Lipsitz, *Time Passages*, 120.

62. Cashmore, "Shades of Black," 264.

63. Christenson and Peterson state that mainstream music is seen in a negative light by most male teenagers (see P. G. Christenson and J. B. Peterson, "Genre and Gender," 298).

64. "You go to a thrash show and you'll be looking at about a 90 percent male turnout." "But if you go to a show like Ratt you'll be looking at about 75 percent women." (Fan quoted in Bruce K. Friesen, "Functional Aspects of Adolescent Socialization through Deviant Subcultures," 10.)

65. Susan Orlean, "The Kids Are All Right."

66. Ernest A. Hakanen and Alan Wells, "Adolescent Music Marginals," 13.

67. W. Spahr, "Teutonic Rock."

68. Robert Love and Jenny Jedeikin, "Wild Wild West Berlin."

69. Edna Gundersen, "Tell Tchaikovsky the News," 16.

70. Francine Du Plessix Gray, "Reflections," 78.

71. Christopher Johnston, "Psst! Hey, Mister, Want to Buy Some Software Cheap?," 139.

72. Handelman, "Money for Nothing," 34.

73. Straw, "Characterizing Rock Music Cultures," 115.

74. Brigadier General James Dozier was made to listen to rock groups, notably AC/DC, for about eight hours per day (Kim Rogal, "Dozier's 42 Days in a Tent").

75. Green, *Music on Deaf Ears*.

76. Les Daly, "Seven Tribes of Britain," 17.

77. That does not mean that the lyrics of some metal bands cannot be described in terms of an integral "artistic vision." For a discussion of the lyrics of Rush and Pink Floyd as artistic vision, see the author's *Serious Rock*.

78. See, for example, Ulrich Frick, "Rock Music as Commodity"; James S. Lem-

ing, "Rock Music and the Socialization of Moral Values in Early Adolescence," 366; and Stephen L. Markson, "Claims-Making, Quasi-Theories and the Social Construction of Rock and Roll," 11. .

79. Leming, "Rock Music and Socialization," 375.
80. Christenson and Peterson, "Genre and Gender," 287.
81. See Roger Jon Desmond, "Adolescents and Music Lyrics," 278; Leming, "Rock Music and Socialization," 375; and Jon Pareles, "Should Rock Lyrics Be Sanitized?," 5.
82. Desmond, "Adolescents and Music Lyrics," 279.
83. See the author's *Serious Rock* for an interpretation of this album.
84. The music for the priests's part was much more stirring than that for the dreamer. The lyrical meaning was confused for the listener by hearing the music. It took me some time to realize this, and when I did I no longer put a tape of the album on reserve for my theory class—they were only given the lyrics.
85. Patricia M. Greenfield et al., "What Is Rock Music Doing to the Minds of Our Youth?"
86. Simon Frith, "Towards an Aesthetic of Popular Music," 145.
87. Ibid.
88. Willis, *Profane Culture*, 155.
89. The Hell's Angels were mainly a youth, though not an adolescent, group in the late 1960s. The club still exists, but its typical member today is well past his youth.
90. For an analysis of tattoos, see Clinton P. Sanders, *Customizing the Body*.
91. Brake, *Comparative Youth Culture*, 113.
92. Gordon MacKay, "Metal Mania: Paul Di'Anno Interview," 19.
93. Kotarba and Wells, "Styles of Adolescent Participation," 399.
94. Brake described the hippies as "flowing-haired and bearded." But the biker boys and the greasers also had long hair. (Brake, *Comparative Youth Culture*, 101).
95. The style appeared before the rise to stardom of Bon Jovi, but John Bonjovi was a major vehicle for its popularization. His father is a hair stylist.
96. Daly, "7 Tribes of Britain," 17.
97. The impact of drugs and alcohol on mentality and sensibility is in part culturally defined; see Howard S. Becker's "Becoming a Marijuana User."
98. One hundred and fifty pounds of kitty litter was laid down at the Nassau Coliseum on Long Island, N.Y., for an AC/DC concert. Those "stuck in the crunch near the stage were openly urinating for all to see" (Lou O'Neill, Jr., "Back Pages," 90.)
99. Paul E. Willis, "The Cultural Meaning of Drug Use," 106.
100. Ibid., 108.
101. Fan clubs are common among girls for all forms of popular music; see Angela McRobbie and Jenny Garber, "Girls and Subcultures."
102. Bashe, *Heavy Metal Thunder*, 8.
103. Fashion throughout the West is intensely gendered, which was why the "unisex" look was so outrageous.

104. "Consciousness of kind" is more basic for males than for females. Mc-Robbie and Garber suggest that teens deal with their sense of inadequacy in different ways: males join gangs and females develop love "obsessions" (Angela McRobbie and Jenny Garber, "Girls and Subcultures").
105. Dolf Zillmann and Azra Bhatia, "Effects of Associating with Musical Genres on Heterosexual Attraction."
106. "Rockin' Forever, Mid-Nebraska: Letters."
107. Cashmore, "Shades of Black, Shades of White," 263.
108. "Dirt Bag," *Concrete Foundations*, 7.
109. Jensen's excellent analysis of the hostility of traditional country music fans to the Nashville sound suggests parallels to the reaction of metal fans in the 1980s to rather similar changes associated with lite metal (see Joli Jensen, "Genre and Recalcitrance").
110. Byrnside, "Formation of a Musical Style," 186.
111. Desmond, "Adolescents and Music Lyrics," 283.
112. Tom Junod, "Surviving High School," 66.
113. Quotation from a 1989 high school graduate from a middle-class Chicago suburb.
114. Quotation from a 1984 high school graduate from an affluent suburb of Indianapolis.
115. Quotation from a 1982 high school graduate from an upper-middle-class Chicago suburb.
116. Quotation from a 1989 high school graduate from an upper-middle-class Chicago suburb.
117. Very few students mentioned that not everyone who listened to this genre of music was a member of a distinctive clique. One said, "You would not be able to pick out all the people who listen to heavy metal. Some dressed in the black T-shirts and spandex, but others were 'preppy.' There was a time that I listened to heavy metal music, but no one would have known it. Also anyone who listened to heavy metal was thought to be a stoner—'F' grade student. I'm proof that this was not always the case" (Quotation from a 1989 graduate of a Chicago Catholic School).
118. See Paul Verden et al., "Heavy Metal Mania and Adolescent Delinquency," 76, and Julian Tanner, "Pop Music and Peer Groups."
119. Tim Schlattmann, "Traditional, Non-Traditional, Emotionally/Behaviorally Disturbed Students, and Popular Musical Lyrics," 26.
120. Lawrence Trostle, "The Stoners."
121. Keith Roe, "The School and Music in Adolescent Socialization," 222.
122. Ibid., 225.
123. Ibid., 223.
124. John Clarke, "Style," 180.

Chapter 5

1. C. Wright Mills use the term "cultural apparatus" to include "all the organizations and milieux in which artistic . . . work goes on, and the means

by which such work is made available to critics, publics, and masses" (*Power, Politics, and People*, 406).

2. Bennett, *On Becoming a Rock Musician*, xi.
3. Foote, "Making It in Metal Mecca," 56.
4. For an excellent analysis of radio's importance, see Simon Frith, "Industrialization of Popular Music."
5. Eric W. Rothenbuhler, "Commercial Radio and Popular Music," 83.
6. For an analysis of FM radio in the 1960s, see Peter Fornatale and Joshua E. Mills, *Radio in the Television Age*.
7. Laurel Leff, "As Competition in Radio Grows, Stations Tailor Programs for Specific Audiences," 48.
8. Michael Goldberg, "The Sedating of Rock 'N' Roll."
9. See David Mills, "Turning Back the Clock on Rock."
10. Bashe, *Heavy Metal Thunder*, 26.
11. Martin and Segrave, *Anti-Rock*, 232.
12. Ibid., 313.
13. For a discussion of radio formats as mechanisms that function to manage audiences for business interests, see Eric W. Rothenbuhler, "Commercial Radio and Popular Music," 81.
14. James Lull, "Popular Music and Communication," 13.
15. Pete Fornatale, *The Story of Rock 'N' Roll*, 146.
16. The numerous and significant impacts of radio on heavy metal due to the absence of the genre from radio needs to be understood in light of later developments in the mass media. When heavy metal was in its first decade radio was the major mode for promoting rock music. Had MTV been in existence during the 1970s the absence of radio play would also have to have been matched by the absence on MTV to have these consequences.
17. Charles Hamm, "The Acculturation of Musical Styles," 147.
18. Metal Mike, "Scorpions," 16.
19. Ozzy Osbourne interview, "The Friday Rock Show on BBC One," Tommy Vance interviewer, broadcast 8 May 1987.
20. Robert Christgau, "Rockism Faces the World," 71.
21. Peter Clarke, "Teenager's Coorientation and Information-Seeking about Pop Music."
22. Pink Floyd is a genre unto itself. Their albums *Animals* and *The Wall* should be included here.
23. Notable examples of live heavy metal albums, which represent only a fraction of the total, include Judas Priest's *Unleashed in the East* (1979), Black Sabbath's *Live Evil* (1983), Ozzy Osbourne's *Speak of the Devil* (1982), Rainbow's *On Stage* (1977), Scorpion's *Tokyo Tapes* (1978), Iron Maiden's *Maiden Japan* (1981), Deep Purple's *Made in Japan* (1973), and UFO's *Lights Out* (1979).
24. *Aardschok America* for August–September 1987, page 48, lists 114 stations with metal programming, the vast majority of which are college stations.
25. As of July 1990 there were seventeen full-time stations. Another seven stations download from the satellite feed the "Countdown" of the top "hits"

for the week (conversation with Pat Dawsey, program director for Z-Rock, 11 July 1990).

26. Conversation with Pat Dawsey, program director for Z-Rock, 11 July 1990.
27. The impact of "power ballads" on heavy metal has some similarity to the effect of crossovers in rhythm and blues's attempt to reach a white audience. According to Nelson George, the search for crossovers destroyed that style's musical and lyrical relevance; see Nelson George, *The Death of Rhythm and Blues*.
28. David Handelman, "Money for Nothing," 58.
29. Goldstein, "Who Among the Living Is Immune to Anthrax?," 67.
30. NA, "Vinnie Vincent," 25.
31. Greg Kot, "Volume Dealers," 6.
32. Ibid., 7.
33. Sue Cummings, "Road Warriors," 59.
34. Ibid., 61.
35. The "Friday Rock Show" on BBC One is celebrated by Saxon in their song "Denim and Leather."
36. Alan Anger, "HM Can Never Die."
37. Dave Ling, "RAW Plugs."
38. Doherty agrees that rock and TV have a long common history (see Thomas Doherty, "MTV and the Music Video").
39. Richard Goldstein, "Tube Rock," 38.
40. R. Serge Denisoff, *Inside MTV*, 96.
41. Gary Burns, "Music and Television."
42. For a full description, see the chapter "Some People Just Don't Get It," in Denisoff, *Inside MTV*, 281–316.
43. Martin and Segrave, *Anti-Rock*, 232.
44. Handelman, "Money for Nothing," 58.
45. Of course it sold the records of the other music that was aired. A headline in *Variety* read "Clip Tunes Help Sell Pix and Records."
46. Frost, "Heavy Metal Rears Its Ugly Head Again."
47. NA, "MTV Overtaking Radio as Motivation of Disc Purchases."
48. Denisoff, *Inside MTV*, 208.
49. Bashe, *Heavy Metal Thunder*, 30.
50. Martin and Segrave, *Anti-Rock*, 232.
51. Kim Neely, "Faith No More," 54.
52. Michael Goldberg, "MTV's Sharper Pictures," 62.
53. Stephanie Gutmann, "Video's Real Music Is in the Moves."
54. Bernard Doe, "Contract Killers."
55. David Housham, "Gross Takings," 42.
56. Cited in Denisoff, *Inside MTV*, 143.
57. Jeff Silberman, "More Propaganda!"
58. For a discussion of licensing, see Frith, "The Industrialization of Popular Music," 75.
59. For a description of the poses symbolizing male camaraderie, see Greil Marcus, "MTV DOA RIP."

60. Cummings, "Road Warriors," 61.
61. Dean Abt, "Music Video," 97.
62. Jon Pareles, "Young vs. MTV," 32.
63. Abt, "Music Video," 97.
64. See, for example, E. Ann Kaplan, *Rocking Around the Clock.*
65. Goldberg, "MTV's Sharper Pictures," 64.
66. Kaplan, *Rocking Around the Clock,* 17.
67. Pareles, "Young vs. MTV," 32.
68. Robert Plant was a pitchman for Coca-Cola in 1989. The video of his "Tall Cool One" was the basis for the Coke spot. However, the song and staging were outside the conventions of metal.
69. Charles M. Young, "Soda Pop," 64.
70. For further discussion, see Leming, "Rock Music and Socialization," 379.
71. Rebecca Coudret, "Rock, Steeped in the Blues, Fits Cinderella like a Favorite Slipper."
72. James Wolcott, "Mixed Media," 30.
73. Desmond, "Adolescents and Music Lyrics," 281.
74. Frith, "Towards an Aesthetic of Popular Music," 140–41.
75. Denisoff, *Inside MTV,* 264.
76. Georg Simmel, *The Sociology of Georg Simmel,* 135.
77. Aerosmith is among the many bands that understood that the increase of women in their audience was due to MTV (David Wild, "The Band that Wouldn't Die," 46). Surveys of record buyers by Street Pulse Group indicate that the ratio of females to males in the metal audience is increasing due, in part, to MTV exposure (Charles M. Young, "Heavy Metal," 44).
78. Handelman, "Money for Nothing," 58.
79. James Lull, "Listeners' Communicative Uses of Popular Music," 156.
80. Richard C. Vincent et al., "Sexism on MTV," 941.
81. Michael Gross, "Frock 'n' Roll."
82. Bashe, *Heavy Metal Thunder,* 8.
83. Denisoff, *Inside MTV,* 299.
84. Markson, "Claims-Making, Quasi-Theories, and the Social Construction of the Rock and Roll," 10–11.
85. Goldberg, "MTV's Sharper Pictures," 64.
86. Desmond, "Adolescents and Music Lyrics," 276.
87. Lull, "Listeners' Communicative Uses," 145.
88. Iron Maiden, *Live After Death* (Capitol, 1985).
89. First released as a movie, the video version came out in 1987 (Warner Bros.). It contains Led Zeppelin's concert at Madison Square Garden in 1973.
90. The title is a take on the band's first album, *Kill 'Em All.* (Metallica, *Cliff 'em All,* [Elektra, 1987]).
91. Sylvie Simmons, "The 80s," 59.
92. Michael Goldberg, "*Spinal Tap:* The Comics Behind the Funniest Rock Movie Ever."
93. Michael Goldberg, "Look out, Spinal Tap: Here Come the Scorpions, Heavy Metal's Latest Heroes," 38.

94. Richard Corliss, "X Rated," 94.
95. Will Straw, "Characterizing Rock Music Cultures," 113.
96. Ibid.
97. Alan Anger, "HM Can Never Die."
98. See Chapter 7 for more discussion of the repudiation of heavy metal by mainstream rock magazines.
99. The ratio of all photos to concert photos is: 44/14 (*Metal Forces*, no. 25), 73/30 (*RAW*, no. 3), and 36/11 (*Kerrang!*, no. 126).
100. Halfin and Makowski, *Heavy Metal*, 7.
101. Handelman, "Money for Nothing," 41.
102. Coffman discusses this relationship in terms of a 'parasocial' interaction maintained by these media (see James Coffman, "Everybody Knows This Is Nowhere.").
103. Advertisement in *Kerrang!*, August–September 1984, 34.
104. Rock fanzines began in the latter half of the 1960s; see Greg Shaw, "The Real Rock 'n' Roll Underground," and R. Serge Denisoff, *Solid Gold*.
105. Denisoff, *Solid Gold*, 286.
106. Michael Goldberg, "Rock & Roll Fanzines," 57.
107. NA, "Zines!"
108. Ibid.
109. Chris Hunt, "Independents' Day," 37.
110. NA, "Zines!"
111. Bruce Britt, "Finding the Antidote."
112. Paul D. Colford, "The Lords of Rock," 5.
113. Ward et al., *Rock of Ages*, 485.
114. Lynn Van Matre, "High-Flying Days of Rock."
115. Eric W. Rothenbuhler and John W. Dimmick, "Concentration and Diversity in the Industry, 1974–80," 145. This work is an extension of the work done by Peterson and Berger; see their "Cycles of Symbol Production."
116. Laura Landro, "Merger of Warner Unit, Polygram Angers Troubled Record," 33.
117. The total American releases dropped to about 60 percent of the 1978 level by the middle of the 1980s (Recording Industry Association of America, *Inside the Recording Industry: A Statistical Overview [Update 1987]*).
118. NA, "Record Business Sees Light Ahead—On Video Screen," 5.
119. Frith, *Sound Effects*, 157.
120. NA, "Record Business Sees Light Ahead," 5.
121. Simmons, "The 80s," 59.
122. This is true for rock music in general. In Great Britain ninety new labels appeared during the first half of 1980 alone (Frith, *Sound Effects*, 155).
123. Barich, "A Reporter At Large," 102.
124. Hunt, "Independents' Day," 36.
125. Gene Khoury, "Metal Industry Report," 10.
126. Daniel Kagan, "A Contractual Cacophony in Music," 52.
127. Hunt, "Independents' Day," 36.
128. Ibid., 37.

129. For an analysis of this concentration, see Burnett and Weber, "Concentration and Diversity in the Popular Music Industry, 1948–86."
130. Todd Barrett, "The Start of a CD Backlash?"
131. This estimate excludes such hard-rock bands as Kiss (Mercury) and Aerosmith and Guns 'n' Roses (Geffen), which are often classed as metal. Were these kinds of bands included the percentage of nonmajor companies would be even smaller. The metal albums counted were released on Mercury, Epic, Capitol, Geffen, Elektra, Atlantic, CBS, Warner, RCA, and Polydor. The only album not on these major labels was Joe Satriani's *Surfing with the Alien,* the number forty-three album of 1988, released by Relativity (source: *Billboard Chart Research, Top Pop Albums of the Year 1948–1989 Given in Rank Order* [New York: Billboard Publications, 1990]).
132. Jon Pareles, "Fringe Fever."
133. Jeffrey Ressner, "Head Bangers."
134. Also, heavy metal came into being in a period characterized by much musical diversity and high industry concentration. That was also the situation in the late 1980s. According to DiMaggio, independent producers are more influential at such times (Paul DiMaggio, "Market Structure, the Creative Process, and Popular Culture").
135. Thrash metal records share punk's standards: they attempt to convey the sweat of the band on their records. They are proud of being able to do their whole album in a day or two. In contrast, classical metal groups may spend months in the studio.
136. Johnson, "Flamin' Tasty."
137. Ibid.
138. Gotz Kuhnemund, "Atrophy," 69.

Chapter 6

1. Erving Goffman, *The Presentation of Self in Everyday Life,* 112.
2. David Housham, "Gross Takings," 42.
3. When all of one's food, lodging, and upkeep are taken care of and one is either in the bus or at a concert most of the time, spending the per diem is not always easy. It is not unusual, I have been told, for the touring crew to walk around with large stacks of cash.
4. Mick Farren and George Snow, "Groupies," in *The Rock'n'Roll Circus,* 61.
5. Georg Simmel, "The Metropolis and Mental Life," in *The Sociology of Georg Simmel,* 412.
6. Roger Dean and Martyn Dean, *Magnetic Storm,* 60.
7. William Foote Whyte, "The Social Structure of the Restaurant."
8. Robert N. Wilson, "Teamwork in the Operating Room."
9. Personal letter from Gary Dray, 27 March 1989.
10. Christopher Small, "Performance as Ritual," 10.
11. Elias Canetti, *Crowds and Power,* 37.
12. Opening bands that are not judged to be within the genre of metal are also

roundly booed, jeered, and often pelted. In the mid-1970s, when the Ramones opened for Black Sabbath, they were booed. Their music and clothing were not very different from the metal style, but their demeanor and lyrical themes, and especially their excessive cool, placed them out of bounds. At a Chicagofest concert (5 August 1982) the band preceding Iron Maiden's appearance on the Rock Around the Dock stage was a typical new-wave group, Bohemia. Throughout their set the hapless band was constantly jeered ("Get off the stage, you ain't metal," "Maiden, Maiden") and pelted with every object available, mainly containers that once held beer.

13. One band has hit upon the idea of playing music that is inherently offensive to the ears of its audience. The tape consists of 45 minutes of Chinese martial music, the sounds and structure of which are alien to Western ears. Not only does the audience express its dislike of the tape, but the music greatly aggravates them. The band has helped the audience interact with one another, has increased its emotional excitement, and has prepared it for cathartic release when the band finally appears on stage.

14. W.A.S.P. concert, 4 August 1989, Vic Theater, Chicago.

15. Anthony Pearson, "The Grateful Dead Phenomenon," 426.

16. Personal letter from Gary Dray, 27 March 1989.

17. See the description of the proxemic rule differences for thrash, below.

18. The ethic of sharing and the proxemic rules of a heavy metal audience are unlike the codes of audiences at pop concerts and concerts for other music-based subcultures, such as punk/hardcore or the Grateful Dead.

19. Manowar made the *Guiness Book of Records* for the peak decibel level at one of their concerts.

20. Harrigan and Dome, *Encyclopedia Metallica*, 13.

21. There seem to be differences among people in their susceptibility to hearing damage. Perhaps the more sensitive auditors dislike metal for that reason, and thus avoid heavy metal concerts. There also seems to be some evidence that one's mood may be an intervening variable conditioning whether loud music does any damage. Reviewing this research, James Frank lamented the fate of the ears of a "Guy Lombardo fan who accidentally stumbles into a Mötley Crüe concert" (see James Frank, "Rock 'n'—Say What? Our Parents May Be Right," 1).

22. He celebrated the precursor to the rock triumvirate (sex, drugs and rock and roll): wine, women, and song.

23. Lull, "Listeners' Communicative Uses," 147.

24. Edward Rothstein, "Edward Rothstein on Music," 30.

25. John Dewey, *Art as Experience*.

26. Joseph Agee Bussulman, *The Uses of Music*, 139.

27. James E. Fletcher, "The Wordless Dimension," 88.

28. Hazel Guild, "Soviet Journal Sez Rock Music Works like a Shot of Morphine."

29. Moshing is done at thrash metal concerts where there is no enforced seating.

30. The origins of the practice and the term are obscure. Headbanging was done and known by that term several years before 1977. The British group Mo-

törhead had a fan club called Motörheadbangers. The Ramone's song "Suzy Is a Headbanger" also celebrates the practice.

31. James E. Fletcher, "Wordless Dimension," 93.
32. Ibid.
33. Stephen Struthers, "Recording Music," 252.
34. Fletcher, "Wordless Dimension," 102.
35. Aldous Huxley, *The Doors of Perception and Heaven and Hell,* 165.
36. Norm N. Nite, *Rock On,* 169.
37. Rob Halford, Forward, ix.
38. Denisoff, *Inside MTV,* 264.
39. The height of the stage, placement of security barriers, and seating/no-seating arrangements, among other factors, are not mute physical details. They establish, indeed define, relationships. They speak most loudly to the power balance between the audience and the performers.
40. Rob Andrews, "Caught in the Act."
41. Simon Frith and Angela McRobbie, cited in John Shepherd, "Music and Male Hegemony," 165.
42. The rear-end slapping practiced by members of professional football teams is another example of this male bonding, which, of course, symbolically extends to the audience as well.
43. W.A.S.P. concert, 4 August 1989, Vic Theater, Chicago.
44. Bennett, *On Becoming a Rock Musician,* 225.
45. For genres in which the code requires the audience to sway to the music, the changes in lighting are far more gradual (private conversation with Tom Celner, lighting technician and designer, 21 July 1989).
46. Scott Hasson, a physical therapist at the University of Texas, reports, "In laboratory tests, after viewing the color red, people performed 15% better on grip-strength tests" (NA, "A Color Is a Color Is a Color?").
47. Halford, Forward, viii.
48. Barry Schwartz, "Waiting, Exchange, and Power."
49. Deborah Frost, "White Noise: How Heavy Metal Rules," cited in U.S. Congress, *Record Labeling (Senate Hearing 99–529),* 32.
50. Carl J. Couch, "Evocative Transactions and Social Order," 5.
51. Helloween at 1988 Monsters of Rock Concert, Castle Donington, Great Britain.
52. George H. Lewis, "The Politics of Meaning," 25.
53. At 1988 Monsters of Rock Concert, Castle Donington, Great Britain.
54. At 1988 Monsters of Rock Concert, Castle Donington, Great Britain.
55. Black Sabbath concert, 31 August 1982, Poplar Creek, in a suburb Chicago.
56. W.A.S.P. concert, 4 August 1989, Vic Theater, Chicago.
57. Considine, "Metal Mania," 104.
58. The acts of appreciation are the same for all audience members, even though different individuals may vary greatly in their subjective understanding and, therefore, appreciation of a particular song. Some fans are rather sophisticated in their understanding of the lyrical expression and/or of the musical

techniques. Others are unsophisticated, interpreting the lyrics literally and failing to understand either the structure or technique of the performance.

59. Alan Lewis, "The Social Interpretation of Modern Jazz," 47.

60. Ronnie James Dio claims responsibility for introducing the malocchio into heavy metal. He learned it from his Italian-born grandmother who invoked it as a means of warding off the evil eye. When Dio replaced Ozzy Osbourne as the singer for Black Sabbath, he substituted the malocchio for Ozzy's well-known peace-sign salute (interview with Dio, broadcast on WZRD, 26 September 1990).

61. Black Sabbath concert, 31 August 1982, Poplar Creek, in a suburb of Chicago.

62. Another specialized sector of the audience does not interact specifically with the band, but serves as cheerleaders for the audience. These are the fanatics, dedicated to the band itself or to a particular song. Their movements and noise, although not intended to do so, stimulate those around them to express their appreciation more strongly.

63. Reported by Michael Wedeven on his reactions to a 7 October 1988 Suicidal Tendencies and Zeotrope concert at the Cubby Bear in Chicago.

64. Kenneth Burke, *Permanence and Change.*

65. Bashe, *Heavy Metal Thunder,* 9.

66. Susan P. Montague and Robert Morais. "Football Games and Rock Concerts," 47.

67. Stephen Davis, *Hammer of the Gods.*

68. Lull, "Listeners' Communicative Uses," 149.

69. Emile Durkheim, *The Elementary Forms of Religious Life,* 470.

70. Mircea Eliade, *The Sacred and the Profane,* 11.

71. For example, instruments need constant attention. They may need retuning, broken strings must be replaced, cymbals come loose, and so on. In blues and folk styles, the musician attends to the maintenance. The collective tuning in a symphony orchestra prior to performing similarly makes backstage activity public. In metal, however, these actions are hidden. Assistants do the maintenance backstage, replace the offending instrument with another one that is sitting at the ready for just such an emergency, or crawl out on stage on their hands and knees to surreptitiously fix the problem.

Chapter 7

1. There are alternative theories for why heavy metal is so despised by the rock critics. In an analysis of the genre for *Musician,* Charles Young suggests that the critics heap scorn on the music in order to show their supposed superiority to its audience ("Heavy Metal," 43).

2. Cited in Joseph A. Kotarba, "Adolescent Use of Heavy Metal Rock Music as a Resource for Meaning," 9.

3. R. Serge Denisoff, "Prozines and Fanzines," in *Solid Gold,* 283–322.

4. Bashe, *Heavy Metal Thunder,* 4.

5. "Black Sabbath 20th Anniversary Special," broadcast on "Metal Shop" WVVX, 7 April 1990.
6. Bangs, "Bring Your Mother to the Gas Chamber, Part 1," 41.
7. Ibid., 78.
8. Robert Palmer, "Dark Metal."
9. Frost, "Heavy Metal Rears Its Ugly Head Again," 83.
10. Chris Heim, "Whitesnake Offers Chapter from a Heavy-Metal Manual."
11. Anthony DeCurtis, "Music's Mean Season," 16.
12. Arion Berger, "No Great Shakes," 9.
13. Cashmore, "Shades of Black," 264.
14. Ibid.
15. Steve Vai, *Guitar Extravaganza.*
16. DeCurtis, "Music's Mean Season," 16.
17. Tim Holmes, *AC/DC*, 75.
18. Halfin and Makowski, *Heavy Metal*, 4.
19. Bashe, *Heavy Metal Thunder*, and "Black Sabbath."
20. Mary Douglas, *Purity and Danger.*
21. The following is a much abbreviated discussion. The topic is more adequately discussed in a growing number of works, including Martin and Segrave, *Anti-Rock*, and John Orman, *The Politics of Rock Music.*
22. Cited by James R. McDonald, "Censoring Rock Lyrics," 297.
23. Richard A. Peterson, "Market and Moralist Censors of a Black Art Form," 238.
24. These were terms used, respectively, by Dwight Macdonald, *Against the American Grain*, Van Wyck Brooks, *America's Coming of Age*, and Edward Shils, "Mass Society and Its Culture."
25. James R. McDonald, "Censoring Rock Lyrics," 299.
26. Cited in McDonald, "Censoring Rock Lyrics," 309.
27. A. Dougherty, "From 'Race Music' to Heavy Metal," 52.
28. Martin and Segrave, *Anti-Rock*, 285.
29. Anonymous interview, November 1989.
30. Charles Hamm, "Changing Patterns in Society and Music," 56.
31. Larry E. Greeson and Rose Ann Williams, "Social Implications of Music Videos for Youth," 179.
32. Nonmetal music was also excoriated, especially that performed by Sheena Easton and Prince.
33. U.S. Congress, *Record Labeling (Senate Hearing 99–529)*, 3.
34. Ibid.
35. Ibid., 11.
36. Ibid., 12.
37. NA, "2 Exorcisms Revealed by N.Y. Cardinal," 1.
38. Corliss, "X Rated," 92.
39. Rob Tannenbaum, "Church Assails Heavy Metal."
40. Testimony by PMRC consultant Jeff Ling, U.S. Congress, *Record Labeling (Senate Hearing 99–529)*, 14.
41. Julia Malone, "Washington Wives Use Influence to Target Sex, Drugs in

Rock Music," cited in U.S. Congress, *Record Labeling (Senate Hearing 99–529)*, 21.

42. U.S. Congress, *Record Labeling (Senate Hearing 99–529)*, 71.
43. "Shoot to Thrill" is a cut on the best-selling album *Back in Black* (Atlantic Records, 1980). Other cuts on that album include "Given the Dog a Bone," "Let Me Put My Love Into You," and "You Shook Me All Night Long." This is the context in which the term "shoot" is understood by fans.
44. Testimony by PMRC consultant Jeff Ling, U.S. Congress, *Record Labeling (Senate Hearing 99–529)*, 13.
45. Ibid.
46. Ibid.
47. U.S. Congress, *Record Labeling (Senate Hearing 99–529)*, 71.
48. Lynn Lisa Kelly, "Mail (Letters)."
49. Paul Verden et al., "Heavy Metal Mania and Adolescent Delinquency," 73.
50. NA, "Dirt Bag."
51. NA, "Heavy Metal Band's Lyrics Focus at Trial."
52. Judy Keen, "Nevada Judge Will Decide Landmark Suit," 2.
53. Mary Billard, "Heavy Metal Goes on Trial."
54. Carol Gentry, "Studies Debunk Message Tapes."
55. Dylan Jones, "Can Subliminal Messages Alter Behavior?"
56. Marilyn Elias, "Missing the Message."
57. Stephen B. Thorne and Philip Himelstein, "The Role of Suggestion in the Perception of Satanic Messages in Rock-and-Roll Recordings."
58. NA, "Band Cleared in Suicides Blamed on Hidden Message."
59. Mary Billard, "Judas Priest."
60. NA, "Band Cleared in Suicides Blamed on Hidden Message."
61. U.S. Congress, *Record Labeling (Senate Hearing 99–529)*, 73.
62. Ibid., 73–74.
63. Ibid., 74.
64. Ibid., 14.
65. For example, King's 1988 study was cited in Elizabeth F. Brown and William R. Hendee, "Adolescents and Their Music."
66. Paul King, "Heavy Metal Music and Drug Abuse in Adolescents," 297.
67. Kotarba, "Adolescent Use of Heavy Metal Rock Music," 18.
68. Nina Darnton, "Committed Youth," 67.
69. Ibid., 66–67.
70. Corliss, "X Rated," 94.
71. Statement of Dr. Joe Stuessy, U.S. Congress, *Record Labeling (Senate Hearing 99–529)*, 123.
72. Richard Peck, *Rock Rock Rock: Making Musical Choices*, 34.
73. Ibid., 34.
74. King, "Heavy Metal Music and Drug Abuse," 298.
75. Carl A. Raschke, *Painted Black*, 38.
76. Phyllis Polack, "Music Censorship Attempts Increase," 72.
77. Robert Pattison, *The Triumph of Vulgarity*, 164.
78. Billard, "Heavy Metal Goes on Trial," 132.
79. Russell, *Mephistopheles*, 256.

80. Desmond, "Adolescents and Music Lyrics," 281.
81. Stuart Goldman, "Rock of Ageds," 59.
82. R. Serge Denisoff, "The Radical Right and the FCC," in *Solid Gold*, 377–421.
83. Laura Canyon, "Kill with Power!," 22.
84. Corliss, "X Rated," 98.
85. Dante Bonutto, "The Friday Rock Show," 1988.
86. Bangs, "Bring Your Mother to the Gas Chamber, Part 2," 48.
87. Pattison, *Triumph of Vulgarity*, 184.
88. Florence Gilder, "Letter of the Month," 26.
89. Bloom, *Closing of the American Mind*, 71.
90. Plato, *The Republic*, 97.
91. Ibid., 98.
92. Ibid., 100.
93. *2112*, (Mercury Records, 1976).
94. Steven Crockett, "Blam! Bam! Bloom! Boom!," 259.
95. Ibid., 260.
96. *Hemispheres* (Mercury Records, 1978).
97. William Greider, "Bloom and Doom," 246.
98. Ibid., 247.
99. Bob Greene, "Scout Finds Merit in Heavy Metal."
100. Ad for *Newsweek* special issue on youth, *Newsweek*, 14 May 1990, 71.
101. U.S. Congress, *Record Labeling (Senate Hearing 99–529)*, 12.
102. Ibid., 12.
103. Patrick Goldstein, "Parents Warn" (cited in U.S. Congress, *Record Labeling (Senate Hearing 99–529)*, 19.
104. Statement of Millie Waterman, U.S. Congress, *Record Labeling (Senate Hearing 99–529)*, 89.
105. Ibid.
106. Ibid.
107. U.S. Congress, *Record Labeling (Senate Hearing 99–529)*, 2.
108. Ibid., 52.
109. Martin and Segrave, *Anti-Rock*, 232.
110. U.S. Congress, *Record Labeling (Senate Hearing 99–529)*, 54.
111. Bruce Iglauer, "Voice of the People."
112. Editors of *Rock & Roll Confidential, You've Got A Right to Rock*, 3.
113. Kim Neely, "Judas Priest Gets Off the Hook."
114. *Louisiana House Bill No. 154*, 1990.
115. Editors of *Rock & Roll Confidential, You've Got A Right to Rock*, 2.
116. Ibid., 10.
117. Ibid., 8.
118. There are bands, such as Trouble and Trixter, that play white metal songs but who are not tied to evangelical movements. They merely express Christian themes in their lyrics.
119. Menconi, "A Serious Look at Christian Heavy Metal," 13.
120. Van Pelt, "Mosh for the Master?" 21.
121. Pierre Bourdieu, "The Forms of Cultural Capital."

Chapter 8

1. *Painkiller* (Columbia), 1990.
2. For example, "It's back, just when the world was supposed to be safe for New Wave, ready at last for SMART music, what should rear its leather-clad, lipstick-smeared image on the nation's TV tubes but that bête noire of rock progressivism, heavy metal."(Deborah Frost, "Heavy metal rears its ugly head again," 83.)
3. Skid Row's *Slave to the Grind*, Van Halen's *For Unlawful Carnal Knowledge*, Metallica's *Metallica*, and Guns N' Roses' *Use Your Illusion II*.
4. Bruce Haring, "Tuning In to Radio's Wired Wave."
5. Chris Mundy, "Nirvana," 40.
6. Chris Mundy, "Nirvana," 40.
7. Chris Mundy, "Nirvana," 40.
8. See Esther Iverem, "Decrying Rap's Influence: Senate Subcommittee Hears Testimony on Dangers of Music," and Paul D. Fischer, "Worse than the PMRC."
9. The PMRC's reign of symbolic terror also gave rise to a wide range of academic research. See, for example, Mary E. Ballard and Steven Coates, "The Immediate Effects of Homicidal, Suicidal, and Nonviolent Heavy Metal and Rap Songs . . . "; Amy Binder, "Media Depictions of Harm in Heavy Metal and Rap Music"; Donna Gaines, *Teenage Wasteland*; Graham Martin and others, "Adolescent Suicide"; James T. Richardson and others (eds.), *The Satanism Scare*; Keith Roe, "Adolescents' Use of Socially Disvalued Media"; Jill Rosenbaum and Lorraine Prinsky, "The Presumption of Influence"; Simon Singer and others, "Heavy Metal Music Preference . . . "; and Marsha Wooten "The Effects of Heavy Metal Music on Affects Shifts . . . "
10. Deena Weinstein, "Alternative Youth."
11 Michael Azerrad, *Come as You Are*, 230.
12. Azerrad, *Come as You Are*, 230.
13. Phone conversation with author, 1992.
14. Phone conversation with author, 1995.
15. Also, a variety of metal bands could also be found on a variety of soundtrack albums in the 1990s, such as *Hellraiser III: Hell on Earth* (1992), *Judgment Night* (1993), and *Tales from the Crypt: Bordello of Blood* (1996).
16. Possibly the earliest concert in the Soviet bloc was in Belgrade, Yugoslavia, where Iron Maiden played in September 1981.
17. Robert Benjamin, "MTV Wannabes Lead Rocky Life in China."
18. N.A., "Hair Farm Report."
19. Kean Wong, "Metallic Gleam," 21.
20. American-based CMC Records mainly deals with the other metal underground, Purgatory, rescuing bands dropped by major labels. At the end of the century some U.S.-based indies, like Metal Blade and Pavement, have European branches.
21. Learning from the majors, metal indies issue CDs of albums long out of print and previously only available on vinyl.

22. Joey Severance of Metal Blade said that in 1998 there were about 500 college radio metal shows. (Phone conversation with author on January 29, 1999.)

23. S. Ian, "Heavy Metal Covers Wide Range."

24. Some local access cable stations show them in video-'zines, like *Mindmelt* in Chicago.

25. Digby Pearson started his metal label, Earache, in his bedroom in Nottingham with a government arts grant.

26. Bethany Bryson ("'Anything but Heavy Metal'") provides evidence that in the United States musical exclusiveness decreases with education.

27. For the history of this style see Michael Moynihan and Dedrik Sønderlind, *Lords of Chaos*, and William Shaw, "Satan in the Sunshine."

28. Of course each band, as well as each song, can be seen to have unique features.

29. Chuck Eddy, *Stairway to Hell*.

30. Lewis Carroll, *Through the Looking-Glass*.

31. Also see Martin Popoff, *The Collector's Guide to Heavy Metal*, and Mark Hale, *The Worldwide Megabook of Heavy Metal Bands*.

32. This category now includes that 1978–1980 style called the New Wave of British Heavy Metal.

33. The innovative pairing of rap and rock bands, including Slayer and Biohazard, on the 1993 *Judgment Night* soundtrack was in this style.

34. For an overview of the subgenre see, for example, Mike Gitter, "Everything You Ever Wanted to Know About Death Metal but Were Afraid to Ask"; Jack Harrell, "The Poetics of Destruction: Death Metal Rock"; and Deena Weinstein, "Death Metal: Distillate/Dead End of Heavy Metal."

35. The title of Joe Carducci's assessment of metal, "Metal: 'Is it Heavy?' Is the Only Question Worth Asking," describes his take on the genre.

36. In the July 1998 *Terrorizer*, 56.

37. The few bands that did gain some coverage were those in the lite-metal MTV-favored style, such as Motley Crüe in the 1980s and Metallica in the 1990s; that is, those with major album sales.

38. Ben Ratliff, "Metal: The Next Generation."

39. Marc Weingarten, "Black Sabbath: The Forum January 5th, 1999."

40. Ali, "The Rebirth of Loud," 88.

41. Ali, "The Rebirth of Loud," 88.

42. Ali, "The Rebirth of Loud," 88.

43. Even musicians playing in other styles grasp this. For example, David Pirner of Soul Asylum quoted in *Request* (July 1995, 26): "I think metal has got this whole self-sustaining element that is great. The allegiance to that shit is so stunning. They don't need the industry; they don't need the press. That will never go away, and, thank god, the industry didn't exploit it to death."

44. It wasn't the year's highest-grossing tour, beaten out of first place by the sharply contrasting Lilith Fair.

45. Deena Dasein, "Never Say Die."

46. Deena Dasein, "Judas Priest: Surviving Decapitation."

47. For a description of both bands and their fans, see Harris M. Berger's *Metal, Rock and Jazz.*

48. Kiss was originally classified as hard rock until MTV's success with lite metal helped put them, and other bands such as Aerosmith and Alice Cooper, into the metal category.

References

Abt, Dean. "Music Video: Impact of the Visual Dimension." In *Popular Music and Communication*, edited by James Lull, 96–111. Newbury Park, Calif.: Sage, 1987.

Ali, Lorraine. "The Rebirth of Loud." *Spin*, August 1998, 87ff.

Andrews, Rob. "Caught in the Act." *Hit Parader*, May 1986, 50.

Anger, Alan. "HM Can Never Die." *Kerrang! Kontaktz*, 1987, 7.

Azerrad, Michael. *Come as You Are: The Story of Nirvana*. New York: Doubleday, 1993.

Ballard, Mary E., and Steven Coates. "The Immediate Effects of Homicidal, Suicidal, and Nonviolent Heavy Metal and Rap Songs on the Moods of College Students." *Youth and Society* 27 (December 1995): 148–68.

"Band Cleared in Suicides Blamed on Hidden Message." *Chicago Tribune*, 25 August 1990.

Bangs, Lester. "Bring Your Mother to the Gas Chamber: Are Black Sabbath Really the New Shamans?, Part 1." *Creem*, June 1972, 40ff.

_____. "Bring Your Mother to the Gas Chamber: Black Sabbath and the Straight Dope on Blood-Lust Orgies, Part 2." *Creem*, July 1972, 47ff.

_____. "Heavy Metal." In *The Rolling Stone Illustrated History of Rock and Roll*, edited by Jim Miller, 332–35. New York: Rolling Stone Press/Random House, 1976.

_____. "Transcendence of the Orgasm: Field Tripping with Deep Purple." *Creem*, June 1974, 33ff.

Barich, Bill. "A Reporter at Large: The Crazy Life." *New Yorker*, 3 November 1986, 97–130.

Barrett, Todd. "The Start of a CD Backlash?" *Newsweek*, 16 July 1990, 48.

Bashe, Philip. "Black Sabbath: Rock's Dinosaur Dogs Its Detractors." *Circus*, 31 March 1981, 29–30.

_____. "Heavy Metal Comes of Age." *Circus*, 31 May 1983, 26.

_____. *Heavy Metal Thunder: The Music, Its History, Its Heroes*. Garden City, N.Y.: Dolphin, 1985.

Baumeister, Roy. "Acid Rock: A Critical Reappraisal and Psychological Commentary." *Journal of Psychoactive Drugs* 16, no. 4 (October–December 1984): 339–45.

Becker, Howard S. "Becoming a Marijuana User." *American Journal of Sociology* 59 (November 1953): 235–42.

Benjamin, Robert. "MTV Wannabes Lead Rocky Life in China." *Chicago Sun-Times*, 13 August 1993, 28.

Bennett, Stith. *On Becoming a Rock Musician*. Amherst: University of Massachusetts Press, 1980.

Berger, Arion. "No Great Shakes." *Village Voice: Pazz & Jop Music Supplement*, 27 February 1990, 9ff.

Berger, Harris M. *Metal, Rock, and Jazz: Perception and the Phenomenology of Musical Experience*. Hanover, N.H.: Wesleyan University Press, 1999.

Billard, Mary. "Heavy Metal Goes on Trial." *Rolling Stone*, 12–26 July 1990, 83ff.

_____. "Judas Priest: Defendants of the Faith." *Rolling Stone*, 20 September 1990, 25.

Billboard Chart Research. *Top Pop Albums of the Year 1948–1989 Given in Rank Order*. New York: Billboard Publications, 1990.

Binder, Amy. "Media Depictions of Harm in Heavy Metal and Rap Music." *American Sociological Review* 58, no. 6 (1993): 753–67.

Bloom, Alan. *The Closing of the American Mind*. New York: Simon and Schuster, 1987.

Blumer, Herbert. "The Mass, the Public, and Public Opinion." In *Reader in Public Opinion and Communication*, 2d ed., edited by Bernard Berelson and Morris Janowitz, 43–50. New York: Free Press, 1966.

Bourdieu, Pierre. "The Forms of Cultural Capital." In *Handbook of Theory and Research for the Sociology of Education*, edited by John G. Richardson, 241–58. New York: Greenwood Press, 1986.

Brake, Michael. *Comparative Youth Culture: The Sociology of Youth Cultures and Youth Subcultures in America, Britain, and Canada*. London: Routledge and Kegan Paul, 1985.

Britt, Bruce. "Finding the Antidote: Poison Dismays Its Critics by Producing Hits—and Loving It." *Chicago Tribune*, 5 September 1990.

Brooks, Van Wyck. *America's Coming of Age*. Garden City, N.Y.: Anchor Doubleday, 1958.

Brown, Elizabeth F., and William R. Hendee. "Adolescents and Their Music: Insights into the Health of Adolescents." *Journal of the American Medical Association* 262 (22–29 September 1989): 1659–63.

Bryson, Bethany. "'Anything but Heavy Metal': Symbolic Exclusion and Musical Dislikes." *American Sociological Review* 61 (October 1996): 884–99.

Buff, Stephen. "Greasers, Dupers, and Hippies—Three Responses to the Adult World." In *The White Majority—Between Poverty and Affluence*, edited by L. K. Howe, 60–77. New York: Vintage Books, 1970.

Burke, Kenneth. *Permanence and Change*. Indianapolis, Ind.: Bobbs-Merrill, 1954.

Burnett, Robert, and Robert Philip Weber. "Concentration and Diversity in the Popular Music Industry, 1948–86." Paper presented at the annual meeting of the American Sociological Association, San Francisco, August 1989.

Burns, Gary. "Music and Television: Some Historical and Aesthetic Considerations." Paper presented at the annual meeting of the American Popular Culture Association, Toronto, April 1984.

Burroughs, William S. *The Soft Machine, Nova Express, The Wild Boys: Three Novels by William S. Burroughs.* New York: Grove Press, 1980. (*Nova Express* originally published 1964.)

Bussulman, Joseph Agee. *The Uses of Music: An Introduction to Music in Contemporary American Life.* Englewood Cliffs, N.J.: Prentice-Hall, 1974.

Byrnside, Ronald. "The Formation of a Musical Style: Early Rock." In *Contemporary Music and Music Cultures,* edited by Charles Hamm, Bruno Nettl, and Ronald Byrnside, 159–92. Englewood Cliffs, N.J.: Prentice-Hall, 1975.

Canetti, Elias. *Crowds and Power.* New York: Viking, 1962. (Originally published 1960.)

Canyon, Laura. "Kill with Power!" *Kerrang!,* 4–17 April 1985, 21–22.

Carducci, Joe. "Metal: 'Is it Heavy?' Is the Only Question Worth Asking." *Details,* July 1991, 111–12.

Cashmore, E. Ellis. "Shades of Black, Shades of White." In *Popular Music and Communication,* edited by James Lull, 245–65. Newbury Park, Calif.: Sage, 1987.

Christenson, P. G., and J. B. Peterson. "Genre and Gender in the Structure of Music Preferences." *Communication Research* 15 (1988): 282–301.

Christgau, Robert. "Rockism Faces the World." *Village Voice,* 2 January 1990, 65–72.

Christian, Harry. "Convention and Constraint among British Semi-Professional Jazz Musicians." In *Lost In Music: Culture, Style, and the Musical Event,* edited by Avron L. White, 220–40. London: Routledge and Kegan Paul, 1987.

Clarke, John. "The Skinheads and the Magical Recovery of Community." In *Resistance through Rituals: Youth Subcultures in Post-War Britain,* edited by Stuart Hall and Tony Jefferson, 99–102. London: Hutchinson and Co., 1975.

———. "Style." In *Resistance Through Rituals: Youth Subcultures in Post-War Britain,* edited by Stuart Hall and Tony Jefferson, 175–91. London: Hutchinson and Co., 1975.

Clarke, John, Stuart Hall, Tony Jefferson, and Brian Roberts. "Subcultures, Cultures, and Class: A Theoretical Overview." In *Resistance Through Rituals: Youth Subcultures in Post-War Britain,* edited by Stuart Hall and Tony Jefferson, 9–74. London: Hutchinson and Co., 1975.

Clarke, Peter. "Teenager's Coorientation and Information-Seeking about Pop Music." *American Behavioral Scientist* 16, no. 4 (March–April 1973): 551–66.

Clifford, Mike. *The Harmony Illustrated Encyclopedia of Rock.* New York: Salamander/Harmony/Crown, 1983.

Cobley, Mike. "Again & Again: The Same Old Song." *Kerrang! Kontaktz,* 1987, 37.

Coffman, James. "Everybody Knows This Is Nowhere: Role Conflict and the Rock Musician." *Popular Music and Society* 1, no. 1 (Fall 1971): 20–32.

Cohen, Ralph. "Do Postmodern Genres Exist?" *Genre* 20 (Fall–Winter 1987): 241–58.

Cohen, Stanley. *Folk Devils and Moral Panics.* London: MacGibbon and Kee, 1972.

Colford, Paul D. "The Lords of Rock: Never Say 'It's Only Rock and Roll' to Mega-promoters—and Fierce Rivals—Ron Delsener and John Scher." *Newsday,* 28 August 1990, 4ff.

"A Color is a Color is a Color?" *Personal Vitality*, 3:11, November 1989, 4.

Considine, J. D. "Good, Bad, & Ugly: A Field Guide to Heavy Metal for Confused Consumers, Outraged Critics, and Wimpy New Wavers." *Musician*, September 1984, 52–53.

_____. "Metal Mania." *Rolling Stone*, 15 November 1990, 100–104.

_____. "Purity and Power." *Musician*, September 1984, 46–50.

Cooley, Charles Horton. *Social Organization: A Study of the Larger Mind*. New York: Schocken, 1962.

Corliss, Richard. "X Rated." *Time*, 7 May 1990, 92–99.

Couch, Carl J. "Evocative Transactions and Social Order." Paper presented at the 1990 Stone Symposium, St. Petersburg Beach, Fla., January 1990.

Coudret, Rebecca. "Rock, Steeped in the Blues, Fits Cinderella like a Favorite Slipper." *Chicago Tribune*, 3 November 1988, 14.

Crockett, Steven. "Blam! Bam! Bloom! Boom!" In *Essays on "The Closing of the American Mind,"* edited by Robert L. Stone, 253–61. Chicago: Chicago Review Press, 1989.

Cummings, Sue. "Road Warriors." *Spin*, August 1986, 59–61.

Cummings, Winston. "Krokus: Set to Attack." *Hit Parader*, May 1986, 54–55.

Daly, Les. "7 Tribes of Britain." *Sun* (London), 2 October 1981, 17.

Darnton, Nina. "Committed Youth: Why Are So Many Teens Being Locked Up in Private Mental Hospitals?" *Newsweek*, 31 July 1989, 66–72.

Dasein, Deena. "Talk This Way," *RAW*, 8–21 February 1989, 4.

_____. "Metal Covers: The Song Remains the Same, or Does It?" *C.A.M.M.*, May 1990, 36–37.

_____. "Never Say Die." *L.A. New Times 2*, 26 June 1997, 90ff.

_____. "Judas Priest: Surviving Decapitation." *Illinois Entertainer*, January 1998, 24ff.

Davis, Stephen. *Hammer of the Gods: The Led Zeppelin Saga*. New York: William Morrow, 1985.

Dean, Roger, and Martyn Dean. *Magnetic Storm*. New York: Harmony Books, 1984.

DeCurtis, Anthony. "Music's Mean Season." *Rolling Stone*, 14–28 December 1989, 15–16.

_____. "Rock & Roll Photo Album." *Rolling Stone*, 21 September 1989, 55.

Denisoff, R. Serge. *Inside MTV*. New Brunswick, N.J.: Transaction Books, 1988.

_____. *Solid Gold: The Popular Record Industry*. New Brunswick, N.J.: Transaction Books, 1975.

Denzin, Norman K. "Problems in Analyzing Elements of Mass Culture: Notes on the Popular Song and Other Artistic Productions." *American Journal of Sociology* 75 (May 1970): 1035–38.

Desmond, Roger Jon. "Adolescents and Music Lyrics: Implications of a Cognitive Perspective." *Communication Quarterly* 35, no. 3 (Summer 1987): 276–84.

Dewey, John. *Art as Experience*. New York: Minton, Balch, 1934.

DiMaggio, Paul. "Market Structure, the Creative Process, and Popular Culture." *Journal of Popular Culture* 11 (1977): 436–52.

"Dirt Bag." *Concrete Foundations*, 29 February 1988, 7.

Dodson, Don. "Differentiating Popular Culture and Mass Culture." Paper presented at the annual meeting of the Association for Education in Journalism, Ottawa, Canada, 1975.

Doe, Bernard. "Contract Killers." *Metal Forces,* 1987, 9.

Doherty, Thomas. "MTV and the Music Video: Promo and Product." *Southern Speech Communication Journal* 52, no. 4 (1987): 349–61.

Dougherty, A. "From 'Race Music' to Heavy Metal: A Fiery History of Protests." *People Weekly,* 16 September 1985, 52–53.

Douglas, Mary. *Purity and Danger.* London: Routledge and Kegan Paul, 1966.

Duke, John. "Intense Innovation." *Metal Hammer,* 29 May 1989, 16–17.

Duncan, Robert. *The Noise: Notes from a Rock 'n' Roll Era.* New York: Ticknor and Fields, 1984.

Durkheim, Emile. *The Elementary Forms of Religious Life.* New York: Free Press, 1965. (Originally published 1916.)

Eddy, Chuck. "Boogie Blunderland." *Village Voice,* 27 March 1990, 79ff.

_____. "Heavy Metal." In *Rock and Roll Confidential Report,* edited by Dave Marsh, 183–90. New York: Pantheon Books, 1985.

_____. "The Ramones." *Rolling Stone,* 20 September 1990, 78–82.

_____. *Stairway to Hell: The 500 Best Heavy Metal Albums in the Universe.* New York: Da Capo, 1998.

Editors of *Flip* Magazine. *Flip's Groovy Guide to the Groups! 2.* New York: Signet New American Library, 1969.

Editors of *Rock & Roll Confidential. You've Got A Right to Rock: Don't Let Them Take It Away.* Los Angeles: Duke and Duchess Ventures, 1990.

Eliade, Mircea. *The Sacred and the Profane.* New York: Harper and Row, 1957.

Elias, Marilyn. "Missing the Message." *USA Today,* 13 August 1990.

Epstein, Jonathon S., David J. Pratto, and James K. Skipper, Jr. "Teenage Behavioral Problems and Preferences for Heavy Metal and Rap Music: The Case of a Southern Middle School." *Deviant Behavior* 2, vol. 11 (1990): 381–384.

Evans, Rick. "Lita Ford Trial by Fire: The Metal Queen Returns with 'The Bride Wore Black.'" *Hit Parader,* May 1986, 34.

_____. "Poison: Fallen Angels." *Hit Parader,* July 1989, 22–23.

Farren, Mick, and George Snow. *The Rock 'n' Roll Circus: The Illustrated Rock Concert.* New York: A&W Visual Library, 1978.

Fischer, Paul D. "Worse than the PMRC: The 1994 Congressional Hearings on Music Lyrics and Commerce." *Journal of Popular Music Studies* 8 (1996): 43–56.

"Fist/Thunder in Rock." *Prairie Sun* (Illinois), 1982.

Fletcher, James E. "The Wordless Dimension: The Nonverbal Messages of Music and the Screen." In *Intermedia: Communication and Society,* edited by Teri Kwal Gamble, 83–117. Durham, N.C.: Moore Publishing, 1979.

Foote, Jennifer. "Making It in Metal Mecca: Heavy Metal Is Now More than a Soundtrack for the Wonder Years, It's a Career Goal." *Newsweek,* 7 August 1989, 56–58.

Fornatale, Peter. *The Story of Rock 'N' Roll.* New York: William Morrow, 1987.

Fornatale, Peter and Joshua E. Mills. *Radio in the Television Age.* Woodstock, New York: Overlook Press, 1980.

Frank, James. "Rock 'n'—Say What? Our Parents May Be Right: That Music Is Way Too Loud." *Chicago Tribune,* 21 July 1989.

Frick, Ulrich. "Rock Music as Commodity." *Osterreichische Zeitschrift für Soziologie* 8, no. 4 (1983): 164–73.

Fricke, David. "Heavy Metal Justice: The Thrash Superstars of Metallica Make It to the Top with Their Integrity Intact." *Rolling Stone,* 12 January 1989, 44ff.

———. "Metal Forefathers: Historical Precedents from the 60s and 70s: Two Bands Who Were Heavy Before It Was Hip." *Musician,* September 1984, 56.

———. "The Year in Records." *Rolling Stone,* 13–27 December 1990, 201–26.

Friesen, Bruce K. "Functional Aspects of Adolescent Socialization through Deviant Subcultures: Field Research in Heavy Metal." Paper presented at the annual meeting of the American Sociological Association, San Francisco, August 1989.

Frith, Simon. "The Industrialization of Popular Music." In *Popular Music and Communication,* edited by James Lull, 53–77. Newbury Park, Calif.: Sage, 1987.

———. *Sound Effects: Youth, Leisure, and the Politics of Rock 'N' Roll.* New York: Pantheon Books, 1981.

———. "Towards an Aesthetic of Popular Music." In *Music and Society: The Politics of Composition, Performance, and Reception,* edited by Richard Leppert and Susan McClary, 133–49. Cambridge: Cambridge University Press, 1987.

Frith, Simon, and Howard Horne. *Art into Pop.* New York: Methuen, 1988.

Frost, Deborah. "Heavy Metal Rears Its Ugly Head Again: A New Generation of Bands Is Dominating the Charts." *Rolling Stone,* 27 September 1984, 83–85.

———. "White Noise: How Heavy Metal Rules." *Village Voice,* 18 June 1985, 46–48.

Gaines, Donna. *Teenage Wasteland: Surburbia's Dead End Kids.* New York: Pantheon, 1991.

Gans, Herbert J. *Popular Culture and High Culture.* New York: Basic Books, 1974.

Gentry, Carol. "Studies Debunk Message Tapes." *Chicago Tribune,* 19 August 1990.

George, Nelson. *The Death of Rhythm and Blues.* New York: Pantheon Books, 1988.

Gilder, Mrs. Florence. "Letter of the Month." *Hit Parader,* October 1989, 26.

Gillett, Charlie. *The Sound of the City: The Rise of Rock and Roll.* New York: Dell, 1970.

Gitter, Mike. "Everything You Ever Wanted to Know About Death Metal but Were Afraid to Ask." *Pulse* 109, October 1992, 79ff.

Goffman, Erving. *The Presentation of Self in Everyday Life.* Garden City, N.Y.: Doubleday Anchor, 1959.

Goldberg, Michael. "Look out, Spinal Tap: Here Come the Scorpions, Heavy Metal's Latest Heroes." *Rolling Stone,* 5 July 1984, 38.

———. "MTV's Sharper Pictures." *Rolling Stone,* 8 February 1990, 61ff.

———. "Rock & Roll Fanzines: A New Underground Press Flourishes." *Rolling Stone,* 29 March 1984, 55–58.

———. "The Sedating of Rock 'N' Roll." *Esquire,* April 1983, 100–103.

———. "*Spinal Tap:* The Comics Behind the Funniest Rock Movie Ever." *Rolling Stone,* 24 May 1984, 37–38.

Goldman, Stuart. "Rock of Ageds: That Old Devil Music." *National Review,* 24 February 1989, 28ff.

Goldstein, Patrick. "Parents Warn: Take the Sex and Shock Out of Rock." *Los Angeles Times,* 25 August 1985. (Cited in *Record Labeling [Senate Hearing 99–529].*)

Goldstein, Richard. "Tube Rock: How Music Video Is Changing Music." *Village Voice,* 24 September 1985, 38ff.

Goldstein, Toby. "Who Among the Living Is Immune to Anthrax?" *Metal Creem Up-Close,* August 1987, 65ff.

Graff, Gary. "Crüe Change: Hard-Driving Band Takes Sober Look at Its Future." *Chicago Tribune,* 17 December 1989, sect. 13, 28.

———. "Sophomore Slump: After 1st Hit, Rising Stars Fear Playing a Sour Note." *Chicago Tribune,* 30 August 1988.

Du Plessix Gray, Francine. "Reflections: Soviet Women." *New Yorker,* 19 February 1990, 48–81. (Excerpted from *Soviet Women: Walking the Tightrope.* Garden City, New York: Doubleday, 1990.)

Green, Lucy. *Music on Deaf Ears: Musical Meaning, Ideology, and Education.* Manchester, England: Manchester University Press, 1988.

Greene, Bob. "Scout Finds Merit in Heavy Metal." *Chicago Tribune,* 21 May 1990.

Greenfield, Patricia M., et al. "What Is Rock Music Doing to the Minds of Our Youth? A First Experimental Look at the Effects of Rock Music Lyrics and Music Videos." *Journal of Early Adolescence* 7, no. 3 (Fall 1987): 315–29.

Greeson, Larry E., and Rose Ann Williams. "Social Implications of Music Videos for Youth: An Analysis of the Content and Effects of MTV." *Youth and Society* 18, no. 2 (December 1988): 177–89.

Greider, William. "Bloom and Doom." In *Essays on "The Closing of the American Mind,"* edited by Robert L. Stone, 244–47. Chicago: Chicago Review Press, 1989.

Gross, Michael. "Frock 'n' Roll." *Chicago Tribune,* 5 February 1986.

Gross, Robert L. "Heavy Metal Music: A New Subculture in American Society." *Journal of Popular Culture* 24, no. 1 (Summer 1990): 119–30.

Grossberg, Lawrence. "Rock and Roll in Search of an Audience." In *Popular Music and Communication,* edited by James Lull, 175–97. Newbury Park, Calif.: Sage, 1987.

Grossman, Loyd. *A Social History of Rock Music: From the Greasers to Glitter Rock.* New York: David McKay, 1976.

Guild, Hazel. "Soviet Journal Sez Rock Music Works like a Shot of Morphine." *Variety,* 24 June 1987, 87.

Gundersen, Edna. "Tell Tchaikovsky the News: The Moscow Music Peace Festival Takes Metal Behind the Iron Curtain." *Rolling Stone,* 5 October 1989, 15–16.

Gutmann, Stephanie. "Video's Real Music Is in the Moves." *Newsday,* 3 September 1990, 5.

"Hair Farm Report." *Pulse,* April 1993, 15.

Hakanen, Ernest A., and Alan Wells. "Adolescent Music Marginals: Who Likes Metal, Jazz, Country, and Classical." Paper presented at the annual meetings of the North Central Sociological Association and Southern Sociological Society, Louisville, Ky., March 1990.

Hale, Mark. *The Worldwide Megabook of Heavy Metal Bands.* Ann Arbor, Mich.: Popular Culture Ink, 1993.

Halfin, Ross, and Pete Makowski. *Heavy Metal: The Power Age.* New York: Delilah, 1982.

Halford, Rob. Forward to *Heavy Metal Thunder: The Music, Its History, Its Heroes,* by Philip Bashe. Garden City, N.Y.: Dolphin, 1985.

Hall, Stuart, and Paddy Whannel. *The Popular Arts.* London: Hutchinson Educational, 1964.

Hamm, Charles. "The Acculturation of Musical Styles: Popular Music, U.S.A." In *Contemporary Music and Music Cultures,* edited by Charles Hamm, Bruno Nettl, and Ronald Byrnside, 125–58. Englewood Cliffs, N.J.: Prentice-Hall, 1975.

―――. "Changing Patterns in Society and Music: The U.S. Since World War II." In *Contemporary Music and Music Cultures,* edited by Charles Hamm, Bruno Nettl, and Ronald Byrnside, 35–70. Englewood Cliffs, N.J.: Prentice-Hall, 1975.

Handelman, David. "Money for Nothing and the Chicks for Free: On the Road with Mötley Crüe." *Rolling Stone,* 13 August 1989, 34ff.

Haring, Bruce. "Tuning In to Radio's Wired Wave." *USA Today,* 7 January 1999.

Harrigan, Brian. *HM A–Z: The Definitive Encyclopedia of Heavy Metal from AC/DC through Led Zeppelin to ZZ Top.* London: Bobcat Books, 1981.

Harrigan, Brian, and Malcolm Dome. *Encyclopedia Metallica: The Bible of Heavy Metal.* London: Bobcat Books, 1980.

Hatch, David, and Stephen Millward. *From Blues to Rock: An Analytic History of Pop Music.* Manchester, England: Manchester University Press, 1987.

Hayakawa, S. I. "Popular Songs vs. The Facts of Life." In *Mass Culture: The Popular Arts in America,* edited by Bernard Rosenberg and David Manning White, 393–403. New York: Free Press, 1957. (Originally published 1955.)

"Heavy Metal." In *The Rolling Stone Encyclopedia of Rock & Roll,* edited by Jon Pareles and Patricia Romanowski, 248. New York: Rolling Stone Press/Summit Books, 1983.

"Heavy Metal Band's Lyrics Focus at Trial." *Chicago Tribune,* 17 July 1990.

Hebdige, Dick. *Subculture: The Meaning of Style.* New York: Methuen, 1979.

Hedges, Dan. "Metallica's Sonic Assault Makes Believers of Ozzy Fans." *Circus,* 31 July 1986, 26–28.

Heim, Chris. "Whitesnake Offers Chapter from a Heavy-Metal Manual." *Chicago Tribune,* 12 February 1988.

Henry, Jules. *Culture Against Man.* New York: Vintage/Random House, 1963.

Holmes, Tim. *AC/DC.* New York: Ballentine Books, 1986.

Housham, David. "Gross Takings." *Q,* November 1987, 38–44.

Hunt, Chris. "Independents' Day." *Solid Rock,* 1987, 36–37.

Hunt, Dennis. "Heavy-Metal Hit Wins New Respect for Iron Maiden." *Chicago Sun-Times,* 9 September 1983.

Huxley, Aldous. *The Doors of Perception and Heaven and Hell.* New York: Harper Colophon, 1963. (Originally published 1954.)

Ian, S. "Heavy Metal Covers Wide Range; Yet Only Pop Rockers Make It on MTV." *Billboard*, 16 March 1991, 9.

Iglauer, Bruce. "Voice of the People: Record Labeling Is Censorship by Fear." *Chicago Tribune*, 21 February 1990.

Iverem, Esther. "Decrying Rap's Influence: Senate Subcommittee Hears Testimony on Dangers of Music." *Washington Post*, 7 November 1997: 2.

Jasper, Tony, and Derek Oliver. *The International Encyclopedia of Hard Rock & Heavy Metal.* New York: Facts On File Publications, 1983.

Jensen, Joli. "Genre and Recalcitrance: Country Music's Move Uptown." *Tracking: Popular Music Studies* 1 (Spring 1988): 30–41.

Johnson, Howard. "Flamin' Tasty." *Kerrang!*, 4 August 1988, 29.

_____. "Hard Nuts: The Rebirth of Raven." *Kerrang!*, 4–17 April 1985, 14–16.

Johnston, Christopher. "Psst! Hey, Mister, Want to Buy Some Software Cheap?: Software Piracy as a Way of Life in Hong Kong." *PC Computing*, October 1988, 136–42.

Jones, Dylan. "Can Subliminal Messages Alter Behavior?" *USA Today*, 19 July 1990.

Junod, Tom, with Melissa Harris. "Surviving High School." *Atlantic*, September 1988, 61ff.

Kagan, Daniel. "A Contractual Cacophony in Music." *Insight*, 4 July 1988, 50–52.

Kaplan, E. Ann. *Rocking Around the Clock: Music Television, Post Modernism, and Consumer Culture.* New York: Methuen, 1987.

Karshner, Roger. *The Music Machine: What Really Goes On in the Record Industry.* Los Angeles: Nash Publishing, 1971.

Keen, Judy. "Nevada Judge Will Decide Landmark Suit." *USA Today*, 6 July 1990.

Kelly, Lynn Lisa. "Mail (Letters)." *Hit Parader*, September 1989, 25.

Khoury, Gene. "Metal Industry Report: Power Metal = Mainstream Metal." *Concrete Foundations*, 29 February 1988, 10.

King, Paul. "Heavy Metal Music and Drug Abuse in Adolescents." *Postgraduate Medicine* 83, no. 5 (April 1988): 295–304.

Klemm, Oliver. "Slayer: Rod of Iron." *Metal Hammer*, Janaury 1987, 30–32.

Kot, Greg. "Nuclear Assault: A Heavy Metal Conscience for the Thinking Kid." *Chicago Tribune*, 30 November 1989, sect. 5, 10.

_____. "Volume Dealers: Heavy Metal Bands Still Break Sound Barriers." *Chicago Tribune*, 18 March 1990, sect. 13, 6–7.

Kotarba, Joseph A. "Adolescent Use of Heavy Metal Rock Music as a Resource for Meaning." Paper presented at the annual meeting of the American Sociological Association, Washington, D.C., August 1990.

Kotarba, Joseph A., and Laura Wells. "Styles of Adolescent Participation in an All-Ages, Rock 'n' Roll Nightclub: An Ethnographic Analysis." *Youth and Society* 18, no. 4 (June 1987): 398–417.

Kuipers, Dean. "Chasing the Dragon." *Spin*, May 1990, 32ff.

Kuhnemund, Gotz. "Atrophy: Beer Bong Thrash from Arizona." *Metal Hammer*, October 1988, 68–69.

Lacey, Liam. "Heavy Metal: A Bluffer's Guide." *The Globe and Mail* (Toronto), 31 March 1984.

Landro, Laura. "Merger of Warner Unit, Polygram Angers Troubled Record Industry." *Wall Street Journal,* 12 April 1984, 33ff.

Leff, Laurel. "As Competition in Radio Grows, Stations Tailor Programs for Specific Audiences." *Wall Street Journal,* 19 November 1980, 48.

Leming, James S. "Rock Music and the Socialization of Moral Values in Early Adolescence." *Youth and Society* 18, no. 4 (June 1987): 363–83.

Levine, Harold, and Steven H. Stumpf. "Statements of Fear through Cultural Symbols: Punk Rock as a Reflective Subculture." *Youth and Society* 14, no. 4 (June 1983): 417–35.

Lévi-Strauss, Claude. *The Savage Mind.* Chicago: University of Chicago Press, 1966.

Lewis, Alan. "The Social Interpretation of Modern Jazz." In *Lost in Music: Culture, Style, and the Musical Event,* edited by Avron L. White, 33–55. London: Routledge and Kegan Paul, 1987.

Lewis, George H. "The Politics of Meaning: Emergent Ideology in Popular Hawaiian Music." *Tracking: Popular Music Studies* 1, no. 2 (Fall 1988): 23–33.

Ling, Dave. "RAW Plugs." *RAW,* 28 September–11 October 1988, 46.

Lipsitz, George. *Time Passages: Collective Memory and American Popular Culture.* Minneapolis: University of Minnesota Press, 1990.

Loren, Todd, Greg Fox, and Mary Kelleher. *Poison,* September 1990. (Revolutionary Comics, San Diego.)

Louisiana House Bill No. 154, 1990.

Love, Robert, and Jenny Jedeikin. "Wild Wild West Berlin." *Rolling Stone,* 11 January 1990, 13.

Lull, James. "Listeners' Communicative Uses of Popular Music." In *Popular Music and Communication,* edited by James Lull, 140–74. Newbury Park, Calif.: Sage, 1987.

——. "Popular Music and Communication: An Introduction." In *Popular Music and Communication,* edited by James Lull, 10–35. Newbury Park, Calif.: Sage, 1987.

Lyotard, Jean-François. *The Postmodern Condition: A Report on Knowledge.* Minneapolis: University of Minnesota Press, 1984.

Macdonald, Dwight. *Against the American Grain.* New York: Random House, 1962.

McDonald, James R. "Censoring Rock Lyrics: A Historical Analysis of the Debate." *Youth and Society* 19, no. 3 (March 1988): 294–313.

McGuigan, Cathleen. "Not the Sound of Silence." *Newsweek,* 14 November 1983, 102.

MacKay, Gordon. "Metal Mania: Paul Di'Anno Interview." *Network,* November 1986, 18–19.

McRobbie, Angela, and Jenny Garber. "Girls and Subcultures." In *Resistance through Rituals: Youth Subcultures in Post-War Britain,* edited by Stuart Hall and Tony Jefferson, 209–22. London: Hutchinson and Co., 1975.

Malone, Julia. "Washington Wives Use Influence to Target Sex, Drugs in Rock Music." *Christian Science Monitor,* 23 August 1985.

Marcus, Greil. "MTV DOA RIP." *Artforum International,* January 1987, 12.

Markson, Stephen L. "Claims-Making, Quasi-Theories and the Social Construction of Rock and Roll." Paper presented at the annual meeting of the American Sociological Association, San Francisco, August 1989.

Marlowe, Chris. "Full Metal Jackets." *RAW,* 21 December–10 January 1989, 36–39.

Martin, Graham, Michael Clarke, and Colby Pearce. "Adolescent Suicide: Music Preference as an Indicator of Vulnerability." *Journal of the American Academy of Child and Adolescent Psychiatry* 32, no. 3 (May 1993): 530–35.

Martin, Linda, and Kerry Segrave. *Anti-Rock: The Opposition to Rock 'n' Roll.* Hamden, Conn.: Archon Books, 1988.

Menconi, Al. "A Serious Look at Christian Heavy Metal: 'Vengeance Is Mine,' Saith the Lord—Or Is It?" *Media Update,* January–February 1989, 12–14.

"Metal Moderators: Brian Slagel." *CMJ Music Marathon Program Guide* (1988): 37.

Mike, Metal. "Scorpions." *Aardschok America,* August–September 1987, 14–17.

Miller, Dale Susan. "Youth, Popular Music, and Cultural Controversy: The Case of Heavy Metal." Ph.D. diss., University of Texas at Austin, 1988.

Mills, C. Wright. "The Cultural Apparatus." In *Power, Politics, and People,* edited by I. L. Horowitz, 405–22. New York: Oxford University Press, 1963.

Mills, David. "Turning Back the Clock on Rock." *Insight,* 31 March 1986, 62–63.

Mills, Joshua E. *Radio in the Television Age.* New York: Overlook Press, 1980.

Milton, John. *"Paradise Lost" and Other Poems.* New York: New American Library, 1981.

Montague, Susan P., and Robert Morais. "Football Games and Rock Concerts: The Ritual Enactment of American Success Models." In *The American Dimension: Cultural Myths and Social Realities,* edited by W. Arens and Susan P. Montague, 33–52. Port Washington, N.Y.: Alfred Publishing, 1976.

Moynihan, Michael, and Didrik Sønderlind. *Lords of Chaos: The Bloody Rise of the Satanic Metal Underground.* Venice, Calif.: Feral House, 1998.

"MTV Overtaking Radio as Motivation of Disc Purchases." *Variety,* 16 February 1983, 113.

Mundy, Chris. "Nirvana." *Rolling Stone,* 23 January 1992, 39–41.

Neely, Kim. "Faith No More." *Rolling Stone,* 6 September 1990, 53ff.

_____. "Judas Priest Gets Off the Hook." *Rolling Stone,* 4 October 1990, 39.

_____. "Wrap Up." *Rolling Stone,* 6 September 1990, 162.

Nite, Norm N. *Rock On: The Illlustrated Encyclopedia of Rock n' Roll—The Video Revolution 1978–Present.* Vol. 3. New York: Harper and Row, 1985.

Oliver, Paul. *The Meaning of the Blues.* New York: Collier Books, 1963. (Originally published 1960.)

O'Neill, Lou, Jr. "Back Pages." *Circus,* 31 December 1986, 90.

Orlean, Susan. "The Kids Are All Right: Bon Jovi Hit the Top with an Image Tailor-Made for Today's Teens." *Rolling Stone,* 21 May 1987, 35ff.

Orman, John. *The Politics of Rock Music.* Chicago: Nelson-Hall, 1984.

Osbourne, Ozzy. "Ozzy Osbourne's Favorite Hard Rock of the Seventies." *Rolling Stone,* 20 September 1990, 72.

Palmer, Robert. "Dark Metal: Not Just Smash and Thrash." *New York Times,* 4 November 1990.

Pareles, Jon. "Fringe Fever." *New York Times Magazine,* 11 September 1988, sect. 6, 52.

_____. "The Rewards of Rock Before the Gloss." *New York Times,* 9 October 1988, 28.

_____. "Should Rock Lyrics Be Sanitized?" *New York Times,* 13 October 1985, 1ff.

_____. "Young vs. MTV: A Case of Modest Revenge." *New York Times,* 14 August 1988.

Pattison, Robert. *The Triumph of Vulgarity: Rock Music in the Mirror of Romanticism.* New York: Oxford University Press, 1987.

Pearson, Anthony. "The Grateful Dead Phenomenon: An Ethnomethodological Approach." *Youth and Society* 18, no. 4 (June 1987): 418–32.

Peck, Richard. *Rock Rock Rock: Making Musical Choices.* Greenville, S.C.: Bob Jones University Press, 1985.

Peterson, Richard A. "Market and Moralist Censors of a Black Art Form: Jazz." In *The Sounds of Social Change,* edited by R. Serge Denisoff and Richard A. Peterson, 236–47. Chicago: Rand McNally, 1972.

Peterson, Richard A., and David G. Berger. "Cycles of Symbol Production: The Case of Popular Music." *American Sociological Review* 40 (April 1975): 158–73.

Pielke, Robert G. *You Say You Want a Revolution: Rock Music in American Culture.* Chicago: Nelson-Hall, 1986.

Plato. *The Republic.* New York: Norton and Company, 1985.

Polack, Phyllis. "Music Censorship Attempts Increase." *Aardschok America,* August–September 1987, 72ff.

Pond, Steve. "The Who Reboards the Magic Bus, but Will It Still Be Magic?" *Rolling Stone,* 13–27 July 1989, 87ff.

Popoff, Martin. *The Collector's Guide to Heavy Metal.* Toronto, Canada: Collector's Guide Press, 1997.

Rabey, Steve. "Heavy Metal Mania: In the Record Bins and on the Concert Stage, Christian Heavy Metal Is Hot. But What Hath Stryper Wrought?" *Newsound,* Spring 1987, 10ff.

Raschke, Carl A. *Painted Black.* New York: Harper and Row, 1990.

Ratliff, Ben. "Metal: The Next Generation." *Rolling Stone,* 4 February 1999, 19–24.

"Record Business Sees Light Ahead—On Video Screen." *Chicago Tribune,* 26 April 1983.

Recording Industry Association of America. *Inside the Recording Industry: A Statistical Overview (Update 1987).* New York: Author, 1987.

Ressner, Jeffrey. "Head Bangers: Learning to Earn." *Rolling Stone,* 16 November 1989, 33.

Richardson, James T., Joel Best, and David Bromley (eds.). *The Satanism Scare.* Hawthorne, N.Y.: Aldine de Gruyter, 1991.

"Rockin' Forever, Mid-Nebraska: Letters." *Circus,* 31 August 1986, 6.

Roe, Keith. "The School and Music in Adolescent Socialization." In *Popular Music and Communication,* edited by James Lull, 212–30. Beverly Hills, Calif.: Sage, 1987.

_____. "Adolescents' Use of Socially Disvalued Media: Towards a Theory of Media Delinquency." *Journal of Youth and Adolescence* 24 (October 1995): 617–31.

Rogal, Kim. "Dozier's 42 Days in a Tent." *Newsweek*, 15 February 1982, 46.

Rosenbaum, Jill L., and Lorraine Prinsky. "The Presumption of Influence: Recent Responses of Popular Music Subcultures." *Crime and Delinquency* 37, no. 4 (1991): 528–35.

Rothenbuhler, Eric W. "Commercial Radio and Popular Music: Processes of Selection and Factors of Influence." In *Popular Music and Communication,* edited by James Lull, 78–95. Newbury Park, Calif.: Sage, 1987.

Rothenbuhler, Eric W., and John W. Dimmick. "Popular Music: Concentration and Diversity in the Industry, 1974–80." *Journal of Communication* 32, no. 1 (Winter 1982): 143–49.

Rothstein, Edward. "Edward Rothstein on Music: Heart of Gould." *New Republic,* 26 June 1989, 28–32.

Russell, Jeffrey Burton. *Mephistopheles: The Devil in the Modern World.* Ithaca, N.Y.: Cornell University Press, 1986.

Sanders, Clinton R. *Customizing the Body: The Art and Culture of Tattooing.* Philadelphia: Temple University Press, 1989.

Sanford, Jay Allen. *AC/DC.* San Diego: Revolutionary Comics, 1990.

Saunders, Mike. Review of *Kingdom Come,* by Sir Lord Baltimore. *Creem,* May 1971, 74.

_____. Review of *Demons and Wizards,* by Uriah Heep. *Rolling Stone,* 23 November 1972, 66.

Schlattmann, Tim. "Traditional, Non-Traditional, Emotionally/Behaviorally Disturbed Students, and Popular Musical Lyrics." *Popular Music and Society* 13, no. 1 (1989): 23–35.

Schwartz, Barry. "Waiting, Exchange, and Power: The Distribution of Time in Social Systems." *American Journal of Sociology* 79 (1973): 841–70.

Schwendinger, Herman, and Julia R. Siegel-Schwendinger. *Adolescent Subcultures and Delinquency.* New York: Praeger, 1985.

Shaw, Greg. "The Real Rock 'n' Roll Underground." *Creem,* June 1971, 22.

Shaw, William. "Satan in the Sunshine." *Details,* March 1995: 133–38.

Shepherd, John. "Music and Male Hegemony." In *Music and Society: The Politics of Composition, Performance, and Reception,* edited by Richard Leppert and Susan McClary, 151–72. London: Cambridge University Press, 1987.

Shils, Edward. "Mass Society and Its Culture." In *Culture for the Millions?,* edited by Norman Jacobs, 1–27. Boston: Beacon Press, 1964.

Silberman, Jeff. "More Propaganda!: LA Firm Aims for Greater Creativity with Its Music Vid Clips." *BAM,* 16 June 1989, 14.

Silverman, Leigh. "Finding Fame without Fortune." *Rolling Stone,* 21 September 1989, 33.

Simmel, Georg. *The Sociology of Georg Simmel.* Edited by Kurt H. Wolff. New York: Free Press, 1950.

Simmons, Sylvie. "The 80s: The Decade in Rock." *RAW,* 12–15 July 1989, 58–60.

Singer, Simon I., Murray Levine, and Susyan Jou. "Heavy Metal Music Preference, Delinquent Friends, Social Control, and Delinquency." *Journal of Research in Crime and Delinquency* 30 (August 1993): 317–29.

Slagel, Brian. "Bitch: A Conversation with One of LA's Best." *New Heavy Metal Revue*, March 1982, 8–9.

Small, Christopher. "Performance as Ritual: Sketch for an Enquiry into the True Nature of a Symphony Concert." In *Lost in Music: Culture, Style, and the Musical Event*, edited by Avron L. White, 6–32. London: Routledge and Kegan Paul, 1987.

Snow, Matt. "Every Man for Herself." *Q*, September 1989, 8–11.

Spahr, W. "Teutonic Rock: Heavy Metal Sales Boosting Industry." *Billboard*, 5 September 1981, 60.

Stivers, Richard. *Evil in Modern Myth and Ritual*. Athens: University of Georgia Press, 1982.

Stoltenberg, J. "Towards Gender Justice." *Social Policy* 6 (May–June 1975): 35–36.

Straw, Will. "Characterizing Rock Music Cultures: The Case of Heavy Metal." *Canadian University Music Review* 5 (1984): 104–21.

Street, John. *Rebel Rock: Politics of Popular Music*. New York: Basil Blackwell, 1986.

Struthers, Stephen. "Recording Music: Technology in the Art of Recording." In *Lost in Music: Culture, Style, and the Musical Event*, edited by Avron L. White, 241–58. London: Routledge and Kegan Paul, 1987.

Tannenbaum, Rob. "Church Assails Heavy Metal: 'Help to the Devil,' Says New York's Archbishop." *Rolling Stone*, 19 April 1990, 32.

Tanner, Julian. "Pop Music and Peer Groups: A Study of Canadian High School Students' Responses to Pop Music." *La Revue Canadienne de Sociologie et d'Anthropologie/The Canadian Review of Sociology and Anthropology* 18, no. 1 (February 1981): 1–13.

Thorne, Stephen B., and Philip Himelstein. "The Role of Suggestion in the Perception of Satanic Messages in Rock-and-Roll Recordings." *Journal of Psychology* 116, no. 2 (March 1984): 245–48.

Trostle, Lawrence Charles. "The Stoners: Drugs, Demons, and Delinquency: A Descriptive and Empirical Analysis of Delinquent Behavior (Satanism, Street Gangs, Occult)." Ph.D. diss., Claremont Graduate School, 1986.

"Two Exorcisms Revealed by N.Y. Cardinal." *Chicago Sun-Times*, 6 March 1990.

Ulrich, Lars, and Malcolm Dome. "Encyclopedia Metallica." *RAW*, 28 September–11 October 1988, 27–34.

U.S. Congress. Senate. *Record Labeling (Senate Hearing 99–529): Hearing before the Committee on Commerce, Science, and Transportation*. United States Senate, Ninety-Ninth Congress, First Session on Contents of Music and the Lyrics of Records. Washington, D.C.: U.S. Government Printing Office, 1985.

Vai, Steve. *Guitar Extravaganza*. New York: Warner Brothers Publications, 1989.

Van Matre, Lynn. "High-Flying Days of Rock: Excess to an Extreme." *Chicago Tribune*, 24 April 1983.

Van Pelt, Doug. "Mosh for the Master? Now that Christians Are Playing Thrash Metal, It's Time to Ask, 'Is Christian Music Getting Out of Control?'" *Contemporary Christian Music*, February 1989, 20–21.

Verden, Paul, Kathleen Dunleavy, and Charles H. Powers. "Heavy Metal Mania and Adolescent Delinquency." *Popular Music and Society* 13, no. 1 (Spring 1989): 73–82.

Vincent, Richard C., Dennis K. Davis, and Lilly Ann Boruszkowski. "Sexism on MTV: The Portrayal of Women in Rock Videos." *Journalism Quarterly* 64 (Winter 1987): 750ff.

"Vinnie Vincent: We Have Lift Off." *Metal Hammer*, 20 June 1988, 24–25.

Ward, Ed, Geoffrey Stokes, and Ken Tucker. *Rock of Ages: The Rolling Stone History of Rock & Roll.* New York: Rolling Stone Press/Summit Books, 1986.

Weber, Max. *From Max Weber: Essays in Sociology.* Edited by H. H. Gerth and C. Wright Mills. New York: Oxford University Press, 1946.

Weingarten, Marc. "Black Sabbath: The Forum January 5th, 1999." *Rolling Stone*, 18 February 1999, 28.

Weinstein, Deena. "The Amnesty International Concert Tour: Transnationalism As Cultural Commodity." *Public Culture* 1, no. 2 (Spring 1989): 60–65.

_____. "Rock: Youth and Its Music." *Popular Music and Society* 9, no. 3 (1983): 2–15.

_____. *Serious Rock: The Artistic Vision of Modern Society in Pink Floyd, Rush and Bruce Springsteen.* Montreal: Culture Texts, 1985.

_____. "Death Metal: Distillate/Dead End of Heavy Metal." Paper presented at the First International Conference on Rock 'n' Rap, Columbia, Mo., February 1993.

_____. "Expendable Youth: The Rise and Fall of Youth Culture." In *Adolescents and Their Music: If It's Too Loud, You're Too Old*, edited by Jonathon Epstein, 67–85. Hamden, Conn.: Garland, 1994.

_____. "Alternative Youth: The Ironies of Recapturing Youth Culture." *Young: Nordic Journal of Youth Research* 3, no. 1 (February 1995): 61–71.

Welch, Chris. *Black Sabbath.* London: Proteus Books, 1982.

_____. "The British (Rock) Empire Strikes Back." *Metal Hammer*, 23 January 1989, 82.

Wells, Alan. "Women and Popular Music: Britain and the United States." Paper presented at the annual meeting of the Western Social Science Association, Reno, Nev., April 1986.

Whyte, William Foote. "The Social Structure of the Restaurant." *American Journal of Sociology* 54 (January 1949): 302–10.

Wild, David. "The Band that Wouldn't Die." *Rolling Stone*, 5 April 1990, 45ff.

Willis, Paul E. "The Cultural Meaning of Drug Use." In *Resistance through Rituals: Youth Subcultures in Post-War Britain*, edited by Stuart Hall and Tony Jefferson, 106–18. London: Hutchinson and Co., 1975.

_____. *Profane Culture.* London: Routledge and Kegan Paul, 1978.

Wills, Geoff, and Cary L. Cooper. *Pressure Sensitive: Popular Musicians under Stress.* Newbury Park, Calif.: Sage, 1988.

Wilson, Robert N. "Teamwork in the Operating Room." *Human Organization* 12 (Winter 1954): 9–14.

Wolcott, James. "Mixed Media: The Noise Boys." *Vanity Fair*, October 1987, 26–30.

"Women in Metal." *New Yorker*, 28 November 1988, 32–33.

Wong, Kean. "Metallic Gleam." *The Wire* no. 110, April 1993, 18–21.

Wooten, Marsha A. "The Effects of Heavy Metal Music on Affects Shifts of Adolescents in an Inpatient Psychiatric Setting." *Music Therapy Perspectives* 10, no. 2 (1992): 93–98.

Wyman, Bill. "Terms of Interment: Retrospecting the Ramones and the Clash." *Reader*, 2 September 1988, 12ff.

Young, Charles M. "Heavy Metal: In Defense of Dirtbags and Worthless Puds." *Musician*, September 1984, 41–44.

———. "Soda Pop: 1986 Was Feeding Time for Hucksters, Hacks, and Hipocrites." *Musician*, January 1987, 64ff.

Young, Jon. "Mean Duds: A Heavy Metal Must." *Musician*, September 1984, 54.

Zillmann, Dolf, and Azra Bhatia. "Effects of Associating with Musical Genres on Heterosexual Attraction." *Communication Research* 16, no. 2 (April 1989): 262–88.

"Zines!" *Solid Rock*, 1987, 43.

Index

About the
Author

Deena Weinstein is Professor of Sociology at DePaul University in Chicago, where she has taught a course on the sociology of rock music for almost two decades and has published numerous scholarly works on rock. She is also a rock critic whose reviews of albums and concerts, as well as interviews with musicians, have appeared in a wide variety of publications. Weinstein places her interest in rock music in the context of cultural theory and has published numerous books and articles on modernism and postmodernism.